Financial Planning
Answer Book

2007 Edition

Financial Planning
Answer Book

2007 Edition

Jeffrey H. Rattiner, CPA, CFP®, MBA, RFC

CCH
a Wolters Kluwer business

ISBN-10: 0-8080-9079-8
ISBN-13: 978-0-8080-9079-3

Preface

The purpose of this book is to provide financial professionals with technical information necessary to practice as a financial planner. The book covers the entire spectrum of financial planning disciplines in a user friendly question-andanswer format. It provides a level of depth worthy of a comprehensive reference guide when handling client issues. The book can certainly be used as a starting point on researching financial planning issues or for in-depth analysis on financial planning topics.

Jeffrey H. Rattiner, CPA, CFP ®, MBA, RFC
Centennial, Colorado

About the Author

Jeffrey H. Rattiner is president and chief executive officer of the JR Financial Group, Inc., which is a financial planning and information holding company with offices in the Denver and Phoenix metro areas serving consumers and financial services organizations. Mr. Rattiner earned his Bachelor of Business Administration (BBA) with an emphasis in Marketing Management from Bernard M. Baruch College of the City University of New York in 1981, his Master of Business Administration (MBA) in Certified Public Accounting from Hofstra University in 1983 and his Certified Financial Planner education from New York University in 1992. He is a Certified Financial Planner (CFP), and a Certified Public Accountant in New York, Colorado, and Arizona.

Mr. Rattiner's extensive *Rattiner's Financial Planning Fast Track*®*(FPFT)* boot camp program, which satisfies the CFP Board educational requirement in only seven months, trains professionals on how to become Certified Financial Planner® (CFP®) licensees, and has won critical acclaim as the cover story in the December 2001 issue of *Financial Planning Magazine*. He also informs and educates financial planners on how to become more successful in practice. Mr. Rattiner authored *Rattiner's Review for the CFP Certification Examination—Fast Track Study Guide* and *"Rattiner's Financial Planner's Bible"* for John Wiley & Sons, as well as *"Getting Started as a Financial Planner"* for Bloomberg Press (now in its second edition), *"Adding Personal Financial Planning to Your Practice"* for the American Management Association, *Personal Financial Planning Library* for Harcourt Brace, and co-authored *"Practicing Financial Planning."*

He has been the Director of Professional Development & Corporate Sponsorship for the Institute of Certified Financial Planners (ICFP); the Director of Technical Standards for the Certified Financial Planner Board of Standards (CFP Board), and was previously employed as Technical Manager in the Personal Financial Planning (PFP) Division of the American Institute of Certified Public Accountants (AICPA) in New York City.

Acknowledgments

When we started writing this book many years ago, I relied on many outside professionals to help me with the organization, information and writings contained throughout this book. Special thanks go to Matthew Bishop, CFP®, who was instrumental with providing the estate and retirement sections, and to Richard Yasenchak, CFP®, who was instrumental with providing the investment sections.

To my family—my wife, Rochele, and children, Brandon, Keri, and Matthew. A special thank you for guiding me with your inspiration.

To my parents—Ronald and Esther. A special thank you for your ongoing persistence.

To my colleagues—a special thank you to those individuals who have worked with me in various capacities for many years and who have contributed in the development of this publication; it is truly appreciated.

To my Financial Planning Fast Track® Students—who challenge me to stay current on the laws, rules, regulations, and information relating to financial planning. A special thank you for keeping me sharp and focused.

Thanks to all the people at Panel, Aspen, and CCH, past and present, without whose efforts the publication of this book would not have been possible.

How to Use This Book

The 2007 edition of the *Financial Planning Answer Book* is designed for practitioners who need quick and authoritative answers to questions concerning financial planning. This book uses simple, straightforward language. The question and answer format, with its breadth of coverage, effectively conveys the complex subject matter of financial planning. In addition, the book provides an extensive index.

List of Questions. A detailed list of questions follows the table of contents in the front of the book in order to help the reader locate areas of immediate interest. This list provides both the question number and the page number on which the question appears. A series of subheadings help to group and organize the questions by topic within each chapter.

Question Numbers. The questions are numbered consecutively within each chapter (*e.g.*, Q 2:1, Q 2:2, Q 2:3).

Index. At the back of the book is an index provided as further aid to locating specific information. All references are to question numbers rather than page numbers.

Contents

CHAPTER 3

Contents

Chapter **5**

Fixed Income **5-1**

CHAPTER 6

CHAPTER 7

List of Questions

Chapter 1 Fundamental to Financial Planning

Financial Planning and Disclosure

Compensation

Financial Planning Process

Planning for the Closely Held Business

Planning for the Executive

Planning for Charitable Giving

Planning for Business Entities

Different Types of Money Market Instruments

Securities Issued by the U.S. Treasury

Federal Agency Debt

State and Local Government Securities

Foreign Bonds

The Risk Structure of Interest Rates

The Term Structure of Interest Rates

Tax Issues When Planning Investments

Tax Issues When Planning for Retirement

Tax Issues When Planning for Employee Benefits

Chapter 8 Characteristics of Retirement Plans

401(k) Plans

SIMPLE IRAs

Nonqualified Plans

Qualified Plan Annuities, Distributions, and Loans

Chapter 1

Fundamental to Financial Planning

The first steps of financial planning can sometimes be the most important. The planner should sit down with the client and discuss the whole process, and make decisions regarding compensation, cash flow, budgeting, and asset allocation. This chapter also covers the formulas necessary to determine the time value of money.

Financial Planning and Disclosure

Q 1:1   What is personal financial planning?

Personal financial planning is a process and not a product. The most comprehensive definition of personal financial planning was developed by the Certified Financial Planner Board of Standards and is contained in its Code of Ethics and Professional Responsibility. The definition reads as follows:

> Personal financial planning or financial planning denotes the process of determining whether and how an individual can meet life goals through the proper management of financial resources. Personal financial planning process or financial planning process denotes the process which typically includes, but is not limited to, these six elements: establishing and defining the client-planner relationship, gathering client data including goals, analyzing and evaluating the client's financial status, developing and presenting financial planning recommendations and/or

alternatives, implementing the financial planning recommendations, and monitoring the financial planning recommendations.

Q 1:2 How do financial planners provide disclosure to prospective clients?

Financial planners provide disclosure to clients through SEC form ADV Part II (*e.g.*, if registered investment advisers) or their own form. The disclosure is to be delivered to the client within 48 hours of entering into an investment advisory agreement or when the contract is signed if the client has the right to terminate the contract within five days of signing. CERTIFIED FINANCIAL PLANNER (CFP®) certificants may also use the Sample CFP® Certificant Disclosure Form provided in the Code of Ethics and Professional Responsibility (Code of Ethics). The Code of Ethics outlines certain disclosures to clients that should be included in whatever form is used by a CFP certificant. The required disclosures and examples developed by the Certified Financial Planner Board of Standards and described in the Code of Ethics read as follows:

> Compliance with the client disclosure requirements of the Code of Ethics is accomplished only when all material information relevant to the professional relationship (which includes everything required pertinent and appropriate to the given client relationship) has been disclosed to the client or prospective client. Such disclosure should include, if material, (1) information about the financial condition of the CFP certificant and/or his or her firm which is reasonably likely to impair the ability of the CFP certificant to meet contractual commitments to the client and (2) any legal or disciplinary event relative to the CFP certificant that is material to a client's or potential client's evaluation of the CFP certificant's integrity or ability to meet contractual commitments to the client. Mere completion of a suggested disclosure form does not in and of itself constitute full compliance with the Code of Ethics disclosure requirements.

Part I of the Sample CFP® Certificant Disclosure Form is a general disclosure provided prior to establishing a client relationship. Part I details relationships that may reasonably compromise the CFP® certificant's objectivity and independence. For example, the planner should state which firms he or she uses to purchase and sell securities or insurance products.

Part II is a general disclosure that is provided at the time of entering into a client relationship. It contains material information that is related to the professional relationship. The first section of Part II is the basic philosophy of the CFP® certificant (or firm) on working with a client. An example of this disclosure by the Certified Financial Planner Board of Standards, and described in the Code of Ethics, reads as follows:

> Our approach to personal financial planning is to obtain from you significant financial and other information including your attitudes, goals and objectives; to analyze the information obtained in order to develop alternatives for your consideration; to educate you about the

implications of selecting a particular alternative; to implement the alternative selected by you; and to periodically update the plan adopted. It is our goal to become your chief financial adviser and to coordinate the efforts of your other advisers in your best interests. We want you to be educated about your own financial affairs and to take an active role in managing them.

The next section under Part II contains the philosophy and principles that will be used by the planner. An example from the Code of Ethics reads as follows:

> Our philosophy of financial planning is to gather adequate reliable information about a client's personal financial situation; to determine the client's goals and objectives, time horizon, and risk tolerance; to analyze all of the foregoing information in an objective manner; and to develop recommendations for our clients based upon this thorough analysis and in the interest of rendering disinterested advice. In a personal financial planning engagement, we endeavor to consistently act in the interest of our client and to place his or her interest ahead of our own. Moreover, we believe that a client should be both informed and proactively involved in his or her personal financial affairs. Accordingly, we believe in holding frequent meetings with our clients to educate them about the financial planning process and their own financial situation.

Part II also requires principals and employees to provide resumes to the client if they are expected to provide financial planning services for the client. This should include educational background, professional and employment history, professional certifications and licenses, and areas of competence and specialization.

The next section is a description of the financial planning process that the CFP® certificant will provide to the client. The Code of Ethics provides two precise examples:

Example 1-1. This engagement is limited in scope to retirement planning only. Other types of personal financial planning services will not be performed by us unless they directly affect your retirement plan, and you give us your express permission prior to performing such additional services.

Example 1-2. You have expressed interest in asset management services. These services include:

- Analysis of your current financial condition, goals and objectives, and development of a personal financial plan.
- Design of an investment portfolio appropriate to your individual circumstances, needs, goals, risk tolerance, investment experience, and time horizon.
- Quarterly written reports on the status of your investment portfolio.
- Two meetings each year to review and update your objectives and financial status and provide an evaluation of your investment portfolio.

- Ongoing monitoring of your investment portfolio.
- Recommendations involving investment repositioning and current opportunities for new investments.
- Availability of our professional staff to answer questions.

The method of compensation must also be disclosed to the client in Part II. This is generally referenced as fee-only, commission-only, or fee and commission. For example, if the compensation is on a fee-only basis, the CFP® certificant should state the hourly rate, and what the expected range of the total cost for the services will be. The CFP® certificant cannot present himself or herself as fee-only if other forms of economic benefit are received from related parties. The compensation arrangement must also be disclosed. This includes sources of compensation (*e.g.*, fees from client, commission from third parties), referral fees (if any), and any contingencies to the fee and/or commission. An example of a contingency is when a planner receives no commission unless the client purchases a product recommended by the planner.

Other categories of disclosure under Part II include agency and employment relationships, potential conflicts of interest, and other material information that is relevant to the relationship. In addition, any information required by laws applicable to the relationship must be provided to the client. For registered investment advisors, the law requires them to file Form ADV with the SEC and provide Form ADV Part II to clients.

Part III details subsequent disclosures. It is provided subsequent to establishing the client relationship. This includes changes to the CFP® certificant's business affiliation, address, telephone number, credentials, qualifications, licenses, compensation structure, and agency relationships, and scope of the CFP® certificant's authority in any agency relationship. In the second section of Part III, any new conflicts of interest are disclosed. For example, it must be disclosed if a firm changes its method of compensation from fee-only to fee plus commission. The final section under Part III states that a client has the right to receive annually the current SEC Form ADV Part II or the amended disclosure that was initially received when the relationship began.

Compensation

(Adapted from Rattiner, *Getting Started as a Financial Planner*, Bloomberg Press, 2005.)

Q 1:3   How are financial planners compensated?

The compensation structure selected by a planner is often a reflection of the type of practice provided. It represents the image, both professional and personal, that is presented to the client. It also represents the types of clients the planner wishes to pursue. The compensation structure should be addressed when the business is originally set up, because it makes sense to commit to one method going forward. It is not something that changes frequently. However, a planner will revisit the issue periodically as his or her practice matures. It is crucial to establish a compensation structure from the beginning that the planner feels comfortable with. There are no right or wrong compensation methods. The selected method must be evaluated on its merits for the type of practice that is desired.

There are five methods of compensation that financial planners can use to charge their clients: commission only, fee only, fee-based (fee and commission), fee offset, and assets under management.

Q 1:4   What is a commission-only financial planner?

Planners working on commission receive payment from a third party, usually an insurance or investment company. The planner's fee, of course, is bundled into the amount the client pays the third party, but the actual payment comes directly from the third-party vendor. The payment can take the form of a lump sum payment made at the time of sale to the client or of a long-term "trailer," in which the planner is compensated every time the client makes a payment on the vendor's product. Commission payments can continue for many years. Some planners discourage this form of compensation because it can skew a planner's objectivity and independence. However, the bottom line is doing what is appropriate for the client, always and forever. Do that, and this type of payment will not present a problem.

Many planners entering the financial planning business work on a commission basis, because it is the easiest way to enter the business and probably the quickest way to earn a living. Commissions (whether alone or in combination with fees) still represent the dominant form of compensation structure in the industry. That is because its origins are in the insurance and stockbrokerage industries, in which that mode of payment has been the most common. Commissions make sense if planners are providing specific product recommendations and want to follow the implementation. The payouts can be large, and planners can make comfortable livings from their practice.

Clients may perceive an inherent conflict of interest, since the income stream of a planner is tied to client trades. Usually, when planners have been in the business for a number of years, they feel a desire to upgrade their practices away from commissions for this reason. This task is difficult for most planners, because they must deplete their income stream—those recurring commissions—until fees are earned. This approach could take some time but may be worthwhile in the long run.

Q 1:5   What is a fee-only financial planner?

Fees are direct charges to the client. They can take one of two forms. In the first, the planner charges the client by the hour (an hourly fee arrangement). For example, planners typically charge anywhere from $100 to $400 per hour. Planners should provide clients with an estimate of how much the client should be expected to pay for the amount of time spent with the planner. Charging by the hour works well when the services vary from client to client. Planners have the ability to handle each of these different client situations. The primary disadvantage is the effort involved in keeping time records and the possibility that clients may dispute a particular activity.

The second type of fee only is a flat fee that depends on the scope of the project (a flat-fee arrangement). For example, planners usually charge $2,000 to $5,000 for a comprehensive financial plan. The planner bases the fee on how many hours it will take to complete the assignment. If the planner determines it will take 10 hours to put together a plan at $300 per hour, the flat fee is $3,000. This method tends to eliminate any conflicts of interest stemming from accepting payments on product recommendations. A flat-fee arrangement also works well if the services provided are relatively uniform for all clients. The fee can be based on any number of factors, such as client income, investment assets, or net worth. Planners may even base the fee on the complexity of the client's situation. The main advantage of this method is the simplicity of determining a fee and the ease of billing. The main disadvantage is that the formula can result in a fee that is grossly disproportionate to the actual cost of delivering the service.

Fee-only means moving with the trends in the profession. It is the direction in which the financial planning marketplace is currently moving. Because planners who practice on a fee basis feel no pressure to sell a product, they may come across to the client as being more objective. This professionalism makes them feel that they are doing a more satisfactory job for the client. However, there are drawbacks. For starters, it takes time to convert to a fee-only basis, and some planners may argue that it is tough to make a living solely on this compensation method. Another concern is that planners have little incentive to see through the implementation of the plan since they are not getting paid specifically for the follow-up. A third drawback is the possibility that the total cost of doing the planning for the client will be higher than what was initially quoted, especially if there is a commission earned by an outside party.

Q 1:6   What is a fee- and commission-based financial planner?

A combination approach allows for the receipt of both fees and commissions from the client. It is easy to double-bill clients under this method. To avoid this problem, make sure that services are completely separate and charge individually for each client.

The total amount of compensation the planner receives could be perceived as being excessive to the client, because it may appear that they are paying twice for the same work, *i.e.*, a fee for meeting with the client and then commissions on recommendations. Planners view this differently, perhaps, since they are getting paid for doing two separate jobs: providing a plan and receiving a commission for the implementation of an insurance or investment product. It can also allow a planner to stay alert to the types of products available in the marketplace. This method indicates that a planner wishes to be paid for all services provided. Some professionals suggest avoiding this approach since it tends to provide less value to the client and does not work well to build a long-term clientele.

Q 1:7   What is fee offset?

A fee-offset compensation program essentially reduces the amount the client is ultimately responsible for paying to the planner by substituting commissions paid by third-party vendors for the client's direct outlay of finds. For example, if the planner charges the client $2,000 and the planner recommends an insurance product that has an $800 commission to the planner, the planner then receives only $1,200 directly from the client. The client pays the remaining $800 as a commission on the insurance policy. The planner still receives the payment to complete the work, yet the client gets a discount. This method usually provides the best of both worlds for the planner and the client. This approach is advantageous if planners want to guarantee themselves a certain dollar amount from the client.

It also works for clients because their fee is capped and can even be reduced if they buy additional products; they pay the net amount (gross fees less commissions). The downside is that this practice may not be legal in all states. Some states consider this rebating and will not permit it. Check with your state investment and/or insurance commissioner. This approach is also difficult for the client to understand and may leave room for disagreement between the planner and the client.

Q 1:8   How are planners compensated for assets under management?

This type of compensation involves receiving a payment from a client based on the assets under management or control. The planner is paid some percentage of the assets or a flat fee for directing the client's assets through several investments, usually in a long-term arrangement. Many planners charge their clients 1 percent as a management fee. If a client has $1 million invested, the planner would receive an annual management fee of $10,000. The fee is deducted from the client account at the beginning of each quarter.

This method provides the most stable income stream of any method. However, this method does have its drawbacks. First, if a planner's clients have a substantial amount of assets in retirement accounts or in real estate investments, these assets are outside the actively managed accounts. These assets must be considered when doing asset allocation, yet may not be included in calculating the fee for the planner. Planners often avoid this situation by charging a higher setup fee for these types of situations. Second, a practice may be short-lived if return is promoted. Planners using this approach must provide value to clients by educating them that investing is a long-term process and not a quick fix, basically stating to the client that the planner can pick and choose the best investments for them and their investment goals. This provides a safe harbor from fluctuating markets and keeps the income stream intact.

Financial Planning Process

(Adapted from Rattiner, *Getting Started as a Financial Planner*, Bloomberg Press, 2005, unless noted otherwise.)

Q 1:9 What is the "Rattiner PIPRIM" system for going through the financial planning process?

In order to translate personal financial needs into goals and objectives, a client-centered financial planning process called PIPRIM is used. PIPRIM is described as:

- Preliminary meeting with a client
- Integrated goal setting and data gathering
- Putting it all together
- Recommending solutions
- Implementing the plan
- Monitoring the plan

Q 1:10 What is the preliminary meeting according to PIPRIM?

The preliminary meeting is the time when a planner learns about the prospect and determines if he or she can meet the prospect's needs. This meeting usually lasts no more than one hour. The planner should be prepared to talk about the prospect's goals and objectives, current financial situation, and immediate and long-term needs. The planner should determine if he or she offers the appropriate services for satisfying the client's needs, and how the prospect will benefit from such services. Planners should try to determine their role in relation to the prospect. That is, are they likely to be teacher, motivator, counselor, or adviser? The most important part of the preliminary meeting is getting the prospect to translate the meeting discussion into his or her own words. The prospect's own words are often requisite to commitment.

If the planner and prospect reach a mutually agreed-upon understanding of the situation, it is best to set up a next meeting no more than two weeks later. Momentum and commitment are important at this stage of the game. It is appropriate to give the prospect some homework to do before the next meeting to keep him or her focused on the financial process. This homework often asks the prospect to rank his or her goals by importance, timeframe, and degree of risk that he or she is willing to accept.

Planners often send an engagement letter to the client no more than two days after the initial meeting. The engagement letter is a summary of the planner's understanding of details from the preliminary meeting, and describes in legal terms the obligations of the client and planner in a contractual relationship. This is often the initial transition from prospect to client relationship. The letter should be signed and returned by the client before the next meeting.

The next meeting usually lasts about 60 minutes, and is used to develop a working relationship with the client. It helps to develop what the next 10 or more hours that are necessary to complete the financial plan will be like with the client. It also covers any homework the client did since the first meeting.

Q 1:11   What is integrated goal setting and data gathering according to PIPRIM?

The third meeting often lasts several hours and is used to collect data to design an effective financial plan. It is important that this meeting be interactive. Planners should probe their clients with closed-and open-ended questions to obtain quantitative and qualitative data used to establish a client's goals and objectives. Goals are broadbased projections of a client's aspirations. For example, a client's goal may be to retire rich. Objectives are a quantifiable way of achieving the goals over a specified time period. For example, saving $5 million by age 65 is an objective, whereas retiring rich is the goal.

Quantitative information tells the planner where the client is and what it will take to get him or her to a specific financial goal. Qualitative information tells clients why they want to reach the goal, what will make them work toward it, and what they are not likely to do. Quantitative data is often found using a fact-finding questionnaire that asks about insurance coverage, liabilities, assets, cash outflows and inflows, and other personal information. Qualitative data is obtained by conducting a goals and objectives interview, asking questions to determine interest in activities and hobbies, risk tolerance levels, good and bad experiences with different investments, retirement plans, children education plans, and other areas. It is good practice to meet with both husband and wife during this meeting.

After the meeting, the planner should schedule the next appointment about four weeks later. Before doing any further work, send a synopsis of the meeting to the client that states the issues and objectives discussed during the meeting and conclusions that were agreed upon. The client should sign and return this synopsis statement.

Q 1:12   What is the process of putting it all together according to PIPRIM?

This is when the planner reviews all the material and information obtained from the goal setting and data gathering session. The planner identifies and forms conclusions on financial strengths and weaknesses. Two financial statements should be developed to summarize the position of the client's financial condition. The first is the Statement of Financial Position, which gives a reflection of the client's assets, liabilities, and net worth. The second is the Cash Flow Statement, which provides information on the client's cash inflows less cash outflows. The planner also revises goal and objectives if necessary.

Q 1:13   How does a financial planner recommend solutions according to PIPRIM?

The next stage is to present recommendations to the client in order to achieve goals and prioritize objectives. It is generally advisable to test your recommendations with the client over an informal lunch or morning coffee. This allows the client to have ownership of the plan and provide you with more direction. Once the planner is satisfied that the client will be in agreement with the recommendations, the planners should develop a precise written proposal. The financial plan should include:

- An overview of the client's short- and long-term goals;
- The client's current financial strengths and weaknesses and how they impact the plan;
- The client's financial objectives based on current resources;
- A clear and precise summation of all recommendations, including positives and negatives;
- The financial plan using recommendations that were agreed upon by both the planner and the client;
- A comprehensive economic overview of the financial plan supported by financial statements; and
- A step-by-step implementation and monitoring of the plan.

Q 1:14   What is the implementation process?

Perhaps the most important part of the financial planning process is the implementation phase. It must explain the tasks and decisions to be made along the way. It should be clear whether the planner or the client will initiate action on each recommendation. Planners should motivate their clients to ensure that the plan is carried out. Planners also draw on outside experts as needed. For example, a planner may be fee-only, so the client will need to be referred to a stockbroker or insurance agent to purchase or sell the selected investment vehicles.

The implementation process is defined by the Certified Financial Planner Board of Standards in its *Financial Planning Practice Standards*, and reads as follows:

> The financial planning practitioner and the client shall mutually agree on the implementation responsibilities consistent with the scope of the engagement.
> The client is responsible for accepting or rejecting recommendations and for retaining and/or delegating implementation responsibilities. The financial planning practitioner and the client shall mutually agree on the services, if any, to be provided by the practitioner. The scope of the engagement, as originally defined, may need to be modified.

The practitioner's responsibilities may include, but are not limited to the following:

- Identifying activities necessary for implementation
- Determining division of activities between the practitioner and the client
- Referring to other professionals
- Coordinating with other professionals
- Sharing of information as authorized; and
- Selecting and securing products and/or services

If there are conflicts of interest, sources of compensation or material relationships with other professionals or advisers that have not been previously disclosed, such conflicts, sources or relationships shall be disclosed at this time.

When referring the client to other professionals or advisers, the financial planning practitioner shall indicate the basis on which the practitioner believes the other professional or adviser may be qualified.

If the practitioner is engaged by the client to provide only implementation activities, the scope of the engagement shall be mutually defined, orally or in writing. This scope may include such matters as the extent to which the practitioner will rely on information, analysis or recommendations provided by others.

The financial planning practitioner shall select appropriate products and services that are consistent with the client's goals, needs and priorities.

The financial planning practitioner shall investigate products or services that reasonably address the client's needs. The products or services selected to implement the recommendation(s) must be suitable to the client's financial situation and consistent with the client's goals, needs and priorities.

The financial planning practitioner uses professional judgment in selecting the products and services that are in the client's interest. Professional judgment incorporates both qualitative and quantitative information.

Products and services selected by the practitioner may differ from those of other practitioners or advisers. More than one product or service may exist that can reasonably meet the client's goals, needs and priorities.

The practitioner shall make all disclosures required by applicable regulations.

Q 1:15   What are monitoring responsibilities?

Planners should evaluate the performance and review changes in the client's circumstances. Revisiting other steps because of new tax laws or client circumstances and objectives should be done.

The monitoring process is defined by the Certified Financial Planner Board of Standards in the 2002 *Financial Planning Practice Standards*, and reads as follows:

The financial planning practitioner and client shall mutually define monitoring responsibilities.

The purpose of this Practice Standard is to clarify the role, if any, of the practitioner in the monitoring process. By clarifying this responsibility, the client's expectations are more likely to be in alignment with the level of monitoring services which the practitioner intends to provide.

If engaged for monitoring services, the practitioner shall make a reasonable effort to define and communicate to the client those monitoring activities the practitioner is able and willing to provide. By explaining what is to be monitored, the frequency of monitoring and the communication method, the client is more likely to understand the monitoring service to be provided by the practitioner.

The monitoring process may reveal the need to reinitiate steps of the financial planning process. The current scope of the engagement may need to be modified.

Q 1:16 How do financial planners work with other outside resources?

There is generally such a tremendous amount of information in the financial industry that it becomes very difficult for a planner to stay current on everything. As a result, financial planning firms often affiliate with other outside resources. Outside resources enable planners to leverage themselves in key areas by using known experts whose opinions can be relied upon. Leveraging often results in a whole that is greater than the individual components.

There are generally four primary areas for leveraging outside resources:

1. CPAs. Surveys have shown that CPAs are practitioners that have the basic trust of Americans. The best way to network with a CPA is to act like one. This means that a financial planner should become involved in their activities, such as a local CPA community group. To maximize a relationship with a CPA, it is best to have an exclusive arrangement with him. This means that all of the planner's tax, accounting, and audit referrals are sent to the CPA. In return, the CPA refers his or her clients that need financial help to the financial planner.

2. Attorneys. State laws prohibit the sharing of commissions with attorneys. However, the benefit of working with an attorney is that he or she will become comfortable with the financial planner's style of personal financial planning and will develop strategies to complement the financial planner's approach to clients.

3. Insurance brokers. When leveraging insurance brokers, the financial planner should never go with just one company. It is necessary to get quotes from many companies. It is ideal for the planner to deal with at least two dozen companies and various product lines.

4. Money managers. Leveraging a money manager eases the burden of diversifying and managing a client's portfolio. The financial planner shifts the responsibility of selecting and managing investments to the money manager. The financial planner's responsibility shifts to managing the money manager.

Q 1:17   What are effective methods for communicating with clients?

Highly successful financial planners are insightful, in that they know more than just the technical side of the business. They are very skilled in handling drawbacks, objections, and miscalculations. This is usually achieved through highly developed communication skills. Communication is central to the client relationship. It gives rise to a cycle of action and reaction. The better a planner can listen to and articulate the client's goals and objectives, the greater the trust and loyalty the planner will enjoy. Communication also involves motivating and teaching clients on the financial process.

Good communication starts with listening to your clients. An effective planner should see the issues through their eyes and not his or her own. Listen carefully to verbal and nonverbal cues. In addition, planners should be positive and establish rapport. Try to show that the glass is half full instead of half empty. The atmosphere should be open and friendly. Do not rush the meeting, and project an accepting, nonjudgmental attitude. The planner should ask open-ended questions to gather insight into the client's financial situation.

Communication is thought of as verbal and nonverbal cues designed to provoke a response. There are five common human traits to know when effectively communicating with clients.

First, clients use verbal and nonverbal actions to communicate facts and feelings. This includes use of words, rate of speech, volume of speech, and bodily and other nonverbal actions. Tone and pitch often signify the client's feelings. For example, angry people tend to speak loudly, and sad people are often low-pitched. In many cases, verbal and nonverbal cues can indicate mixed signals. The client may say one thing, but act in a different way. Both of these messages may be important, so the planner should conduct more probing to find a mutual understanding.

Second, men and women, husbands and wives, and young and older people all communicate differently. Men tend to use informal words and phrases, and women use more formal ones. It is best to communicate the message to both spouses at the same time, because the message can become skewed if one spouse relays it to the other.

Third, initial impressions stick with a client for a long period of time. In the book, *Contact: The First Four Minutes*, authors Leonard Zunin and Natalie Zunin conclude that the first four minutes of an interpersonal relationship are vital to its continued success.[1]

Fourth, communication is constantly being influenced by multiple factors. This means that communication is impacted by motivation, credibility, and style. It is critical to motivate clients to stay focused on the big picture. Credibility is reached over time as your client gains trust in the relationship. Also, the organization of communication is important. It is recommended that planners present their best and most important points first or last. Planners should be

---

[1] Ballantine Books, 1986.

authoritative when they speak, emphasize the client's understanding of information to create self-confidence, and emphasize a low-pressure approach. The responsibility for actions should be placed in the hands of the client.

Lastly, personal life experiences leave hidden marks on everyone. For example, if a planner inherits a client who lost considerable money through a stockbroker, he will initially find it difficult to obtain this individual's trust. It is critical to set expectations up front, and be open, honest, and sincere.

Cash Flow and Budgeting

Q 1:18   How do you help clients manage cash flow?

Cash flow management serves two purposes. First, it allows for the management of income and expenditures. It does this by establishing a reserve of cash or cash equivalents to meet unanticipated or emergency needs. Second, it allows for the systematic creation of a surplus of cash for capital investment.

Clients manage cash flows through budgeting, cash flow planning, and determining net worth. (See Q 1:19 below.) After a budget is established, cash flow planning is used to maximize discretionary income by implementing specific strategies. The current net worth of a client is critical to determine the appropriate cash flow necessary to save for future objectives.

Q 1:19   What is budgeting?

Budgeting is an analysis of how clients are spending money and at what rate they are investing to reach short- and long-term goals. To manage money, clients should learn to plan a budget from the bottom up. To accomplish this, clients need to document actual and estimated income, document actual and estimated spending and investing, and compare actual to projected figures. It is critical for the client to maintain accurate and detailed accounts of income and spending patterns. A planner should help clients successfully manage and control their spending. The planner should make realistic estimates as to how much a client should spend, and if this figure exceeds income, the planner should reduce or eliminate certain expenses.

When preparing personal budgets and performing analysis, the planner should establish reasonable goals and objectives for the client. In addition, objectives should be measurable and specific. It may be the client's goal to become rich, but the objective may be to have $2 million within 20 years.

The planner should also determine the client's current financial situation by analyzing expenses and income flows over the last six months, and help the client realistically forecast future expenses and income. Start by determining the family's annual income by calculating gross salaries, dividend and interest income, rental income, inheritances, and other incoming cash flows. Next, develop estimates for both fixed and discretionary expenses. Fixed or nondiscretionary expenses can be changed, but must be paid. Discretionary expenses are flexible and can be prevented or planned for. The next step is to determine the excess of shortfall of income within the budget period. If net income is positive, the client can increase discretionary expenses. Next, the planner should consider available methods of increasing income or decreasing expenses. The final step may be to calculate income and expenses as a percentage of the total to determine a better allocation of resources.

Q 1:20   What tools are available to help clients increase their discretionary income?

1. *Debt Restructuring.* The process of paying off all outstanding credit cards by consolidating debt into one low personal line of credit by refinancing the house, discontinuing the use of credit cards, and deferring major purchases on credit for a specified period of time.

2. *Asset Reallocation.* This process involves the change in assets from underperforming assets to more productive investment assets to improve return and income. Growth investments can be reallocated to income investments for more cash inflow. Concentrate on tax savings by investing in municipals.

3. *Qualified Plan Vehicles and Other Personal Retirement Accounts.* The process of utilizing a qualified plan to benefit from saving programs and deductibility. The planner should demonstrate the long-term benefits of tax-deferred savings.

4. *Control and Monitor Spending.* The process of reducing spending by emphasizing the savings element.

5. *Separate Treatment of Children's Assets.* The process of saving for a child in a custodial account or trust to benefit from the lower tax rate of the child.

Q 1:21   What are the ways to borrow money to improve the client's financial situation?

The primary way to pay off all outstanding debt is through debt restructuring. This involves either paying off all outstanding credit card balances and student loan balances or consolidating debt into one loan or mortgage.

Taking a cash-out refinance will give a new first mortgage by paying off the current first mortgage and provide additional cash. If current mortgage rates are lower than that on the existing first mortgage, a new first mortgage will allow the borrower to save on the current debt. The combined loan to a value of 80 percent is recommended to avoid mortgage insurance. Interest is taxdeductible as with all home mortgages.

Another option is taking out a home equity loan or a home equity line of credit. A home loan is a good choice for satisfying credit card debt because interest is tax-deductible. A home equity loan is cash that is given up front (interest charged from the start) at a fixed interest rate. In contrast, home equity credit line allows the individual to use the money only when needed (no interest charged until used), but at a variable rate that is usually tied to the prime rate. If current mortgage rates are higher than that of the existing first mortgage, a home equity will allow the borrower to keep the current low first mortgage rate. The homeowner generally can take out cash up to 125 percent of property value. Interest is fully tax-deductible on home equity loans up to $100,000.

Other ways to borrow money include using the cash value of a life insurance policy for a loan. Interest rate charges are generally less than personal or credit card loans. A loan from a life insurance product also does not have to be repaid. Tapping into a company savings plan is also a choice. Many companies allow their employees to borrow against their qualified plan, up to $50,000. Another alternative is using after-tax money from a Roth IRA. This generally allows a client to take money out without penalty or tax consequences.

Portfolio Management and the Asset Allocation Decision

Q 1:22   What are the life cycle stages?

There are generally four life cycle stages. These stages are not exclusive and there is possibility for overlap. The first stage is the accumulation phase, which is during the early to middle years (generally before 40 years old) of working careers. In this stage, families try to protect themselves from a potential financial disaster resulting from death or disability. It is important to build cash reserves and emergency funds to meet unexpected situations and take out appropriate insurance. Families often find themselves saving for a home and car. In addition, they should start saving for their retirement and children's education. During the accumulation phase, individuals are generally accepting of high-risk investments for above-average returns.

The second stage is the consolidation phase, when individuals are generally past the midpoint of their careers (generally 40 to 60 years old). In this phase, they have paid off most or all outstanding loans and have assets for their children's education. It is important that they continue to save for retirement. In the consolidation phase, individuals are generally accepting of moderate-risk investments.

The third phase is the spending phase, which begins when an individual retires. In this phase, individuals seek greater capital preservation. They are accepting of low-risk investments. The overall portfolio should be less risky than during the consolidation years, but there is still need to have some risky growth investments, such as common stock, for inflation protection. The final phase is the gifting phase. This phase is very similar to the spending phase, and, in fact, may mirror it. Estate planning becomes the most critical function for families. Any excess assets are transferred to children, friends, and charitable organizations.

Q 1:23   What is the portfolio management process?

The portfolio management process never ends. It is a lifelong process of monitoring a portfolio to ensure it is consistent with the plan. There are four primary steps. The first step in this process is to establish an investment policy statement. The investment policy statement is a road map for an individual. It lists the risks, objectives, and the constraints of a portfolio. It is reviewed and updated yearly for an individual. The second step is to evaluate current economic conditions and forecast future trends. The third step in the portfolio management process is to construct the portfolio. This involves allocation among different asset classes and countries. The final step is the constant monitoring of an investor's needs and changing capital market conditions.

Q 1:24   What is the investment policy statement and its inputs?

The investment policy statement is a road map for the investor. The construction of a policy statement is critical to the investment process, serving three purposes. First, it is designed to impose an investment discipline on the client and the portfolio manager. Thus, a portfolio manager will not hastily make decisions that do not conform to the policy statement. Second, it helps educate the investor on the risks and returns associated with investing. It helps the investor decide on realistic goals that can be expected, given different levels of risk. Third, it creates a standard to measure the performance of a portfolio manager.

An investment policy statement should answer:

- Is the policy statement designed to meet the specific needs and objectives of a particular client? One policy does not fit all investors.
- Is the policy clearly and precisely written so that a competent stranger can manage the portfolio?
- Would the client have been able to remain committed to the policy statement over the past 50 or so years? This means the client should fully understand all investment risks and the discipline required in the investment process.
- Would the portfolio manager have been able to remain committed to the policy statement over the past 50 or so years?
- Would the policy statement be expected to meet the client's objectives if implemented?

The inputs to an investment policy statement include investment objectives and investment constraints.

The objectives of an investor are his or her investment goals in terms of risk and return. A portfolio manager should educate the client to understand that risk and return are positively correlated. Higher returns mean more risk; lower returns mean less risk.

Risk comes in two forms, systematic and unsystematic. Systematic risk is defined as nondiversifiable risk. Investors should understand that systematic risk cannot be reduced or eliminated. It is risk that the market rewards, and is divided into three types: (1) market risk, or risk present for being in the market; (2) interest rate risk, or risk that interest rates will adversely affect the price of stocks and bonds; and (3) purchasing power risk, or the risk that inflation will adversely affect the price of stocks and bonds. On the other hand, unsystematic risk is defined as diversifiable risk. It is risk that the market does not reward. A planner should help investors diversify appropriately to eliminate unsystematic risk. Unsystematic risk includes business risk, or the risk inherent in the industry or business itself; and financial risk, or the risk incurred through debt.

Return is described in three forms. The first is expected return, which is the return that an investor would normally anticipate to earn from an investment. Expected return is directly correlated with risk. The higher the risk, the higher the return an investor can expect; the lower the risk, the lower the return an investment will achieve. The second, minimum required rate of return, is the return an investment must produce in order to invest in it. The minimum required rate of return should be calculated before investing funds. The third is actual return, the real return earned by the investments, including capital appreciation, interest, and dividends.

It is critical that the actual returns be compared to an appropriate benchmark when monitoring the performance of a portfolio. An investor who specifies low-risk (low return) investments in the policy statement should compare the portfolio manager's performance against a low-risk benchmark. In contrast, an investor who specifies high-risk (high return) investments should compare the performance of the portfolio against a high-risk benchmark. For example, if a client were seeking capital preservation, an appropriate benchmark would not be the S&P 500 index.

The investment constraints of an investment policy statement include liquidity and marketability needs, time horizon, tax consequences, legal and regulatory factors, and unique needs and preferences.

Liquidity is the ability to convert an asset into cash with no loss of principal. Marketability is the ease in which an asset can be bought or sold. Real estate is often marketable but not liquid. For example, a home can be sold if the price is right, but the price may be lower than the original cost of the home. Stocks are both liquid and marketable. An investor may require that a percentage of cash be available at all times in order to meet needs, such as paying taxes, unemployment, or buying a home.

The time horizon among investors will be different depending on their age. Younger investors have a long-term horizon, whereas older investors have a shorter time horizon. There is a relationship between time horizon, liquidity, and risk. Younger investors require less liquidity and can handle more risk over a longer time horizon. Older investors require more liquidity and less risk over a shorter time horizon.

The portfolio manager must evaluate the tax consequences of different investments. This means that the after-tax return and equivalent taxable yield should be considered. In addition, the manager should stay current to changes in the Tax Code. Certain investments are more appropriate for a tax-deferred account while others are not. For example, municipal bonds are not appropriate for an IRA.

Legal and regulatory factors also affect the investment process. For example, insider trading prohibits clients and portfolio managers from a breach of duty or misappropriation of information. There is generally a 10 percent penalty imposed when taking money out of retirement accounts before age 59½.

The final input into an investment policy statement is the unique needs of an individual investor. All investors are different and have special needs. Some investors want socially responsible stocks as part of their portfolio. Some investors have no time to manage their portfolios, while other investors wish to take an active role in the management process. The implications of these constraints differ among investors.

Q 1:25   What is the asset allocation decision?

Asset allocation is the process in which investors divide funds into different asset classes. This is found in the investment policy statement. Asset allocation is usually broken down into ranges instead of fixed percentages. This provides some flexibility in a variable market. For example, the policy statement may require that 60 to 80 percent of the value of the portfolio be invested in common stocks. In this way, if market conditions allow, the portfolio manager may find it appropriate to invest 80 percent in common stocks. If market conditions look unfavorable, the portfolio manager can decrease his or her holdings in stocks to 60 percent.

The investment strategy for asset allocation under the policy statement includes:

- Asset classes to consider for investment;
- Normal policy weights to assign to each asset class;
- The permissible allocation ranges per asset class;
- Type of diversification within each asset class;
- Specific securities to purchase for the portfolio.

Modern portfolio theory has recognized that the risk of a portfolio is less than the simple weighted risk of each individual asset, unless the correlation among stocks is one. In addition, several studies have shown that the asset class (investment policy) is the single most important function to achieving superior returns. Market timing and security selection are unlikely to produce high returns over a period of time.

Q 1:26   How can you manage client expectations?

Financial planners should help clients feel comfortable with investing, and set expectations for realistic returns for a given level of risk.

Risk comes in two forms, systematic and unsystematic. Systematic risk is defined as nondiversifiable risk. Investors should understand that systematic risk cannot be reduced or eliminated. It is risk that the market rewards, and is divided into three types: (1) market risk, or risk present for being in the market; (2) interest rate risk, or risk that interest rates will adversely affect the price of stocks and bonds; and (3) purchasing power risk, or the risk that inflation will adversely affect the price of stocks and bonds. On the other hand, unsystematic risk is defined as diversifiable risk. It is risk that the market does not reward. A planner should help investors diversify appropriately to eliminate unsystematic risk. Unsystematic risk includes business risk, or the risk inherent in the industry or business itself; and financial risk, or the risk incurred through debt.

Return is described in three forms: (1) expected return, which is the return that an investor would normally anticipate to earn from an investment. Expected return is directly correlated with risk. The higher the risk, the higher the return an investor can expect; the lower the risk, the lower the return an investment will achieve. (2) Minimum required rate of return is the return an investment must produce in order to invest in it. The minimum required rate of return should be calculated before investing funds. (3) Actual return is the real return earned by the investments, including capital appreciation, interest, and dividends.

Time Value of Money

Q 1:27 How do you calculate the present value of a fixed sum?

The present value of a fixed sum is determined by taking the future value of a sum of money and calculating what it is worth today, using a discount rate. The more frequent the compounding, the smaller the present value. The formula used is:

$$PV = FV / (1 + r)^n$$

Where,

PV = Present value or value of investment today

FV = Future value of an investment at the end of n years

r = interest rate during each compounding period

n = number of compounding periods

The present value function found on a calculator is often used in place of the formula.

Example 1-3. Calculate the present value of $15,000 to be received in 5 years using an annual interest rate of 10%. Solution: 15,000 FV, 10 R, 5 N, calculate PV $\Rightarrow$ $9,313 (ignore the sign)

Example 1-4. Calculate the present value of $15,000 to be received in 5 years using an interest rate of 10%, compounded monthly. Solution: 15,000 FV, 8333 R (10/12), 60 N (5×12), calculate PV ⇒ $9,116 (ignore the sign)

Q 1:28   How do you calculate the future value of a fixed sum?

The future value of a fixed sum is the amount invested today that will grow over time when it is compounding interest. The formula for finding the future value of a single cash flow is:

$$FV = PV(1+r)^n$$

Where,

   PV = Present value or value of investment today

   FV = Future value of an investment at the end of n years

   r = interest rate during each compounding period

   n = number of compounding periods

The present value function found on a calculator is often used in place of the formula.

Example 1-5. Calculate the future value of $15,000 invested for 5 years using an annual interest rate of 10%. Solution: − 15,000 PV, 10 I, 5 N, calculate FV ⇒ $24,157

Example 1-6. Calculate the future value of $15,000 invested for 5 years using an interest rate of 10%, compounded monthly. Solution: −15,000 PV, .8333 I (10/12), 60 N (5×12), calculate FV ⇒ $24,679

Q 1:29   How do you calculate the FV and PV of an ordinary annuity and annuity due?

An annuity is a series of equal cash flows that occur at equal intervals over a period of time. For example, receiving $1,000 at the end of each year for the next 15 years is an annuity. An ordinary annuity is when cash flows begin at the end of each year. An annuity due is when cash flows begin on the same day as the initial investment.

Example 1-7. Finding the future value of an ordinary annuity.

Calculate the future value of an ordinary annuity that will pay $1,000 per year for each of the next 15 years while earning a 10% rate of return. Solution: 15 N, 10 I, 1000 PMT, CPT FV ⇒ $31,772

Example 1-8. Finding the future value of an annuity due.

Calculate the future value of an annuity paying $1,000 beginning today and continuing each year for the next 15 years while earning a 10% rate of return. Solution: Your calculator should be set at beginning mode; 15 N, 10 I, 1000 PMT, CPT FV ⇒ $34,949

Example 1-9. Finding the present value of an ordinary annuity.

Calculate the present value of an ordinary annuity of $1,000 received annually for 15 years using a 10% rate of return. Solution: 15 N, 10 I, 1000 PMT, CPT PV ⇒ $7,606

Example 1-10. Finding the present value of an annuity due.

Calculate the present value of an annuity of $1,000 received annually beginning today and continuing for 15 years earning a 10% rate of return. Solution: Your calculator should be set at beginning mode; 15 N, 10 I, 1000 PMT, CPT PV ⇒ $8,366

Example 1-11. Finding the annual payment in an ordinary annuity.

Calculate the annual payments required to fund your retirement plan in order to have $250,000 at the end of 15 years while earning a 10% rate of return. Solution: 15 N, 10 I, FV 250,000, CPT PMT ⇒ $7,868

Example 1-12. Finding the monthly payment in an annuity due.

Calculate the annual payments received at the beginning of each month for 15 years from an investment of $500,000 earning at annual return of 7% compounded monthly. Solution: Your calculator should be set at beginning mode; 180 N (15 × 12), .5833 (7/12) I, −500,000 PV, CPT PMT ⇒ $4,468

Q 1:30   How do you calculate the net present value (NPV)?

Net present value is the amount of cash flow (in present value terms) that a project generates after repaying the invested capital and required rate of return on that capital. It is the present value of future cash flows discounted at the firm's cost of capital less costs from the project. If the project generates a positive NPV, then shareholder wealth increases. In contrast, a negative NPV will decrease shareholder wealth. The decision rule holds that if NPV is greater than zero, accept the project; if NPV is less than zero, reject the project.

NPV is considered better than the internal rate of return (IRR) because it measures profitability in terms of dollars added to shareholder value. In contrast, IRR measures profitability as a rate of return. NPV assumes the reinvestment rate of cash flows is the cost of capital, while IRR assumes the reinvestment rate is the IRR. When the IRR is equal to the cost of capital, the NPV will be zero. If the IRR is less than the cost of capital, the result is a negative NPV.

Example 1-13. Calculate the NPV of a project with an initial cost of $25,000 that produces the following cash flows: year 1, +5,000; year 2, +5000; year 3, +12,000; year 4, −3000; year 5, +4000. The cost of capital is 5%. Solution: −25,000[CF0]; 5,000 [CFj]; 5,000 [CFj]; 12,000 [CFj]; −3,000 [CFj]; 4,000 [CFj]; 5 [i]; CPT NPV ⇒ −$4,670

Q 1:31   How do you calculate the internal rate of return (IRR)?

The IRR calculates the rate of return at which the present value of a series of cash inflows will equal the present value of the project's cost: PV (Inflows) equals PV (Investment costs). It is also defined as the rate of return in which the net present value of a project is zero. It assumes that all cash flows are reinvested at the IRR. The IRR is equivalent to the yield to maturity (YTM), the geometric average return, and the compounded average rate of return. The decision rule holds that if IRR is less than cost of capital, reject the project; if IRR is greater than cost of capital, accept the project.

Example 1-14. Calculate the IRR of a project that has an initial outflow of 25,000, and will generate the following cash flows: year 1, 7,000; year 2, −5,000; year 3, 9,000; year 4, 7,000; year 5, 15,000. Solution: −25,000 [CF0]; 7,000 [CFj]; −5,000 [CFj]; 9,000 [CFj]; 7,000 [CFj]; 15,000 [CFj]; CPT IRR ⇒ 7.64%

Q 1:32   How do you calculate the FV and PV from irregular cash flows?

It is common for the stream of cash flows to change from year to year for projects or investments—so it's not an annuity. The uneven cash flow is simply just a stream of (annual) single cash flows. To determine the FV/PV of irregular cash flows, you need to find the FV/PV of each cash flow and then add them up. The PV only of an uneven cash flow stream is also calculated using the NPV function on your calculator.

Example 1-15. Calculate the future value of an uneven cash flow series using a 10% discount rate and PV_1 though PV_5. Assume cash flows are:

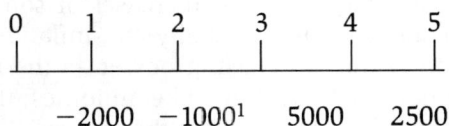

```
0     1     2     3     4     5
|     |     |     |     |     |

   −2000  −1000¹  5000   2500
```

Solution:

    FV1: enter PV = −2000; I/Y = 10; N = 4; CPT⇒ FV1 = −2928.20

    FV2: enter PV = −1000; I/Y = 10; N = 3; CPT⇒ FV2 = −1331.00

    FV3: enter PV = 0; I/Y = 10; N = 2; CPT⇒ FV3   = 0.00

    FV4: enter PV = 5000; I/Y = 10; N = 1; CPT⇒ FV4 = 5500.00

    FV5: enter PV = 2500; I/Y = 10; N = 0; CPT⇒ FV5 = 2500.00
                     Add up the FVs   = 3740.80

Example 1-16. Calculate the present value of an uneven cash flow series.

    PV1: enter FV = −2000; I/Y = 10; N = 1; CPT⇒ PV1 = −1818.18

    PV2: enter FV = −1000; I/Y = 10; N = 2; CPT⇒ PV2 = − 826.44

    PV3: enter FV = 0; I/Y = 10; N = 3; CPT⇒ PV3   = 0.00

    PV4: enter FV = 5000; I/Y = 10; N = 4; CPT⇒ PV4 = 3415.07

    PV5: enter FV = 2500; I/Y = 10; N = 5; CPT⇒ PV5 = 1552.30
                     Add up the FVs   = 2322.75

Regarding Example 1-16, what you are really doing is finding the NPV of a series of cash flows: Solution: 0 [CF0]; −2000 [CFj]; −1000 [CFj]; 0 [CFj]; 5000 [CFj]; 2500 [CFj]; 10 [i]; CPT NPV ⇒ 2322.75

Q 1:33   How do you determine the inflation-adjusted interest rate?

The inflation premium is an adjustment to the real risk-free rate to compensate investors for expected inflation and tightening or easing of monetary policy due to inflationary expectations.

Nominal rate of return investors require is:

Nominal risk-free rate = (1 + real risk-free rate) (1 + inflation rate) − 1

The nominal risk-free rate is the real risk-free rate adjusted for expected inflation and the relative tightening or easing in capital markets:

Real risk-free rate = [(1 + nominal risk-free rate) / (1 + inflation rate)] − 1

Calculate the nominal risk-free rate if the real rate is 5 percent and the expected inflation rate is 3 percent: (1.05) (1.03)−1 = 8.15%. The nominal rate is usually estimated by adding the real rate to the inflation premium. The estimate of the nominal risk-free rate is 5% + 3 % = 8%.

Q 1:34   What are serial payments?

A serial payment is a payment that increases at some constant rate on an annual basis. The constant rate is usually the inflation rate. The last serial payment will have the same purchasing power as the initial serial payment. Serial payments are not fixed payments like annuities; the first serial payment will be less than an annuity payment, but the last serial payment will be more than an annuity payment.

Example 1-17. Assume Jeff wants to start a business in 5 years. He needs to have $150,000 (today's dollars) in 5 years to finance his business. Inflation is expected to average 3%, and Jeff can earn a 7% annual compounded rate on his investments. In order to determine what serial payment he should invest at the end of the first year, he uses the following formula: Solution: 150,000 FV; 5 N; 0 PV; [(1.07 ÷ 1.03) −1] × 100 [i]; CPT PMT [x] 1.03 ⇒ 28,591

Example 1-18. What is Jeff's payment in the second year? Solution: 28,591 [x] 1.03 ⇒ 29,449

Chapter 2

Planning for the Professional

Financial planning should cover not only present needs, but possible future ones as well. Present needs include planning for the client's business and charitable giving. The financial planner also needs to help the client make decisions regarding long-term care, Social Security, and retirement.

How to Plan for the Professional

Professionals, such as physicians, dentists, attorneys, and accountants, can only transfer their practice to another professional. Their licenses are not transferable. The selling price is often depressed because there is a small buildup of capital value. There is also no guarantee that excess goodwill will pass on to the buyer, because the buyer is generally someone who is new to the profession with limited capital. These factors present a challenge in planning for the professional, but it is the job of the financial planner to guide the professional into making rational choices and good decisions when possible.

The planner must help the individual build and preserve income, and prepare for estate planning issues.

Q 2:1   How to plan for corporate and noncorporate practice?

Professionals can choose to practice in various legal and tax forms. They can form a C corporation, S corporation, general partnership, limited liability partnership, or a sole proprietorship. Many professionals are adopting a limited liability company (LLC), if their state permits it. An LLC is taxed as a partnership with the limited liability of a corporation. An LLC can elect to be taxed as a corporation by filing Form 8832. Operating as a partnership requires at least two partners. The other forms operate with just one person. There is a limit to the number of shareholders under an S corporation.

The professional's choice of whether or not to incorporate is based on tax decisions. Most of the tax benefits of incorporation come from fringe benefits. The professional corporation is often used as a tax shelter by retaining earnings taxed at corporate rates that are lower than the individual's marginal tax rate. Professional corporations also take advantage of a minimum deduction of 70 percent for dividends received from other corporations. However, a personal service corporation does not benefit from graduated corporate income rates. Personal service corporations have a flat tax rate of 35 percent. A personal service corporation is substantially owned by its current and retired employees, and its activities involve services in the field of health, law, accounting, consulting, and engineering.

There is an opportunity for corporations to avoid double taxation by accumulating earnings (but watch out for the accumulated earnings tax), which increases the value of the stock. The unrealized appreciation of stock is not taxable. When the stock is sold or liquidated at some future time, owners can recognize a taxable gain while indirectly paying a second tax on the accumulated earnings. This strategy reduces the present value of the second tax. Three factors create tax savings: (1) spread between the corporate and individual tax rates; (2) deferral of tax payments; and (3) conversion of ordinary income (dividend payments) to capital gain income.

Professionals of a corporate entity can get cash out of the corporation by serving as corporate executives whose salary that is taxed only once at the individual level, and which provides a tax deduction for the corporation. Shareholders serve as creditors by lending money to a corporation, as the interest paid to the shareholder becomes a deductible expense for the corporation. By leasing property to the corporation, the shareholders receive rent payments that are deductible expenses for the corporation. Dividends are paid with aftertax dollars (double taxation), but salaries, interest, and rent are paid with before-tax dollars.

A C corporation can use tax-favored fringe benefits that are not available, or only on a limited basis, under other tax forms. Benefits that are nontaxable to the employee and immediately deductible by the corporation include: (1) health and accident plan exclusion from income; (2) employer payments to health and accident plan exclusion from income; (3) group term life insurance exclusion from income; (4) travel and entertainment; and (5) meals and lodging for convenience of the employee. Benefits that are tax-deferred to the employee and immediately deductible by the corporation include qualified pension and profit-sharing plans. Benefits that are immediately taxable to the employee and immediately deductible by a C corporation include (1) group term insurance greater than $50,000; (2) additional cash salary; and (3) group legal services.

Q 2:2   How to plan for shareholder-professionals?

Shifting income and stock ownership within a professional corporation has tax consequences. Corporate profits generally shift from senior members to junior members in the form of stock ownership. As a result, senior members will incur taxes from the gain realized, and junior members often find it difficult to pay for the stock. The sell of stock often occurs on credit.

The biggest obstacle is often the valuation of the stock price. There are four primary valuation methods: (1) book value at the termination date, which is often impractical for professionals; (2) fixed price agreed upon by the stockholders, which must be updated periodically; (3) price fixed by appraisal after death, which causes delays; and (4) self-adjusting formula set forth in the agreement, such as a value indicated by the capitalization of earnings or present value of cash flows. The fourth way is the preferred way to value a business.

If a professional corporation chooses to buy the stock of a departing shareholder, there is generally no tax deduction. To benefit from a tax deduction, the corporation may prefer to pay the departing shareholder deductible severance pay. The amount of pay should be based on a conservatively valued stock price.

Provisions should be made for the sale of the business upon death, disability, or retirement of the professional. A professional generally can sell shares using a buy-sell agreement either as a stock redemption agreement or a crosspurchase agreement. In a stock redemption agreement, the corporation agrees to buy the decedent's stock. In a cross-purchase agreement, the business partners each buy their respective interest in the decedent's stock. The buy-sell agreement is the sale of stock upon the happening of a specified event, which is not limited to death. It can provide for the sale upon retirement or disability. The funding used to pay for the stock is usually from life insurance. Also making periodic contributions to a sinking fund is a choice for accumulating earnings, but the corporation must exercise care to avoid the accumulated earnings tax.

Planning for the Closely Held Business

Q 2:3   What are some of the issues that a financial planner should be alert to when planning for a closely held business?

There are specific rules surrounding a closely held business that financial planners should follow:

- **Successor management.** The successor management must be determined. This should be a person with knowledge, talent, and drive similar to the current owner. Time may be required to find someone with these traits or the transfer of the business may occur within the family.

- **Building the second estate.** This means that an owner should not keep all assets in the business. There are several techniques for transferring assets out of the business. These techniques include profit-sharing plans, ESOPs, stock bonus plans, 401(k) plans, stock redemptions, sale of stock to trusts, and charitable contributions.

- **Reserve fund for business.** The business owner should determine what amount of cash is necessary upon death to ensure the business continues to operate. This may require building up a cash reserve. However, the owner should do so only by paying attention to the accumulated earnings credit of Code Sections 535(c)(2) and 537(b). The former provides for a credit of $250,000. The latter allows accumulations under Section 303 redemptions.

- **Outside market.** The business owner should determine if there is a public or private market for the company. The owner and planner can also determine ways in which to make the company more marketable.

- **Sale of stock to insiders.** The owner can use a buy-sell agreement to dispose of stock to other employees. The owner can also take advantage of an ESOP to dispose of a major stock interest with very favorable tax consequences.

- **Estate tax implication and liquidity.** Liquidity needs must be addressed. Also, determining to what extent an estate will rely on stock redemptions under Sections 302 and 303 is important. There are many questions surrounding the distribution of assets and ownership. Stock retained until death receives a step-up basis equal to its fair market value for estate tax purposes.

- **Valuation of company stock.** The valuation of the company stock should be determined.

Q 2:4   How to plan for stock redemptions?

Converting stock of a corporation into cash with little loss of value is a challenge for financial planners and business owners. The tax law might treat redemptions as dividends, which are taxed as ordinary income. A stock redemption can also be treated as a sale or exchange. This is what the estate would prefer since a sale or exchange is treated as a capital gain with a tax-basis recovery. If the stock is transferred at the death of the owner, its tax basis is its fair market value at date of death or alternative valuation date.

The IRS defines a stock redemption as an acquisition by a corporation of its own stock from a shareholder in exchange for property, whether or not stock so acquired is canceled, retired, or held as Treasury stock. For tax planning purposes, the primary objective in arranging a stock redemption is to achieve capital-gain treatment, as opposed to dividend treatment, on the exchange of stock for money or other property.

The redemption proceeds will be taxable as ordinary income if the transaction is treated as a dividend distribution. There is a three-part tax treatment that applies to a corporate distribution to a shareholder. The rules apply regardless of whether the distribution to the shareholder is made pursuant to a redemption of stock or paid with respect to the shareholder's ownership in stock. First, the portion of the distribution not in excess of the corporation's current and accumulated earnings and profits is treated as a dividend and taxed as ordinary income. Second, the portion of the distribution in excess of the corporation's current and accumulated earnings and profits is then treated as a nontaxable return of capital to the extent of the shareholder's basis in his or her stock. Third, the portion of the distribution not treated as a dividend that exceeds the shareholder's basis in his or her stock is taxed as capital gain.

Example 2-1. Steve is sole shareholder of a corporation that has $50,000 in current accumulated earnings and profits. His basis in the stock is $5,000. The corporation distributes $70,000, which is not compensation. $50,000 is treated as dividends and taxed as ordinary income, $5,000 is treated as a return of capital investment (basis is reduced to zero), and $15,000 is treated as capital gain.

Qualifying a redemption as a sale or exchange and not as a dividend is very important. There are two routes by which to do this under the Code. The first is Section 302, which deals with distributions in redemption of stock. The second is Section 303, which applies to distributions in redemption of stock to pay death taxes.

Code Section 302 allows for capital gain treatment of four types of redemptions, in which the redemption materially affects a shareholder's percentage of ownership: (1) a redemption not essentially equivalent to a dividend; (2) a substantially disproportionate redemption; (3) a termination of the shareholder's interest; and (4) redemptions from noncorporate shareholders in partial liquidations.

Code Section 303 redemptions apply to estates in which stock of a closely held corporation constitutes a substantial portion of the total assets. For these redemptions, the beneficiary or estate receives a stepped-up basis in a decedent's assets that is generally equal to the value of the assets at the date of death of the decedent. If the stock increased in value between the time of redemption and the decedent's death, any amount in excess of the adjusted basis will be taxed as long-term gain.

There are certain requirements that must be met to qualify for Code Section 303 tax treatment:

1. The stock to be redeemed must be included in the decedent's gross estate.

2. The value of the stock included in the gross estate must exceed 35 percent of the decedent's AGI. Stock in two or more corporations may be combined for this percentage requirement if 20 percent or more of the outstanding stock of each corporation is included in the decedent's gross estate. This percentage test must be met both before and after adding to the gross estate the property transferred within three years of death.

3. One cannot redeem more than the total of federal and state death taxes, GSTT, administration and funeral expenses. The executor cannot use the Section 303 redemption to pay debts of the estate.

4. Only those beneficiaries responsible for the paying of estate taxes can employ the Section 303 redemption. If stock is left to one heir and the taxes are payable out of the residuary estate passing to a different heir, the Section 303 redemption is not available.

The corporation must have money to prepare for the Section 303 redemption. Life insurance carried on the decedent is often used to provide this liquidity to a corporation. In this way, the corporation can redeem the shares from the decedent. Another alternative is for the corporation to give a shareholder its note. The redemption is made when the note is provided, not when it is paid. ESOP plans are also used to raise capital by borrowing to purchase stock from the company. The company's tax-deductible contributions to the plan enable it to pay off the loan. In this way, the company pays off the loan with tax-deductible dollars.

Q 2:5   How to plan for a business disposition?

The planning of a business disposition is often complex, but a financial planner should be aware of some options available to their clients.

The liquidation of a business is when the corporation's properties are distributed to shareholders and the corporate stock is cancelled. Liquidations are often an inappropriate way to sell the business because the tax treatment is unfavorable. The corporation pays tax on its capital gain when it sells assets or distributes assets to shareholders. Shareholders are taxed on the gain equal to the difference between the fair market value of what they receive from the corporation and their basis in their stock. S Corporations avoid double taxation on liquidations because of the pass-through of corporate income to shareholders and the basis rule.

The vast majority of business sales are taxable. The stock sale results in a taxable gain to the business's selling shareholders that is equal to the difference between the selling price and their basis. The sale of stock does not affect the cost basis of assets. Asset sales result in a taxable gain to the corporation if the selling price exceeds the corporation's basis, and the shareholders are also taxed on the capital gain when the proceeds from the sale are distributed to them in liquidation. Asset sale may result in a new cost basis for assets.

Stock sales qualify for tax-free dispositions if at least 80 percent of the voting power and at least 80 percent of the other stock of the seller are transferred to the acquiring organization in exchange for only voting stock in the buyer. The asset sale will qualify if substantially all of the seller's net assets are transferred to the acquiring organization in exchange for only voting stock in the buyer. The tax consequences of a tax-free sale are: (1) there is no tax to the seller or to the selling corporation at the time of the transaction; (2) the seller receives stock in the acquiring corporation at a basis equal to the seller's basis in the property sold, that is, a carryover basis; and (3) the exchange is tax-free, but the seller will be taxed when he or she goes to sell the stock. The gain on the sale can be avoided if the stock is held until death.

Planning for the taxable sale includes installment sales and private annuities. In installment sales, the seller's gain can be spread ratably over the period during which installment payments are made. The buyer's interest payments are deductible (within limits) when made and taxable to the seller when received. Imputed interest rules apply, as interest on an installment note is regulated by a minimum rate of interest defined in the Code. Imputed interest is imposed for tax purposes if an installment sale does not provide for an adequate rate of interest, and it is taxed over the installment period by a complex set of rules. In sum, the sale cannot be planned to avoid the tax on interest to the seller by understating the interest at artificially low rates. The private annuity allows payments to be made for the remainder of seller's life, based on actuarial factors. Part of each annuity payment is a tax-free return of basis, part is capital gain, and part is interest—similar to an installment sale—but only until the seller reaches life expectancy, and the annuity factor makes the calculations somewhat different, so the amount of income tax payable may be significantly different from an installment sale.

Q2:6   How to plan for business continuation (buy-sell)?

Buy-sell agreements make sure an estate can sell a business interest for a reasonable price. The contract contains wording that binds the owner of a business to sell his or her share of the business at a specified price to a designated buyer, usually the partners in the business. There are numerous benefits to constructing a buy-sell agreement:

- Guarantees a market for a closely held business;
- Provides a source of liquidity for estate taxes owed;
- Allows for the continuation of the business with the other owners; and
- Improved credit risk.

The buy-sell agreement is the sale of a business interest (*e.g.*, stock) upon the happening of a specified event, which is not limited to death. It can provide for the sale upon retirement or disability. The funding used to pay for the stock is usually from life insurance. Also, making periodic contributions to a sinking fund is a choice for accumulating earnings, but the corporation must exercise care to avoid the accumulated earnings tax.

There are two types of buy-sell agreements: cross-purchase agreement and stock redemption agreement. In a cross-purchase agreement, each owner purchases an insurance policy on the other owners. The policy owner is also the beneficiary. Upon the death of an owner, the owner's estate will sell, and the other owners will buy, the business interest of the deceased. For example, assume three equal partners and one of them dies. The two surviving partners will each purchase one-half of the deceased partner's interest. In a stock redemption agreement, the business buys (redeems) the insurance on the owners. The firm is the beneficiary and carries life insurance on each partner. Upon the death of an owner, the business will buy the business interest from the deceased owner's estate.

There are advantages and disadvantages to a cross-purchase agreement. The surviving stockholders pay for the stock with after-tax dollars. It is easy to form when there are a small number of stockholders, although it becomes burdensome when the number of shareholders increases. For example, if a corporation has five stockholders at the time the buy-sell agreement is executed, the last survivor would have to buy the shares of the five predeceased stockholders. Also, the obligation to purchase the shares falls on younger shareholders who are often not in a position to buy the shares. Finally, this agreement results in fewer legal problems and tax consequences.

There are also advantages and disadvantages to a stock redemption agreement. It is easy to form when there are a large number of stockholders. The corporation, not the stockholders, pays the life insurance premiums under the agreement. This means that premiums are paid with money that has only been taxed once to the corporation. Under a cross-purchase agreement, premiums are paid with money that might have been taxed both to the corporation and to stockholders. In addition, no dividend treatment results despite using the corporation's earnings and benefits for buying the benefit. The corporation may not have enough cash to redeem shares if life insurance is not used; however, the corporation can use installment payments on the purchase price to redeem shares.

Planning for the Executive

Q 2:7   What are the issues facing the executive?

Corporate executives have financial planning issues quite different from other individuals. They have packages filled with stock options and deferred compensation plans. Most of their assets are tied up in the stock of the employer. Executives generally have a need for diversification. They often have liquidity problems at death. In addition, executives are very mobile, moving from city to city or country to country during the course of their careers. Property that was acquired in community property states will need to be looked at. Executives also are in the top marginal tax brackets. In 2006, the tax rate for the highest bracket is 35 percent. Finding ways to save on taxes is critical for them. Executives are also known for being apathetic about saving. They generally feel that the corporation will take care of them. It is vital that the financial planner guide the executive into saving money in qualified plans and other tax-advantaged accounts.

Q2:8 What are the different types of executive compensation?

Qualified plans. The executive pays no current income tax on the amounts contributed by the employer on his or her behalf. Earnings are tax-exempt, which allows for tax-free accumulation of income and gains on investments. For defined benefit plans, the highest "annual benefit" payable under the plan (or in the aggregate if the employer has more than one plan) must not exceed the lesser of (a) 100 percent of the participant's average compensation in the highest three years of service, or (b) $175,000 (in 2006 as indexed). Annual benefit refers to a benefit that is payable annually in the form of a straight annuity. The $175,000 limit (as indexed for 2006) is adjusted downward if the annuity starting date occurs before the participant reaches age 62. If the annuity starting date occurs after the participant reaches age 65, the limit is adjusted upward. In 2006, the maximum compensation base that can be used is $220,000. The retirement benefit is certain for defined benefit plans. For defined contribution plans, the maximum allowable annual contribution is the lesser of 100 percent of salary or $44,000 (in 2006). As with defined benefit plans, the maximum compensation base that can be used for defined contribution plans is $220,000 (in 2006). Retirement benefits are uncertain for defined contribution plans.

Nonqualified deferred compensation plan. Nonqualified plans are often limited to executives. They are designed to defer the payment of income taxes by employees until benefits are paid out. Employer deduction is deferred to the time of payout, and the deduction is matched to employee income. The assets must be available to pay claims of creditors in order to avoid current taxation. There are generally two types of nonqualified compensation plans. Salary reduction plans give participants the option to defer regular compensation, bonuses, or commissions. They are appropriate when executives are in the highest tax bracket but anticipate a lower tax bracket upon retirement. Supplemental executive retirement plans (SERPs) contain additional, employer-provided benefits. They complement an existing qualified plan that is not already stretched to the maximum limits.

Traditional IRAs/Roth IRA. Executives can contribute to a traditional IRA; however, their contributions will most likely not be deductible because of their income level. Roth IRA contributions are allowed but are eliminated beyond certain AGI levels.

Incentive stock options (ISOs). Incentive stock options offer favorable tax treatment to an executive. When the options are granted, they are not reported as income and there are no taxes due. When the options are exercised, there is no income for reporting regular tax. However, the difference between FMV at exercise and exercise price (the bargain element or "spread") is an adjustment item for calculating alternative minimum tax (AMT). Upon a qualifying sale of stock, for AMT, the long-term capital gain is the difference between FMV at time of sale and FMV at time of exercise. For regular tax, the long-term capital gain is the difference between FMV at time of sale and exercise price. An employer receives no deduction unless the holding period requirement is satisfied. The holding period requirements for a qualifying sale is that shares must be held for at least one year after the option is exercised and for at least two years after the option was granted. If the holding period is not met, a disqualifying disposition occurs and the appreciation on the sale (untaxed bargain element plus other appreciation) will be taxed as ordinary income. In addition, an employee receiving the ISO is required to continue as an employee from the time of the grant of the options until at least three months before the exercise. If not, the options are converted to NSOs. Also, ISOs cannot be issued to any beneficiary of the executive.

Non-qualified stock options (NSOs). There is no special tax treatment for NSOs given to an executive. When the options are granted, there is no income tax due. Upon exercise of the options, the employee realizes income equal to the difference between grant (exercise) price and FMV at time of exercise. This difference is called the bargain element. The FMV at time of exercise becomes the new cost basis. The company must withhold federal and state taxes as well as Social Security taxes. Depending on the individual's tax situation, too much or too little tax might have been withheld. If the employee holds the stock and sells after exercise, the employee recognizes capital gain or loss; it could be short- or long-term, depending on whether it is held for more than one year. The sale will not trigger additional tax unless the selling price exceeds the share basis. NSOs may be granted to an employee, member of the board, an independent contractor, a family member, or any other beneficiary of the employee or independent contractor, in connection with the performance of services.

Group term life insurance. Group term life insurance is generally tax-free to the executive on coverage up to $50,000. However, a key employee in a discriminatory plan will have premiums that are taxed based on a rate schedule, referred to as Table 1, provided by IRS regulations. For amounts over $50,000, the executive receives a break on the portion of the employer-paid premium that is taxable. That is, premiums are taxable to the employee based on Table 1 costs less employee contributions.

Group permanent life insurance. Premiums are taxable to the executive using complex formulas for computing the amount taxable.

Split dollar life insurance. This insurance allows an employer to provide life insurance protection for an executive. The employer has full discretion on the amount of insurance to be provided and which individuals are covered. The employer and employee split the premium. The executive pays the portion of premium that is attributed to the "economic benefit"(lesser of P.S. 58 cost or "standard risk," one-year individual term rates) of the insurance protection in that year. The employer pays the remaining portion of the premium attributed to the cost of insurance (the amount equal to the annual increase in the cash surrender value). The death benefit is also split between the employer and beneficiary of the executive. The employer receives a return of its contributions, which is the cash surrender value. The beneficiary receives the net amount at risk.

Table 2-1

Charitable Contribution Deduction Limitation

Type of property	Donee	Limitations of AGI	Amount deductible
Cash	Public	50%	Full deduction
	Private	30%	Full deduction
Capital gain property			
Real and intangible	Public	30%, or	Full deduction for FMV
personal property		50% on election	Donor's cost basis
	Private	20%	Full deduction for FMV
Tangible personal property			
Use-related			
	Public	30%, or	Full deduction for FMV
		50% on election	Donor's cost basis
	Private	20%	Donor's cost basis
Use-unrelated			
	Public	50%	Donor's cost basis
	Private	20%	Donor's cost basis
Ordinary income property			
	Public	50%	Donor's cost basis
	Private	30%	Donor's cost basis

Adopted from Ivers III, James. (2002). *Fundamentals of Income Taxation*(3d ed.). The American College; Huebner School Series.

Below-market interest loans. Employers sometimes offer below-market interest loans to executives, which is an attractive executive benefit. However, imputed interest is imposed for tax purposes if a loan does not provide for an adequate rate of interest.

Q 2:9   What are planning strategies for executives with both incentive stock options and nonqualified stock options?

Consideration should be given to exercising options and selling stock over a period of time to take advantage of price averages and risk reduction. Executives in high tax brackets should consider early exercise for appreciating stocks to benefit from lower taxes because the bargaining element is taxed as income for NSOs and there are possible AMT consequences for ISOs. After exercise, executives should hold the stock for more than one year to benefit from long-term capital gain tax treatment. In addition, diversification and meeting financial goals may be good reasons for selling options sooner than the end of the exercise period. Liquidating the options at time of exercise ensures positive cash flow without tying up funds.

Planning for Charitable Giving

Q 2:10 What are the advantages of and requirements for charitable gifting?

There are often many advantages of gifting to a charity. The decision to gift should only be made if the individual has financial security for his or her family. An unlimited amount of property can be transferred to qualified charities without incurring federal gift taxes. As with the marital deduction, there is no limit to the size of the gift tax charitable deduction. The charitable organization incurs no income tax liability as a result of the gift and is not subject to income tax on the income derived from the property transferred. A charitable transfer made during an individual's lifetime will not only provide an income tax deduction, but will also remove property from the taxpayer's estate. By contrast, a testamentary bequest to a qualified organization will only remove property from the taxpayer's estate. The reasons for making a lifetime gift to a charity (rather than to a noncharitable beneficiary) are to use the unlimited charitable deduction to either reduce or avoid gift tax liability while removing the value of the asset (including any appreciation) from the donor's potential gross estate.

Contributions qualifying as charitable deductions for income tax purposes must meet several requirements. They must be made to qualifying organizations. They must be a gift of property and not the value of time or services provided. They must be made before the close of the year in which the deduction is to be claimed. They must have a value greater than any benefit received from the qualifying organization (only the value in excess of the benefit received is deductible). They must be a gift of the donor's entire interest in the property, unless made in accordance with special rules. They must be claimed by the taxpayer as an itemized deduction (no charitable deduction has been allowed to nonitemizers since 1986).

Q 2:11 What are the income tax deduction limits for public and private charities?

Public Charity. These charities are listed in Code Section 170(b)(1)(A). They generally include churches, educational organizations, hospitals and medical research organizations, government entities, and publicly supported organizations that receive a substantial amount of support from the general public or governmental units (*i.e.*, Red Cross, Salvation Army, and Boys/Girls Clubs of America). Contributions to public charities cannot exceed 50 percent of the taxpayer's AGI. A 30-percent ceiling generally applies to long-term capital gain (LTCG) property. There is one exception to this rule. A 30-percent limit does not apply if election is made to reduce the FMV of the property by the amount of the long-term capital gain if the property had been sold.

Private Charity. Private charities generally include veteran's organizations, fraternal orders, and certain private nonoperating foundations. Contributions to private charities cannot exceed 30 percent of the taxpayer's AGI. A 15-percent ceiling applies to all LTCG property.

Capital gain property for purposes of charitable contributions is property that has been held for more than 12 months. There are two types of capital gain property: (1) real and intangible personal property, and (2) tangible personal property.

Real and intangible personal property. A gift of stock is considered intangible personal property, and appreciated land is an example of real property. For contributions made to public charities, the deduction cannot exceed 30 percent of AGI if the full market value of the gift is deducted. The 30-percent limit can be increased to 50 percent of AGI for public charities if the donor is willing to decrease the value of the gift by 100 percent of the potential gain. This means reducing the fair market value to the property's cost basis.

Example 2-2. Mark donates stock worth $45,000 to the Red Cross (public charity). The stock cost $25,000 when it was purchased five years ago. Mark has an AGI of $50,000. Therefore, his maximum deduction for the year is $15,000 ($50,000 × 30%). The remaining $30,000 ($45,000 FMV − $15,000 current deduction) can be carried forward for five years and applied against future income. Exception: If Mark excludes 100% of the potential gain, the deductible value is decreased to $25,000 (cost basis). Mark could deduct the entire $25,000 because 50% of his AGI is $25,000. The current year deduction is increased with this election.

For contributions to private charities, the deduction cannot exceed 20 percent of AGI. There is a full deduction for fair market value only.

Tangible personal property. A car or jewelry is tangible personal property. A distinction is made between gifts that are used by the charity and those gifts that are not used. Use-related gifts include a painting given to a museum that is shown in public galleries. For contributions to public charities, the deduction cannot exceed 30 percent of AGI if the full market value of gift is deducted. The 30-percent limit can be increased to 50 percent of AGI if the donor is willing to reduce the value of the gift by 100 percent of the potential gain. For contributions to private charities, the deduction is 20 percent of the donor's cost basis.

The painting from the earlier example would be use-unrelated if given to the Boy Scouts, or if it was sold by the museum. For contributions made to public and private charities, the fair market value of the gift must be reduced by 100 percent of the potential gain. This means that the amount of deduction is the donor's cost basis. For contributions to public charities, the deduction cannot exceed 50 percent of AGI. For donations to private charities, the deduction cannot exceed 20 percent of AGI.

Ordinary income property. Ordinary income property is an asset that would have resulted in ordinary income (rather than capital gains) on the date of contribution if it were sold. Ordinary income property includes capital assets held 12 months or less at time of contribution; art, books, and jewelry, but only if given by the person who created them; and a business person's stock-intrade and inventory. The deduction for ordinary income property is limited to the donor's cost basis.

Q 2:12 What is the carryover period for charitable contributions?

Contributions that exceed the AGI limit for the current tax year can be carried over to each of the next five years. Carryover contributions are subject to the original percentage limits in the carryover years, and are deducted after deducting allowable contributions for the current year. It's best to use the earlier year carryover if there are carryovers from prior years.

Q 2:13 What are the substantiation requirements for charitable contributions?

If the gift is less than $250, cash donations need a receipt or other reliable written records with date, amount, and name of organization. Noncash donations do not require a receipt where it is impractical to get one. Cash donations of $250 or more in any one day to any one organization must have written substantiation from the organization. Noncash donations require a written acknowledgement from the charitable organization. For contributions over $500, the taxpayer must show the means of acquisition of the property, the date acquired, and the adjusted basis. Most contributions over $5,000 require a written appraisal. Form 8283 must be filed for noncash contributions over $500. Individuals should not combine separate contributions. For example, giving $25 each week to a church is considered as making separate payments that should not be combined.

Q 2:14 What are the estate and gift tax consequences of charitable contributions?

A charitable contribution to a qualified charity reduces current income taxes (assuming the donor itemizes deductions). No federal gift tax is payable on a gift to a qualified charity, regardless of the size of the gift. Gifts to qualified charities can reduce the federal estate tax, with the amount of the deduction limited only by the value of the gift (i.e., the donor's entire estate can be left to charity and a deduction will be allowed for the entire gift). The charity itself will pay no tax upon the receipt of either a lifetime gift or a bequest. Generally, no income tax will be payable by a qualified charity on income earned by donated property.

Q 2:15 What techniques are used for charitable gifting?

A charitable remainder trust (CRT) in which an income interest is retained. The donor retains a limited right to enjoy the property while receiving an income tax deduction and reducing federal estate tax. The funding date is critical for determining if a trust qualifies as a CRT. If the trust is not funded, an income tax charitable deduction cannot be claimed and the assets are included in the estate. The beneficiary may receive the income for a period not exceeding 20 years or life, and the remainder goes to the charity. In addition, the CRT must have an irrevocable remainder interest to be held for or paid to a charity.

A gift of a remainder interest in a personal residence or farm. A general rule is that an individual cannot receive a deduction for gifts of a future interest in property. One exception to this rule is the gift of a personal residence or farm. An individual can gift a house or farm to a charity, and have the right to live in it or use it for the rest of his or her life, or a period of years. This can be accomplished without setting up a trust. However, the gift must be irrevocable. The individual will receive an income tax deduction for the contribution. The personal residence is not limited to a permanent residence. It can include a vacation home.

A transfer of property to charity in exchange for an annuity. This often involves the transfer of money or property from the donor in exchange for the charity's promise to pay an annuity. The annuity is usually paid for the life of the donor. The difference between the value of the annuity and the value of property transferred is the amount allowed for the charitable deduction. The annuity provides for immediate or deferred payments. A portion of the annuity payments are subject to income tax. Once the full investment in the annuity is received, there are no further tax deduction.

A gift of an income interest to charity through a charitable lead trust. The charitable lead trust differs from the charitable remainder trust in that the donor in the charitable lead trust gives away an income stream and receives a remainder interest. The donor places income-producing property in a reversionary trust and directs that the trust income be transferred to a designated charity for a period of time not to exceed 20 years. At the end of this "lead" time, the property reverts to the donor or to some other noncharitable beneficiary. The benefit the donor receives is a very large income tax deduction in the year that the trust is funded, the value of the deduction being the present value of the total anticipated income during the lead period when the charity receives the income. If set up correctly, the value of the remainder interest can equal zero, resulting in a full deduction of the current value of property transferred to the trust. The trust must be set up as a grantor trust, making the annual income taxable to the donor (but can purchase tax-exempt securities to lower the tax liability of the donor), unless it is established at the grantor's death. These trusts are generally established at the transferor's death.

A gift of a remainder interest through a wealth replacement trust. This is when an irrevocable life insurance trust is used in conjunction with a charitable remainder trust to replace the asset the heirs of the donor would be losing.

A gift of life insurance to a charity. The deduction amount for a paid-up life insurance policy is the replacement cost for a comparable contract with the same company. If the gift is a new policy that is transferred immediately after purchase, the value of the gift is the gross premium paid by the donor. If the gift is an existing policy for which future premiums are payable, its value is the policy's "interpolated terminal reserve" plus the unearned portion of the paid premium (the value of the policy's reserve at date of gift plus the amount of the gross premium paid, which is not yet earned by the insurer). Two provisions apply to estate tax consequences. Code Section 2035(a) includes in the gross estate life insurance proceeds on the life of the decedent if the decedent made a transfer of any incidents of ownership in the policy within three years before death. Section 2042 includes in the gross estate life insurance proceeds receivable by the personal representative or receivable by other beneficiaries if the decedent possessed any of the incidents of ownership at death. Ownership of insurance policies may be transferred from the decedent to exclude the proceeds of the policies from the decedent's estate. The insured must survive three years after the transfer in order for the insurance to be effectively moved from the estate [IRC § 2035(a)].

A bargain sale to charity. This is when an individual wants to donate a piece of appreciated property, but not all of it. Generally the appreciation above the cost basis is donated to the charity. However, the donor faces tax liability from a bargain sale to charity. The transaction is split in two under Code Section 1011 (b), a sale portion and a contribution portion. The sale portion is taxable to the donor. To calculate the capital gain on the sale portion: (1) take the tax basis of the property; (2) multiply it by a fraction where the numerator is the sale proceeds and the denominator is the property's fair market value; and (3) subtract (2) from the sale proceeds.

Example 2-3. Steve sells a piece of real estate for $45,000 to his university, which represents his cost basis in the property. The property is currently worth $90,000. The realized capital gains are calculated as:

(1) Tax basis of property	$50,000
(2) Less: basis allocable to sale portion	$22,500 [$45,000 × ($45,000/$90,000)]
(3) Taxable gain	$27,500

On the bargain sale, he makes a donation of $45,000 to the university. If he sold the property for $90,000, he would have a realized capital gain of $45,000 ($90,000 − $45,000). The bargain sale saves tax on $17,500 ($45,000 − $27,500).

Planning for Business Entities

Q 2:16   How to plan for business entities?

Business owners have many choices when selecting the form of enterprise. They may choose to operate unincorporated as a sole proprietorship, partnership (general partnerships, limited partnerships, and limited liability partnerships), or limited liability company; or they may choose to incorporate under a C corporation or an S corporation. The choice of business form is not irrevocable and owners often change from one type of business form to another.

The choice of business form is complex. When selecting between business forms, an owner should consider several basic factors. This includes the ease and expense of formation, control of the closely held business, flexibility of operations, ability to raise capital, liability of owners, income taxation, and compensation and fringe benefits of owners.

Q2:17   How to select a business entity when expense and ease of formation are important?

A sole proprietorship is the most common form of business ownership. This is due to its relative administrative simplicity. By definition, it is an unincorporated trade or business owned by a single individual. Sole proprietorships are easy to establish and require no special forms. Sole proprietors file just a schedule C in addition to their personal tax forms.

A partnership consists of two or more owners doing business together with the intent to divide the income and profits. Partnerships are formed with a formal written partnership agreement. The legal aspects of general partnerships are governed by state partnership statutes, most of which are in conformity with the Federal Uniform Partnership Act and the Revised Uniform Limited Partnership Act. Partnership agreements can range in complexity. Regardless of the complexity of the agreement, a professional's help is highly recommended. The cost will depend on the amount of legal assistance that is required to draft the document. The cost can be low for simple documents and high for complex documents.

Limited liability partnerships (LLPs) are formed and operate pursuant to state LLP statutes. They require at least two owners, but no maximum. In some states, partners have to reregister as a limited liability partnership each time a partner dies or the entity dissolves. This may result in the LLP being more expensive than an LLC, since filing fees in most states are per partner, not per entity.

Limited liability companies (LLCs) are the fastest growing form of business. LLCs are formed under state laws. Member of an LLC file Articles of Organization and an Operating Agreement with the state authorizing the business. This is complex in nature and requires a knowledgeable tax and business law attorney to assist in the formation, which can be costly. In general, the start-up costs exceed those of a simple partnership or corporation. LLCs are treated as a partnership under federal income tax rules. An LLC can elect to be taxed as a corporation by filing Form 8832. Operating as a partnership requires at least two partners. The other forms operate with just one person.

A corporation comes into existence upon the proper filing of Articles of Incorporation and issuance by the state of a Certificate of Incorporation. Its formation is very similar to an LLC. Employment contracts must be prepared. Subscription agreements are commonly formed with original shareholders. There will be legal fees that are paid for advice and formation. The cost of incorporation is several hundred dollars, which may increase, depending on the complexity of the incorporation. In general, incorporation often requires higher start-up costs than unincorporated businesses.

Q2:18   How to select a business entity when control is important?

The sole proprietor runs the business and has power that is only limited by the state. In this way, a sole proprietorship offers maximum control over the business.

A partnership is formed by two or more partners who enter into a voluntary agreement. The general rule is that a partner has actual and apparent authority to bind other partners to a contract made in the ordinary course of business. This means that a partner can represent the other partners in a manner contrary to their wishes. To prevent this from happening, the control of the partner can be spelled out in the partnership agreement. The other partners are also able to ratify a contract that has been made. Each partner has duties to every other partner that are similar to an agent's duties to a principal. These include fiduciary duties and a duty to act in good faith. Notice to one partner is viewed as notice to all partners. However, each partner can effectively prevent outsiders from exerting control over the partnership. If one partner transfers his or her interests to a third party, the existing partners must agree to accept the buyer as partner. This ensures that the control of the partnership will not be diluted without the consent of the other partners.

For an LLC, control of the corporation is governed by the Operating Agreement. The control can be centralized under one or more members. Most LLCs are set up so as not to allow for free transferability of an ownership interest. The control of current owners is certain.

The control of a corporation is with the Board of Directors, which is often chosen (and influenced) by majority shareholders. Therefore, a corporation is under the control of its majority shareholders. This is generally not a problem for smaller corporations. However, difficulty exists when there is no clear majority owner. In addition, in the absence of any restrictions on the transfer of stock, the owners of the corporation can transfer stock to outsiders and introduce new shareholders to the corporation. Control of a corporation often depends on individual characteristics and planning.

Q 2:19 How to select a business entity when flexibility of business operation is important?

Flexibility is often important to business owners. Flexibility allows owners to quickly abandon unprofitable projects and move into more profitable businesses. Sole proprietorships offer maximum flexibility to an owner. The sole proprietor can expand or contract the business whenever he or she decides to do so.

A partnership is more restricted than a sole proprietorship because the agreement of all partners is required for major business decisions. The partnership agreement also controls what types of business or operations the partners can participate in. This can be amended without much disruption, but any changes to the partnership agreement require mutual consent of all partners.

The flexibility provided by an LLC is very similar to that provided by a partnership, where decisions to expand or contract the business generally require the consent of all partners. Changes to the operating agreement must have approval from all members.

The corporate form of ownership offers the least amount of flexibility. The powers of the corporation are limited to its original charter. Major business decisions must be approved by the Board of Directors and, in some cases, the shareholders. This can result in time delays and restrictions on various changes.

An S corporation is subject to the following strict eligibility requirements: (1) it must be a domestic corporation; (2) it cannot have more than 100 shareholders; (3) it must have no shareholders other than individuals who are U.S. citizens or resident aliens, estates, or certain types of trusts; and (4) it can have only one class of stock. If these requirements are not met, the resulting profits are subject to double taxation.

Q 2:20   How to select a business entity when ability to raise capital is important?

A sole proprietorship is built on the individual's own money and assets. Sole proprietors are often limited to the amount of capital that can be raised. By definition, a sole proprietorship is not permitted to raise funds through expanding its equity base by adding owners.

A partnership also has restrictions similar to a sole proprietorship for raising money, but a partnership has a larger equity base—two or more partners— on which to raise capital. This generally means that a partnership can raise more money than a sole proprietorship. In addition, a partnership can expand its equity base with approval from all partners.

While regular partnerships are owned solely by general partners, limited partnerships can raise capital by selling partnership interests to limited partners in exchange for a share of future income without diluting the control of the general partners. Thus, partnership ventures that require a large sum of money are often formed as limited partnerships.

LLCs provide an excellent means for raising capital. They permit an unlimited amount of members (unlike an S corporation) in order to increase the equity base. Unlike a partnership, each member of an LLC has limited liability for the capital that is raised.

Corporations are an excellent choice if a business needs a large amount of funds and expects to expand rapidly. A corporation is a separate legal entity for which various sources of commercial credit can be used to raise capital. However, owners of a closely held corporation may be required by commercial lenders to personally guarantee loans. In this respect, the corporation is similar to other unincorporated businesses in raising funds. The biggest advantage of a corporation is its ability to raise capital by expanding its equity base, either by issuing new stock or merging with other companies. An advantage that an S corporation and a C corporation have over LLCs and other unincorporated forms is that the owners of the corporation can merge tax-free with another corporation.

Q 2:21　How to select a business entity when the liability of owners is important?

The sole proprietor has the greatest liability of all business forms. The owner is responsible for all debts. The failure of the proprietorship will result in the creditors satisfying their claims by going after the proprietor's personal assets. In this way, there is unlimited liability with a sole proprietorship.

General partners have unlimited liability similar to a sole proprietorship. The partners are jointly and severally liable for any tort action. Joint liability means that all partners must be sued together. In this way, each partner is jointly liable with all other partners for the contracts of the partnership. Several liability means that a party may sue any partner for the full amount of the claim. Thus, a partner who commits a tort in the ordinary course of partnership business has both a personal liability and has created a liability for all the other partners.

Limited partnerships must have one or more general partners and one or more limited partners. Like shareholders in a corporation, limited partners have limited liability. Limited partnerships are distinguished from limited liability partnerships (LLPs) in the liability exposure of the general partners. Under an LLP, the partnership is similar to a general partnership, but all general partners have limited liability. Each partner's liability under a LLP is limited to his or her investment in the partnership (the same holds for limited partners under a limited partnership). LLP partners may be personally liable for their own tort-related acts and their own professional errors, omissions, and negligence. An LLP partner may also be personally liable for the professional errors, omissions, and negligence of others who are under the partner's direct supervision or who should have been. LLP partners generally are not liable for any debt, obligations, or liabilities of other partners.

An LLC offers limited liability protection to all members but still is treated as a partnership under federal income tax rules. An LLC can elect to be taxed as a corporation by filing Form 8832. Operating as a partnership requires at least two partners; the other forms operate with just one person. There is a limit to the number of shareholders under an S corporation. The owner of an LLC is often forced to take personal risk for any credit obtained by the LLC. To this extent, an LLC does not completely shelter an owner from liability. One of the principal differences between an LLC and an LLP is the level of limited liability protection for the owners and the entity. Each LLP partner remains liable for the malpractice of people he or she directly controls or supervises, whereas, members of an LLC are not so liable.

A corporation is a separate legal entity. It is separate from the persons who formed the corporation or who currently own it. Corporations provide limited liability protection that is unavailable to sole proprietors and general partners. The liability arising out of the operations of a corporation is satisfied by corporate assets. In this way, the shareholders can lose only what they invest in the corporation (what they pay or promise to pay for the stock of the corporation). However, shareholders of closely held businesses often find themselves personally guaranteeing loans unless their corporation has substantial assets. A corporation, as with an LLC, does not completely shelter an owner from liability.

The decision made by a professional when deciding a form of business is not greatly influenced by liability protection. The primary risk of a professional is malpractice liability. Malpractice liability cannot be avoided because all individuals remain liable for their own actions, regardless of liability protection found in LLCs, LLPs, or other forms. However, LLCs and LLPs do limit an individual's liability for the actions of others, which can be a significant benefit. Often, liability is shifted to forms of insurance.

Q 2:22   What is the income taxation of sole proprietorship and pass-through entities?

All income is taxed to the owner as self-employment income. The business is not a separate entity and does not file its own tax return. Sole proprietors file just a schedule C in addition to their personal tax forms. Expenses incurred from the business are deductible from the owner's gross income under tax laws. A sole proprietor can use its business structure to employ and shift income to other family members, which could result in lower taxes.

Partnerships, LLPs, and S corporations are categorized as pass-through entities. LLCs can elect to be taxed as a corporation, but generally an LLC will elect to be taxed as a partnership. With this election, an LLC is also a pass-through entity.

Tax basis. A partner's initial basis equals the initial investment of cash or property plus the share of partnership debt for which the partner may ultimately be held responsible. For example, three individuals each deposit $10,000 into a partnership in which they are equal general partners. The partnership borrows $15,000 from a bank to buy supplies and equipment. Each partner's basis is $15,000—the initial cash contributions plus a proportionate share of the partnership debt. A shareholder's initial basis in the stock of an S corporation equals the cash plus the adjusted basis of any property transferred in exchange for the stock. No debt is included in the shareholder's stock basis because there is no personal liability in S corporations. However, a shareholder can have a separate basis in a debt obligation.

Reporting requirements. Partnerships and S corporations are not taxable entities. Taxable income generated by partnerships is measured and characterized at the entity level, and taxed directly to the partners.

Tax consequences to partners. Each partner receives a Schedule K-1 that details information about the partner's distributive share of the partnership's income or loss from business items and separately stated items, such as dividend income, capital gains, and charitable donations. The cash flow from the business is irrelevant to the computation of the partner's tax liability. Thus, the partner is taxed on his or her distributive share of the partnership income whether or not the amount is actually distributed or not. General partners are required to pay self-employment (SE) tax on their distributive share of ordinary business income. Limited partners are not considered selfemployed and are not required to pay SE tax on their distributive share of ordinary income.

Tax consequences to shareholders. Shareholders receive a Schedule K-1 (same as partnerships) to incorporate into their individual tax returns. The cash flow from the S corporation is irrelevant to the computation of the shareholder's tax liability. Shareholders can also be employees of the corporation. The employee and corporation pay FICA payroll taxes, and the corporation withholds federal income tax. The corporation issues a W-2 to any shareholder/employee along with a K-1. Shareholders are not subject to SE tax.

Adjusting the basis in a partnership. The basis in a partnership increases by ordinary business income, capital gains, and dividend income; and decreases from ordinary business loss, capital loss, and cash distributions. If a partner is allocated income (taxable), but receives no cash distribution of that income, the partner is making an additional investment in the partnership. The cash distribution in future years is considered a nontaxable return of investment. Thus, cash distributions are generally nontaxable for pass-through entities. Partners may deduct their distributive share of partnership losses for the year. However, this results in a reduction of their cost basis in the partnership interest. The basis cannot be reduced below zero. If a partner's share of loss exceeds the basis, the excess cannot be deducted in the current year. It can be carried forward to future years, but the basis must be restored in order to deduct the carry-forward.

Adjusting the basis of S corporation stock. Shareholders increase the basis of stock by their share of the corporation's income and gain, and decrease the basis of stock by their share of the corporation's losses. The cash distribution is considered a nontaxable return of investment that reduces their stock basis. Thus, cash distributions are generally nontaxable for pass-through entities. Losses are deductible to the extent of the owner's equity investment and debt obligation. In both cases, the basis cannot be reduced below zero. For example, Steve has a basis in stock of $90,000 and a basis in debt of $30,000. Therefore, Steve has an equity investment and an investment as a corporate creditor. If the corporation passes through a loss of $150,000 to Steve (reflected on his K-1), the most that can be deducted is $125,000 on his Form 1040. The $25,000 non-deductible loss is carried forward.

Maximizing tax benefits of start-up firms. All losses that are incurred immediately pass through to partners or shareholders. For a C corporation, losses may be trapped at the entity level as loss carry-forwards.

Partnerships offer the ability to shift income to family members. By dividing income among a number of family members, the total tax burden may shrink to the extent that the division causes income to be taxed at a lower tax bracket. Family partnerships are common for shifting income, but the IRS closely restricts their use as income-shifting devices.

Use of losses. It was mentioned earlier that partners and shareholders are allowed to deduct losses that are passed through against income from other sources. The basis cannot be reduced below zero. If a partner's or shareholder's share of loss exceeds the basis, the excess cannot be deducted in the current year. It can be carried forward to future years, but the basis must be restored in order to deduct the carry-forward.

Q 2:23   What is the income taxation of C corporations?

A corporation is a separate legal entity with its own tax status and tax rates. Only corporations pay income tax at the entity level. Corporations report taxable income on Form 1120, and are not subject to the passive activity loss rules. Taxable income paid and net income reported on financial statements is usually not the same. Corporations generally have tax rates that are more favorable than individual rates.

Dividends received deduction. If a corporation receives dividends from another corporation, it is entitled to a deduction. If the recipient corporation owns less than 20 percent of the stock of the paying corporation, the deduction is 70 percent of dividends received. If the recipient corporation owns 20 percent but less than 80 percent of the stock of the paying corporation, the deduction is 80 percent of dividends received. If the recipient corporation owns 80 percent or more of the stock of the paying corporation, the deduction is 100 percent of dividends received.

Net operating losses. Net operating losses can only be carried back two years or forward 20 years to offset other corporate income. They are not passed through to shareholders.

Capital gain and loss treatment. Capital gains and losses recognized by corporations are taxed at the same rate as ordinary income and are not subject to the reduced capital gains rate. Deductions for capital losses can only offset capital gains, and no amount can be used to offset ordinary income. Net capital losses can be carried back three years and forward five years to offset capital gains.

Flow-through of income and losses to corporations. Shareholders can get cash out of a corporation in four ways:

1. Shareholders can serve as corporate executives being paid a salary that is taxed only once at the individual level, and provides a tax deduction for the corporation.
2. Shareholder can serve as creditors by lending money to a corporation, in which case the interest paid to the shareholder becomes a deductible expense for the corporation.
3. Shareholders can serve as creditors by leasing property to the corporation, in which case the shareholders receive rent payments that are deductible expenses for the corporation.
4. Shareholders can pay salaries, interest, and rent with before-tax dollars, whereas dividends are paid with after-tax dollars (double taxation).

Using closely held corporations as a tax shelter. Corporations generally offer lower tax rates than the high individual tax rates. Corporations can avoid double taxation by accumulating earnings, thus increasing the value of the stock.

The unrealized appreciation of stock is not taxable. When the stock is sold or liquidated at some future time, the shareholder can recognize a taxable gain while indirectly paying a second tax on the accumulated earnings. This strategy reduces the present value of the second tax. Three factors create tax savings: (1) spreading between the corporate and individual tax rates; (2) deferral of tax payments; and (3) conversion of ordinary income (dividend payments) to capital gain income.

Accumulated earnings tax. The tax advantage of corporate tax rates on earnings accumulated by the corporation is limited somewhat by the accumulated earnings tax. The accumulated earnings tax is a penalty tax designed to prevent tax avoidance through the accumulation of earnings within the corporation beyond the expected needs of the business. A corporation can accumulate up to a minimum credit of $250,000 of earnings and profits without encountering any problem with the accumulated earnings tax. If the corporation accumulates more than this amount, the corporation must demonstrate to the IRS that the accumulation is for the reasonable needs of the business. If it cannot demonstrate this need, the IRS imposes the accumulated earnings tax at a rate of 35 percent (in 2006) on all accumulated taxable income.

Q 2:24   How to select a business entity when compensation and fringe benefits of owners are important?

Regular corporations can use tax-favored fringe benefits that are not available, or only on a limited basis, under other tax forms.

Benefits nontaxable to the employee and immediately deductible by the corporation include: (1) health and accident plan exclusion from income; (2) employer payments to health and accident plan exclusion from income; (3) group term life insurance exclusion from income; (4) travel and entertainment; and (5) meals and lodging for the convenience of the employee.

Benefits that are tax-deferred to the employee and immediately deductible by the corporation includes qualified pension and profit-sharing plans.

Benefits that are immediately taxable to the employee and immediately deductible by the corporation include (1) group term insurance greater than $50,000; (2) additional cash salary; and (3) group legal services.

Planning for the Elderly

Medicare Planning

Q 2:25   What is the Medicare planning process?

Medicare is a federal health insurance program for persons age 65 or older, persons of any age with permanent kidney failure, and disabled persons covered after two years of disability benefits. It is administered by the Centers for Medicare & Medicaid Services within the Department of Health and Human Services. Social Security offices take applications and provide information about Medicare.

Medicare is broken down into Hospital Insurance (Part A) coverage, Medical Insurance (Part B) coverage, and Medicare + choice (Part C) coverage. Many people under the Part A plan have a Medigap policy to pay for costs that the original plan does not cover. Medigap policies are supplemental insurance policies sold by private insurance groups to fill gaps in the original Medicare plan health coverage.

Q 2:26   What is Medicare Part A hospital insurance?

All persons age 65 or older who are entitled to Social Security retirement benefits (or would be entitled for retirement benefits but the application has not been filed), or those persons receiving monthly cash benefits under Railroad Retirement programs (whether retired or not), are eligible for benefits. Individuals age 65 and over can receive Medicare benefits even if they continue to work. Enrollment in Medicare will not affect the amount of future Social Security benefits. Medicare Part A coverage includes the following four areas of coverage: hospital coverage, skilled nursing care, home health care, and hospice benefits.

Hospital coverage means that Medicare pays hospital benefits for up to 90 days in each benefit period. A benefit period begins when a Medicare recipient is hospitalized and ends only when a recipient has been out of the hospital or skilled nursing facility for 60 consecutive days. Hospital expenses are paid in full for 60 days during the benefit period. However, a patient must pay a deductible of $952 for the first 60 days. This is followed by 30 additional days with copayment, and a 60-day lifetime reserve. A patient must pay a coinsurance of $238 per day (in 2006) for the 30-day period. The 60-day lifetime reserve may be used if the 90-day period has been exhausted. Daily coinsurance of $476 a day (in 2006) is paid for these 60 additional lifetime reserve days. There is no limit on the amount of benefit periods (90-day benefit periods) a person can have in a lifetime. However, the 60-day lifetime reserve may only be used once.

The specific inpatient services that are covered under Medicare Part A hospital coverage include:

- Bed and board in a semi-private room, which includes two to four beds;
- All meals, including special diets;
- Nursing services;
- Use of regular hospital equipment, such as wheel chairs, surgical dressings, and crutches;
- Services from medical social workers;
- Diagnostic and therapeutic items and services supplied by the hospital;

- Operating and recovery room costs;
- Drugs and biologicals furnished by the hospital (however, coverage of outside drugs is limited in duration and must be a medical necessity that facilitates the patient's departure from the hospital);
- Services from interns and residents-in-training;
- X-rays and other radiology services;
- Respiratory or inhalation therapy;
- Blood transfusions, after the first three pints;
- Lab tests;
- Independent clinical laboratory services;
- Alcohol detoxification and rehabilitative services;
- Custodial special care units, such as intensive care and coronary care;
- Dental service when the individual requires hospitalization because of the dental condition;
- Rehabilitation services, such as physical therapy, speech therapy, and occupational therapy;
- Appliances that are permanently installed, such as a pacemaker or artificial limbs; and
- Lung and heart transplants.

Hospital insurance does not provide coverage for the following:

- Services of physicians and surgeons, which include the services for pathologists, radiologists, anesthesiologists, and physiatrists;
- Services of private duty nurses, unless the patient's condition requires it and the nurse is a resident of the hospital;
- The first three pints of blood received in a calendar year;
- Personal convenience items supplied at the patient's request, which includes a radio and television rental; and
- Supplies, appliances, and equipment for use outside of the hospital, unless it is required as part of the patient's hospitalization (*i.e.,* pacemaker).

Another area covered by Medicare Part A is a skilled nursing facility. A skilled nursing facility provides benefits when a patient no longer requires hospital care but may not be well enough to go home. A skilled nursing facility may be a skilled nursing home, or a wing of a hospital or nursing home. However, not all nursing homes qualify. Those nursing homes that only offer custodial care are excluded. The facility must be primarily engaged in providing skilled nursing care or rehabilitative services under the supervision of a fulltime nurse and a physician, and the physician must be available at all time for emergencies. In addition, the facility generally must be certified by the state, and the facility must have a written agreement with Medicare.

Sole custodial care is not provided under any part of Medicare, because coverage is limited to patients in need of skilled nursing care and rehabilitative services on a daily basis. Most nursing homes are not skilled nursing facilities and are not certified by Medicare. Medicare does not provide coverage for custodial care when it is the only type of care needed. In general, custodial care involves helping the patient walk, bath, dress, eat, and take medicine.

Benefits in a skilled nursing facility are only provided if (1) a physician certifies that skilled nursing care or rehabilitative services are needed for a condition that was treated in the hospital resulting in a stay of at least three days; (2) the patient is admitted to a skilled nursing facility within 30 days of leaving the hospital; (3) the patient's care in the skilled nursing facility is for a condition that he or she was treated for in the hospital; and (4) a medical professional certifies that the patient needs skilled nursing care.

Benefits for a skilled nursing facility are paid in full for 20 days, and an additional 80 days are covered with a copayment. For patients in a skilled nursing facility in 2006, the coinsurance is $119 per day. After 100 days of coverage, the patient must pay the full cost of skilled nursing facility care. The plan pays the cost of 100 days post-hospital care in each benefit period, regardless to how many benefit periods there are.

Benefits covered for skilled nursing care include:

- Bed and board in a semi-private room, unless isolation is required;
- Nursing care under the supervision of a registered nurse (but not private duty nursing);
- Drugs, biologicals, supplies, appliances, and equipment for use in the facility;
- Medical social services;
- Medical services by interns-in-training;
- Other diagnostic or therapeutic services provided by the facility;
- Rehabilitation services, such as physical therapy, speech therapy, and occupational therapy;
- All meals, including special diets; and
- Blood transfusions.

Home health care is also allowed under Medicare Part A and fully covers the cost of 100 home health visits made on an "intermittent" basis under a plan established by a physician. A patient can receive home health care benefits indefinitely if the services are given seven days a week for four hours per day. Benefits are provided if (1) a person must be confined to his or her home; (2) the care follows a hospital or skilled nursing facility stay; (3) the care includes intermittent skilled nursing care, physical therapy, and speech therapy; (4) the care is under the supervision of a physician; (5) services are provided by a home health care agency certified by Medicare; and (6) the services are provided on a visiting basis to the individual's home. A home health care agency specializes in providing skilled nursing care and rehabilitative care in the home of the patient.

Home health services not covered under Medicare Part A include the following:

- Drugs and biologicals;
- Blood transfusions;
- Meals delivered to the home;
- Homemaker services; and
- 24-hour nursing care at home.

The final area of Medicare Part A coverage is hospice benefits. Hospice benefits are available under Medicare for individuals who are certified as being terminally ill with a life expectancy of less than six months. A hospice is a public agency or private organization whose primary purpose is to provide pain relief, symptom management, and supportive services to the terminally ill. Benefits are provided primarily in the patient's home by a Medicare-approved hospice. The focus of a hospice is on the care and not the cure. A person loses all other Medicare benefits if they elect hospice benefits.

The following are benefits covered under hospice care:

- Nursing care under a registered nurse's supervision;
- Medical social services provided by a social worker under a physician's supervision;
- Counseling, including dietary counseling;
- Short-term inpatient care, including respite care;
- Services of a home health aide and homemaker services;
- Medical appliances and services;
- Drugs, including outpatient drugs for pain relief and symptom management; and
- Physical therapy, speech therapy, and occupational therapy.

There is no deductible paid for hospice benefits. Medicare pays all benefits for the terminally ill, except for small coinsurance amounts for outpatient drugs and inpatient respite care.

Q 2:27   What is Medicare Part B Medical Insurance?

All persons entitled to Part A may enroll for Part B for a fee. The monthly premium for Part B coverage beginning January 1, 2006 is $88.50. Social Security and Railroad Retirement beneficiaries age 65 or over are automatically enrolled at the time they are eligible for Part A Hospitalization Insurance. Any other person age 65 or over may enroll, provided they are a citizen of the United States, or an alien lawfully admitted for permanent residence and resident in the United States for the last five years. Enrollment is done at the local Social Security office.

The initial enrollment period is a period of seven full calendar months. The start of the enrollment period is on the first day of the third month before the month a person first becomes eligible to enroll and ends with the close of the last day of the third month following the month a person first becomes eligible to enroll. For example, if a person turns 65 on April 5, 2007, the initial enrollment period begins January 1, 2007, and ends July 31, 2007.

If a person does not enroll during the initial enrollment period, he or she may enroll during the special enrollment period. The special enrollment period is seven full calendar months beginning with the first month during which a person's employer plan coverage ends, or employment ends, whichever occurs first.

If an individual declines to enroll during his or her initial enrollment period, he or she may enroll during the general enrollment period. The general enrollment period is given each year from January 1 through March 31.

Medicare Part B is a voluntary program and, if chosen, a participant must pay monthly premiums. In September of each year, the government announces new premium rates for the following year. Premiums are set by the government each year in order to cover 25 percent of the program's total cost. Payment for the monthly premium is automatically deducted from the individual's Social Security check. Premiums are in addition to deductibles and co-payments that may exist. Medicare usually pays 80 percent of costs covered under Medical Insurance after an individual pays the first $124 of such covered services each calendar year.

The benefits provided under Medical Insurance include:

- Doctors' services wherever provided in the United States;
- Home health services not directly covered under Part A;
- Services of clinical psychologists within limits;
- Services of licensed chiropractors for spine manipulation only (it does not include X-rays by the chiropractor);
- Services of podiatrists, but this does not include routine foot care;
- The cost of diagnosing eye and ear conditions (examinations for eyeglasses and hearing aids are not covered);
- Plastic surgery for repair (not cosmetic reasons);
- Radiological and pathological services;
- Outpatient physical therapy and speech therapy;
- Drugs that cannot be self-administered;
- Dentist bills for facial or jaw surgery (bills for ordinary dental care are not covered);
- X-rays;
- Surgical dressings, casts, and splints; medical equipment, such as wheels chairs and hospital beds; prosthetic devices, such as artificial limbs;
- Ambulance services;

- Outpatient rehabilitative services;
- Vaccines for the flu, pneumococcal, and hepatitis B;
- Liver or lung transplants;
- Screening pap smears;
- Screening mammography and diagnostic mammography;
- Prostate screening;
- Colorectal screening;
- Diabetes screening;
- Screening pelvic exams;
- Services of nurse practitioner and clinical nurse specialist in rural areas;
- Oral cancer drugs;
- Prescription drugs used in immunosuppressive therapy for preventing or treating the rejection of a transplanted organ or tissue;
- Bone mass measurements for some individuals; and
- Rural health care services.

Q 2:28   What is Medicare Advantage (Part C)?

Medicare Advantage covers all the services under Part A and Part B, plus extra benefits in a basic package or other supplemental benefits priced separately from the basic package. It permits contracts between the Centers for Medicare & Medicaid Services and a combination of different managed care and fee-for-service entities. Benefits often include coverage for prescription drugs. Beneficiaries entitled to Medicare Part A and enrolled in Medicare Part B are eligible for Medicare Advantage.

There are two types of Medicare Advantage plans: Medicare managed care plans, such as Health Maintenance Organizations (HMOs), Preferred Provider Organizations (PPOs), and Provider Sponsored Organizations (PSOs); and Medicare Private Fee-for-Service plans. Each plan requires a monthly premium that varies among companies.

Q 2:29   What is Medicare Prescription Drug Insurance (Part D)?

Effective January 1, 2006, Medicare Prescription Drug Insurance (Part D) was added to Medicare by the Medicare Prescription Drug, Improvement, and Modernization Act of 2004. Part D is a voluntary program of health insurance, offered through private health carriers, that covers a portion of prescription drug costs not generally covered by other Medicare programs. Participants could keep traditional Medicare and enroll in a drug-only plan, or may choose a Medicare Advantage Plan with comprehensive benefits. Eligible participants (who qualify under Part A and Part B) qualify for Part D coverage and are required to pay a monthly premium averaging $32.20 for 2006.

Q 2:30 What services are not covered by Medicare?

The original Medicare plan does not cover health care when you travel outside the United States. There are some exceptions for emergency situations in Mexico and Canada. In addition, Medicare doesn't cover one of the most expensive out-of-pocket cost for Americans: long-term nursing home care. Nursing home care can cost an individual an average of $60,000 per year. Medicare does not cover routine physical exams and ordinary dental work. In addition, Medicare provides no coverage for cosmetic surgery, routine foot care, eye and hearing exams, prescription glasses and hearing aids, private rooms in hospitals or nursing homes, services covered under workers' compensation, acupuncture, and most immunizations.

Q 2:31 What is Medigap insurance?

Medigap insurance is offered from private companies and groups. Medigap fills gaps from Part A and Part B of Medicare. Medigap cannot be used with Medicare Advantage. Medigap premiums vary by state and are dependent on your age and the different prices among companies.

There are ten Medigap policies that offer different levels of coverage. No other form of Medicare supplement can be sold unless it existed before the ten plans were designed and provides at least comparable benefits. These ten were created because there had been a multitude of Medicare supplement plans available, and it was virtually impossible to compare them. Additionally, some aggressive sales agents sold seniors more than one plan. These plans were created and laws were passed that prohibited seniors from owning more than one supplement, and made it a crime to attempt to sell seniors on having more than one plan. The ten plans are identifies by the letters A-J and insurance companies cannot provide benefits that differ from these available options, with two exceptions:

1. Companies can offer high-deductible Medigap standard policies when used with medical savings accounts. These are identical to plans A-J except in the amount of the deductible.

2. The Medicare SELECT program can limit or exclude benefits for medical services if a non-network provider is used. A Medicare SELECT policy is identical to plans A-J except in the treatment of benefits when using nonnetwork providers.

The three basic benefits provided under A-J include hospitalization, medical expenses, and blood. Each Medigap plan differs in its treatment of skilled nursing facility, Part A deductible, Part B deductible, Part B excess charges, foreign travel emergency, at-home recovery, preventive medical care, and prescription drugs. For prescription drugs, Medigap plans H, I, and J pay 50 percent of outpatient drug charges after a $250 deductible with either a $1,250 (plans H and I) or $3,000 (plan J) calendar-year limit.

Table 2-2

Medicare Supplement (Medigap) Insurance

Benefits	*A*	*B*	*C*	*D*	*E*	*F*	*G*	*H*	*I*	*J*
Basic	X	X	X	X	X	X	X	X	X	X
Skilled-nursing facility			X	X	X	X	X	X	X	X
Part A deductible		X	X	X	X	X	X	X	X	X
Part B deductible			X			X				X
Part B excess charges						100%	80%		100%	100%
Foreign travel emergency			X	X	X	X	X	X	X	X
At-home recovery				X			X		X	X
Preventive medical care					X					X
Prescription drugs								$1,250	$1,250	$3,000

Chart taken from Beam, Burton; Bickelhaupt, David; Crowe, Robert; Poole, Barbara (2002). *Fundamentals of Insurance for Financial Planning* (3rd ed.). Bryn Mawr, Pennsylvania: The American College, Huebner School Series.

Social Security Planning

Q 2:32 Who receives Social Security benefits?

Social Security is administered by the Social Security Administration and provides old age, survivor's, and disability benefits. In contrast, Medicare provides hospital and medical benefits for aged or disabled individuals. Medicare is administered by the Centers for Medicare & Medicaid Services. The benefits under Social Security are paid as child's benefits, mother's or father's benefits, and lump sum death benefit. Benefits for a widow(er) age 60 and over, or for a dependent parent, are only payable if the worker was fully insured.

A general list of who receives Social Security benefits includes the following:

- A disabled insured worker under age 65;
- A retired insured worker age 62 or over;
- The spouse of a retired or disabled worker entitled to benefits who (1) is age 62 or over, or (2) has in care a child under age 16 or over age 16 and disabled, who is entitled to benefits;
- The divorced spouse of a retired or disabled worker entitled to benefits, if age 62 or over and married to the worker for at least 10 years;

- The divorced spouse of a fully insured worker who has not yet filed a claim for benefits, if both are age 62 or over, were married for at least 10 years, and have been fully divorced for at least two continuous years;

- The dependent, unmarried child of a retired or disabled worker entitled to benefits or of a deceased insured worker, if the child is: (1) under age 18, or (2) under age 19 and a full-time student, or (3) age 18 or over but has a disability, which began before age 22;

- The surviving spouse (including surviving divorced spouse) of a deceased insured worker if the widow(er) is age 60 or over;

- The disabled surviving spouse (including a surviving divorced spouse) of a deceased insured worker if the widow(er) is age 50-59 and becomes disabled within a specified period;

- The surviving spouse (including a surviving divorced spouse) of a deceased insured worker, regardless of age, if caring for an entitled child of the deceased who is either under age 16 or disabled before age 22;

- The dependent parents of a deceased insured worker at age 62 or over.

Q 2:33 What is fully insured and currently insured?

Insured status is measured by the number of quarters. These quarters are earned by paying taxes on wages. Individuals will not receive all benefits unless they are fully insured. Fully insured is 40 quarters of coverage, which equals a total of 10 years in covered work. Some benefits are paid if a worker is currently insured, which equals six quarters of coverage during the full 13-quarter period ending with the calendar quarter in which he or she died, became entitled to disability benefits, or became entitled to retirement benefits. In 2006, workers receive one quarter of coverage for each $970 of earnings, up to a maximum of four quarters.

Q 2:34 What are the retirement benefits of Social Security?

An individual is entitled to retirement benefits if he or she is fully insured and at least age 62. The retirement benefit at normal retirement age (age 65, but gradually increasing to age 67 for those born after 1960) equals the worker's primary insurance amount (PIA). If benefits are received prior to normal retirement age, the worker will receive a monthly benefit equal to only a percentage of PIA. For a retired worker, PIA is reduced by 5/9 of 1 percent for each of the first 36 months the worker is under normal retirement age when payments commence and by 5/12 of 1 percent for each such month in excess of 36. There are advantages and disadvantages to taking retirement benefits before full retirement age. The advantage is that a person collects benefits for a longer period of time. The disadvantage is that his or her benefit is permanently reduced. An individual can obtain a higher retirement benefit by working past normal retirement age up to age 70.

Q 2:35   What is the definition of disability under Social Security?

A person is entitled to disability benefits if all of the following conditions are met:

1. Is insured for disability benefits;
2. Is under the age of 65;
3. Has been disabled for 12 months, or expects to be disabled for 12 months;
4. Has filed an application for disability benefits; and
5. Has completed a five-month waiting period or is exempted from this period.

A person must be so severely impaired, physically and mentally, that he or she cannot perform any gainful work. The impairment must last 12 months or more, and the determination is based on medical evidence. To qualify for disability, an individual must be fully insured and have at least 20 quarters of coverage during a 40-quarter period ending with the quarter in which the person is disabled. The quarterly period is met if a person worked five years out of the last 10 years before disability. Special insured status is required to qualify for disability benefits if an individual is disabled before age 31. Special insured status is met if a person is disabled before the quarter in which age 31 is attained, and has credits in one-half of the quarters during the period beginning with the quarter after the quarter in which the person attained age 21 and ending with the quarter in which the person became disabled. If disabled before age 24, the person must have six quarters of coverage in the preceding 12-quarter period.

Q 2:36   Who receives survivor benefits under Social Security?

The survivor of a deceased insured worker receives benefits under Social Security. Mother's and father's benefit is a monthly benefit for a widow(er), regardless of age, if caring for at least one child, under 16 or disabled before age 22, of a deceased worker. Child's benefit is a monthly benefit for each child who is under age 18, over age 18 and disabled before age 22, or under age 19 and a full-time student. Widow(er)'s benefit is a monthly benefit for a widow(er), or surviving divorced widow(er), age 60 or older. Disabled widow(er)'s benefit is a monthly benefit for a disabled widow(er), age 50-60. Parent's benefit is a monthly benefit for a parent age 62 or older who was dependent upon the deceased worker for support. There is a lump-sum death payment of $255 (in 2006) paid to the surviving spouse or children of the deceased worker.

Q 2:37   What are family limitations to Social Security benefits?

The spouse is entitled to receive 50 percent of the employee's full retirement benefit. The spouse's benefit ends when certain events happen:

- The spouse dies;
- The worker dies (in which case the spouse is entitled to a widow(er)'s, mother's, or father's benefits);

- The worker's entitlement to disability benefits ends and he or she is not entitled to retirement benefits;
- The spouse is under age 62 and there is no longer a child of the worker under 16 or disabled who is entitled to a child's benefits;
- The spouse becomes entitled to retirement or disability benefits and his or her PIA is equal to or larger than one-half of the worker's PIA;
- The spouse and worker are divorced before the spouse reaches age 62 and before the spouse and worker had been married for 10 years; and
- The divorced spouse marries someone other than the worker.

Each qualified child may receive a monthly payment up to 50 percent of the employee's full retirement benefit amount, but there is a limit to the amount that can be paid to the family as a whole. This total depends on the amount of the benefit and the number of family members who also qualify on the employee's record. The total varies, but it is generally equal to about 150 to 188 percent of PIA for retirement and survivors. The child's benefit ends when certain events happen:

- The child dies;
- The child marries (but not if the child is a disabled child over age 18 and the child marries another Social Security beneficiary);
- The child's parent is no longer entitled to disability benefits, unless entitlement ended because the insured parent became entitled to retirement benefits or died; or
- The child reaches age 18 and is neither under disability nor a full-time student.

A grandchild is considered the child of the worker if the grandchild's natural parents are deceased or disabled at the time the worker became entitled to retirement or disability benefits or died, the grandchild was legally adopted by the worker's surviving spouse, and the grandchild is dependent on the insured.

The spouse can lose benefits if he or she is under normal retirement age and has earnings exceeding $12,480 (in 2006). A child can lose benefits if he or she works and earns over $12,480 in 2006. A widow or widower may receive the employee's full benefit (100 percent PIA) at 65 or older or reduced benefit as early as age 60 (or at age 50-59 if disabled). Children under age 18 also receive 75 percent of the deceased employee's benefit.

Q 2:38   How are Social Security benefits calculated?

The primary insurance amount (PIA) is the basic unit used to determine the amount of each monthly benefit. A disabled or retired worker receives the full PIA if benefits start at normal retirement age. The Average Indexed Monthly Earnings (AIME) is needed to calculate PIA. AIME is based on an individual's lifetime earnings history. Social Security benefits depend on an average of 35 years of the worker's best earnings (after indexing) to figure AIME. If there are fewer than 35 years of earnings, zero is used for each remaining year. The index factors given for each year make past earnings comparable to the level of earnings today. AIME is computed by dividing the total earnings (sum of the

Table 2-3

Benefits for workers and their families

Benefits for family members

Benefits for survivors of deceased workers

Spouse not caring for child

| FRA retirement benefit or disability benefit | Age 62 retirement benefit | Spouse not caring for child | | Child or spouse caring for child | Age 65 | Age 60 age 50-59 or and disabled | One Child | Spouse and one child or two children | Maximum family benefit for retirement and survivor | Maximum family benefit for disability |
		FRA	Age 62							
100% of PIA	77½% of PIA	50% of PIA	36¼% of PIA	50% of PIA	100% of PIA	71½% of PIA	75% of PIA	150% of PIA	150–188% of PIA	100–150% of PIA

Adapted from Mercer (2006). *2005 Guide to Social Security and Medicare* (31st ed.). Louisville, Ky: Mercer Human Resource Consulting, Inc.

highest 35 years of indexed earnings) by 420 (35 year × 12 months). This number is then used to find PIA.

The dollar amount in the PIA formula is adjusted annually by changes in the national indexing average wage. The PIA resulting from the formula is increased annually to reflect changes in the cost of living.

Q 2:39   How does working after retirement affect Social Security benefits?

If an individual continues to work after normal retirement age, Social Security benefits are not lost. If under the normal retirement age, the following applies:

- If $33,240 or less is earned in 2006 by a worker who reached normal retirement age in 2005, no benefits are lost for that year.
- If more than $33,240 is earned in 2006 before the month the beneficiary reaches normal retirement age, $1 of benefits is lost for each $3 of earnings over $33,240.
- If $12,480 or less is earned in 2006 by a worker under normal retirement age for the entire year, no benefits are lost for that year.
- If more than $12,480 is earned in 2006 by a worker under the normal retirement age for the entire year, $1 of benefits is lost for each $2 of earnings over $12,480. The under-normal-retirement test applies if the worker does not reach normal retirement age on or before the last day of the taxable year.

Q 2:40   What is the taxation of Social Security?

Social Security is funded by FICA and self-employment taxes. The FICA tax is 7.65 percent, and is paid by both employer and employee. The 7.65 percent is a combined 6.2 percent Social Security tax and 1.45 percent Medicare tax. In 2006, the Social Security tax is computed on the first $94,200 of the employee's wages. The Medicare tax is computed on the employee's total wages. Self-employment tax is imposed on self-employed people at a rate of 15.3 percent. This is comprised of a 12.4 percent Social Security tax (up to $94,200 in 2006) and a 2.9 percent Medicare tax (no ceiling).

An individual may have to pay taxes on his Social Security benefit if he has income that exceeds a certain dollar amount. In 2006, 50 percent of benefits are included in gross income if a person's income plus half of his or her Social Security benefits are more than the following base amount for his or her filing status:

- $32,000 for married couples filing jointly;
- $0 for married couples filing separately, and the filer lived with the spouse at any time during the year;
- $25,000 for all other taxpayers.

Eighty-five percent of benefits are included in gross income if a person's income plus half of his or her Social Security benefits are more than the following base amount for his or her filing status:

- $44,000 for married couples filing jointly;
- $0 for married couples filing separately, and the filer lived with the spouse at any time during the year;
- $34,000 for all other taxpayers.

Medicaid Planning

Q 2:41   What is Medicaid planning?

Medicaid is a joint federal and state program that provides assistance for health care to certain aged, disabled, or blind individuals. The intent is to provide help to needy individuals. This can be integrated with the requirements for Supplemental Security Income (SSI).

If a client's assets exceed a certain dollar value, the individual will be ineligible to receive Medicaid benefits, or if the income of an individual and spouse exceeds a specified dollar amount, the individual will not receive Medicaid benefits. Any distribution from an annuity will count for purposes of the income test, but such distributions do not count under the asset test. Depending on state law, an individual's personal residence may be included as an asset for purposes of Medicaid eligibility.

There are strict limits imposed on asset transfers to achieve Medicaid eligibility. For example, the value of any transfer of assets within 36 months before the individual makes an application for Medicaid will be considered an available resource. There are some exceptions, including transfers to children who are caretakers for their parents. In general, assets transferred to trusts have a look-back period of 60 months from the date the individual makes a Medicaid application or the date an individual enters a nursing home. Assets in a revocable trust are considered a source of funds, regardless of when the trust was created. A 60-month look-back period applies to transfers between trusts.

A financial planner may consider an irrevocable special needs trust to qualify a client for Medicaid. This is a bypass trust that is excluded from the gross estate of the beneficiary. Therefore, its assets are not counted for purposes of eligibility under Medicaid. The settlor (also called grantor) retains the following powers:

- While competent, the power to act as trustee;
- When not competent, the right to invade principal on the basis of health, education, maintenance, and support;
- The power to appoint an unlimited amount of trust property to family members other than the trustor; and
- The power to change beneficiaries so as to reallocate the estate amount for the children.

Long-Term Care Insurance

Q 2:42 What does long-term care insurance provide for the older client?

Long-term care (LTC) insurance provides for an individual in the event that he or she becomes incapacitated or otherwise needs lengthy, skilled health care, such as that provided by a nursing home. Long-term care insurance can be expensive, but this expense must be weighed against the daily cost of care in a nursing home.

The Health Insurance Portability and Accountability Act (HIPAA) created a definition for qualified LTC plans. HIPAA provides favorable tax treatment to qualified long-term care insurance contracts only. There are specific conditions that apply in order for a policy to meet HIPAA requirements:

1. Only qualified long-term care insurance can be provided under the contract. No other insurance can be issued under the policy.

2. If expenses are reimbursable under Medicare, the policy cannot pay for them.

3. The contract must be guaranteed renewable or noncancellable.

4. The policy cannot have a cash surrender value or loan provision.

5. Refunds of premiums and policy dividends must be used to reduce future premiums or increase future benefits.

6. The policy must comply with consumer protection provisions, such as those adopted in the NAIC Model Act.

In a qualified long-term health care plan, individuals can deduct premiums paid for LTC in excess of 7.5 percent of adjusted gross income. There are limits to the maximum amount that can be deducted, subject to the covered individual's age. Employer contributions are deductible by the employer and result in no taxable income to the employee. Benefits are received tax-free with one exception: for contracts written on a per diem basis, only portions of the proceeds are excludible from income.

HIPAA defines qualified long-term care services as necessary diagnostic, preventive, therapeutic, curing, treating, and rehabilitative services, and maintenance or personal care services that are required by a chronically ill person and are provided by a plan of care prescribed by a licensed health care practitioner. A chronically ill person is someone that meets one of two conditions:

1. The inability to perform at least two activities of daily living (ADLs) for a period of at least 90 days. The act identifies ADLs as eating, bathing, dressing, transferring from bed to chair, using the toilet, and maintaining continence. A qualified long-term care policy must contain at least five of the six.

2. Substantial and adequate services are required to protect the individual from threats to his or her health and safety due to cognitive impairment.

A financial planner should consider the following when helping a client find a good long-term care insurance policy:

- The policy should be guaranteed renewable for life.
- A three-month waiting period generally offers the best value for the premium dollars paid.
- The policy should provide coverage for skilled and intermediate care, and also for custodial care, which does not require the engagement of licensed medical professionals.
- Long-term care at home can be more attractive than a residential or nursing facility.
- Select a policy that does not require the insured to be hospitalized before entering a nursing home.
- Select a policy that provides long-term care coverage for Alzheimer's disease.
- Choose a policy that provides for the anticipated rise in the cost of long-term care.
- Select a policy that provides for a waiver of premiums in the event of disability, and provides level premiums for life.
- Select a policy that provides a favorable benefit period.

Life Insurance as an Alternative

Q 2:43   How can life insurance be used in the estate plan?

A financial planner should consider the use of life insurance in an estate plan. Its use is generally most beneficial when preparing for aging and death. There are several advantages to life insurance. Life insurance is used to provide income to a decedent's family. It provides liquidity for the estate at the death of the decedent. It is often used to fund business continuation agreements. However, a life insurance policy can have unfavorable estate and gift tax consequences if the policy is poorly planned.

Ownership and beneficiary designation of a life insurance policy is critical when an estate exceeds the applicable exclusion amount (AEA). If the estate is less than the AEA, there are no transfer taxes, so the selection of an owner and beneficiary is easy. If the estate is likely to exceed the AEA, two rules should be considered when naming a spouse as owner and beneficiary of an estate:

1. Naming either spouse as owner or beneficiary of a policy on the life of the other spouse will subject the proceeds to transfer taxation at least at the second death. To minimize taxes, neither spouse should be designated owner or beneficiary of an insurance policy on the life of the other.

2. A taxable gift occurs when the noninsured spouse is named owner and someone else is beneficiary. To minimize taxes, name whichever spouse is selected as both the owner and beneficiary to avoid gift tax consequences.

If a child is named owner and beneficiary, he or she can turn over the proceeds to provide liquidity to the estate. However, any transfer of funds to the estate is treated as a gift unless the child is the sole beneficiary of the estate. To avoid making a gift, the child could purchase estate assets or lend money to the estate.

Q 2:44   What is the use of an ILIT?

A financial planner should also consider for his or her clients the use of an irrevocable trust as the owner and beneficiary of a life insurance policy. An irrevocable life insurance trust (ILIT) is generally the best choice in selecting an owner and beneficiary. The trust must be irrevocable, or, under Code Section 2038, the insurance proceeds will be pulled back into the trustor's estate. The trustor cannot be named as beneficiary because it will be deemed as a Section 2036(a) transfer with a retained interest. Therefore, the trustee is both the owner and beneficiary, which is usually the uninsured spouse. A second-todie policy should be considered if the sole purpose is to pay estate taxes at the death of the second spouse. A term policy should be considered if the couple is younger and has less wealth, and the purpose is to replace the financial contribution of the deceased spouse.

An ILIT has several impressive outcomes. It excludes both the insurance proceeds from income taxation and estate taxation for both spouses and the insurance proceeds from the probate estates of both spouses. The annual exclusion can be used for gifts to the trust to pay premiums. It ensures that the responsible party will have the needed liquidity after death. Finally, it makes proceeds available to the surviving spouse for health, education, maintenance, and support.

Q 2:45   What is the gift and estate taxation of life insurance?

There are several sections of the Code that apply to life insurance. Section 2001 states that the decedent's adjusted taxable gift include the date-of-gift value less the annual exclusion for any life insurance policy the decedent transferred after 1976 and more than three years before death. Section 2033 states that if the decedent owned a life insurance policy on the life of another person, the replacement cost of the policy is included in the decedent's gross estate. The three-year rule does not apply to a policy on another's life. Section 2035(a) includes in the gross estate all life insurance proceeds on the life of the decedent if the decedent made a transfer of any incidents of ownership in the policy within three years before death. Section 2042 includes in the gross estate life insurance proceeds receivable by the personal representative or receivable by other beneficiaries if the decedent possessed any of the incidents of ownership at death. Ownership of insurance policies may be transferred from the decedent to exclude the proceeds of the policies from the decedent's estate. The insured must survive three years after the transfer in order for the insurance to be effectively moved from the estate [IRC § 2035(a)]. The transfer of a life insurance policy may be subject to federal gift taxes. Obviously, to be a gift, the transfer must be complete and irrevocable. The donor must give up all incidents of ownership.

Q 2:46 What is the income taxation of life insurance?

The general rule is that the proceeds of a life insurance policy paid by reason of death are not includible in the deceased's or the beneficiary's gross income for federal income tax purposes. There is an exception to this general rule. If the life insurance policy is acquired by another owner for a valuable consideration (money-purchase price), the difference between the policy's death proceeds and the purchaser's cost basis (purchase price plus net premiums paid) is includible in the beneficiary's gross income. This tax assessment is in accordance with the so-called "transfer-for-value rule."

Estate Planning Documents

Q 2:47 What is the importance of a will when planning for the elderly?

The most critical purpose for establishing a will is to provide the testator with an opportunity to control the passing of his or her property and thus avoid intestacy. A will is revocable, which means it can be altered, amended, or completely rewritten numerous times until the individual's death. Wills are generally amended through the use of codicils. Codicils are supplements to wills, and must be executed following the same rules and guidelines as the original will. An *in-terrorem* clause can be added to a will. This clause states that if a beneficiary contests the validity of a will, the beneficiary's bequest is void. This may deter an unsatisfied beneficiary from contesting a will.

Q 2:48 How is a power of attorney used in planning for the older client?

A power of attorney is created by an individual, giving authority to another entity to act on behalf of the individual. The power of attorney is usually witnessed and accredited. The person executing the power is called the principal, and the person appointed by the power is the attorney-in-fact. A durable power of attorney is not terminated by disability or incapacity of the principal. It is designed to cover a situation where the principal becomes incompetent. A power of attorney that is not a durable power of attorney terminates upon disability or incompetence. A durable power of attorney takes effect upon execution, and continues until revoked by the principal or upon the death of the principal. A springing power of attorney does not become effective until the occurrence of a specified event. The purpose of a springing feature is to avoid giving another person powers to act on behalf of the principal when the principal is capable of making decisions.

A durable power of attorney for health care appoints a person to make decisions concerning medical treatment for an incapacitated principal. It apples to all situations where the principal is unable to give informed consent with respect to a particular medical decision. It often gives the power to use or not to use artificial life support systems. It always springs on incapacity. These powers are recognized in almost all states. State law varies in terms of the scope of authority of the attorney-in-fact. One major drawback is that it is so powerful. It can place reluctant family members in the position of making a decision that may be regretted later on in life.

Q 2:49   What is the use of living wills when planning for the older client?

Living wills are used to identify medical situations in which the testator no longer wants life-sustaining treatment (*i.e.*, life support systems to prolong life). Living wills are medical life support directives. They do not designate an agent to make medical decisions. There are several drawbacks to living wills. They are generally very brief and vague, only covering a narrow range of outcomes, which are mostly in the area of life-sustaining treatment. They cannot cover all possible medical outcomes. Planners might want to consider executing both a living will and durable power of attorney for health care to cover all areas.

Q 2:50   How are trusts used when planning for the older client?

Living trusts should be considered for clients to manage their property in cases of incapacity or death. If the affected party was serving as trustee at the time of the disability or death, most state laws allow a successor trustee to immediately take over the administration of the estate. A living trust can be used to manage the disposition of property at disability or death.

A living trust is similar to a will in that both guide the disposition of property, both have a fiduciary that is responsible for managing the property, and both instruments are revocable and amendable, at least up until the death of the person creating the instrument (living trusts generally become irrevocable at the death of the grantor). However, there are major differences between a living trust and a will. A living trust disposes of property owned by the trustee in trust for the trustor (decedent). A will disposes of probate property owned by the decedent at death. A living trust appoints a trustee while a will nominates an executor. The execution requirements are stricter for a will. The signing of trust documents does not require witnesses. However, the mental capacity necessary for setting up a trust is at a higher standard than that for making a will.

A living trust can be set up as a revocable living trust or as an irrevocable living trust. A revocable living trust is subject to the right to rescind and amend. This means that a grantor can change the conditions and beneficiaries of the trust during his or her lifetime. The revocable living trust becomes irrevocable at the grantor's death, and is included in the decedent's taxable estate. There is no gift tax when the trust is created. In contrast, an irrevocable living trust cannot be revoked by the grantor after its creation except upon the consent of all the beneficiaries. Gift tax may apply at time of transfer to an irrevocable living trust. However, it does offer income and estate tax benefits.

A testamentary trust is also used as a principal document of property disposition. This trust takes effect after death at the end of the probate process. It contains all provisions commonly found in a will, and includes unique cases that relate to the trust documents. A testamentary trust must appoint a trustee and nominate an executor.

Using the Family Home

Q 2:51   What are strategies for the older client owning a home?

The home is often the largest asset of an older couple. It is generally paid off when the couple retires, and most senior citizens are homeowners. Planning for the home can involve several strategies:

- The older couple can stay in the home and plan to leave it to a child or grandchild. The problem with this strategy is that the child may not be interested in living in the home. In addition, there is generally more than one child or grandchild. To simplify this problem, the will should direct the executor to sell the home and allocate the proceeds to all the children. However, this may result in a hurried sale, which generally does not get the best price.
- Stay in the home and fix it up to make it more in line with the current needs of an older couple. This would mean adding security features, adding a response system for health emergencies, and widening doors.
- Stay in the home and transfer ownership of the home to a trust. This is often done to remove the home from the estate.
- Stay in the home and have a son or daughter move into the home. The older couple can also sell the home and move into one of their children's homes.
- Obtain a home equity loan or reverse mortgage to provide income for home care, vacations, and living expenses.
- Sell the home and use the proceeds to buy admission into a retirement community that offers no equity ownership.

Q 2:52   What is the capital gains exclusion when selling a home?

The Taxpayer Relief Act (TRA '97) provides capital gain tax relief when selling a home. Up to $500,000 in capital gains for joint filers ($250,000 for single individuals) on home sales can be excluded from income. There is an ownership test and a use test that must be met in order to receive the preferential tax treatment. The ownership test requires owning the home for two out of the last five years before the sale. The use test requires having used the property as the taxpayer's primary residency for two out of the last five years prior to sale. The use test is modified to allow for exclusion from the two-year requirement if absence from the home was caused by sickness or being in a nursing home, and the taxpayer used the home for one year as a primary residence. A widow or widower satisfies the test if the deceased spouse satisfied the ownership and use test prior to death. The exclusion is only to be used every two years.

If there are changes in employment or health problems before reaching two years, the gains included in income are on a pro rata basis. The numerator of the ratio is the shorter of (1) the aggregate time period of ownership/use of the residence, or (2) the time period between the earlier sale of a residence for which gain was excluded and the current sale. The denominator is equal to two years.

Example 2-4. A single taxpayer has lived in her first house for 18 months. She is forced to sell the house because of health reasons. The amount of gain excluded cannot exceed $187,500 (($250,000 $\times$ 1.5) $\div$2). If she realizes a gain of $75,000, the entire amount is excludible.

Q 2:53   How can the older client access home equity?

Older clients can access capital through a conventional home equity loan or credit line, and through a "reverse mortgage." A reverse mortgage is an agreement between a bank or insurance company and the elderly homeowner. The senior citizen receives periodic payments, and, in return, the lender receives an equity interest in the house. If the payments are in the form of an annuity, the arrangement is known as a Reverse Annuity Mortgage (RAM).

Payments continue for a fixed number of years or for the life of the homeowner. If the homeowner sells the home, the proceeds are immediately used to pay off the loan. The loan also becomes payable at the death of the homeowner. Repayment, therefore, has to wait until the consumer dies, vacates the home, or transfers ownership of the dwelling.

One advantage of this type of loan is that it does not count against Medicaid and Supplemental Security Income (SSI). These funds are not considered income, because the arrangement is a loan. The typical reverse mortgage payments are under $10,000 per year, which may assist in paying expenses but more certainly won't cover all expenses.

FHA-insured mortgages provide a fixed annuity for the life of the homeowner. The percentage of the value of the home that can be borrowed under FHA depends on the homeowner's age. The older the person is, the more that can be borrowed. This is because the life expectancy of the person is less, so the payments will be larger. The maximum amount of the loan is set regionally and ranges from $115,200 to $208,800 for single-family homes.

The Federal National Mortgage Association ("Fannie Mae") also offers reverse mortgages. The value of the loan is limited to one-third to one-half of the amount of equity in the home. Fannie Mae has a toll-free number, (800) 572-4562, for information on reverse mortgages.

Q 2:54   What is the use of house trusts: PRTs and QPRTs?

In a house trust, the home is transferred into an irrevocable trust, where the grantor (*i.e.*, parents) retains the right to the house for a period of years, after which the trust ends and the home is transferred to the remaindermen. If the transferor survives the period, all beneficial interest in the trust ceases, and the asset is out of the transferor's estate. The advantages of transferring a home into the trust is to remove the asset from the estate at a far less than fair market value, thus removing any potential appreciation. This allows for the transfer of the home to the couple's children while fully utilizing the applicable exclusion amount (AEA).

The primary purpose of this trust is to leverage the AEA to avoid estate tax, not gift tax. The value of the gift made is calculated by taking the FMV of the property and reducing it by the retained interest. This equals the remainder interest that is considered a gift. This remainder interest is a future interest, and is discounted. Therefore, the longer the term of the trust and the higher the Section 7520 rate, the smaller the gift value. The result is to freeze the value in the grantor's interest and transfer growth in value to the children, escaping larger gift and estate taxes.

Two types of trusts for such a transfer are the Personal Residence Trust (PRT) and the Qualified Personal Residence Trust (QPRT). The PRT only contains the house, whereas the QPRT contains the house and a limited number of other assets. The other assets in a QPRT generally generate enough income to pay the taxes on and other expenses of the house.

The parents can continue to live in the house. The grantor (*i.e.*, the parent) who survives the term of the QPRT does not have to vacate the residence since he or she can rent it as a remainderman. However, the house must be rented at a fair market rental value. If the parents use the house and rent it for less than fair market value, the value of the house reverts back into the estate. In this case, it is considered a transfer with a retained interest. If the parents both die during the term of the PRT or QPRT, then the house is included in their estates. If only one dies during the term, then only a half interest is included in the estate of the deceased parent. In addition, the residence cannot be purchased back from the trustee by the settlor, the settlor's spouse, or an entity controlled by them.

There is no reason to create a PRT or QPRT of any kind with a term that goes beyond 2009 because the estate tax will be repealed at that time. In the post-EGTRRA era, a PRT or QPRT is only beneficial if the term ends before the settlor dies and the settlor dies before 2010. If a settlor dies after 2009, assuming the estate tax remains repealed, the now distributed PRT or QPRT turns out to be a waste of time. The remaindermen receive the trust assets with a carryover basis.

If the settlor had simply held onto the assets, the increase in basis would have been allocated to him or her.

Q 2:55   What is the use of a private annuity for the older client?

A private annuity is an exchange of an asset for an unsecured promise by the buyer to pay an annuity for the life of the transferor. In this way, a private annuity (sometimes called a sale-leaseback) involves the sale of a residence to a family member or friend, while the donor continues to live there and pay rent. The private annuity commonly provides life payments to the annuitant. Taking the payments in this way allows the annuitant to spread the capital gains from the sale, rather than accepting them in one lump sum. A private annuity allows a person with a large estate to remove possible future appreciation from the estate, and spread out capital gains (although the sale will probably escape taxation because of the capital gain exclusion for home-sale profits). The private annuity contract must be unsecured, so the annuitant-to-be should make sure the entity making the annuity payments is sound financially.

In contrast, a gift-leaseback involves the gift of a residence, while the donor continues to live there and pay rent. This results in the use of the donor's unified credit against gift and estate taxes, and possibly, in some cases, a need to pay gift tax.

Q 2:56   What is the treatment of a residence by Medicaid?

The value of the homestead is not considered in determining initial Medicaid eligibility. The home is considered an exempt asset under Medicaid. Property no longer qualifies as a homestead if a single person who is in a nursing home is too sick to return home. However, the property maintains its homestead status as long as a nursing home resident's spouse or dependent relative continues to live in it.

Gifting Strategies for the Older Client

Q 2:57   What should be considered when designing a gifting strategy?

The following should be considered when designing a gifting strategy:

1. Consider gifting assets that yield higher amounts of income versus those that yield lower amounts of income. This will prevent a build-up of income in the estate.
2. If the donee is in a lower income tax bracket than the donor, consider gifting assets that produce as much taxable income as possible. The donor should retain assets that do not produce as much taxable income, such as municipal bonds.
3. Give growth assets instead of nongrowth assets. This prevents post-gift appreciation from being taxed in the donor's gross estate.

4. Give high basis assets instead of low basis assets. The donee receives the same basis as the donor's. If an asset is held until death, the asset receives a step-up in basis equal to the fair market value at the decedent's death or alternative valuation date.

5. Sell assets whose value is less than their basis. Selling these assets results in a loss to the owner, which could possibly be deducted from the donor's income taxes. If these assets are retained, the basis for determining the loss is lost:

   a. If given during the owner's life, the basis equals the fair market value at the time of the gift.

   b. If the estate owner dies holding the assets, the basis becomes the fair market value at time of death.

6. Avoid gifting installment obligations. The donor will have to recognize the entire untaxed profit at the time of transfer.

7. Before gifting stock in an S corporation to a trust, make sure the gift will not cause the loss of S corporation status. This generally means that the trust must be a qualified subchapter S trust (QSST).

Q 2:58   What are gifts of present and future interests?

The gift tax exclusion is available only for gifts of present interest; the exclusion does not apply to gifts of future interest. To be considered a gift of present interest, the donee must have the immediate right to use, possess or enjoy the property. A gift will be considered one of future interest if the right to use, possess or enjoy property is delayed. When making gifts to a trust, the gift will be considered of present interest only if the beneficiary has the right to demand immediate custody of the property transferred.

The most common types of future interests include reversions and remainders. A reversion is a future interest in property that is retained by the transferor after he or she transfers an interest in property. The reversion becomes a present interest of the transferor (or transferor's estate) at some point when the donor gets the property back.

Example 2-5. Ben transfers property in trust to Samantha for her life. The document does not explain what will happen to the property after Samantha's death. Ben has retained a reversionary interest. The trust property will belong to Ben when Samantha dies. If Ben dies before Samantha, the property will belong to his estate.

Remainders are the right to use, possess, and enjoy property after all prior owners' interests end. They usually arise from trusts, where the remainderman is entitled to the remaining assets at the termination of the trust.

Example 2-6. If a business person gave money to a trust, which states that the income is to be paid currently to his or her child and, upon termination of the trust, the principal is to be transferred to his or her grandchildren, the value of the remainder interest to the grandchildren would not be eligible for the annual gift tax exclusion.

Example 2-7. A father pays the premiums on an insurance policy on his life that is owned by the son. This payment of premiums is a gift of a present interest. On the other hand, if the father transfers an insurance policy to a trust for the benefit of his son, when the father dies, the insurance proceeds will be invested and the son will be entitled to the income from the investments. The son has a future interest in the insurance policy.

The income beneficiaries receive a life estate or estate for years in the trust income. In contrast, the remaindermen receive the remainder at termination of the income interests. Therefore, the life estate and estate for years are usually a present value interest, whereas the remainder is a future interest.

Helping the Older Client Plan for Retirement Plan Distributions

Q 2:59   What questions should be asked when planning for retirement distributions?

A client should consider all available options when planning for a retirement distribution. This means the client must have a clear understanding of the retirement plan distribution rules. An advisor can assist his or her client by asking five primary questions.

1. What kind of distributions does his or her current plan allow? This may mean that the advisor will have to review plan documents to determine the options that are available. All qualified pension plans must provide two forms of survivorship benefits for spouses: (1) the qualified preretirement survivor annuity and (2) the qualified joint and survivor annuity. Profit sharing plans, ESOPs, and stock bonus plans generally do not provide these options if the nonforfeitable account balance of the participant is payable as a death benefit to the spouse. Other distribution options generally include "direct rollover" of certain distributions.

2. Should the distribution be made as a lump sum or in a series of deferred payments? The advantages of lump sum distributions include 10-year averaging for eligible distributions to an individual born before 1936, and freedom to invest proceeds at the participant's discretion. In contrast, the advantages of periodic payments are deferral of taxes until money is distributed; continued tax shelter of income; and security of income. There is no best alternative, but rather competing advantages of each one. A complex analysis, especially for large sums of money, should be done to determine which alternative to choose.

3. If periodic payments are chosen, what type of payment schedule is best? This means the client and advisor need to determine four important factors: (1) if the minimum distribution requirements are satisfied; (2) consideration of "electing out" of the survivorship benefit in favor of an optional benefit form selected by the participant is significantly important as the participant nears retirement age; (3) if the payment is subject to a

10 percent early distribution penalty; and (4) the tax consequences of the payments.

4. If a lump sum payment is chosen, what are the consequences to the client? The advisor will need to determine if (1) the client is eligible for 10-year averaging; (2) the election for 10-year averaging, if available, is beneficial to the client; and (3) how much tax is payable.

5. What are the potential future estate tax consequences of the different forms of distributions?

Q 2:60 What are the required spousal benefit provisions under a qualified pension plan?

All qualified pension plans must provide two forms of survivorship benefits for spouses: (1) automatic lifetime survivor benefit in the form of a qualified joint and survivor annuity (QJSA); and (2) automatic lifetime survivor benefit in the form of a qualified preretirement survivor annuity (QPSA).

A QJSA must provide an annuity for the life of the participant with a survivor annuity for the life of the participant's spouse. It must provide a survivor annuity that is not less than 50 percent nor greater than 100 percent of the annuity payable during the joint lives of the participant and spouse. For example, if $1,000 per month is payable during the joint lives, the annuity to the surviving spouse can be any specified amount from $500 per month to $1,000 per month. The spouse's annuity must continue even if the spouse remarries. For a QPSA, it must provide a survivor benefit if the participant dies before retirement. The survivor annuity payable is the amount that would have been paid under a QJSA.

The nonparticipant spouse can "elect out" of the benefits from a QPSA and QJSA. The consent of the nonparticipant spouse to waiver (or electing out) of a QPSA and QJSA in favor of an optional benefit form selected by the participant must (1) be in writing; (2) acknowledge the effect of the waiver; and (3) be witnessed, either by a plan representative or a notary public.

Stock bonus, profit sharing, and ESOPs generally are exempt from the QJSA and QPSA requirements if two conditions are satisfied: (1) there are no annuity options, and (2) the plan participant's account balance is payable to the participant's spouse in the event of the participant's death.

Other Benefit Options under Plan Provisions. Qualified plans generally offer a wide range of distribution options. However, administrative costs increase as more options are available. In addition, the IRS makes it difficult to withdraw a benefit option when one is chosen. As a result, qualified plans try to limit the menu of distribution choices..

As a general rule, all qualified plans must have a provision for direct rollovers. Pension plans often provide a life annuity for an unmarried participant. It provides monthly payments for life. As an option to the joint or single life annuity, plans often offer a period certain annuity. A period certain annuity is an annuity form that proves payments for a specified period of time. Profit sharing, ESOPs, and stock bonus plans often provide a lump sum benefit at retirement or termination of employment. These plans also offer an option to take out nonannuity distributions over the retirement years. This allows the participant to take out money as he or she needs it, which is subject to the minimum distribution rules.

Q 2:61　Which alternative is best: lump sum or deferred payments?

There is not one simple answer when determining if a lump sum or deferred payment is the best choice. A complete analysis is necessary to calculate the alternative that is best for the client. The analysis will require the planner to predict future tax rates and investment returns. The factors involved in determining which alternative is best include:

1. The age of the participant (or participant and beneficiary), which impacts the expected number of years of payments.
2. The health of the participant (and beneficiary), which further impacts the expected number of years of payments.
3. The expected return on investment.
4. The current and future expected tax rates.
5. The amount of income needed and when it is needed.
6. The total amount of benefit to be received.

Q 2:62　What are the rules under RMD?

RMD applies to qualified plans, IRAs, SEPs, SIMPLE IRAs, and Section 457 government deferred compensation plans. Minimum distributions must begin no later than April 1 of the calendar year following the later of (a) the calendar year in which the employee attains age 70½ or (b) the employee retires (not available for 5 percent owners of a business or for an IRA owner). Participants use the balance as of December 31 of the year prior to the distributions year as the RMD calculation base. RMD is calculated separately for each IRA, but distributions can be taken from any account to satisfy the minimum.

Q 2:63　How is RMD calculated?

RMD is calculated using the participant's life expectancy. The required minimum is determined by dividing the owner's account balance by the appropriate life expectancy. To satisfy RMD rules, the entire interest must be distributed by the required beginning date, or the interest must be distributed over one of the following periods:

1. Over the lifetime of the participant;
2. Over the joint and survivor lives of the participant and a designated beneficiary;
3. Over a period that does not extend beyond the life expectancy of the participant; or

4. Over a period that does not extend beyond the joint and survivor life expectancy of the participant and a designated beneficiary.

Three life expectancy tables are used to determine RMD:

1. Uniform Lifetime Table is used to determine the minimum required distributions during the lifetime of the participant when the retirement benefit is in the form of an account balance. It is often used in situations where the employee's spouse is either (a) not the sole designated beneficiary; or (b) is the sole designated beneficiary but is not more than 10 years younger than the employee.

Example 2-8. Jim reaches age 72 in 2007. His account balance in an IRA was 500,000 as of the end of 2006. His required distribution for 2005 is $19,532 (500,000 ÷ 25.6).

Table 2-4 Uniform Lifetime Table

Age of employee	Distribution period	Age of employee	Distribution period
70	27.4	93	9.6
71	26.5	94	9.1
72	25.6	95	8.6
73	24.7	96	8.1
74	23.8	97	7.6
75	22.9	98	7.1
76	22.0	99	6.7
77	21.2	100	6.3
78	20.3	101	5.9
79	19.5	102	5.5
80	18.7	103	5.2
81	17.9	104	4.9
82	17.1	105	4.5
83	16.3	106	4.2
84	15.5	107	3.9
85	14.8	108	3.7
86	14.1	109	3.4
87	13.4	110	3.1
88	12.7	111	2.9
89	12.0	112	2.6
90	11.4	113	2.4
91	10.8	114	2.1
92	10.2	115	1.9

2. The Joint and Last Survivor Table is used to determine the minimum

required distributions during the lifetime of the participant when the employee's spouse is either (a) sole designated beneficiary, or (b) more than 10 years younger than participant. If the designated beneficiary is changed to anyone other than the spouse, this table cannot be used.

3. The Single Life Table is used for designated beneficiaries, including the spouse. The spouse can recalculate each year. Non-spouse beneficiaries do not recalculate but determine life expectancy for first year of distributions and subtract one year for each subsequent year. This table also applies to Roth IRA non-spouse beneficiaries.

Example 2-9. Jim dies in 2006 at age 63. He owns a Roth IRA worth $35,000. His son, Bill, inherits the Roth IRA at age 25. Bill must begin taking minimum distributions (tax free) by December of 2007, using the Single Life Table. The initial life expectancy of 58.2 years is given from the table.

Table 2-5 Single Life Table

Age	Life expectancy	Age	Life expectancy
0	82.4	36	47.5
1	81.6	37	46.5
2	80.6	38	45.6
3	79.7	39	44.6
4	78.7	40	43.6
5	77.7	41	42.7
6	76.7	42	41.7
7	75.8	43	40.7
8	74.8	44	39.8
9	73.8	45	38.8
10	72.8	46	37.9
11	71.8	47	37.0
12	70.8	48	36.0
13	69.9	49	35.1
14	68.9	50	34.2
15	67.9	51	33.3
16	66.9	52	32.3
17	66.0	53	31.4
18	65.0	54	30.5
19	64.0	55	29.6
20	63.0	56	28.7
21	62.1	57	27.9
22	61.1	58	27.0
23	60.1	59	26.1
24	59.1	60	25.2

Table 2-5 Single Life Table (*cont'd*)

Age	Life expectancy	Age	Life expectancy
25	58.2	61	24.4
26	57.2	62	23.5
27	56.2	63	22.7
28	55.3	64	21.8
29	54.3	65	21.0
30	53.3	66	20.2
31	52.4	67	19.4
32	51.4	68	18.6
33	50.4	69	17.8
34	49.4	70	17.0
35	48.5	71	16.3
72	15.5	92	4.9
73	14.8	93	4.6
74	14.1	94	4.3
75	13.4	95	4.1
76	12.7	96	3.8
77	12.1	97	3.6
78	11.4	98	3.4
79	10.8	99	3.1
80	10.2	100	2.9
81	9.7	101	2.7
82	9.1	102	2.5
83	8.6	103	2.3
84	8.1	104	2.1
85	7.6	105	1.9
86	7.1	106	1.7
87	6.7	107	1.5
88	6.3	108	1.4
89	5.9	109	1.2
90	5.5	110	1.1
91	5.2	111	1.0

Q 2:64   What is the penalty for not making a distribution by the required beginning date (RBD)?

There is a 50 percent penalty on the amount not distributed that should be distributed by the required beginning date. If the account value has decreased below the calculated minimum based on the December 31st balance, the account can be depleted with no 50 percent penalty for not taking the full amount required. The 50 percent penalty for shortfalls in RMD applies to traditional IRAs and may pertain to Roth IRAs. Roth IRAs are not subject to minimum required distributions during the lifetime of the participant. There-fore, there is no required beginning date during the lifetime of the participant. However, Roth IRAs are subject to minimum required distributions after the death of the participant.

Q2:65   What are beneficiary considerations?

The designated beneficiary must be determined by September 30 of the year following the year of death, and must be beneficiary as of the date of death. The beneficiaries can be eliminated by disclaimer but not replaced or added after the owner's death. Disclaimers are often used to stretch IRAs. For example, the primary beneficiary disclaims and allows the IRA to pass to a much younger contingent beneficiary. The executors or trustees do not have the ability to choose a beneficiary after the date of death. The first required distribution must be withdrawn by December 31 of the year following the year of death. If a beneficiary dies during the period between the owner's death and the desig-nation date for beneficiaries, the required distributions are calculated using the life expectancy of the beneficiary (as if designated).

> **Example 2-10.** Assume the father dies in 2006 and names his daughter as beneficiary. The daughter dies later in 2006 prior to being named as desig-nated beneficiary (September 30, 2007). The grandchild inherits the retire-ment plan, and must use the daughter's life expectancy in the new tables.

Beneficiaries must be named under the plan documentation. If a beneficiary is named by the estate or will, he or she cannot be a designated beneficiary and cannot use the single life expectancy table for calculating distributions.

Q2:66   What distribution choices are there when the death of the owner is prior to the required beginning date (RBD)?

The entire benefit must be distributed within five years of the death of the participant. This rule has been dubbed the five-year rule. An exception to the fiveyear rule exists. The life expectancy rule applies in all cases in which the deceased owner has a designated beneficiary. This means that distributions are made over the life expectancy of the designated beneficiary.

If the designated beneficiary is not the surviving spouse of the participant, to satisfy the life expectancy rule, the entire interest of the participant must be distributed over the life expectancy of the designated beneficiary. The minimum required distributions must begin by December 31 of the year following the year when the participant died. The applicable distribution period is determined by using the life expectancy table. For each subsequent distribution calendar year, the previous year's life expectancy is reduced by one.

If the designated beneficiary is the surviving spouse of the participant, to satisfy the life expectancy rule, the entire interest of the participant must be distributed over the life expectancy of the spouse. The minimum required distributions must begin by December 31 of the later of (1) the year following the year in which the participant died; or (2) the year in which the participant would have attained age 70½, had the participant survived. If the surviving spouse dies before benefits must begin under the life expectancy rule, the surviving spouse will be treated as if he or she was the participant. This means that the next beneficiary is the designated beneficiary of the now-deceased surviving spouse. This successor beneficiary is subject to the life expectancy rule or the five-year rule.

If no designated beneficiary is named by the participant, the five-year rule applies.

If Roth IRA owners die before their required beginning dates, the distributions must be made in accordance with the five-year rule or the life expectancy rule.

Q 2:67 What distribution choices are there when the death of the owner is after the required beginning date (RBD)?

The entire balance must be distributed at least as rapidly as was the case before the participant died. The "at least as rapidly" rule is satisfied by using the longer of (using the single life table):

- The life expectancy of the designated beneficiary determined as of the year following the year when the participant died; or
- The remaining life expectancy of the participant using the participant's birthday during the year of death, reduced by one.

If the sole designated beneficiary is the surviving spouse of the participant, he or she must take distributions over his or her life expectancy by December 31 of the year following the owner's death. The distributions should be recalculated for each subsequent year using a single life table.

If the designated beneficiary is not solely the surviving spouse of the participant, the "at least as rapidly" rule is satisfied by using the larger of the two numbers. For each subsequent distribution calendar year, the number should be further reduced by one.

If no designated beneficiary is named, the distribution period is the deceased owner's life expectancy calculated in the year of death and reduced by one for each subsequent year.

In the year of death, the heirs must take the decedent's required distribution based on the method under which the decedent had been taking distributions. In later years, the required distributions depend upon who is the chosen beneficiary.

If the designated beneficiary is older than the owner, the designated beneficiary can use the owner's remaining life expectancy. For example, if the daughter dies after RBD and the father is the beneficiary, the father can use the daughter's life expectancy for calculating RMD.

Q 2:68 What happens if the surviving spouse makes an election of an IRA rollover?

If the surviving spouse makes a spousal rollover to an IRA, minimum distributions for the surviving spouse's life expectancy do not have to begin until April 1 of the year following the year the surviving spouse attains age 70½. The minimum distribution is based on the uniform lifetime table of the surviving spouse. The surviving spouse can name a new beneficiary, such as a child.

> **Example 2-11.** Steve dies at age 82, having named his spouse, Sarah, age 75, as the beneficiary of his IRA. Sarah names their child, Bart, as the sole beneficiary. Sarah uses the uniform lifetime table to calculate the minimum distribution. In the year following Steve's death, Sarah is age 76 and her distribution period is 22. When Sarah dies, minimum distributions to Bart are determined based on his single life expectancy.

Q 2:69 What happens when there are multiple beneficiaries and separate accounts?

If more than one beneficiary is designated, required distributions are based on the age of the oldest beneficiary. Separate accounts can be established for each beneficiary at any time, but for each beneficiary to use his or her own life expectancy to calculate distributions, the separate accounts must be established by December 31 of the year following the year of the owner's death. Post-death investment gains and losses are allocated to the separate accounts on a pro rata basis.

Beneficiaries must establish the separate accounts by designation date of September 30 to avoid the possibility of calculating a first-year distribution based on the life expectancy of the oldest designated beneficiary. If separate accounts are not created and beneficiaries that cannot be designated exist (charity), the account will be subject to the five-year rule. The beneficiaries should consider paying off the charity's portion in full and then set up separate accounts for the designated beneficiaries.

Q 2:70 What happens when the trust is beneficiary?

The beneficiary documentation certifying designated beneficiaries on September 30 must be provided to the plan administrator by October 31 of the year following the year of the employee's death. If a trust is named beneficiary and a spouse is the sole beneficiary of the trust, the spouse cannot roll over the account into his or her own IRA account. Individual trusts cannot split into separate accounts, but if the IRA is payable to multiple trusts, then the rules for separate accounts can be used if divided prior to December 31. A beneficiary can be disregarded in determining the oldest beneficiary if the individual is a successor to the interest of another beneficiary. Clients should review documents to ensure designated beneficiaries are correct, especially if multiple IRAs exist or multiple beneficiaries have been designated.

Q 2:71 What are eligible retirement plan rollovers?

Rollovers are often used when a retirement plan participant receives a plan distribution, either through retirement or termination from employment, and wants to defer tax payments on part or all of the distribution.

Rollovers must be completed within a 60-day period following the date of distribution. If not completed within the 60 days, the amount withdrawn is considered a taxable distribution, unless the IRS allows the rollover to stand, based on extenuating circumstances.

Only one rollover is permitted from an account in any one-year period, beginning on the distribution date. However, if an individual owns multiple IRAs, he or she can make one rollover from each account in a one-year period. The one-a-year rule only applies to rollovers, not transfers. A transfer is when the trustee of one fund moves the funds directly to another fund. An individual can do an unlimited number of transfers each year.

For distributions after 2001, tax-free rollovers to and from qualified plans, Section 403(b) tax-deferred annuity plans, traditional IRAs, SEPs, and eligible Section 457 governmental plans are allowed under the Internal Revenue Code. As a result, rollovers between retirement plans are permitted.

A rollover of a distribution from a SIMPLE IRA during the first two years of participation is only allowed to another SIMPLE IRA. Thus, SIMPLE to SIMPLE is permitted at any time. After two years in a SIMPLE Plan, a participant may roll over to a qualified plan, Section 403(b) tax-deferred annuity plan, traditional IRA, SEP, or eligible Section 457 governmental plan.

The surviving spouse who is beneficiary can roll over distributions into his or her own qualified plan, Section 403(b) tax-deferred annuity plan, traditional IRA, SEP, or eligible Section 457 governmental plan.

Table 2-6 Permissible Rollovers

Fund may be rolled over from any of these funds:	*To:*
IRA	IRA, SEP, Qualified plan, 401(k), 403(b), or governmental 457 plan
Roth IRA	Roth IRA
SIMPLE IRA (during the first two years)	SIMPLE IRA
SIMPLE IRA (after a two-year participation period)	SIMPLE IRA, IRA, SEP, Qualified plan, 401(k), 403(b), or governmental 457 plan
Any qualified plan	IRA, SEP, Qualified plan, 401(k), 403(b), or governmental 457 plan
SEP	IRA, SEP, Qualified plan, 401(k), 403(b), or governmental 457 plan
SIMPLE 401(k) plan	IRA, SEP, Qualified plan, 401(k), 403(b), or governmental 457 plan
403(b)	IRA, SEP, Qualified plan, 401(k), 403(b), or governmental 457 plan

Governmental 457 plan	IRA, SEP, Qualified plan, 401(k), 403(b), or governmental 457 plan

Taken from College of Financial Planning (2002). *Retirement Planning and Employee Benefits. Denver,* Colorado: College of Financial Planning.

In order to qualify for tax-deferred treatment on the entire rollover amount, rollovers from qualified plans or TSAs must be completed by means of a direct rollover. This means that the plan's trustee must transfer the funds directly from the qualified plan to another qualified plan or IRA. If funds are made by check, the payment should be made to the trustee of the rollover account. If a check is made out to the participant-employee, a mandatory 20 percent withholding will be imposed on the qualified plan or TSA distribution.

The 20 percent withholding results in the recipient receiving a distribution of 80 percent of his or her account balance. In this situation, the recipient can roll over the 80 percent amount and, depending on his or her tax situation, receive a portion of the withheld 20 percent back as a refund when filing his or her tax return for the year. The full 20 percent amount is treated as a taxable distribution and possibly subject to a 10 percent early withdrawal tax, but this can be avoided if the recipient deposits an equal amount into the rollover account.

IRAs can be used as conduit accounts for moving funds from one qualified retirement plan to another. To qualify, the IRA account must consist of funds that are solely from the employer-sponsored qualified plan. The main objective of creating a conduit IRA is to preserve the qualified plan status of the assets in order to take advantage of loan availability and eligibility for 10-year forward averaging tax treatment.

Q2:72   What distributions are not eligible for a rollover?

Distributions not eligible for rollover include:

- Amounts distributed that satisfy the required minimum distribution (RMD generally begins at age 70½);
- Amounts which are part of a series of substantially equal periodic payments payable for a period of 10 years or more, or for the life or life expectancy of the employee (or employee and designated beneficiary);
- A hardship withdrawal;
- Nontaxable portion of a distribution;
- Elective contributions that are returned as a result of Section 415 limitations;
- Corrective distributions of excess contributions and excess deferrals;
- Loans in default that are deemed distributions;
- Dividends on employer securities in an ESOP; and
- Cost of life insurance coverage.

Chapter 3

Insurance

Insurance is a key part of any financial planning. This chapter first examines life insurance: the risks, the selection process, the different types available, tax consequences, and its use in estate planning. Other types of insurance may also be necessary and/or desirable for the client. These include disability, homeowners, automobile, and umbrella liability insurance.

Insurance Risk

Q 3:1   What is risk management?

Risk is defined as the "possibility of loss." Risk management is a process to deal with pure risks by anticipating possible accidental losses and designing and implementing procedures that minimize the occurrence of loss or the financial impact of the losses that do occur.

The risk management process entails identifying actual and potential risks facing an individual or organization; analyzing the impact potential risks have on the organization or individual; evaluating potential treatment options, including risk control and risk financing techniques; and implementing the decisions made on different treatment options. Selected options need to be monitored to see how effective they are, and if needed, adjustments should be made accordingly.

Q 3:2   What are the methods of handling risk?

There are four options when handling risk: electing to avoid the risk, retaining the risk oneself, transferring the risk to other parties without employing an insurance transaction, and transferring the risk through insurance. Electing to avoid a risk is accomplished by merely not engaging in the action that gives rise to the risk. Virtually every important business decision involves a calculated risk. If the potential benefits cannot be proven to exceed the risk, the endeavor should not be undertaken.

The decision to voluntarily retain a risk oneself is typically made because there are no other more attractive alternatives. For small, frequent, predictable losses, retention is far less expensive than insurance.

Transferring the risk to other parties without employing an insurance transaction is accomplished through contracts such as hold-harmless and indemnification agreements. Hold-harmless agreements effectively remove the non-liable party from the risk altogether, while indemnification agreements state that once the loss is adjudicated and paid by one party, the other will provide indemnification. There is a limit to the types of liability that can be transferred with a contract. For example, tort liability cannot be transferred to another party.

A final option is to transfer the risk through insurance. Risks that cannot be avoided, retained, or transferred via contract should be transferred to an insurance company.

For those risks that are retained by the organization or individual, the costs can be reduced by looking at methods of loss prevention and control. Such methods include safety programs, night security guards, sprinkler systems, and burglar alarms. These items are methods that can be used to prevent the loss all together, or to reduce the chance it will occur.

Insurance Regulation and Compensation

Q 3:3   What are the landmark decisions of insurance industry regulation, McCarran-Ferguson, and other acts?

In the 1869 landmark decision *Paul v. Virginia*, [75 U.S. (8 Wall.) 168] the United States Supreme Court determined that insurance was not interstate commerce and hence not subject to federal jurisdiction under the congressional power over interstate commerce. In a series of subsequent cases in which insurers sought to avoid features of state law to which they objected, the Court upheld the right of a state to regulate the business of insurance.

In the 1944 landmark case of *U.S. v. South-Eastern Underwriters Association*, [322 U.S. 533], the Supreme Court overturned 75 years of legal precedent that had commenced with *Paul* when it found that insurance can fall within the embrace of Congress's power over interstate commerce. The decision sent shock waves through the insurance industry and the insurance regulatory communities.

The McCarran-Ferguson Act was enacted in 1945, through which it opted to preserve the state regulatory system and invited the states to preempt the federal antitrust laws by regulating the business of insurance. The act retained the role as federal overseer for Congress. Since 1945, insurance regulation has evolved within this framework. State regulation of insurance involves the legislature, the regulator, the courts, and the National Association of Insurance Commissioners.

Q 3:4   What is the National Association of Insurance Commissioners (NAIC)?

The National Association of Insurance Commissioners is an organization of state insurance department regulators. It was founded in 1871. The NAIC helps to promote uniformity among the states. The NAIC also develops model laws and regulations that each state is encouraged to pass. The NAIC has also codified statutory accounting practices into policy manuals and produces an annual statement guide that covers the information to be included in every report, schedule, and exhibit that make the NAIC blanks.

Q 3:5   What is the state guaranty fund?

Individual states have passed legislation creating guaranty funds to protect the policyholders of insolvent companies. These guaranty associations, or guaranty funds, provide mechanisms to pay for covered claims filed against insolvent insurers in an effort to protect their policyholders from catastrophic financial loss. All states except New York have created post-assessment guaranty associations, which assess solvent insurers for funds to pay claims after an insolvency of an insurer has occurred.

Q 3:6   How are agents compensated?

Life insurance agents are appointed by the insurer with the authorization to solicit and deliver contract of insurance. Agents are compensated primarily on a commission basis from the insurance company they represent. Compensation is higher in the first year that the policy is in force, and is reduced in subsequent years. If the agent achieves a certain level of production, the agent may receive additional bonuses or other types of compensation.

Q 3:7   How are brokers compensated?

A broker represents the client directly and can show illustrations from many different companies. The commissions earned by brokers are typically larger than agents, since they are not housed by the insurer, and their expenses are not being reimbursed by the insurance company.

Brokers also earn subsidies for their office and production bonuses. They can also earn overrides based on being an agency manager (individuals who oversee an office of insurance representatives).

Q 3:8   How do insurance professionals sell insurance?

Life insurance professionals use graphs as illustrations to help explain differences among life insurance policies. These graphs aid the agent and the client since they allow them to "picture" the differences among policies. Graphs can be used. They can also be used to show dividend comparisons, rate of return comparisons, how the cash values of competing products grow over different time ranges, and how death benefits are calculated in permanent policies.

Evaluating Insurance Companies

Q 3:9   What are the rating companies?

There are five insurance rating companies: A.M. Best Company, Standard and Poor's Corporation, Fitch, Inc. (formerly Duff and Phelps), Moody's Investors Service, Inc., and Weiss Ratings, Inc. Each company uses a slightly different classification system; however, all of them distinguish between insurers whose financial condition is strong, and those that are classified as vulnerable or weak.

Q 3:10   Who is A.M. Best?

A.M. Best Company is the original ratings company and has been around approximately 100 years.

The objective of Best's rating system is to provide an opinion on an insurer's financial strength and ability to meet ongoing obligations to their policyholders. Their ratings are based on an evaluation of a company's balance sheet strength, operating performance and business profile. A.M. Best uses both public and private information to arrive at its ratings.

A.M. Best's rating categories are:

- A++, and A+ (Superior)
- A, and A− (Excellent)
- B++, and B+ (Very Good)
- B, and B− (Fair)
- C++, and C+ (Marginal)
- C, and C− (Weak)
- D (Poor)
- E (Under Regulatory Supervision)
- F (In Liquidation)
- S (Rating Suspended)

For more details on what each category means, check out A.M. Best's ratings guide at http://www.ambest.com/ratings/guide.html.

Q3:11   Who is Standard & Poor's?

Standard & Poor's Corp. rates its companies on their claims-paying ability (Financial Strength Rating). This rating is a current opinion of an insurance organization's financial security characteristics with respect to its ability to pay in accordance with the terms of its insurance policies and contracts.

Standard & Poor's rating categories are:

- AAA (Extremely Strong)
- AA (Very Strong)
- A (Strong)
- BBB (Good)
- BB (Marginal)
- B (Weak)
- CCC (Very Weak)
- CC (Extremely Weak)
- R (Under Regulatory Supervision)
- NR (Not Rated)

Ratings from "AA" to "CCC" may be modified by the addition of a plus or minus sign to show the relative standing within the major rating categories. For more information go to www.standardandpoors.com.

Q3:12 Who is Fitch (formerly Duff and Phelps)?

Fitch, Inc. provides the Insurer Financial Strength Rating for insurance companies. This rating takes a look at the financial strength of an organization, and its capability to meet senior obligations to policyholders and contractholders on a timely basis. The rating is based on an analysis of relevant factors that in a large part determine an insurance organization's financial strength, including its regulatory solvency characteristics, liquidity, operating performance, financial flexibility, balance sheet strength, management quality, competitive positioning, and long-term business viability.

Fitch's rating categories are:

- AAA (Exceptionally Strong)
- AA (Very Strong)
- A (Strong)
- BBB (Good)
- BB (Moderately Weak)
- B (Weak)
- CCC, CC, and C (Very Weak)
- DDD, DD, and D (Distressed)

Ratings from "AA" to "CCC" may be modified by the addition of a plus or minus sign to indicate the relative position within the major category. For more information go to www.fitchratings.com.

Q3:13 Who is Moody's?

Moody's Investor Service provides Insurance Financial Strength ratings, which are opinions on the ability of insurance companies to repay punctually senior policyholder claims and obligations. Moody's rating symbols for Insurance Financial Strength ratings are identical to their ratings used to show the credit quality of bonds.

Moody's rating categories are:

- Aaa (Exceptional)
- Aa (Excellent)
- A (Good)
- Baa (Adequate)
- Ba (Questionable)
- B (Poor)
- Caa (Very Poor)
- Ca (Extremely Poor)
- C (Lowest)

Ratings from "Aa" to "Caa" may be modified with the numbers 1, 2, and 3 (e.g., Aa2). These modifiers indicate the relative position within the major category. For more information, go to www.moodys.com.

Q3:14   Who is Weiss?

Weiss Ratings, Inc. Insurer Safety Ratings represent an independent opinion of an insurance company's financial safety—now, and in the future. These ratings are derived, for the most part, from annual and quarterly financial statements obtained from state insurance commissioners. This data is supplemented by additional information requested from the insurance companies themselves.

Weiss's rating categories are:

- A (Excellent)
- B (Good)
- C (Fair)
- D (Weak)
- E (Very Weak)
- F (Failed)
- U (Unrated companies)

Ratings from "A" to "E" may be modified by the addition of a plus or minus sign to indicate the relative position within the major category. For more information go to http://www.weissratings.com.

Q3:15   How do you evaluate an insurance company's financial strength?

Other than using the ratings companies discussed above, there are several other ways to evaluate an insurance company's financial strength. The information discussed below relies on publicly accessible financial information from the insurance company.

One factor that can be looked at is the average policy size issued by the company. Statistics show that larger policies, which are purchased by more affluent people as part of estate or business continuation planning, lapse less frequently than smaller policies. Policies that have been in force longer tend to have lower average expenses.

Another factor that should be looked at is the quality of the company's investment assets. The most critical asset categories to look at are bonds, mortgages, real estate, and policy loans. Many insurers who have had financial difficulties have had a large portion of their assets invested in junk bonds. Companies that are heavily invested in junk bonds should be avoided.

A third factor is the policy lapse ratio, which tells how many ordinary policies are lapsing annually. As a general rule, planners should look for companies with lapse ratios less than 11 percent. Greater than average lapse ratios will usually mean higher than average expenses and may mean less than average service to policy owners.

Evaluating and Comparing Insurance Products

Q 3:16   What is the traditional net cost method?

The basic technique is to make a summation of the total premiums paid over a period of time (usually 20 years), subtract the projected dividends, and then subtract the projected cash value of the policy. This is the total net cost of the policy over the selected period. Now divide the result by the face amount of the policy (in thousands), and again by the number of years in the period to arrive at the net cost of insurance per thousand dollars of coverage per year.

Among the weaknesses of this approach are:

1. The net cost method ignores the time value of money.
2. It can assume inaccurate assumptions based on the ledger statement for projected dividends and cash value.

Q 3:17   What is the interest adjusted net surrender cost method?

The interest adjusted net surrender cost method applies an interest adjustment to the yearly premiums and dividends. The surrender cost method measures the cost of $1,000 of insurance assuming that the policy is surrendered at a specific time. The surrender cost is calculated by the following method:

1. Calculate the future value of total premiums over a selected period, such as 10, 15, or 20 years. Most policy illustrations use a 5 percent interest rate.
2. Calculate the future value of the projected dividends using the same time period and interest rate.
3. Subtract the future value of the dividends from the future value of the total premiums to arrive at the net premiums paid over the specified period.
4. Subtract the total cash value and terminal dividends from the future value of the net premiums to arrive at the total net cost of the policy over the specified period.
5. Divide the result by the future value of the annuity due factor for the rate assumed and the period selected. The result is the level annual cost for the policy.
6. If necessary, divide the level annual cost for the policy by the face amount of the policy (in thousands) to arrive at the interest adjusted net annual cost per thousand dollars of coverage.

Among the weaknesses of this approach are misleading results if the policies being compared are not similar, and the unreliability of the projected cash values and dividends 10 and 20 years into the future.

Q3:18   What is the interest-adjusted net payment cost method?

The interest adjusted net payment cost method applies an interest adjustment to the yearly premiums and dividends. The net payment cost method measures the cost of $1,000 of insurance assuming that the policy remains in force during the selected period. The net payment cost is similar to the net surrender cost, and is calculated by the following method:

1. Calculate the future value of total premiums over a selected period, such as 10, 15, or 20 years. Most policy illustrations use a 5 percent interest rate.
2. Calculate the future value of the projected dividends using the same time period and interest rate.
3. Subtract the future value of the dividends from the future value of the total premiums to arrive at the net premiums paid over the specified period.
4. Divide the result by the future value of the annuity due factor for the rate assumed and the period selected. The result is the level annual cost for the policy.
5. If necessary, divide the level annual cost for the policy by the face amount of the policy (in thousands) to arrive at the interest adjusted net annual cost per thousand dollars of coverage.

Among the weaknesses of this approach are misleading results if the policies being compared are not similar and the unreliability of the projected cash values and dividends 10 and 20 years into the future.

Q3:19   What is the equal outlay method?

The equal outlay method compares two policies by looking at the amount the client pays out for each policy and making them equal by taking the difference in the two premiums and investing it at a specified interest rate in a "side" fund.

To determine which policy is better, compare the cash values including the side fund amounts and the total death benefits including the side fund amounts.

This method can be used to compare fixed premium contracts with flexible premium policies.

Some of the weaknesses of this approach are:

1. When working with a flexible premium policy, the number of adjustments can quickly become burdensome.

2. You cannot rely on the projected cash values and dividends 10 and 20 years in the future.

Q 3:20   What is the cash accumulation method?

The cash accumulation method is ideal for comparing term with permanent insurance.

This method works like this:

1. The outlays for both policies must be the same.
2. Change the face amount of the lower premium policy so that the sum of the side fund plus the face amount equals the face amount of the higher premium policy. This forces the two policies to have the same death benefit.
3. Accumulate the differences in the two premiums at an assumed rate of interest in the side fund mentioned in #2.
4. Compare the cash value plus side fund differences over given periods of time to see which policy is preferable to the other.

Weaknesses of this approach:

1. Selection of the interest rate for the side fund, since a higher assumed interest rate will favor a lower premium and side fund combination.
2. It relies on the investment and accumulation of a side fund.

Q 3:21   What is the Linton yield method?

The Linton yield method works like this: the rate of return that a policy owner must earn on a hypothetical side fund, assuming that the death benefits and outlays are held equal, for each insurance policy, for every year over the period being studied, is computed. The policy with the highest Linton yield should be selected. This indicates the policy with the highest rate of return, given an assumed schedule of costs (term rates).

The Linton yield is a variation on the cash accumulation method. It is the rate of return that equates the side fund with the cash surrender value for a specified period of years.

Q 3:22   What is the Belth method?

The Belth method is actually comprised of two methods: (1) the yearly rate of return method; and (2) the yearly price of protection method. These methods are computed for all years that a policy is in force.

The yearly rate of return is calculated by the following method:

1. Compute the "benefits" from the policy by adding the cash value at the end of the year, the dividends paid during the year, and the net death benefit for the policy year.

2. Compute the "investment" in the policy for the year by adding the premium paid for the year with the cash value at the beginning of the year.

3. Divide the benefits for the year by the investment for the year and subtract one from the result. This is the yearly rate of return.

4. Repeat the calculation for each year over the desired duration period.

The policy with the highest yearly rates in the greatest number of years is generally the best choice. Since the calculation is done for each year, this method is especially useful in comparing policies over many different duration periods.

The yearly price of protection is calculated by:

1. Accumulating the "investment" in the policy for one year at an assumed rate of interest. The investment is the sum of the cash surrender value at the end of the previous year, and the current premium.

2. Computing the year-end policy surrender value by adding the year-end cash surrender value and any dividend received that year.

3. Subtracting the year-end policy surrender value from the year's accumulated investment.

4. Dividing the result of (3) by the year's net amount at risk (the face amount minus the current year's cash surrender value) in thousands. The result is the cost of protection (per thousand dollars of coverage) for the year.

The result is an estimate of the cost in any given year of the net death benefit. The policy with the lowest yearly price of protection in the most years is generally the contract that should be selected under this method.

Q 3:23 What is the Baldwin method?

The Baldwin method is a somewhat more complete variation of the Belth yearly rate of return method. It combines both rate of return with the value of the insurance into one measure. In order to calculate the measure:

1. Calculate the amount of insurance provided by the policy in any given year by subtracting the cash surrender value from the total death benefit. This amount is the net amount at risk.

2. Determine what has been paid to keep the life insurance policy in force for the year. This is calculated by adding the premium, the net after-tax loan interest cost (if any), and the net after-tax (opportunity) cost of cash left in the policy (the cost of not borrowing from the policy and investing at a rate greater than the after-tax return).

3. Calculate the cash benefits received as a result of maintaining the policy for another year. This is computed by adding the current year's dividend with the current year's increase in the cash value.

4. Compute the investment in the contract by subtracting any loans outstanding, plus any unpaid interest, from the total cash value.

5. Determine the dollar amount of return (gain or loss) earned in the current year by subtracting the costs calculated in (2) from the benefits found in (3).

6. Determine the cash-on-cash return for the year by dividing the net gain or loss from (5), by the amount invested in (4).

7. Determine the before-tax equivalent return by dividing the return found in (6) by one minus the combined tax rate. For example, if the combined local, state, and federal tax rate is 40 percent, then divide the return in (6) by 0.6.

8. Determine the value of the life insurance protection received for the year. This can be accomplished by finding out the retail value of a term insurance policy in the same face amount (cost per thousand dollars), and multiplying it by (1), also in thousands of dollars.

9. Determine the total value of benefits received by continuing the policy. This value is equal to the year's net gain or loss (5), plus the life insurance value calculated in (8).

10. Compute the percentage return on this total benefit by dividing the value from (9) by the amount invested (4).

11. Determine the equivalent taxable return that the policy owner must earn to match the tax-deferred/tax-free return from the life insurance contract by dividing the rate of return calculated in (10) by one minus the combined tax rate.

The Baldwin method overcomes some of the problems associated with other comparison methods, but still depends on the values taken from the policy ledger statement.

Legal Aspects of a Life Insurance Contract

Q 3:24   What is offer and acceptance?

To have a legally enforceable contract, there must be a definite offer by one party, and the other party must accept this offer in its exact terms. The offer is usually made by a request for coverage by the prospect, or applicant. The acceptance takes place when the agent binds the coverage or when the policy is issued.

Q 3:25   What is consideration?

The consideration of a contract is the items of value that each party gives to the other. In insurance, the consideration given by the applicant is usually the premium, plus an agreement to abide by the conditions in the contract. The insurer's consideration is its promise to pay valid claims submitted for specified losses.

Q 3:26   What is legal object?

A contract must be legal in its purpose. The courts will not enforce an insurance contract if it has an illegal purpose or is contrary to public policy. A contract in which one party agreed to commit murder for a specified amount would not be enforceable in court because its object is not legal.

Q 3:27   What are competent parties?

A valid contract requires that the party making the offer and the one accepting the offer be legally competent to make the agreement. This means that the parties involved must be capable of understanding the contract they are entering into. The most common problem occurs when applicants are under the age of legal majority (18 or 21 in some states). When this occurs, the minor's contract is voidable at his or her option (*See* question 3:31 "What are void and voidable contracts?").

Q 3:28   What is legal form?

Legal form means that a contract must use the same wording as the legal standard policy, or that it at least approximates the intent of the standard provisions. The insurer must also follow the proper procedure for filing and gaining state approval of its contracts.

Although most insurance contracts are different, they are all composed of three basic parts:

- *Declarations page.* This section contains information about whom or what is insured, the amount of insurance, the premiums, the period of coverage, etc.
- *Insuring agreement.* This section contains the promises of the company to pay for a loss if it results from the perils covered. In a named perils policy, the policy will list the covered perils, while in an open perils policy, the perils excluded from coverage are listed.
- *Conditions.* This section lists in detail the duties and rights of both parties. An example would be the timely payment of premiums, or the time period within which the insured must file a formal proof of loss.

Q 3:29   What are torts?

Torts include all civil wrongs not based on contracts. A tort may be intentional, unintentional, or a strict liability imposed by law. Strict liability imposed by law occurs where certain persons are held liable for damages, regardless of whether or not fault or negligence can be proved against them. Examples include injury from blasting operations by contractors, and injury caused by any type of wild animal kept in captivity.

An intentional tort is one that is deliberately performed, such as assault, battery, libel, slander, false arrest or imprisonment, trespass, or invasion of privacy.

Unintentional torts are those that result from negligence or carelessness.

Q 3:30   What is negligence?

Negligence is the failure to exercise the proper degree of care required under the circumstances. It can occur either by doing what a reasonably prudent person would not do under the circumstances, or by not doing what such a person would do under the same circumstances.

There are four requirements that must be met before negligence liability is present:

- A legal obligation to act or refrain from acting according to the circumstances. For example, a bystander has no legal duty to try to prevent a mugging, whereas a police officer does.
- A failure on the part of the person who has the legal obligation to do what a prudent person would do, or not do.
- The voluntary act of the wrongdoer must have been the proximate cause of the injury. For example, if a fire was started negligently by person A, and person B deliberately pushed person C into the fire, person A would not be liable for the injury to person C.
- An injury or damage to property occurred.

Also, depending on the state, a negligent party may escape liability, or have his or her liability reduced through certain defenses. They are:

- *Contributory negligence.* If the injured party was also negligent, the negligent party has no liability.
- *Comparative negligence.* If the injured party was also negligent, the negligent party has a reduced liability.
- *Last clear chance.* If a person can avoid an accident and does nothing to prevent it, he or she should be legally liable for damages, regardless of the contributory negligence of the injured party.

Q 3:31   What are void and voidable contracts?

A void contract is not a contract at all, but simply an agreement without legal effect. It lacks one or more of the requirements specified by law for a valid contract. A void contract cannot be enforced by either party. For example, a contract having an illegal object is void, and neither party can enforce it.

A voidable contract is one that, for reasons satisfactory to the court, may be set aside by one of the parties. It is binding unless the party with the right to void it decides to do so. For example, a contract between an adult and a minor child is voidable by the child, but not by the adult.

Q 3:32   What is adhesion?

Adhesion is the legal recognition that the policy owner was not in a position to negotiate with the insurer on the terms of the contract. There was none of the usual "give and take" negotiating and bargaining found in a standard contract. The applicant either accepts the policy as prepared by the insurer (adheres to it), or doesn't purchase the insurance. Since insurance is a contract of adhesion, courts will typically resolve any ambiguity in the favor of the policy owner or the beneficiary.

Q 3:33   What is aleatory?

Aleatory means that the outcome is affected by chance and that the number of dollars given up by the contracting parties will be unequal. For example, the insured pays the required premium, and if no loss occurs, the insurance company pays nothing. If a loss does occur, then the insured's premium is most likely small compared to the amount the insurer will have to pay.

Q 3:34   What is utmost good faith?

Insurance is a contract of utmost good faith because the applicant must make full and fair disclosure of the risk to the agent and the company. If the insured fails to inform the insurer of any facts that would influence the issue of the policy or the rate at which it would be issued, the insurer could have grounds for avoiding coverage.

Q 3:35   What does unilateral mean?

Insurance is a unilateral contract because only one party, the insurer, has made a legally enforceable promise, such as to pay covered claims. The insured makes no promises that can be legally enforced. If the insured decides to stop making payments, the policy will lapse.

Q 3:36   What is insurable interest?

An insurance contract is only binding if the insured has an interest in the subject matter of the insurance and this interest is in fact insurable. In most instances, an insurable interest exists only if the insured would suffer a financial loss in the event of damage to or destruction of the subject matter of the insurance.

To be more specific, an insurable interest involves a relationship between the person applying for the insurance and the subject matter of the insurance, such as a dwelling or a person's life, so that there is a reasonable expectation to benefit more from the continuation of the dwelling or the person's life than from the loss or detriment from its cessation.

The purposes of requiring insurable interest in insurance contracts are to prevent gambling and to decrease the moral hazard.

Q 3:37   What is indemnity?

The principle of indemnity maintains that an individual should not be permitted to profit from the existence of an insurance contract, but should be restored to the same financial condition that existed prior to the loss. The insured is only indemnified up to the policy limits and is subject to policy provisions and limitations, such as deductibles.

Selecting the Appropriate Type of Life Insurance

Q 3:38   What is term insurance?

Term insurance provides temporary protection for a limited period of time. The period of time is typically 1 year, 5 years, 10 years, or 20 years. If the insured dies during the period of the contract, the beneficiaries receive the face amount of the insurance policy. If the insured survives the period, the contract expires and no payment of any kind is provided to the policy owner.

Term insurance allows a person to acquire the greatest death benefit for the lowest premium outlay when the policy is first issued. However, this does not mean that term insurance is necessarily the least expensive form of insurance over the full duration of needed coverage. Since term premiums increase at each renewal, at the later ages the premium cost will far exceed the level premium that would have been charged for an ordinary whole life policy issued at the same age as the original policy.

Term insurance is the best alternative for temporary life insurance needs. Usually term insurance is the best alternative if protection is needed for less than 10 years.

Q 3:39   What is annual renewable term insurance?

Annual renewable term insurance is a one-year term contract renewable for successive periods of one year each. The benefit of the renewable feature is the right to renew without a medical exam or other evidence of insurability. The policy owner usually can renew the policy up to the age of 65 or 70. The premium will increase with each renewal and is based on the attained age of the insured at the time of the renewal. However, within the contract period the premium is level.

Q 3:40   What is level term insurance?

Level term insurance is term insurance where the period is greater than 1 year (typically 5, 10, or 20 years) and the premium is level or constant throughout the whole period. Generally, premiums for level term insurance increase each time the contract is renewed even though the face amount stays the same. This is due to the increasing age and higher mortality rates of the insured at the time the policy is renewed.

Q 3:41   What is decreasing term insurance?

Decreasing term is a popular form of term coverage frequently used to assure that a family will have the resources to pay off a home mortgage and/or other loans in the event the family's primary breadwinner dies. The policy owner selects an amount of initial coverage. Then, over a specified period, the death benefit decreases steadily until it reaches 0 at the end of the term. The duration of the policy is typically specified in years, such as 10, 15, or 20 years, or until the insured reaches a certain age. The duration is usually selected to coincide with the time required to repay the loan.

Premiums typically remain constant and are payable for the duration of coverage, even though the coverage is decreasing.

Q 3:42   What Is whole life insurance?

Whole life insurance is permanent insurance for the entire lifetime of the insured. It has a fixed level premium that is paid throughout the lifetime of the insured. Because the cost of insurance is less than the premium in the early years, the excess builds up a reserve (cash value) which is used to keep the premiums level in the later years of the insured.

The cash value of the whole life policy can be used for several purposes:

- As collateral for an insurance company loan.
- If the insured decides to terminate the policy, he or she can elect to receive the policy's cash value at that time.
- To purchase a reduced paid-up insurance policy.
- If the policy isn't canceled, the cash value at time of death becomes part of the death benefit.

With a whole life insurance policy, the cash value is invested in the company's general account through the purchase of long-term bonds and mortgages. The account pays a guaranteed interest rate. One disadvantage to this type of policy is that because the interest rate is fixed, the cash values tend to lose purchasing power during periods of higher-than-normal inflation.

Q 3:43   What is limited pay whole life insurance?

Limited payment whole life is a form of whole life insurance where the premiums are paid for only a limited number of years. The policy becomes a paid-up policy at the end of the premium-paying period. Thus, permanent protection is provided for the insured's entire life, but the premiums are only paid for a limited period.

Q 3:44 What is universal life insurance?

Universal life is another type of permanent insurance where the premiums, cash values, and level of protections can be adjusted up or down to meet the owner's need. The interest credited to the policy's cash value is geared to current interest rates, and is also subject to a minimum interest rate, such as 4 percent.

Like whole life insurance, the cash value is invested in the company's general account, however the investment is in short- to medium-term money markets.

There are two death benefit options under a universal life policy: option A and option B. Option A pays the face amount of the policy. Option B pays the face amount plus the cash surrender value of the policy. There is a higher cost for option B, which reflects the higher mortality charge based on the higher death benefit.

Since the premiums are flexible, if there is a desire to build more tax-sheltered cash in the policy, the premiums can be increased to accomplish this.

Since the death benefit is also flexible, if the amount of needed death protection changes, the benefit may be decreased or increased. However, increases in the death benefit will usually require evidence of insurability.

Q 3:45 What is variable life insurance?

Variable life insurance is a whole life contract for which the insured has the right to direct how the policy's cash value will be invested. The insured bears the investment risk in the form of fluctuations in the cash value and the death benefit. The amount of the premium is fixed, but the face value of the policy varies, subject to a guaranteed minimum, which is the original face amount. As the cash value increases over time, the face value of the policy will also increase.

Unlike whole life and universal life insurance, the cash values for variable life are in a separate account of the company. The insured typically can choose between stock funds, bond funds, and money market funds. In addition, there is no guaranteed minimum cash value, as there is in a whole life policy.

Variable life products are most suitable for those individuals who want control over their cash values and need or desire increasing life insurance protection. They should have a basic understanding of investments, and be willing to bear the entire risk of their investments, since cash values are not guaranteed.

Q 3:46 What is universal variable life insurance?

Universal variable life insurance combines the flexible premium features of universal life with the investment component of variable life. The policy owner decides how the cash value will be invested, and the performance is directly related to the performance of the underlying investments.

The death benefit of a universal variable life policy (or variable universal life) is not variable in the same sense as the death benefit of a variable life policy. There are two options for the death benefit. Under option A, the death benefit is level. Under option B, the death benefit varies directly with changes in the cash value. In this case, the death benefit is equal to a level pure insurance amount plus the cash value.

Variable universal life policies offer greater certainty of death benefits than do variable life policies, as long as premiums continue to be paid at the level needed to maintain the death benefit. In addition, variable universal life offers more investment options than do universal policies, and thereby more potential for greater cash values. However, as with variable policies, the policy owner bears all of the investment risk.

Q 3:47 What is survivorship (second-to-die) life insurance?

Survivorship (or "second-to-die") life insurance is a variation of whole or universal life that insures two lives with the promise to pay only at the death of the second person. This type of policy has increased in popularity as a result of the unlimited marital deduction, which permits married couples with large estates to defer estate tax liabilities until the second death. Survivorship life insurance is a practical approach to this exposure; it automatically provides life insurance proceeds to cover the estate tax when it occurs, at the death of the second spouse.

Since the death benefit is paid only once, and is paid only at the second death, the premium burden for a survivorship policy is significantly lower than having two separate policies.

Q 3:48 What is first-to-die life insurance?

A first-to-die life insurance policy is one written on the lives of two or more people, and payable upon the death of the first person to die. A first-to-die policy may provide a cost effective means of replacing income at the first spouse's death. It is often used to fund specific goals and objectives that depend on the presence of the second of two incomes. The policy could be used to pay off the mortgage, or fund a child's education in the event one spouse dies.

One disadvantage of a joint-life or first-to-die policy is that all coverage ceases upon the first death. For this reason, a first-to-die policy is often coupled with a survivorship (second-to-die) policy when dealing with a married couple, and can often be a better plan than two single-life policies.

Business Aspects of Life Insurance

Q 3:49   What is a buy-sell arrangement?

A buy-sell arrangement is an agreement under whose terms each owner of a business agrees that his or her share of the business is to be sold to the remaining owners at his or her death, and each of the remaining owners agrees to buy the shares of the deceased owner. In a sole proprietorship, the agreement is usually between the owner and an employee, or the owner and a competitor.

Without an appropriate continuation plan, the executor of the deceased's estate might have to sell the business interest in order to satisfy the federal estate taxes and or state inheritance taxes. Under these circumstances, the executor might not receive the full value of the business.

Several other reasons to have a buy-sell arrangement are that it (1) provides liquidity for the payment of death taxes or other settlement costs; (2) provides a means for the business to continue in the hands of the remaining owners or employees; and (3) it guarantees a market to sell the business interest.

The buy-sell arrangement is usually funded with life insurance in one of two forms: a cross-purchase plan or an entity plan. Under the crosspurchase plan, each partner or stockholder carries enough life insurance on the other owners to permit him or her to purchase a pre-defined share of the deceased's business interest. For example, if owners A, B, and C each own a third of a business valued at $600,000, then A would buy a $100,000 policy on both B and C, and B would buy a $100,000 policy on A and C, and owner C would buy a $100,000 policy on both A and B. If A were to die, then B and C would have sufficient funds to purchase owner A's one-third interest in the business.

Under the entity plan, instead of the owners purchasing the life insurance policies, the business entity purchases the policies and also is the beneficiary. When an owner dies, the business purchases the deceased's business interest. Then the remaining owners' share of the business is increased proportionately.

Q 3:50   What is key-person life insurance?

Key-person or key-employee life insurance is a life insurance policy owned by a business and payable to the business, which insures the life of a key person in the organization, upon whose death there would be a substantial loss to the business. The insurance provides money that allows the business to weather the adjustment period after the death of a key employee. It can also provide capital to cover the expenses of recruiting a replacement and providing training for that person.

The premiums for key employee insurance are nondeductible, while the benefits are generally received tax free.

Q 3:51 What is an executive bonus (Section 162) plan?

An executive bonus, or Section 162 plan, involves the purchase of a life insurance policy on the life of one or more employees, as chosen by the employer. The employer pays the premiums for the policy by giving the employee a bonus in the amount of the policy premium.

The employee purchases the policy using the bonus dollars, and is therefore the owner of the policy, and also designates the beneficiaries. Therefore, the policy owner has full rights in the policy.

The employer never has any right to any part of the policy's cash value or dividends, or to the death proceeds. Also, the corporation has at no time any incidents of ownership in the policy.

The plan is called a Section 162 plan because the business will take an income tax deduction under Code section 162 for the amount of the bonus charged to the employee. In addition, the amount received as a bonus by the employee is reported as income to the insured.

Q 3:52 What is a split-dollar life insurance arrangement?

A split-dollar life insurance arrangement is an arrangement, usually between an employer and an employee, where the cost of an insurance policy on the employee is shared.

In a traditional split-dollar plan, the corporation contributes an amount equal to the annual increase in the cash surrender value, while the employee pays the remainder of the annual premium. The death benefit is then split between the employer and the employee's beneficiaries. The corporation receives a return on their payments that is equal to the cash surrender value. The balance of the death benefit is paid to the beneficiary selected by the employee.

The purpose of this arrangement is typically to make the purchase of life insurance easier for the employee, or to provide a fringe benefit to the employee where the corporation is making a significant portion of the payment.

Typically the employer is the owner of the policy and a beneficiary to the policy to the extent of the cash value. In addition, the employer may not change the portion of the beneficiary designation dealing with the employee's personal beneficiary without the consent of the employee.

One drawback to the split-dollar arrangement is that the death benefit payable to the insured's beneficiary decreases year by year, as the cash value of the policy, and therefore the employer's interest, increases.

Q 3:53 What is a reverse split-dollar arrangement?

A reverse split-dollar arrangement is one whereby the traditional ownership of cash values and death benefits are reversed. The employee pays the share of the premium equal to the yearly increase in the cash value, and the employer pays the balance.

This plan gives the employee the right to the policy cash value up to the total of his or her premium payments. The employer is the beneficiary to the death proceeds that are in excess of the employee's share.

Reverse split-dollar plans are designed so that after a number of years, the employee can amass a large sum of cash that can be used for retirement or other purposes.

Q 3:54   What are typical beneficiary designations for business policies?

In a cross purchase buy-sell arrangement, the beneficiary of the policy is the same as the owner since the policy proceeds will be used to purchase the business interest of the deceased owner or partner.

In the entity form of a buy-sell arrangement, the entity or business is the beneficiary of the policy so that the policy proceeds can be used to purchase the business interest of the deceased owner or partner.

In a key-person life insurance policy, the business purchasing the policy on the key person is the beneficiary of the policy so that the proceeds can be used to help the business through the adjustment period when the key-person is no longer around to contribute to the business.

In an executive bonus plan, the employee is able to designate the beneficiary of the policy, and should choose a beneficiary that is in line with his or her estate plan.

In a split-dollar arrangement, the company is typically a partial beneficiary (up to its investment in the policy), and the employee can designate to whom the remainder of the death benefit should go. This selection should be in line with his or her estate plan.

Q 3:55   What is transfer of ownership?

Transfer of ownership occurs when a life insurance policy is transferred from one owner to another for "valuable consideration." When such a transfer for value has occurred, the income tax exclusion is lost. Upon the death of the insured in such cases, only the amount paid for the policy and any subsequent premiums are recovered income tax free by the transferee-owner.

The transfer-for-value rule is not limited to situations where a sale of the policy has occurred; it can also apply when a non-cash consideration for a policy transfer can be inferred.

A transfer for value does not cause this loss of tax-free benefit if it falls under one of the following transfers:

- A transfer to the insured

- A transfer to a partner of the insured or a partnership in which the insured is a partner
- A transfer to a corporation in which the insured is a shareholder or officer

Determining How Much Life Insurance Is Necessary

Q 3:56   What is the human value approach?

The human value approach to estimating the amount of life insurance needed by a client focuses on the earnings of the individual that will be lost in the case of premature death. Basically, the present value of the insured's future earnings is used to support his or her dependents.

For example, assume that the individual takes home $60,000 per year, and that $10,000 of that is attributed to his or her expenses. That would leave $50,000 to support his or her family. Assuming the individual is 40 years today, and will retire at the age of 65, the dependents will lose the present value of $50,000 per year for the next 25 years. The present value of an annuity due for 25 years using the $50,000 shortfall as the payment, and a discount rate of 5 percent, is $704,697.

Q 3:57   What is the financial needs approach?

The financial needs approach begins with an estimate of the various financial needs a family would experience if the insured were to die today. These needs are broken down into two main categories: (1) lump sum needs at death, and (2) ongoing income needs after death.

The usual lump sum cash needs at death include such items as funeral expenses, repayment of outstanding debt, estate taxes due, final hospitalization costs not covered by insurance, short-term needs for food, clothing, transportation costs, and an emergency fund to cover unexpected items. Another item that could be included in the lump sum needed at death would be the amount needed to pre-fund the children's educational needs.

The ongoing income needs typically falls into four areas: (1) a readjustment income for the period immediately after death; (2) an income needed until the youngest child becomes self-sufficient; (3) the income for the surviving spouse, if any, after the children have become self-sufficient and before the spouse is eligible for retirement or social security benefits; and (4) the retirement income needed in addition to social security benefits.

The amount of life insurance needed can be calculated by summing up all these two categories of needs and offsetting them with investments and any existing group or individual life insurance policies.

For ongoing income needs, the present values of future income needs are calculated. First, the difference between the needed income during each period and the available income at that time (from current employment or social security) is calculated for each time period. Then the present value of this income stream can be easily calculated with a financial calculator's net present value (NPV) function.

Common Provisions with Life Insurance Policies

Q 3:58   What is the disability waiver of premium?

If the insured becomes totally disabled, as defined in the rider or policy, the insurance company will waive payment of premiums on the policy during the continuance of the disability, provided that it lasts beyond a specified period of time, usually six months. Typically the rider stipulates that the disability must occur before some age, such as age 60 or 70.

The reason for this waiver is that once an individual becomes disabled, it will undoubtedly be difficult, if not impossible, for the person to obtain insurance coverage. It is therefore essential to be able to continue the existing coverage during this time of possible financial hardship.

During the period of disability, and the continuation of the contract as if the premiums were being paid, the cash value of the policy will continue to increase, and any dividends will still be paid to the insured.

If this waiver is not an automatic provision by the insurance company, the insured should certainly elect to have it included.

Q 3:59   What is the contestable period?

The contestable period is the period of time, typically two years, in which the insurance company can challenge the validity of the life insurance policy.

The courts have generally recognized three exceptions to the contestable period. They include instances in which:

- there was no insurable interest at the inception of the policy
- the policy was purchased with the intent to murder the insured
- there was a fraudulent impersonation of the insured by another person, *i.e.*, for the purposes of taking the medical exam.

The purpose of this clause is to give insurance companies a reasonable opportunity to investigate the validity of the contract. After the contestable period has lapsed, the insurance company relinquishes its right to challenge.

If the insured dies during the contestable period, the operation of the clause is suspended. If this is not the case, and if the beneficiary knows that the insured made material misrepresentations in the application, he or she could wait until the end of the two-year period before submitting the claim, and thus would be protected against voidance of the contract because of the insured's fraudulent acts.

Q 3:60   What is the guaranteed insurability option?

The guaranteed insurability option allows the insured to purchase additional amounts of insurance at stated intervals or ages without providing evidence of insurability. Typically, the policy provides a three-year interval for additional purchases, up to a maximum age of 40 or 45.

Once the insured passes an interval that triggers the right to purchase additional insurance and does not exercise the option, that option lapses, but future options are not affected.

One benefit of this option is that the new coverage is normally not subject to a new suicide provision or a new contestable period.

Finally, this option is only applicable to permanent types of insurance, such as whole life.

Q 3:61   What is the grace period?

The grace period allows for coverage to continue even if the premium payment is late, as long as the premium is paid within the stipulated time period, usually 31 days. No reinstatement is necessary. (See Q 3:63.)

The premium due date and the grace period are defined in the policy.

The purpose of this clause is not to encourage procrastination, but rather to keep the policy from lapsing when the owner of the policy inadvertently neglects to pay the premium.

Q 3:62   What is an automatic premium loan?

If the insured does not pay the premium on the due date, the company will automatically pay the premium and charge it against the cash value of the policy. This loan will have an interest rate that is stipulated in the contract. The effect of this provision is that the face value of the policy is reduced by the loan amount plus interest. It will also keep the policy from lapsing.

This provision may be very beneficial to the policyholder, particularly for one who forgets to pay the premium within the grace period, or one who cannot pay the current premium because of financial difficulties. When the insured is again financially able, he or she can start paying the premiums and will not be subject to the condition imposed in the event of a reinstatement.

Each company handles this provision differently. Some companies specify that the insured must notify the company if he or she wants the provision to apply, while others make the provision automatic and the insured must specify if it is not wanted.

Q 3:63   What is reinstatement?

Reinstatement provisions allow the policy owner to reacquire coverage under a policy that has lapsed. This can be accomplished if the insured:

1. Provides evidence of insurability that is satisfactory to the company;
2. Pays all overdue premiums plus interest; and
3. Repays any policy loans outstanding at the time the policy lapsed, plus interest.

In addition, insurers won't typically reinstate a policy that has been surrendered for its cash value.

It is apparent that reinstatement is not an unconditional right of the insured. It can be accomplished only if the risk has not changed for the insurance company, and if the reinstated policy would have the same reserve (through repayment of premiums and interest) as it would have had if the policy had not lapsed.

Q 3:64   What is a common disaster clause?

If the insured and beneficiary are in a common disaster, the common disaster clause states that the beneficiary must survive the insured by some specified period of time (usually 30 days) in order to receive the settlement. If the beneficiary doesn't survive the specified period of time, the contingent beneficiaries will receive the settlement.

This clause is needed to clear up cases when it isn't known who predeceased whom in a common accident. This clause helps to insure that the settlement will go to the contingent beneficiaries, instead of to the primary beneficiary's estate.

Q 3:65   What is a spendthrift clause?

The spendthrift clause denies the beneficiary the right to commute, alienate, or assign his or her interest in the policy proceeds. This provision is used only in conjunction with an installment settlement option, and provides some protection against claims made by creditors of the beneficiary.

This provision protects the policy proceeds only while the insurer is holding them. However, once the proceeds have been paid, creditors are free to attempt to obtain them.

Q 3:66   What is an accidental death benefit?

The accidental death benefit typically pays twice the face value of the policy in the event that the insured died from an accident, and not some other cause such as disease. For instance, if the insured is in an automobile accident but dies from a heart attack, the accident death benefit will be payable only if the accident can be proven to have triggered the heart attack.

The problems caused by cases in which there might be more than one cause of death are mitigated somewhat because the accidental death benefit provision includes a time limit. The death of the insured typically must occur within 90 days of the accident.

Lastly, the accident and resulting death must occur before the age of 70. This is because the probability of an accident increases substantially as one gets older, and the coverage would become too expensive relative to its value.

Q 3:67   What is a cost-of-living rider?

A cost-of-living rider allows the insured to get an increase in the coverage amount due to increases in inflation. Typically, the insurer offers the insured additional coverage, for an added premium, when the consumer price index increases. The principal advantage is that the additional insurance is offered without evidence of insurability by the insured. However, to continue eligibility the insured must accept each additional offering of coverage. If the insured rejects any of the increases, the insurer may require evidence of insurability for the next increase.

Other Options Are Available to Policy Owners and Beneficiaries

Q 3:68   What are the non-forfeiture options?

When the insured decides to stop the payment of premiums on the life insurance policy, the insured is entitled to the cash value of the policy. This cash value, or non-forfeiture value, may be taken in one of three ways:

1. The insured may take the value in cash, less any policy indebtedness, and plus any accumulated dividends.
2. The insured can use the cash value to purchase a reduced amount of paid-up whole life insurance, payable upon the same conditions as the original policy. The amount of insurance that can be purchased is based on the insured's current age.
3. The insured can use the cash value to get a paid-up term insurance with the same face amount as the original policy. However, the length of the term is based on the insured's age and by applying the cash value as a single premium.

Q 3:69   What dividend options are available to policyholders?

Participating life insurance companies offer the policy owner a variety of options for the use of his or her dividend. The dividends payable to the insured reflect the difference between the premium charged for a given class of policies, and their actual cost based on the experience of the insurer. The savings in mortality, the excess interest received, and the savings in expenses will yield a surplus each year, which is paid back as a dividend. The most common dividend options are:

1. **Cash.** Receive the dividend as cash.

2. **Reduction of premiums.** The insurer applies the dividend to the premium payment currently due, and remits the difference to the insurer.

3. **Paid up-additions.** The dividend is used to purchase paid-up whole life insurance based on the insured's attained age. This is done with no additional evidence of insurability, and with rates that don't contain a loading for expenses.

4. **One-year term insurance.** The dividend is used to purchase paid-up one-year term insurance with a face amount based on the insured's attained age. This option also uses net rates.

5. **Accumulation of interest.** The dividend is left with the insurance company in the equivalent of an interest-bearing savings account for the policy owner. A minimum rate of interest is guaranteed. The accumulated dividends with interest can be withdrawn at any time. If they are not withdrawn, they are added to the death proceeds or to the cash surrender value, if the policy is surrendered.

Q 3:70   What settlement options are available to beneficiaries?

There are several different settlement options available to the life insurance beneficiary. Normally, the owner of the policy elects the option under which the proceeds for the policy are to be paid. If the owner has made no election, then the beneficiary is entitled to select the option most beneficial to him or her. In addition, if the owner has made no provision that denies the right, the beneficiary may also change the option elected by the owner.

The different methods for receiving a life insurance settlement are:

1. **Cash or lump-sum.** Receive the death benefit in one lump sum of cash.

2. **Interest option.** The death benefit may be left with the insurance company to be paid out at a later date. Until it is paid out, the beneficiary will receive a periodic interest-only payment based on the guaranteed interest rate defined in the policy.

3. **Fixed-Period option.** The death benefit and the interest on the proceeds are paid out as installment payments of some specified interval, such as five or 10 years. Again, the guaranteed interest rate is used in determining the payment value.

4. **Fixed-Amount option.** The proceeds of the policy are paid out in fixed payments, such as $500 or $1,000, per month for as long as the principal and the interest on the unpaid portion of the principal will last.

5. **Life Income options.** The death proceeds of the policy are used as a single premium to purchase an annuity for the beneficiary. Various forms of annuities may be available, but the most common are:

   a. **Straight life income.** The beneficiary will receive a specified amount, based on their life expectancy, for as long as he or she lives, and nothing more.

   b. **Life income with period certain.** The beneficiary will receive a life income for as long as he or she lives, with a minimum number of guaranteed payments. If he or she dies before the minimum number of payments has been made, the payments are continued to the contingent beneficiaries.

   c. **Life income with refund.** The beneficiary receives a life income for as long as he or she lives, and if the proceeds haven't been paid out by the time the beneficiary dies, the remainder of the proceeds will be paid to the contingent beneficiaries. There also might be an option to receive the remainder amount as a lump sum.

   d. **Joint and survivor income.** This option provides income to the beneficiary based on two lives, and is paid out until the second of the two people dies.

How Life Insurance Policies Are Priced

Q3:71   What method should be used to analyze expenses?

There are several ways to analyze expenses charged by insurance companies: (1) determining if the policy limits by contract the amount of expenses the insurance company can charge the policy owner and if so, either (a) using these maximums to compare the policy expenses or (b) comparing the current charges versus the maximums stipulated in the policy; (2) for mortality charges, comparing the cost per thousand for the net amount at risk; and (3) comparing the first-year guaranteed costs of each policy.

Q3:72   What are mortality charges?

Mortality charges are the pure insurance costs of the life insurance protection within the policy. These charges are based on mortality tables, which attempt to determine the average number of deaths each year, at each specific age.

Q3:73   What are operating expenses?

Operating expenses are charges assessed on an insured for a portion of the administrative costs of issuing and maintaining a policy. Expenses are based on the insured's age, face amount, premium loads (both front and back), initial policy fees, and administrative fees.

These expenses are not charges related to the management of the investment capital within the policy.

Q 3:74 What is a cash surrender value?

The cash surrender value is the amount available to a policy owner when a permanent life insurance policy is surrendered. It is also the amount upon which a policy loan is based. If the insured surrenders the policy for its cash value, the entire contract is terminated and the life insurance company has no further obligations.

When Life Insurance Policy Should Be Replaced

Q 3:75 What are 1035 exchanges?

Federal income tax law allows certain exchanges to be made without the immediate recognition of gain. These are considered Section 1035 exchanges, after the section of the Internal Revenue Code.

Life insurance and annuities may be exchanged for a similar product with no income tax consequences if the funds are transferred from company to company without the individual receiving any of the funds. The new policy must cover the same insured(s) or annuitant(s), and the new policy cannot have a later maturity date. This means that an endowment at age 65 cannot be exchanged for a whole life policy that endows at age 100. In addition, the basis in the original policy becomes the basis for the new policy.

Just as a life insurance product can be exchanged for a similar life insurance product, and an annuity for an annuity, a life insurance policy can be exchanged for an annuity. However, an annuity cannot be exchanged for a life insurance policy.

Some of the reasons a client might want to exchange policies are:

1. A client feels that a higher rate of return can be realized with a new policy.
2. A client is concerned with the stability of the current insurer.
3. A client would like to change an ordinary life policy into a single premium policy in order to eliminate the premium-paying burden.
4. A new developed policy (perhaps with a more flexible premium structure) is more suitable to the client's need or circumstances than the current policy.

Q 3:76 What are other ways to replace policies?

One alternative to replacing the policy would be to use the cash value in the policy to purchase a reduced amount of paid-up whole life insurance, and then use the freed-up premium payments to purchase the new policy.

Another alternative would be to use the dividends from the policy to purchase new life insurance coverage.

Tax Consequences of Life Insurance Policies

Q3:77   What are the income tax consequences for the cash surrender value?

At the time that the life insurance policy is surrendered, the amount by which the cash surrender value is greater than the net premiums paid is taxable as income. The net premium paid is the total premiums paid minus the dividends received.

If there is an outstanding loan on the policy, this amount is added to the current cash value before subtracting the net premiums.

Q3:78   What are the income tax consequences for dividends?

Dividends are not taxable as income since they are viewed as a return of excess premium paid. However, it the insured elects for the dividends to be held by the insurance company and interest to be paid out on the dividend amount, this interest amount is considered taxable income. (See Q3:69 for more information on the accumulation of interest dividend option.)

Q3:79   What are the income tax consequences for loans?

A policy owner will not have taxable income until loans, including any previous loans, plus any dividends received, exceed the policy owner's total amount of premiums paid. Therefore, until the policy owner has recovered his or her aggregate premium cost, he or she will generally be allowed to receive withdrawals tax-free.

Q3:80   What are the income tax consequences for 1035 exchanges?

Section 1035 exchanges that are allowed by code are considered tax-deferred exchanges. Any gain in the exchange is deferred because the new contract takes the cost basis of the policy it was exchanged for. If there are any losses in the exchange, they are not deductible.

Exchanges that are allowed for tax-deferred status are: (1) a life insurance contract for another life insurance contract; (2) a life insurance contract for an annuity; (3) and an annuity for and annuity. (See Q3:75 for more information on 1035 exchanges.)

Q3:81   What are the income tax consequences for modified endowment contracts?

To the extent that there are gains in the modified endowment contract, such amounts, when withdrawn, are taxed on an income-first basis. In other words, the first distributions out of the contract are not considered a tax-free return of the policy owner's cost but rather the investment earning on the contract. Only after all income or gain in the policy has been received are additional amounts treated as a nontaxable return of the policy owner's investment in the contract.

In addition to the tax on the distributions under the contract, a 10-percent penalty tax can be imposed too. This 10-percent penalty tax is not applied to any distributions made after the taxpayer reaches the age of 59½ years, after the taxpayer is disabled, or as a part of a series of substantially equal periodic payments made for the life of the taxpayer.

Q 3:82   What are the income tax consequences for transfer for value?

When life insurance is transferred for "valuable consideration," a transfer for value has occurred. If the transfer is (1) to the insured; (2) to a partner of the insured or a partnership in which the insured is a partner; (3) to a corporation where the insured is a shareholder or office; or (4) where the transfer occurs and the basis for the new owner is the same as the basis for the original owner (usually in a gift to a spouse or child), then the transfer is done income tax free.

If the transfer is to someone not listed above, then upon the death of the insured only the amount paid for the policy and any subsequent premiums are recovered income tax free by the transferee-owner. The remainder is subject to ordinary income tax.

Q 3:83   What are the income tax consequences for viatical settlements?

Under section 1019(g) of the Code, accelerated benefits and payments from a viatical settlement are treated as though the benefits were paid by reason of death. Since death benefits are generally received free of income tax, the accelerated benefits and viatical settlement will be received income tax free.

The benefits received during the insured's lifetime are tax free if the insured is considered terminally or chronically ill. An individual is considered terminally ill if a doctor certifies that his or her life expectancy is 24 months or less. A person is considered chronically ill if within the past 12 months, a physician has certified that the individual was unable to perform, without substantial assistance, at least two activities of daily living for at least 90 days.

The terminal illness or chronic illness condition need only be met at the time of payment to the policy owner. Therefore, if the insured lives beyond the 24 months, he or she won't be liable for any income tax liability at that point.

The accelerated benefits and viatical settlement are also income tax free to a policy owner that is not the insured, such as a spouse or trust.

Q 3:84   What are the gift tax consequences when qualifying for the annual exclusion?

To qualify for the annual gift exclusion, the donee must be given a present interest, an unrestricted right to the immediate use, possession, or enjoyment of the property, or income from the property. If the gift qualifies, then the donor can deduct the annual exclusion amount ($12,000 in 2006) from the value of the gift in order to determine the gift value.

There are three methods of obtaining the annual exclusion for the gift without really giving a minor control of the property transferred. They are the 2503 (b) trust, the 2503(c) trust, and the *Crummey* trust.

Q3:85   What are the gift tax consequences for future interest gifts?

When giving a gift of a future interest, the donor does not get to use the annual exclusion ($12,000 in 2006), and the full value of the gift will be taxable. Therefore part or all of the donor's unified credit will have to be used. A future interest gift is one that has some condition attached that either might cause some delay, or does cause a delay in the donee's possession and enjoyment of the transferred property.

One exception to this rule is found in the IRC Section 2503(c) trusts. The annual exclusion is allowed for gifts placed in the trust for the benefit of a person who is under age 21.

Q3:86   What are the estate tax consequences regarding incidents of ownership?

Estate taxation of life insurance is influenced by ownership. If an insured owns a policy on his or her life, then at his or her death, the death benefit will be included in the value of his or her estate. This is the case if there is "any incident of ownership" in the policy. An incident of ownership can be any right: the right to borrow, the right to cancel the policy, the right to approve a beneficiary change, even the right to prevent the current owner from borrowing against the policy. If the insured had an incident of ownership within three years of death, the proceeds of the policy will be included in his or her estate.

Policy proceeds will be included in the insured's estate if the insured transferred the policy to another but retained a lifetime right to alter, amend, revoke, or terminate the policy.

If the decedent owns a policy on the life of another, the value of the life insurance policy will be included in the decedent's estate, if the decedent dies before the insured.

Q3:87   What are the estate tax consequences when the proceeds are payable to the estate?

If the policy proceeds were paid to (or for the benefit of) the insured's estate, the proceeds will be included in the insured's gross estate. The insurance proceeds will be considered payable for the benefit of the estate if used to pay federal estate taxes, state death taxes, debts of the estate, or any other taxes payable by the estate.

For the proceeds to be included when the estate isn't the named beneficiary, the beneficiary must be legally obligated to use the insurance money to pay one or more of the items listed above. If there is no legal obligation for the beneficiary to use the money to meet an estate obligation, then there should be no inclusion of the proceeds in the deceased's estate.

Beneficiaries

Q 3:88   How should personal beneficiaries be selected?

If the estate of the insured is not likely to be above the applicable exclusion amount, then naming a beneficiary is much simpler since there will be no transfer taxes at the death of the insured.

If the estate is likely to be above the applicable exclusion amount, then more care should be taken in naming beneficiaries. If you name the uninsured spouse as the owner and the beneficiary, then it is possible to postpone estate taxes on the proceeds until the death of the spouse (provided he or she is the second to die).

To remove the proceeds from the estates of both spouses, an Irrevocable Life Insurance Trust (ILIT) should be considered. This will only work if the insured transferred the policy prior to three years before his or her death, or the ILIT purchased the initial policy.

Finally, if a minor is named as a primary or contingent beneficiary, a guardian should be named in the deceased's will so he or she can receive the payment of proceeds. It is then the guardian's responsibility to manage and conserve the minor's estate.

Q 3:89   How should ILIT beneficiaries be selected?

In an Irrevocable Life Insurance Trust, the trust should be the beneficiary of the life insurance policy; that way the disposition of the insurance proceeds are dictated by the trust documents. In addition, the trust should also be the owner of the policy.

The trust can then define its own beneficiaries, and document how and when the life insurance proceeds will be distributed to the trust's beneficiaries. The trust could specify that the proceeds could be paid out when the children get to certain ages (such as 25, 40, or 50), or when they reach some milestone in their life (such as getting married, buying their first house, or having their first child). As you can see, the use of a trust allows more detailed definition of who will receive the benefits and when they will receive them.

Q 3:90   Can a financial planner give advice about beneficiary designations?

A financial planner may give practical advice about how to fill in the beneficiary information requested in life insurance or retirement plan forms. However, he or she must not give advice about the legal effect of a beneficiary designation.

Except when done by a properly admitted lawyer, giving legal advice, even for free, is a crime or offense in every jurisdiction in the United States. Even if the nonlawyer explicitly states that he or she is not a lawyer, it is still a crime to give legal advice.

Life Insurance in Retirement Plans

Q 3:91   What types of life insurance are appropriate for qualified plans?

Traditionally, whole life insurance was used to provide insurance protection within qualified plans. However, with the increased popularity of universal life and variable life, these choices are available in more policies today. Term insurance is another possibility too, however it is rarely used.

Which plan is better? It is really up to the employer that is considering adopting a plan or making life insurance available to its employees to determine which type of policy is better for his or her organization.

Proponents of whole life insurance will point to the fact that whole life provides better guarantees that the death benefit will be paid as long as the premiums are paid. However, proponents of universal life will point to the premium flexibility, while proponents of variable life will point out the myriad of investment choices that are available. In the end, it is up to the employer to define what options are more important to him or her.

Q 3:92   Can a defined benefit plan be funded with life insurance?

A qualified plan can be funded in whole or in part through the purchase of individual life insurance policies. A plan that is fully funded with life insurance contracts is referred to as a fully insured plan while a plan that is partially funded with life insurance contracts is called a split-funded plan. In a split-funded plan, the remainder of the benefits comes from an investment fund.

The amount of life insurance that can be held in a defined benefit plan is based on the death benefit of the life insurance contracts. The death benefit must be an "incidental" benefit to the plan. To be incidental, the death benefit must not be more than 100 times the monthly retirement benefit, or the aggregate premiums paid over the life of the plan for any insured's death benefit must be less than 50 percent (for ordinary and variable life; 25 percent for term and universal life) of the overall cost to provide plan benefits for that participant.

Q 3:93 Should life insurance be used in a nonqualified deferred compensation plan?

Life insurance is an ideal funding method if the nonqualified deferred compensation plan includes a death benefit. The insurance can be used to provide the funds to the corporation at the death of the participant. These funds are then used for payment of the death benefit in the plan.

The life insurance proceeds will be received by the corporation tax free, but as with all deferred compensation plan benefits, the death benefit will be fully taxable to the participant or to the participant's estate or beneficiary.

The employer should be the owner of the policy and the beneficiary of the entire policy.

The advantages to using life insurance as a funding vehicle include the fact that the cash values grow tax deferred, and the death proceeds will be received tax-free. In addition, if the contract is not a modified endowment contract, the company will not be taxed on withdrawals of cash value, up to their basis.

Q 3:94 Can life insurance be included in a Section 457 plan?

For a deferred compensation plan of a non-government employer, any investment the employer permits can be used in the plan.

For a plan of a state or local government employer, state law will regulate what investments are allowed in the plan. Almost all states permit life insurance.

Under an unfunded deferred compensation plan, the employer is the full owner of the policy and is also the sole beneficiary under the policy. In this case, the death proceeds are taxed as ordinary income to the beneficiary upon receipt of that amount.

Q 3:95 Can life insurance be included in 403(B) plans?

IRS regulations provide that an individual contract, which provides incidental life insurance protection, may be purchased as an annuity contract. Incidental benefit rules require that a proportion of the contributions used for life insurance be limited in relation to all contributions made under the 403(b) plan. For an ordinary life policy, no more than 49 percent of the total contributions can be used to pay for life insurance. For all other types of policies, such as term, whole life, and universal life, not qualifying as ordinary life policies, no more than 25 percent of the total contributions can be used for life insurance.

The cost of the life insurance purchases with 403(b) funds can be included in the employee's gross income in the year the premium is paid. The amount included is the lesser of the cost determined with the PS-58 tables, or the published premium rates charged by the insurer for individual one-year term insurance available for standard risks.

If the participant dies before retirement, the difference between the face amount of the policy and its cash surrender value, if any, is exempt from income tax as death proceeds, provided the insurance cost has been taxed to the employee as PS-58 costs. The amount of the cash surrender value that exceeds the PS-58 costs already taxed to the employee is treated as a taxable distribution.

When the employee retires, he or she must (1) surrender the life insurance policy for the cash value; (2) elect an annuity payment under the life insurance policy that satisfies Code Section 401(a)(9); (3) cash out of the policy and transfer the entire value to a 403(b)(1) annuity or a 403(b)(7) custodial account; or (4) receive a taxable distribution of the life insurance policy (taxable amount is the portion that exceeds the PS-58 costs already taxed to the employee).

Q 3:96   What is a pension subtrust?

A pension subtrust is simply an irrevocable life insurance trust established within a pension plan trust to hold any life insurance policies on the plan participant's life. If the participant does not control the pension subtrust trustee, and the participant does not have any incidents of ownership in the policy held in the subtrust, the policy proceeds generally should not be includible in the participant's federal gross estate.

Q 3:97   What is a voluntary employees' beneficiary association?

Voluntary employee beneficiary associations (VEBAs) are set up as funding arrangement for employee benefits. A VEBA may be used to provide a funding vehicle for benefits including life, sickness, accident benefits, vacation benefits, childcare, legal services, education and job training, severance pay, and supplemental unemployment benefits. A VEBA is not permitted to provide retirement benefits, commuter benefits, or miscellaneous fringe benefits.

A VEBA permits the employer to deduct contributions and to avoid taxation for the investment income earned on those contributions. In contrast, under a self-insured plan, the employer is only allowed to deduct actual benefit payments.

Employees have the option of becoming members of the VEBA, and membership is voluntary. Membership is also available to former employees who are retired, disabled, or laidoff, and to those former employees' dependents. Benefits must also be nondiscriminatory.

Q 3:98   What is pension maximization?

If an individual participates in a qualified defined benefit plan or other pension plan maintained by the employer, the participant's spouse is generally entitled to a "survivor annuity" under the plan. If the participant dies before the spouse, the plan pays the spouse an annuity at least equal to 50 percent or more of the joint annuity paid to the participant. The spouse also has the option to waive the right to this spousal benefit, and then the participant receives a larger monthly benefit during his or her lifetime.

With pension maximization, in some cases it may be better to provide security to the spouse using insurance. The spouse can waive the survivor annuity, and the extra monthly income received during the participant's lifetime can be used to cover the cost of the life insurance.

There are several factors one should consider when looking into pension maximization. First, if the participant's benefits are capped by Code limitations, payments might be equal whether on a joint and survivor or life annuity basis. In this case, it makes sense to take the joint and survivor payout.

If the employee health is poor, the joint and survivor benefit is more attractive since it provides a death benefit for the spouse without the employee proving evidence of insurability.

If the participant's spouse is ill, then life insurance and the life annuity should be selected.

If the couple has ample investments outside of the pension plan, there may be no need to select the joint and survivor annuity or to buy the life insurance policy on the participant.

Underwriting, Rate Making, Loss Adjustment, and Reinsurance Considerations

Q 3:99   What are some of the considerations in underwriting group policies?

While the applicant for individual insurance must generally show evidence of insurability, for group policies the individual members usually are not required to show evidence of insurability. The underwriting process for group insurance focuses on the characteristics of the group instead of the insurability of the individual.

The general underwriting considerations for a group include the reason for the group's existence, the stability of the group, the persistency of the group, the method of determining benefits, the provisions that determine eligibility, the source and method of premium payments, administrative aspects of the plan, prior experience of the plan, the size and composition of the group, and the industry represented by the group.

The group must be formed for some purpose other than to obtain insurance for its members. This rule helps to protect the insurance company from adverse selection that would likely exist if poor risks were to form a group just to obtain insurance.

The stability or turnover rate of a group affects the underwriting process too. A turnover rate that is higher than average will likely result in increased administrative costs for the insurance company. On the other hand, the turnover rate that is lower than normal results in an increasing average age of the members of the group, which in turn results in an increased premium for the group.

The persistency of the group (the length of time the business stays with an insurance company) is a cause for some concern since most of the costs to the insurance company are in the initial expenses. If a business has a history of frequently changing insurance companies the underwriter might avoid this business.

If the determination of benefits or eligibility were left in the hands of the employees or employers, there would be a tendency of those with poorer risks to select greater amounts of coverage or shorter probationary periods. This can also lead to issues with adverse selection.

The prior experience of a company will have some effect on their rates. If the company is transferring its business due to poor claims service or due to rate increases, the underwriter will want to determine the underlying cause. Was the rate increase due to a higher-than-normal claims experience, and will the new insurance company be able to provide better service? The answers to these questions will affect the new premium and/or maybe even denial of coverage.

The size and composition of the group are a significant factor in the underwriting process. With large groups there usually is prior experience that can be used as a determining factor in setting a premium. However, with small groups, it typically is the first time coverage is being written, and administrative expenses tend to be higher with a small group. The age and sex of the group will also affect the resulting premium.

The nature of the industry represented by the group is also a significant factor in the underwriting process. Different industries have different occupational hazards, and different death claim rates. These differences are taken into consideration when setting the premium rates.

Q 3:100 What is reinsurance?

Reinsurance is a concept under which one insurer transfers part of all of certain risks that it has agreed to insure to one or more other insurers. Reinsurance is used by many companies to help stabilize loss ratios and underwriting results, and to help protect against overwhelming financial impact from catastrophes. It can also be used when an insurance company is exiting a line of business.

There are two types of reinsurance: treaty reinsurance and facultative rein-surance. A treaty is a contract governing what portion and types of risks are transferred to the reinsurer. It is negotiated between the primary insurer and the reinsurance company. Under the treaty, the reinsurer automatically assumes part of each risk that meets the criteria of the contract.

Facultative reinsurance is negotiated separately as direct insurers underwrite risks. The direct insurer is not obligated to cede any risks, and the reinsurer is not obligated to accept any risk. Facultative reinsurance is used to reinsure specific polices rather than an entire book of business.

Valuing a Life Insurance Policy

Q 3:101   How is life insurance valued for gift tax purposes?

When a policy is transferred from one party to another, to the extent that the transferor receives less than full and adequate consideration, the transfer is a gift. The difference between the value of the policy and the amount received in exchange for it is the gift value.

If the transaction involves a policy on which further premiums are payable, the value of the policy is the sum of (1) the "interpolated terminal reserve," plus (2) the value of any "unearned premiums," less (3) the amount of any out-standing loan. The interpolated terminal reserve is the reserve held by the insurer to meet its claims under the policy but adjusted from the contract's anniversary date to the date of the gift. The unearned premium is the value of the unearned portion of the last premium made prior to the gift.

If the transaction involves a paid-up policy or a previously purchased single premium policy, the gift tax value is the single premium the insurer would charge for a contract of the same face value on the life of a person that is the insured's age at the time of the gift.

If the transaction involves a new policy that is transferred as a gift immedi-ately after its purchase, the gross premium paid to the date of the transfer is the value of the gift.

Q 3:102   How is life insurance valued for estate tax purposes?

The estate tax value of third-party-owned un-matured life insurance policies includable in the estate of someone other than the insured is generally the replacement cost of the policy. The replacement cost is ascertained using the same rules governing valuation of policies for gift tax purposes. (See Q 3:101.) In most cases this approximates the sum of the cash surrender value plus the unearned premium.

Estate Planning Issues

Q3:103   How does community property affect life insurance?

Life insurance policies purchased during marriage are community property, and if the insured dies, one-half of the death benefit will be included in the insured's gross estate.

If the life insurance policy was separate property but the premiums were paid during marriage with community property, the states have made different rules. In California and Washington, the portion of the premiums paid from community property determines the portion of the death proceeds that are community property. In Texas, Louisiana, and New Mexico, the policy remains the separate property of the original purchaser despite the payment of premiums from community property. The surviving spouse can receive reimbursement for the amount of premiums paid from community property, but does not share in the growth of the policy's value.

Q3:104   What is a disclaimer?

A disclaimer is a written document in which a beneficiary states that he or she does not want to receive the benefit. The disclaimer must be made before the beneficiary receives or uses the property. In addition, as stated above, the disclaimer must be written and signed by the disclaimant, and the disclaimant must not direct where or to whom the property goes next. Finally, the disclaimer document must be delivered to the plan administrator or insurance company no later than nine months after the participant's (or insured's) death.

Typically, a disclaimer is used when someone has no need for the property and does not want to have it added to his or her estate. When the property is disclaimed, it will go to the next beneficiary in line, or directly to the estate, to be disposed of using the requests in the will.

Q3:105   Can a charity be a beneficiary?

Yes, a charity may be a beneficiary for a life insurance contract. The proceeds of the policy will still be included in the decedent's gross estate. However, the estate will receive a charitable deduction for the amount that passes to the charity.

Q3:106   What is an Irrevocable Life Insurance Trust?

An Irrevocable Life Insurance Trust, or ILIT, is a trust in which a life insurance policy is owned by the trust. The trust is irrevocable, which means that once created, it cannot be changed. The purpose of an irrevocable life insurance trust is typically to remove the proceeds of the life insurance policy from the insured's estate. In order for this to be successful, the insured must not have had any incidents of ownership in the policy within the last three years. In addition, having the trust own the policy also removes the proceeds from the estate of the insured's spouse, provided he or she does not have any powers that constitute incidents of ownership.

Having the trust as the beneficiary to the life insurance policy allows the insurance proceeds to be coordinated with the overall estate plan of the deceased, and allows the funds to be managed on behalf of the trust's beneficiaries.

Finally, the trust can be structured so that the initial gift to the trust, either the policy or the initial premium, can qualify for the annual gift tax exclusion. It can also be structured so that any subsequent gifts of cash to pay premiums can qualify for the exclusion too. Generally, this is accomplished by giving the beneficiaries a *Crummey* withdrawal power.

Q3:107   Why is life insurance important in estate planning?

Life insurance is important in estate planning because the insurance proceeds provide support for the insured's family after his or her death. It is also important because it can provide needed liquidity to pay the estate taxes and other debts of the insured.

The latter purpose is important where the estate consists of assets that are not very liquid but have significant value for estate tax purposes, such as a family business, or family property.

Q3:108   What are the benefits of lifetime gifts?

There are several benefits that make the giving of gifts throughout one's life advantageous. Lifetime gifts within the $12,000 (2006) annual exclusion can be made without any gift tax. In addition, any appreciation in the value of the property between the date of the gift and the date of the donor's death escapes gift taxes.

There is an added benefit for life insurance. The value of the gift is the cost of replacing the policy, not the face value of the policy. By contrast, if the donor died owning the policy, the full amount of the death benefit would be includible in the estate.

Q3:109   How is second-to-die insurance used in estate planning?

Since the estate tax marital deduction is unlimited, there is generally no need to pay estate taxes when the first spouse dies. Postponing the estate taxes until the death of the second spouse is generally advantageous; however, this means that the entire estate tax burden falls on the estate of the second spouse to die. Second-to-die insurance is a useful option to provide funds to cover the estate taxes due on the second death.

Life Insurance and Creating Wealth

Q3:110   How can life insurance create wealth?

A life insurance policy can be used to create wealth for a family through providing a lump sum death benefit for the family's use after the death of the insured. Unfortunately, the insured has to die. However, the proceeds can be used to provide education funds and living expenses, to pay off the home mortgage, and can be put to many other uses that help those left behind. The funds can even be used to create trusts for the deceased's children that can be used to help them throughout their lifetime, thereby leaving a legacy to the children.

Q3:111   What is a wealth replacement trust?

A wealth replacement trust is typically an Irrevocable Life Insurance Trust where the death benefit proceeds are used to replace the wealth that the deceased donated to charities at his death. The death benefit is then paid to the beneficiaries of the trust, which is typically his or her family. This way the deceased is able to donate property to charities and still provide an inheritance to his heirs.

Disability Insurance

Evaluating Disability Policies

Q3:112   What is a short-term disability policy?

Short-term disability (STD) insurance provides coverage for disabilities for up to two years. The typical benefit periods written in the policies are 13, 26, 52, and 104 weeks. The elimination period can be as short as 0 days for an accident and 7 days for sickness, but it is rarely more than 15 or 30 days.

The policy typically covers for any disability that prevents the person from performing the duties of their normal occupation.

Q3:113   What is a long-term disability policy?

Long-term disability (LTD) insurance provides coverage for disabilities for some specified period. Benefit periods are typically to retirement age, but lesser benefit periods of 2, 5, or 10 years are also available. The elimination periods are usually a minimum of 30 days and are frequently 30 months or even one year. Benefits are coordinated with other governmental plans and with any other employer-sponsored plans, including group short-term disability policies.

The policy typically covers for any disability that prevents the person from performing the duties of their normal occupation for the first two years of disability, and thereafter disability coverage will continue if he or she is unable to perform the duties of any occupation to which he or she is reasonably suited by education, training, and experience.

Q3:114 What are the ways to compare policies?

There are many different items used to compare disability policies. Listed below are items to look at when doing the comparison:

- What is the definition for disability in the policy?
- What are the amount and frequency of total disability benefits?
- What is the elimination period prior to receiving disability benefits?
- What is the duration of the total disability benefits?
- Are partial disability benefits covered? If so, what is the definition of partial disability, and what period of total disability is required before benefits are payable?
- Are residual disability benefits covered? If so, what is the benefit amount, and how long are they payable? Is there a prior total disability period required before benefits are paid?
- What is the annual policy premium amount?
- Are there any cost-of-living increases for the benefits paid? If so, what is the basis on which the increased amount is determined?
- What is the renewability provision?
- Does the policy contain any riders? If so, what do they cover, and is there an additional premium for the rider?

These should help in determining which policy is better for the circumstances of the insured.

Q3:115 What perils are covered?

The disability income policy may provide coverage for loss of income caused by accident, or it may cover loss of income that results from either an accident or illness. Most companies will not write a policy that covers loss of income due to illness only. This is because it is much easier to feign sickness than it is to feign an accidental injury.

When a disability policy is written to cover sickness and accidents, the intervals for which benefits are payable may be different. For example, one policy might pay benefits for two years if the disability is from an illness, and for 5 years if the disability is the result of an accident.

Q3:116 What is the change in occupation provision?

The change of occupation provision, while relatively uncommon, allows the insurer to reduce the benefit payable if the insured changes to a more hazardous occupation. The benefit is usually reduced to the benefit the premium paid would have purchased at the more hazardous employment classification. If the insured changes to a less hazardous occupation, the premium is reduced, but the benefit remains the same.

Q3:117   How is the cost determined?

There are a large number of factors affecting how disability insurance is priced. They vary not only by the insured's age, but also by smoker status, sex, occupation class, geographic area, and the elimination period. In addition there are different riders or provisions that can be added to the policy, such as guaranteed renewable, non-cancelable, and cost-of-living adjustments.

Another factor that affects the cost of the policy is the type of policy. Is it a group policy or an individual policy? Is the policy a short-term or a long-term policy? Since most disabilities are short term in duration, coverage for longer periods of disability costs proportionately less than coverage for short periods.

Definition of Disability

Q3:118   How has the term "disability" traditionally been defined?

Disability has traditionally been defined as the insured's inability to engage in a designated occupation due to accident or sickness. Disability will typically be defined in one of four ways:

1. The insured's inability to work at his or her own occupation
2. The inability of the insured to work at his or her own occupation or to work in any gainful or reasonable employment
3. The inability of the insured to engage in any reasonable occupation for which he or she might become qualified for
4. The inability of the insured to work in any occupation

Some insurers are using a two-part definition of disability that defines disability as the inability of the insured to work in his or her own occupation for some period of time, such as two years, followed by the inability to engage in any occupation for which he or she is qualified for or could be qualified for.

Q3:119   What does the term "own occupation" mean?

Own occupation is defined as the inability of the insured to engage in his or her own occupation. The insured is guaranteed payment of benefits even if he or she is able to work at other occupations.

Although this definition provides the broadest coverage, unfavorable loss experience with this definition has caused may insurers to shift to a second definition, referred to as *modified own occupation*. Under this definition, if the insured cannot perform the duties of his or her own occupation, benefits will be payable unless the insured enters another occupation.

Q3:120   What does the term "any occupation" mean?

Any occupation is defined as the inability of the insured to work at any occupation, even an occupation that you are not specifically trained to do, or qualified to work in. This is the strictest definition of disability.

Q3:121   How is disability defined for Social Security?

Social Security uses the strictest of the definitions for disability. Social Security essentially requires that the claimant be unable to engage in any occupation. If you are able to work at any occupation then you are not considered disabled.

Other Provisions

Q3:122   What is a noncancelable provision?

A noncancelable provision in a disability policy guarantees the insured the right to renew the policy for a stated number of years, or until a stated age (normally 60 or 65), with the premium guaranteed at renewal. Since the insurer is unable to adjust the rates for a particular class of insureds, most insurers have adopted a guaranteed renewable provision instead of the noncancelable provision.

Q3:123   What is a guaranteed renewable provision?

The guaranteed renewable provision provides the insured with a guaranteed right to renew the policy, but with a provision permitting the insurance company to adjust the premium for an entire class of insureds. The company is not allowed to increase the rate for a single individual.

Q3:124   What is a partial disability rider?

Partial disability is usually defined as the inability to perform some specified percentage of the duties for the insured's occupation. The partial disability rider allows the insured to receive partial benefits (typically one-half the benefit of total disability) in the event that he or she is considered partially disabled following a period of total disability in which the he or she received benefits. Usually the benefit is payable for the period of partial disability, but not exceeding a specified term, such as 5 or 6 months.

Q3:125   What is a residual disability rider?

As is the case with the partial disability rider, the residual disability rider provides coverage for partial disabilities but focuses on the amount of income lost rather than on the physical inability to work. Insureds must usually have a 20 percent income loss to be eligible for the residual disability income benefit. The payment for residual disability is a percentage of the total disability benefit based on the percentage reduction in the insured's income. For example, if the insured's income is reduced by 40 percent, he or she will receive a benefit that is 40 percent of the total disability monthly amount.

Residual disability benefits are usually not limited in duration, other than the maximum benefit period under the policy. This is different from the partial disability rider. Also, some policies for residual disability benefits cover income lost because of an accident or sickness, even in the absence of a prior total disability.

Q 3:126   What is the cost-of-living adjustment (COLA) benefit?

The cost-of-living adjustment benefit is designed to offset the decline in the purchasing power of disability benefits that result from inflation. Some policies base the increase in indemnity on a flat percentage after the individual has been disabled for a year, while other policies tie the increase to the change in the consumer price index. Note that the cost-of-living factor is applied only at claim time, and after the claimant's recovery, the benefits under the contract revert to the original contractual benefit level.

Q 3:127   What is the Social Security rider?

The Social Security rider allows for the integration of Social Security disability and worker's compensation benefits with the benefits from the disability insurance policy. The rider is designed to provide additional monthly disability benefits when Social Security or worker's compensation benefits are not payable under their programs. The rider will also provide monthly benefits above those provided by Social Security or worker's compensation if their benefits do not rise to the level purchased in the disability policy. Since the rider does not pay, or pays a reduced amount, when social insurance benefits are being paid, the premiums for the disability policy will be less expensive than those policies that do not contain the Social Security rider.

Q 3:128   What is the elimination (waiting) period?

The elimination or waiting period is the amount of time that must elapse during the disability prior to receiving any benefits. The logic behind the need for an elimination period is that most people have some financial resources to call upon and therefore do not need immediate coverage, and secondly, the sooner benefits are provided, the greater the cost of the coverage.

Typical elimination periods are 3, 7, 15, 30, 60, 90, 180, and 365 days. As might be expected, short-term disability policies have shorter waiting periods than do long-term disability policies. Lowering the cost by extending the waiting period has become an increasingly necessary strategy as the rates for disability coverage have increased. The 90-day waiting period is today by far the most commonly selected by applicants.

Taxation

Q 3:129   What are the income tax consequences for an individual disability policy?

Premiums paid by a person for individually owned disability insurance is not deductible for federal income tax purposes. However, since the individual pays the premiums, all benefits received are tax free. Since the individual will not have to pay taxes on the disability income, something less than 100 percent of the individual's gross income needs to be replaced.

Q 3:130   What are the income tax consequences for a group disability policy?

First, employer contributions for disability income insurance result in taxable income to the employee. However, the payment of benefits might not be received tax free. In order to determine whether the benefits received are received tax free or not, we need to look at who paid the premiums.

If the employer paid all of the premiums for the policy, then the benefits are considered ordinary income, and are fully taxable.

If the employee paid all of the premiums, then the benefits are received income tax free.

It is more complicated if both the employer and employee share the cost of the premiums. In this case, benefits that are attributable to employer contributions are subject to income taxation, while benefits that are attributable to the employee's contributions are received income tax free. For example, if the employer paid 75 percent of the cost of the plan, then 75 percent of the benefits received by the employee would be taxable, and the other 25 percent would be received income tax free.

Finally, employer contributions for an employee's disability income insurance are fully deductible to the employer as an ordinary business expense. Contributions made by an individual for the disability income insurance are not tax deductible.

Homeowners Insurance

Q 3:131   What is an HO-1 policy?

HO-1 is a homeowners policy that provides basic fire and extended coverage on buildings and personal property for loss caused by 12 named perils. They are fire, lightning, windstorm, hail, explosion, riot, aircraft, theft, damage by vehicles, smoke, vandalism, and volcanic eruption.

Q3:132   What is an HO-2 policy?

An HO-2 policy provides a broader form of coverage than an HO-1 policy. It covers the buildings and personal property of the insured for the named peril of an HO-1 policy, and includes coverage for falling objects; weight of ice, snow, or sleet; accidental discharge of water or steam; freezing; sudden and accidental tearing apart, cracking, burning, or bulging; and sudden and accidental discharge from electrical current.

Q3:133   What is an HO-3 policy?

An HO-3 policy provides open perils coverage on the building and broad form (HO-2) coverage on personal property. The policy excludes damages caused by:

- Collapse
- Freezing of plumbing and certain fixtures
- Vandalism while the house is vacant or unoccupied
- Certain losses to fences and patios
- Theft or vandalism to a house under construction
- Leakage or seepage
- Wear and tear
- Smoke from agricultural or industrial operations
- Birds, rodents, insects, smog, rust, and animals of the insured.

Q3:134   What is an HO-4 policy?

An HO-4 policy is for tenants of apartments or houses and provides broad form coverage of personal property. It does not provide any coverage for buildings, since the insured does not own the building. This policy is also known as renter's insurance.

Q3:135   What is an HO-5 policy?

An HO-5 policy provides open perils coverage on the building and other structures, along with open perils coverage on the personal property. The same exclusions in an HO-3 policy apply to this policy too.

Q3:136   What is an HO-6 policy?

An HO-6 policy is designed to cover the loss exposures of a condominium owner, or an owner of a cooperative unit. This policy provides broad form coverage of personal property (HO-2) and a minimum of $1,000 for structures interior to the condo (such as interior walls, wall-to-wall carpeting). This amount can be increased if needed.

Q 3:137   What is an HO-8 policy?

An HO-8 policy is a modified homeowners policy for homes whose market value is less than their replacement cost. This is typically used for older homes where the cost to rebuild the structure due to its construction material exceeds the market value of the home. Other than this, an HO-8 policy is similar to a HO-1 policy.

Q 3:138   What is an HO-15 policy?

An HO-15 policy provides open peril coverage of personal property, and is used in combination with an HO-3 policy (which provides open peril coverage for the dwelling and other structures).

Q 3:139   What coverage is available in a homeowners insurance policy?

Homeowners insurance provides both property and liability insurance coverage. Property coverage includes the coverage of the dwelling, coverage for other structures on the property, coverage for personal property, and coverage for loss of use. Liability coverage includes coverage for personal liability and coverage for the medical payments to others.

Dwelling coverage (Coverage A) specifies that a dwelling includes structures attached to the dwelling and also covers material and supplies located on the premises, or adjacent to the premises, which are intended for use in construction, alteration, or repair of the dwelling. Coverage A does not include the land. Structures attached to the dwelling include a garage, decks, or fences.

The amount of coverage on the dwelling uses a *replacement cost* basis. This provides that if at the time of the loss the amount of insurance covering the dwelling is at least 80 percent of the dwelling's replacement cost, the loss will be paid on a replacement cost basis rather than on an actual cash value basis.

Other Structure coverage (Coverage B) applies to structures that are separated from the dwelling by a clear space. If there is no clear space, then they are a part of the dwelling, and covered under Coverage A. Examples of other structures include swimming pools, detached garages, and garden sheds. There is no coverage if the structure is used in whole or in part for business purposes or if it is rented to any person that is not a tenant of the dwelling, unless it is used solely as a private garage. Losses to other structures are covered on a replacement cost basis.

Personal Property coverage (Coverage C) provides insurance for personal property owned or used by any insured while it is located anywhere in the world. The coverage is provided on both owned and borrowed property. For example, the insured or a family member borrows property from a friend, and the property is damaged as a result of the peril, the homeowners policy will cover the property as if it had been owned by the insured.

The coverage limit for personal property is 50 percent of the dwelling coverage. However, coverage on personal property located at a secondary residence is limited to 10 percent of the Coverage C limit, or $1,000.

Personal property is covered on an actual cash value basis instead of on a replacement cost basis. However, replacement cost coverage is frequently added through the use of an available endorsement. Some personal property is quite valuable and can be insured for its appraised value with a *scheduled personal property endorsement*. This provides open peril coverage on designated items and allows the insured to arrange for more coverage than is otherwise available under the unscheduled coverage, particularly for theft.

Coverage C limits the amount of insurance available to certain classes of property. These limitations apply to the total loss of property from any single category. They include:

- $200 for money, bank notes, coins, medals, and gold and silver (other than goldware or silverware)
- $1,000 for securities, accounts, deeds, evidences of debt, notes other than bank notes, personal records, passports, tickets, stamps, and manuscripts
- $1,000 for watercraft, including trailers, furnishings, equipment and motors
- $1,000 for trailers not used with watercraft
- $2,500 for property on the residence premises used for business purposes
- $250 for property away from the building used for business purposes

The following limitations apply to theft but not other perils:

- $1,500 for jewelry and furs
- $2,000 for firearms
- $2,500 for silverware, goldware, and pewterware

The following is a list of property that is excluded from personal property coverage:

- Articles that are separately described and specifically insured under the homeowners policy or any other insurance policy, such as those covered under floaters or inland marine coverage
- Animals, birds, and fish
- Motorized land vehicles subject to motor vehicle registration (except those used to service the insured's residence or to assist the handicapped), including (while in or on the vehicle) accessories and equipment plus TVs, CBs, or tape players that may be operated by the electrical system of the vehicle. Tapes for use with excluded tape players are also excluded
- Aircraft and their parts
- Property contained in an apartment regularly rented or held for rental to others by the insured (this can be covered with a commercial form of insurance)

- Property of roomers, boarders, and other tenants not related to the insured
- Property rented or held for rental to others away from the premises (this is a business purpose and needs to be covered under a commercial lines policy)
- Business property, including books of account, drawings, paper records, and EDP software media containing business data
- Credit cards or fund transfer cards (except as provided under the additional coverage)—these are typically covered for losses up to $1,000

Loss of Use coverage(Coverage D) provides coverage when the named insured's residence cannot be occupied as a result of a covered loss. If the named insured and family must live elsewhere while the portion of the residence that they normally occupy is being repaired or rebuilt, they are entitled to benefits for additional living expenses. In addition, there is coverage for the fair rental value, less any noncontinuing expenses, of the portion of the residence that is rented to others. Lastly, there is up to two weeks' coverage for the expense of living elsewhere when civil authorities prohibit the insured from using the residence because a neighboring property is damaged by a named peril. An example would be if the insured were evacuated from their property because of a nearby brush fire.

Personal Liability coverage(Coverage E) provides protection for damages that arise out of bodily injury or property damage for which an insured is legally liable. The limit of coverage is typically $100,000 per occurrence, but can be increased. Although this coverage is very broad, it is subject to numerous exclusions. These exclusions are for bodily injury and property damage and include ones that:

- Arise out of or in connection with a business engaged by the insured
- Arise out of the failure to render professional services
- Arise out the ownership, or use of aircraft
- Arise out of most motorized land vehicles, except for those designed for recreational use off public roads (not subject to motor vehicle registration) and motorized golf carts
- Are caused by war
- Arise from the use, sale, manufacture, deliver, transfer, or possession of a controlled substance

Medical Payments to Others coverage(Coverage F) provides up to $1,000 of coverage for the necessary medical expenses of persons other than the insured who are injured while on the insured's premises with the permission of the insured. Benefits are paid regardless of fault. Injuries off an insured location are also covered if they are caused by activities of the insured, or are caused by an animal owned by the insured. The coverage does not apply to the insured and members of the insured's household.

Coverage amounts for different types of policies:

Coverage	Form HO-2	Form HO-3	Form HO-4	Form HO-6	Form HO-8
A: Dwelling	Amount based on replacement cost, $15,000 minimum	Amount based on replacement cost, $20,000 minimum	Not covered	$1,000 on owner's additions and alterations to the unit	Amount based on actual cash value of the home, $15,000 minimum
B: Other Structures	10% of Part A	10% of Part A	Not covered	Included in Part A coverage	10% of Part A
C: Personal Property	50% of Part A	50% of Part A	$6,000 minimum	$6,000 minimum	50% of Part A
D: Loss of Use	30% of Part A	30% of Part A	30% of Part C	40% of Part C	10% of Part A
E: Personal Liability	$100,000	$100,000	$100,000	$100,000	$100,000
F: Medical Payments to Others	$1,000 per person	$1,000 per person	$1,000 per person	$1,000 per person	$1,000 per person

Q 3:140   What is named peril coverage?

Homeowners insurance is normally written on a named perils basis. Perils are events that cause a loss. There are two forms of named perils, *basic form* and *broad form*. These forms refer to the number of perils covered under the policy.

Basic Form covers loss due to fire, lightning, windstorm, hail, riot or civil commotion, aircraft, vehicles, smoke, vandalism, explosion, theft, and volcanic eruption.

Broad Form covers the same twelve perils in the basic form, and adds the following 6 perils:

- Falling objects
- Weight of ice, snow, and sleet
- Accidental discharge or overflow of water or steam
- Sudden and accidental tearing apart, cracking, burning, or bulging of a steam, hot water, air conditioning, or automatic fire protective sprinkler system, or from within a household appliance
- Freezing of a plumbing, heating, air conditioning, or automatic fire sprinkler system, or of a household appliance
- Sudden and accidental damage from artificially generated electrical currents

Q 3:141   What is open peril coverage?

An open peril policy provides coverage for all perils except those that are explicitly excluded. Open peril policies exclude damages caused by:

- Collapse
- Freezing of plumbing and certain fixtures
- Vandalism while the house is vacant or unoccupied
- Certain losses to fences and patios
- Theft or vandalism to a house under construction
- Leakage or seepage
- Wear and tear
- Smoke from agricultural or industrial operations
- Birds, rodents, insects, smog, rust, and animals of the insured

In addition to this list of perils, there are several types of losses that are specifically excluded regardless of any other cause or event that contributes to the loss. These include losses resulting from:

- **Ordinance or law.** Losses caused by the enforcement of any ordinance or law regulating construction, repair, or demolition of buildings. Thus, the insurer will not be responsible for reimbursing the insured for any increased costs incurred in order to comply with the changes in a municipality's building code that come after the original construction.
- **Earth movement.** Losses caused by earth movement, including landslides, mudflow, earth sinking, rising, or shifting. These would have to be covered by separate flood and/or earthquake insurance for an additional premium.
- **Flood and/or water.** Losses caused by water damage including flood damage, back-up through sewers or drains, or seepage through basement walls and foundation floors. This is water that enters from the outside. Water damage caused by a broken pipe or appliance within the home will be covered.
- **Power failure.** Losses caused by power failure if the power interruption takes place away from the residence premises. Food freezer loss would be covered if a tree falls on the insured's home and disrupts electric power, but not if the tree was at the end of the block and knocked out the entire neighborhood.
- **Neglect.** Losses caused by the neglect of the insured to use all reasonable means to save the property at or after the occurrence of an insured peril. If a tree falls on the house and breaks out a window, the homeowner should attempt to cover the window to prevent losses to personal property by the intrusion of rain or snow, or the theft of property because of the destroyed window being an access to the house.
- **War.** Losses caused by war or act of war.
- **Nuclear accident.** Losses caused by nuclear accident. However, if fire results because of a nuclear accident, the loss attributable to the fire

would be covered. The damage caused directly by the nuclear accident would be the liability of the owner of the nuclear device (reactor, etc.).

- **Intentional losses.** Losses that results from or at the direction of any insured (e.g., arson).

Q 3:142 What is replacement cost?

The coverage on the dwelling and other buildings under the homeowners insurance policy is on a *replacement cost* basis. Replacement cost is simply the cost of rebuilding the structure with material of like kind and quality. If at the time of the loss the amount of insurance covering a building is at least 80 percent of the replacement cost, the loss will be paid on a replacement loss basis rather than on an actual cost basis.

If the 80 percent requirement is not met, the payment will be the larger of:

- Actual cash value of the damaged property (replacement cost less depreciation), or
- Coverage A amount divided by 80 percent of the replacement cost, multiplied by the replacement cost of the loss less the deductible

If the loss is more than $2,500 or 5 percent of the amount of insurance, the building must actually be repaired or replaced before the insured can collect on a replacement cost basis.

Q 3:143 What is a scheduled personal property endorsement?

The Homeowners Scheduled Personal Property Endorsement provides open peril coverage on nine classes of property under the same terms as if separate contracts were purchased for each type of property. The coverage is worldwide.

There are two versions of the endorsement: one that provides coverage on a valued basis and one that provides coverage on either an actual cash value basis or on a replacement cost basis. For property covered on a valued basis, the amount for which an item is insured is agreed to be the value of the item for loss settlement purposes.

Insurers often require an appraisal of each article before it is insured; however, the sales slip on a recently purchased item is sufficient to establish the value of the item.

Listed below is information about each of the nine classes of property.

1. **Personal furs.** Items eligible for coverage include garments made of fur or trimmed with fur. It must be the dressed pelt of an animal and not a manmade fabric. There are three exclusions: (1) loss caused by wear and tear, gradual deterioration, and insects; (2) loss by nuclear radiation or radioactive contamination; (3) and loss due to war.

2. **Personal jewelry.** Personal jewelry is covered essentially the same as with furs. Each item must be scheduled with an amount of insurance

applicable to the item. In addition to the normal exclusions, the insured cannot collect for a total loss if one item in a pair or set is lost or destroyed.

3. **Silverware.** Coverage is provided on valuable silverware, silverplated ware, and the like. The coverage is essentially the same as that provided for jewelry.

4. **Golfer's equipment.** Eligible equipment includes clubs, golf clothing (excluding watches and jewelry), and other clothing that is contained in a locker in a clubhouse or other building used in connection with the game of golf. The coverage is on an open peril basis for most items, except golf balls, which is limited to perils of fire and burglary.

5. **Cameras.** Eligible equipment includes cameras, projection machines, moveable sound equipment, films, binoculars and telescopes. The only exclusions are those of the wear and tear variety, war, and radioactive contamination.

6. **Fine arts and antiques.** Items eligible for coverage include objects such as paintings, statuary, are manuscripts, and antiques. The coverage is open peril with the usual exceptions for wear and tear, insects, war, and radio-active contamination. In addition to these, fine arts and antiques are subject to three additional exclusions: (1) damage caused by repairing, restoration, or retouching processes; (2) breakage of certain breakable objects except when caused by a named peril; (3) loss by any cause to property on exhibition at fair grounds or premises of national or international expositions unless the premises are covered by the policy. It is customary to insure antiques and fine art on a valued rather than an actual cash value basis.

7. **Postage stamps.** Eligible items comprise postage stamps including due, envelope, official, revenue, match and medicine, covers, locals, reprints, essays, proofs, and other philatelic property owned by the insured including the books, pages, or mountings. In addition to the customary exclusions, damage resulting from fading, creasing, denting, scratching, tearing, thinning, transfer of colors, or damage arising while the property is being worked on is excluded. Loss by theft from an unattended auto is also excluded except while being shipped by registered mail. In addition, the policy also excludes mysterious disappearance of individual stamps unless the item has been specifically scheduled, or unless mounted in a volume and the page to which the stamp is attached is also lost. The policy also contains a limit of $250 on any unscheduled stamp, pair, block, or series.

8. **Rare and current coins.** Items eligible for coverage includes rare and current coins, medals, paper money, bank notes, tokens of money, and other numismatic property. In addition to the customary exclusions, damage resulting from fading, creasing, denting, scratching, tearing, thinning, transfer of colors, or damage arising while the property is being worked on is excluded. Loss by theft from an unattended auto is also excluded except while being shipped by registered mail. The policy also contains a limit of no more than $1,000 on unscheduled numismatic property.

9. **Musical instruments.** The only unusual condition in this coverage involves an agreement on the part of the insured that none of the

instruments insured will be played for remuneration during the term of the policy unless permitted by endorsement and the payment of an additional premium.

Q3:144 What is an inflation guard endorsement?

The inflation guard endorsement is an option that automatically increases the amount of insurance under the policy by some percentage of dwelling coverage amount every quarter. The purpose of the endorsement is to help the insured meet the provisions regarding the replacement cost of the dwelling, and to help protect against underinsurance that might result from inflation.

Q3:145 What other options are available to homeowners?

There are a large number of other options, riders, and endorsements available to homeowners insurance policies. Listed below are some of the available options:

1. **Additional limits of liability.** This endorsement amends Coverages A, B & C of the policy to provide replacement-cost coverage at the time of loss, regardless of the stated policy limit.
2. **Increased special limits.** This endorsement to Coverage C can be used to increase coverage for some of the items that have specific limit amounts, such as jewelry, firearms, securities, and money.
3. **Increased limits on Business Property.** This endorsement allows a policy owner to increase the $2,500 limit that applies to business property on the premises.
4. **Increased limits of Other Structures.** This endorsement is used to increase the amount of insurance for other structures on the property (Coverage B).
5. **Business Pursuits coverage.** This endorsement provides coverage for liability that arises out of or in connection with a business engaged in by an insured.
6. **Watercraft coverage.** This endorsement provides coverage for boats that are longer or more powerful than those covered by the standard homeowners coverage.

Automobile Insurance

Q3:146 What coverage is available in a personal auto policy?

The personal auto policy provides four types of insurance coverage:

1. Part A—Liability Coverage
2. Part B—Medical Payments Coverage
3. Part C—Uninsured Motorists Coverage
4. Part D—Coverage for Damage to your Auto

A personal auto policy can be written on eligible vehicles owned or leased by an individual, or by a husband or wife residing in the same household. Eligible vehicles include private passenger automobiles, such as cars, vans, and sports utility vehicles. Pickups are also eligible, provided their gross weight is less than 10,000 pounds. Vans and pickups are ineligible for coverage if they are used for the transportation or delivery of goods and materials, except when they are used for farming or ranching, or their use is incidental to the named insurer's business. Other vehicles such as motor homes, motorcycles, golf carts, and snowmobiles can also be insured by endorsement in most states.

Liability Coverage Part A of the personal auto policy provides bodily injury and property damage liability protection to any insured that is legally responsible for an automobile accident. The coverage protects the insured in case of a claim or lawsuit up to the limits provided in the policy.

The liability limits are selected by the policy owner and apply to each covered accident. The policy typically provides for split limits, such as $25,000/$50,000/$25,000. The first limit is the maximum amount that will be paid to any one person for bodily injury. The second limit is the aggregate that will be paid for all bodily injury claims. The third limit is the aggregate that will be paid for all property damage claims. Again, these numbers are for each accident.

Generally, the liability insurance "follows the auto." This means that the policy that lists the car involved in an accident covers the accident first, followed by the policy that covers the driver, but not the specific car.

The personal auto policy covers the named insured, his or her spouse, and family members living with the named insured or spouse. Other persons are covered only while using a covered auto with permission.

The liability portion of the insurance policy also includes some supplementary payments for bail bonds ($250), appeal bonds, post-judgment interest, loss of earnings by the insured for testifying (up to $200 per day), and the reasonable expenses incurred at the request of the insurer.

Medical Payments Coverage Part B of the personal auto policy provides payment for the reasonable and necessary medical expenses of an insured as a result of an automobile accident. Only those expenses that result from medical services rendered within three years of the date of an accident are covered. The benefits are also paid without regard to fault.

The limit for coverage typically ranges from $1,000 to $10,000, and applies separately to each person injured in an accident.

Part B covers the named insured, spouse, and any family members while occupying an auto or as a pedestrian, if struck by a motor vehicle designed for use mainly on public roads. The policy also covers any other person while occupying the covered automobile.

Uninsured Motorists Coverage Under Part C of the personal auto policy, the insurer agrees to pay compensatory damages that an insured is legally entitled to recover from the owner or operator of an *uninsured motor vehicle* due to bodily injury sustained by an insured and caused by the accident. Some states will also pay for property damage due to the accident.

An uninsured motor vehicle is defined as:

- A vehicle that has no automobile insurance;
- A vehicle that is insured for less than the limits of the financial responsibility laws of the state where the auto is principally garaged;
- A hit-and-run vehicle whose operator cannot be identified that hits the named insured, a family member, a vehicle that any of the insured persons are occupying, or a covered auto; or
- A vehicle to which insurance applies at the time of the accident, but the insurance company either denies coverage, or is insolvent.

Coverage for Damage to Your Auto Part D of the personal auto policy provides coverage for direct and accidental physical damage (including theft) to the covered auto and any non-owned auto. Coverage includes *collision* and *other than collision*. Collision refers to the impact of the covered auto or a nonowned auto with another object, or if the auto is overturned. Other than collision, formerly known as comprehensive coverage, is a form of open perils coverage that covers items such as, fire, falling objects, windstorm, hail, breakage of glass, and contact with a bird or animal.

Coverage in Part D of the policy is on an actual cash value basis, and is usually subject to a deductible per occurrence.

Certain property within the vehicle is not covered under Part D. This includes:

- Electronic equipment designed for the reproduction of sound this is not permanently installed in the automobile;
- Electronic equipment, such as citizens band radios, telephone, two-way mobile radios, scanning monitor receivers, television monitor receivers, video and audio cassette recorders, and personal computers;
- Radar detectors; and
- Tapes, records, compact discs, and other media.

Q3:147   What other endorsements are available?

There are many different endorsements that are available for your automobile insurance. Listed below are several of these endorsements:

- **Underinsured Motorists coverage.** This endorsement amends Part C of the policy to provide coverage similar to the uninsured motorists coverage. An underinsured motorist is one who is insured, but whose own liability limits are less than those listed in the endorsement. For example, if an insured that is covered for $100,000 of underinsured motorists coverage were injured by a negligent motorist who only carried $25,000 of liability coverage, the insured would have $75,000 of coverage under this endorsement.

- **Named non-owner coverage.** This endorsement is available for persons who do not own an automobile but want to have protection when they drive non-owned vehicles, such as a neighbor's car. This also pertains when borrowing a car that is inadequately insured. Parts A, B, and C of the personal auto policy are available to the insured. The coverage is excess over any other coverage applicable to the borrowed auto, and does not apply to the owner of the auto.

- **Miscellaneous type vehicle endorsement.** This endorsement is used to cover miscellaneous types of owned vehicles, such as motor homes, motorcycles and similar type of vehicles, all-terrain vehicles, dune buggies, and golf carts. Each vehicle is listed in a schedule, and the same coverage that applies to the automobiles can be purchases.

- **Towing and labor costs coverage.** This endorsement pays for towing and labor if a covered auto or a non-owned auto is disabled for any reason. The limit of coverage is a stated amount, such as $50, or $100 per occurrence. The labor costs of repair work, such as changing a flat tire, are covered only at the place the auto is disabled.

Q3:148　Can you buy coverage for an antique or classic automobile?

Yes. Depending on the insurance company, you can purchase an endorsement to your personal auto policy, or purchase a separate policy for the antique or classic vehicle. The endorsement or policy is usually written to cover the automobile for a specified dollar amount, instead of up to the actual cash value of the automobile. This is done because the value of an antique or classic auto can vary significantly.

An antique auto is defined as a motor vehicle of the private passenger type that is 25 years old or older and is maintained primarily for use in exhibitions, club activities, parades, and other functions of public interest. It may occasionally be used for other purposes. A classic auto is a motor vehicle of the private passenger type that is 10 years old or older and may be used on a regular basis.

Q3:149　What is no-fault coverage?

Under a no-fault system, there is no attempt to fix blame or to place the burden of the loss on the party causing it; each party collects for any injuries sustained from his or her own insurance company. Under a pure no-fault system, the right to sue the driver who caused an accident would be abolished, and both the innocent victim and the driver at fault would recover their losses directly from their own insurance company. Compulsory first-party coverage would compensate all accident victims regardless of fault.

Although the basic no-fault concept is simple, several modifications to the idea have developed, and three different approaches are listed below.

1. **Pure no-fault proposals.** Under a pure no-fault plan, the tort system would be abolished for bodily injuries arising from auto accidents (some policies would abolish tort actions for auto damages too). Anyone suffering a loss would seek recovery for medical expenses, loss of income, or other expenses from his or her own insurer. Recovery for general damages (pain and suffering) would be eliminated.

2. **Modified no-fault proposals.** Modified no-fault proposals would provide limited immunity from tort action to the extent that the injured party was indemnified under a first-party coverage. For losses above the recovered amount, tort action would be retained. In some proposals, payment for pain and suffering would be limited or eliminated.

3. **Expanded first-party coverage.** In this case there is no exemption from tort liability, and the injured party collects benefits under a first-party coverage, retaining the right to sue for losses more than the amount paid. The insurer paying the first-party benefits retains subrogation.

Umbrella Liability Insurance

Q3:150   What is umbrella liability insurance?

The personal umbrella liability policy is designed primarily to provide liability coverage for catastrophic legal claims or judgments. The smallest limit of coverage available from most insurers is $1 million, and limits up to $5 or $10 million are typically available. The policy covers not only bodily injury and property damage liability but also personal injury liability.

The personal umbrella liability policy requires the policy owner to carry certain underlying liability coverages in auto, homeowners, boat, or motorcycle policies. For example, one may be required to have automobile liability coverage of $250,000/$500,000/$50,000 and homeowners liability of $300,000. If a claim is made under an underlying policy, the umbrella policy will pay only after the limits of the underlying policy are exhausted. For example, assume an individual has a $1 million umbrella policy and carries an automobile liability policy of the required amount of $250,000 per person. If a legal judgment of $600,000 is obtained against the insured, the underlying auto policy will pay $250,000 and the umbrella policy will pay the remaining $350,000.

If the policy owner fails to maintain the required underlying coverage, the insurer will pay only the amount it would have been required to pay if the underlying policies had been in force. Using the same example above, assume that the insured only had an auto liability policy limit of $50,000 per person, rather than the required $250,000 limit. In this case the auto policy would pay $50,000, the umbrella policy would still only pay $350,000. The remaining $200,000 would have to be paid by the insured.

The personal umbrella policy provides coverage for the named insured, spouse, and family members living in the household. Other residents of the household who are under the age of 21 and in the care of an insured are usually covered too.

Q 3:151   What exclusions apply to umbrella liability insurance?

Although the coverage under the umbrella liability policy is far broader than that of the individual contracts, it does not cover all risks. There are exclusions, and some of them are rather important. Some of the exclusions often found in personal umbrella policies include liability arising from the following:

- Government programs such as worker's compensation
- Intentional injury unless it results from actions to prevent or eliminate danger or to protect persons or property
- Damage to property owned by an insured
- Damage to certain types of non-owned property in an insured's care, custody, or control, e.g., automobiles, watercraft, and aircraft
- The use of watercraft, and possibly other recreational vehicles, unless covered by underlying policies
- The use of aircraft
- Business pursuits, other than those arising out of a personal automobile or when underlying coverage exists
- Transmission of communicable diseases
- Sexual molestation, corporal punishment, and physical or mental abuse
- Directors' and officers' activities, other than those performed for a notfor-profit organization but only if the insured receives no compensation other than reimbursement of expenses.

Chapter 4

Equities

A thorough understanding of the equities market is essential to the financial planner. This Chapter provides an overview of the securities market, and includes the technical knowledge necessary to invest successfully in equities.

Organization of Security Markets

Q 4:1   What is the primary market?

The *primary market* is composed of government bonds, municipal bonds, and common stocks as they are originally sold. An initial public offering (known as an IPO) occurs when a security is sold to the public for the first time. The IPO often involves an investment banker introducing a new security to the public. Investment bankers generally specialize in selling securities in the primary market while simultaneously operating in the secondary markets, as discussed in Q 4:2. The bankers tend to act as intermediaries between the issuer and the investors. The issuer sells securities to the investment bankers, who than sell the securities to the public in a process called *underwriting*. Sales of new common stock for a company whose shares are already traded in the market are called *seasoned issues*. In addition, under Rule 415 the Securities & Exchange Commission (SEC) permits companies to file a short-form registration for securities that are to be sold over a period of time. These are called *shelf offerings*. Shelf offerings provide cost savings and flexibility because securities can be sold when conditions are favorable and not sold when conditions are unfavorable.

Q 4:2   What is the secondary market?

The secondary market is where securities are traded after the original sale. Secondary markets are very important to investors because they provide liquidity. The more liquidity a security has, the more willing an investor is to buy it. Therefore, investors are also more willing to buy securities in the primary market because those securities can later be sold in the secondary market. The transfer of securities may occur through an organized exchange, where the market price of securities is determined by buyers and sellers. Organized exchanges are auction markets, such as the New York Stock Exchange (NYSE), the American Stock Exchange (ASE), and other regional exchanges. Investors are represented by brokers who attempt to get the best possible price and act as intermediaries representing both buyers and sellers. In contrast, the "over the counter" (OTC) market is an unorganized market consisting of a network of dealers who buy and sell securities for their own accounts. Unlike brokers, dealers have a vested interest because the securities are bought and sold by the dealers. The dealers earn a profit between the buying and selling prices, which is called the *spread*. Most major OTC companies trade on the NASDAQ, an acronym for National Association of Security Dealers Automatic Quotation system. Consisting of a network of market makers competing freely with each other and unlike the NYSE, the NASDAQ does not have a specific location.

Q 4:3   What are the third and fourth markets?

The *third market* is not a location but a system in which NYSE-listed stocks are traded in the OTC market. The third market provides investors with the flexibility to trade while the NYSE is closed. These trades are usually large—consisting of blocks of 10,000 shares or more. The participants are often institutional investors such as pension plans, mutual funds, or insurance companies. The institutional investors work through large brokerage firms who match buyers and sellers and sometimes take positions themselves to facilitate trading.

The *fourth market* involves transactions between financial institutions without the use of a broker dealer. The fourth market is a communication network between investors consisting of larger block trades. There are several privately owned networks in which to trade, with the largest being a computerized network called the Instinet (institutional network). Instinet is always open for trading stocks, thereby saving investors on transaction costs. Instinet also allows large traders to bypass brokers and prevent leaks about who is transacting the trade.

The Mechanics of Investing in Securities

Q 4:4   What does it mean to "sell short"?

A *short sell* is the sale of borrowed securities in anticipation of a price drop. The short seller profits by selling the securities first with the intention of purchasing them back at a lower price. For example, an investor sells 100 shares on *XYZ* short at $100 and later buys those shares back at $70, resulting in a $3,000 profit.

Q 4:5   When should an investor sell short?

An investor should sell short when he or she believes a stock is overpriced and expects the price to drop. The investor does not own the securities that are being sold short. These securities are sold short with a contract for future delivery. In effect, the broker borrows shares held in a margin account and lends them to the short seller (shares held in a cash account cannot be lent to a short seller). These shares are sold in the open market. The proceeds are not delivered to the seller; they are held by the broker. These proceeds are used at a later date to buy back the shares (covering the short). In addition, the short seller must deposit money to cover the margin requirement for buying the shares back. The money is returned to the short seller minus any losses or plus any gains when the short position is covered.

Q 4:6   What are the technical points affecting short sales?

Three technical points affect short sales. First, if the price of a stock moves up from the previous trade, it is called an *uptick*. If the price of a stock declines from the previous trade, it is called a *downtick*. If the price of a stock does not change from a previous uptick, it is called a *zero uptick*. Investors may sell short only when the last trade for a stock is an uptick or zero uptick, which is called the uptick rule. The reason for this rule is to prevent traders from manipulating the market. Without the rule, short sellers could borrow large quantities of stock to sell short, thereby driving down the market. Second, short sellers must pay all dividends that are owed to the lender of the security. Third, the short seller must deposit margin money to guarantee the repurchase of the security. For example, assume the margin requirement is 50 percent. If an investor sells short 100 shares of *XYZ* at $70, the initial deposit must be $7,000 × 50 percent, or $3,500. This money is returned to the short seller with any gain or loss when the short position is covered.

Q 4:7   How is stock bought on margin?

When an investor purchases stock on margin, he or she makes an initial payment similar to a down payment on a house and borrows the remaining funds necessary to make the purchase. The investor is buying securities with borrowed money. The minimum required equity position is called the *margin requirement* and is set by the Federal Reserve Bank. For example, if the initial margin requirement is 35 percent, this means that the borrower must provide 35 percent of the funds, and the brokerage firm lends the remaining 65 percent. The investor pays interest on the borrowed funds. Buying on margin provides significant leverage to an investor. If the price of a stock goes up, the customer's profits accumulate much faster. If the price of a stock drops, the percentage of the loss is greater. The leverage factor can be calculated as 1 ÷ margin %. For example, at a 35 percent margin requirement, the leverage rate is 2.85 (1 ÷ .35). If the rate of return on the stock is 10 percent, the rate of return using a 2.85 leverage rate is 28.5 percent or 185 percent more.

Q 4:8   How is the rate of return calculated on a margin transaction?

Assume the investor purchases 100 shares of *XYZ* at $70 per share. The 100 shares of *XYZ* stock are later sold at $90 per share. The investor's return is 28 percent (($90 ÷ $70)−1 × 100). Assuming the same shares were purchased with an initial margin requirement of 50 percent, the cost of the investment is $3,500 ($7,000 × 50%). The shares are later sold at $90. The position is worth $5,500 ($9,000 − $3,500). The return is 57 percent on the investment (($5,500 ÷ 35,000)−1 × 100).

Q 4:9   What is the maintenance margin and how is a maintenance call calculated?

The *maintenance margin* is the minimum equity required for a margin position. If the customer's balance drops below the maintenance margin, the investor will get a margin call and must deposit additional funds or sell shares of the stock to cover the call. The maintenance margin protects the firm from being exposed to too much risk. The following formulas are used to indicate what stock price will trigger a margin call. [Schweser, 2000]

$$\text{Long} = \frac{[\text{original price } (1 - \text{initial margin} \%)]}{1 - \text{maintenance margin} \%}$$

$$\text{Short} = \frac{[\text{original price } (1 + \text{initial margin} \%)]}{1 + \text{maintenance margin} \%}$$

For example, an investor buys stock at $50. The initial margin requirement is 50 percent, and the maintenance margin requirement is 35 percent. If the stock drops to $38 the investor will get a margin call. The calculation is

$$\text{Long} = \frac{\$50 \ (1 - .50)}{1 - .35} = \$38.50$$

Investing Internationally in Equities

Q 4:10   What are American depository receipts?

Foreign firms are permitted to have their shares traded on U.S. exchanges. One way is to have their shares directly available for trading by listing them on the exchanges. These shares are traded exactly like those of any U.S. company. The other way that foreign firms may trade is by issuing American depository receipts (ADRs). ADRs represent indirect ownership in shares of a foreign company. ADRs are tradable receipts issued by U.S. banks that have physical possession of shares held on deposit by correspondent banks in the home country of the company whose shares are issued. The correspondent bank holding the shares receives the dividends and converts them into U.S. dollars after paying all foreign withholding taxes. ADRs are an effective way to invest in foreign companies without having to worry about currency risks.

Security Market Indicators

Q 4:11   What is a price-weighted series?

A price-weighted series is the arithmetic average of current values. Two stock prices are considered equal regardless of the number of shares outstanding. The price-weighted series will add the price of all stocks and divide it by the total number of stocks. For example, a $10 stock and $20 stock have an average price of $15 ($10 + $20 ÷ 2). A price-weighted series is adjusted for stock splits. The denominator would adjust downward to make sure the $15 value is maintained. The adjustment for a split is calculated by the following:

Stock	Prices	Prices
A	$10	$10
B	$20	$10 (2:1 stock split)
	$30	$20

The new index value equals the current stock price divided by the number of stocks adjusted for splits. The price-weighted average before the split is $30÷2=$15. After the split, the price-weighted average is still $20 ÷ X= $15, therefore, X= 1.3333 (X is the new divisor).

The major problem with this series is that higher-priced stocks tend to carry more weight than lower-priced stocks. The problem is more evident with rapidly growing stocks that split often, because the denominator is adjusted downward to look the same as before the split. Therefore, fast-growing successful firms lose weight in the index because of stock splits. The Dow Jones industrial average is a price-weighted index. See Q 4:39. The following example represents why the Dow Jones is not a good indicator of stock movement:

Stock	Price	Shares Outstanding	Market Value
A	$100	100	$10,000
B	$ 1	10,000	$10,000

The price-weighted index equals $50.50 (i.e., ($100 + $1) ÷ 2). If stock A doubles, the index goes to $100.50 (i.e., ($200 + $1) ÷ 2). If stock B doubles, the index goes to $51 (i.e., ($100 + $2) ÷ 2). Both stocks have the same market value; they differ only in shares outstanding. However, if A doubles in value, the index goes up 50 points; while if B doubles in value it goes up only 0.50 points. In general, this is a poor indicator of market movement. However, if an investor's portfolio contains an equal number of shares of each stock, it can be measured against a price-weighted index.

Q 4:12   What is a value-weighted series in an index?

A value-weighted index allows for a stock's total number of outstanding shares to be used in a series. The value is derived by taking the market value of all stocks. Market value equals current market price multiplied by total number of shares outstanding. The current market value is compared to the prior "base" value to determine the percentage of change, which then is applied to a beginning index value. The value is often considered a base and is assigned an index value of 100 (or it can be 10, 50, etc.). The new index value is shown in the following equation. [Reilly & Brown, 2000]

$$\frac{\text{Market price today} \times \text{total number of outstanding shares}}{\text{Market price in base year} \times \text{total number of outstanding shares in base year}} \times \text{Beginning Index Value}$$

An example is

Stock	Share Price	Number of Shares	Market Value
Prior Year Market Value			
A	$ 8	12,500,000	$100,000,000
B	$40	10,000,000	$400,000,000
			$500,000,000
Current Market Value (After 2-for-1 stock split by Stock B)			
A	$10	12,500,000	$125,000,000
B	$20	20,000,000	$400,000,000
			$525,000,000

$$\text{New Index Value} = \frac{\text{Current Market Value}}{\text{Market Value in BaseYear}} \times \text{Beginning Index Value}$$

$$= \frac{\$525,000,000}{\$500,000,000} \times 100 = 105$$

Therefore, the value-weighted percentage return is 5 percent (*i.e.*,$(105 \div 100-1)$ $\times$ 100). This shows that there is an automatic adjustment for splits in a value-weighted series. In a value-weighted series, wealth is equally influenced by price changes in stocks. The following example demonstrates this relationship. [Schweser, 2000]

Stock	Price	Shares Outstanding	Market Value
A	$100	100	$10,000
B	$ 1	10,000	$10,000

Assume market value in base year equals $20,000.

$$\text{The market value} - \text{weighted index equals} \frac{\$20,000}{\text{Base of }\$20,000} \times 100 = 100$$

$$\text{If stock } A \text{ doubles, the index equals} \frac{\$30,000}{\text{Base of }\$20,000} \times 100 = 150$$

$$\text{If stock } B \text{ doubles, the index equals} \frac{\$30,000}{\text{Base of }\$20,000} \times 100 = 150$$

However, the problem with a market value-weighted series is if the market capitalization for stock A and B is different, then the index is biased in the direction of the larger company. If a portfolio is built as a weighting of shares purchased by capitalization, then performance can be measured against a value-weighted index. Value-weighted indexes include Standard & Poor's 500 Index, New York Stock Exchange Index, Nasdaq Index, AMEX Market Value Index, Wilshire 5000 Equity Index, and Russell 2000 Index.

Q 4:13   What is an unweighted (equal-weighted) price indicator series?

An unweighted price indicator series assumes that an equal dollar amount is invested in each stock. For example, assume $100 is invested in each stock. That is, 10 shares for a $10 stock, and 5 shares for a $20 stock. The total cost of 15 shares is $200.

Thus:

$$\frac{\$200}{15} = \$13.33$$

If the stocks rise to $17 and $25, respectively, the value changes to:

$$\$170 + \$125 = \$295$$

Therefore, the new average value is $295 ÷ 15 = $19.67.

If a portfolio is built by buying the equal dollar amount for each stock, then it can be measured against an equal weighted index. The value line composite average is an equally weighted geometric average.

Q 4:14   How does the geometric average compare to the arithmetic average?

A geometric mean is found by multiplying the different stock prices and then taking the n th root, where n equals the number of stocks. The geometric mean tends to produce a downward bias in the index when compared to the arithmetic mean. This is illustrated by taking two stocks priced at $10 and $20:

$$\text{The geometric average is } (\$10 \times \$20)^{1/2} = \$14.14$$

$$\text{The arithmetic average is } \frac{\$10 + \$20}{2} = \$15$$

We find that the geometric average is lower than the arithmetic average. Most annual returns are calculated using the geometric average because n represents the number of compounding periods. Compounding allows for the true yearly return to be determined. The value line composite average uses the geometric mean to average its stock returns.

The Role of Dividends

Q 4:15   Why are dividends important?

Dividends are important because they signify management's ability to generate income. They also play a large part in the valuation process. Dividend growth is a component of stock valuation models used by analysts to find the intrinsic value of a company. Dividends may also influence external financing plans by financial managers. If too many dividends are paid out by the firm, this can lead to fewer internal funds for growing the business. In return, management may have to go to external sources to raise capital, such as new stock or bond issues. This can change the firm's capital structure and cost of capital. Therefore, it is important for management to find a balance between what the firm pays out in dividends to attract investors and what the firm reinvests in internal sources to maximize the price of the firm's stock. Finally, because management seeks to maximize investor wealth, it must determine who may earn a greater return on the funds. If management earns a greater return on the funds, then reinvesting the earnings makes more sense than paying them out.

Q 4:16   What is the dividend yield?

The dividend yield is the relationship between the current dividend payment and the current price of the stock.

$$\text{Current dividend yield} = \frac{\text{Current dividend}}{\text{Current price of stock}}$$

If a company pays out $5 in dividends and is trading at $100, the dividend yield is 5 percent ($5 ÷ $100). The yield is often compared with other yields in the same industry to see if it is comparable to others.

Q 4:17   How is the growth rate of dividends obtained?

First, it is important to understand the role of dividends in determining the value of a stock. The value of a stock is often found by using the *constant divi- dend growth model*. The model assumes that current dividends (D_0) will grow (g) at the same rate each year to infinity. Therefore, when calculating the value of common stock (V_0), it is necessary to estimate the growth rate of dividends. In addition, the required rate of return or discount rate (k) also needs to be estimated to be used in the model. Finally, the dividend (D_0) is adjusted for one year's growth. The equation is

$$V_0 = \frac{D_0(1+g)}{k-g} \text{ or } \frac{D_1}{k-g}$$

where V_0 is the price of the stock, D_0 is the latest dividend paid per share, D_1 is the expected dividend per share for Year 1, k is the required rate of return on the stock, and g is the expected growth rate of dividends. The stock's present value is the current dividend multiplied by the growth rate in earnings and dividends divided by the required rate of return.

The discount rate (k) can be calculated by using the capital asset pricing model (CAPM) equation:

$$K_{stock} = R_{risk\,free} + Beta_{stock}\,(R_{market} - R_{risk\,free})$$

The growth rate of dividends can be calculated two ways.

Method I

Valuation models for common stocks depend heavily on the growth rate for estimating a stock's price. Growth is influenced by how well a company utilizes retained earnings and how much is paid out in dividends. The growth rate of earnings is equal to the percentage of net earnings retained times the rate of return on equity capital.

$$\text{Growth Rate (g)} = \text{Return on Equity} \times \text{Retention Rate}$$

where

$$\text{Retention rate} = 1 - \text{Payout ratio}$$

$$\text{Payout ratio} = \frac{\text{Dividends}}{\text{Earnings}}$$

$$\text{Return on Equity (ROE)} = \frac{\text{Net Income}}{\text{Equity}}$$

The relationship between growth, the retention rate, and return on equity is summarized by the following example:

Example 4-1: The firm earns $2, distributes $0.85 in dividends, and retains only $1.15. The payout ratio is 42 percent, and the retention ratio is 58 percent. The return on equity is 20 percent. The growth rate is

$$g = .58 \times .20 = 11.6\%$$

This means that future earnings (and future dividends) are expected to grow at 11.6 percent. There are some interesting dynamics resulting from this relationship. If the firm increases its return on equity, the dividend can be increased without a corresponding increase in the growth rate. For example, if the return on equity increases to 33.14 percent, the firm can distribute 65 percent of its earnings and still achieve an 11.6 percent growth rate. If the firm were to increase the dividend without a corresponding increase in the return on equity, the growth rate would decrease because fewer earnings are retained for future business needs. If the firm distributes $1.25 in dividends and retains only $0.75 in earnings, the retention ratio becomes 38 percent and, correspondingly, the growth rate drops to 7.6 percent. Therefore, an increase in return on equity will increase the rate of growth, and the spread between the required return (*k*) minus rate of growth (*g*) will decrease. Alternatively, a firm may increase its growth rate by increasing its retention rate. The result is a rising stock price.

Method II

An alternative way to estimate the growth rate is to compute the historical growth rate using time value. Assume that dividends increased from $0.20 to $.85 over a 10-year period. To calculate the growth rate using a calculator

$$PV = -.28; \; FV = .85; \; PMT = 0; \; N = 10; \; \text{Solve I}$$

The growth rate given is 11 percent. Note that the growth rate is the same as that computed in Method I when using a future value table for 10 years.

**Q 4:18   How is the payout ratio found and how is it used in valuation?
(Groppelli & Nikbakht, 2000)**

The payout ratio is found by comparing dividends per share to earnings per share.

$$\text{Dividend payout ratio} = \frac{\text{Dividends per share}}{\text{Earnings per share}}$$

Assume that Company A pays a $2.50 dividend and Company B pays $1.50. Company A's EPS are $5.00 and Company B's are $2.00. To solve:

$$\text{Payout ratio of Company } A = \frac{\$2.50}{\$5.00} = 50\%$$

$$\text{Payout ratio of Company } B = \frac{\$1.50}{\$2.00} = 75\%$$

Company A pays out 50 percent of earnings and Company B pays out 75 percent. The payout ratio is used to determine the price/earnings ratio (P/E) of a stock. The calculation is

$$P/E = \frac{\text{Payout ratio}}{k - g}$$

where k is the required rate of return on the stock and g is the expected growth rate of dividends. The payout ratio should be used in conjunction with the discount rate and growth rate. If both companies had the same g and k, then Company B would have a higher P/E than Company A.

$$P/E_a = \frac{.50}{.15 - .10} = 10 \text{ times} \qquad P/E_b = \frac{.75}{.15 - .10} = 15 \text{ times}$$

The payout ratio varies from company to company and industry to industry. Generally speaking, fast-growing companies pay few to no dividends. In this case, the payout ratio may be very low. The opposite can be said about utility companies, who pay a large amount of earnings as dividends.

The payout ratio may not be a good indication of earnings and dividend stability. When business is bad, the payout ratio may greatly increase because companies try to pay out the same amount in dividends even though earnings are falling. However, a stable dividend policy sends a message that the company is able to generate income, and the dividend is not going away even in tough times. This can result in a loyal base of investors in the company's stock. Erratic dividends create uncertainty about a firm's future. Also, reducing dividends may send a negative signal to the capital markets and improperly drive the stock price down.

Before setting the dividend policy, management should (1) determine the growth of future earnings and cash flows (operating income $(1 - \text{tax rate}) + \text{depreciation}$); (2) find out how sensitive earnings are to economic influences and changes in the business cycle; and (3) calculate the dividend yields and payouts of other firms in the industry. Cash flows reflect more accurately than earnings the ability of a company to pay dividends. Setting the right dividend policy is very important for determining stock value. The ultimate goal is to signal that dividends will be maintained even in tough times. However, the dividend policy chosen must be in conjunction with the firm's capital structure and investment goals.

Q 4:19   What are the declaration date, ex-dividend date, and payment date?

Declaration Date. The declaration date is the date when the board of directors passes a resolution to pay a dividend.

Ex-Dividend Date. In return, brokerage firms and stock exchanges establish the ex-dividend date to make sure the right people get the dividend. The exdividend date is two business days before the date of record. If an investor buys the stock before the ex-dividend date, he or she is entitled to receive the dividend. If the investor buys the stock after this date, he or she will not receive the dividend. Before the date, the stock trades "cum dividend."

The price of the stock declines by the amount of the dividend per share on the ex-dividend date. Assume a $100 priced stock that pays a $1.00 dividend. On the ex-dividend date, the stock's price will drop to $99, but the stockholder will receive $1.00 in dividends, so there is no change in overall value to the stockholder. A firm's balance sheet will be adjusted too. Both cash and retained earnings decline by the amount of dividends paid.

Date of Record. The corporation prepares a list of all individuals believed to be stockholders. The date of record is then the date on which holders of record are designated to receive the dividend.

Date of Payment. The date of payment is when dividends are mailed out to stockholders.

Q 4:20   What changes occur when a stock is split?

A stock split is an increase in a firm's number of shares outstanding and is expressed as a ratio. For example, a two-for-one stock split means that a stockholder who has owned 100 shares will now own 200 shares. A three-for-two stock split means that 100 shares increase to 150 shares ($(3 \div 2) \times 100$).

Q 4:21   What is a stock dividend and when is it paid?

A stock dividend is a payment made by the firm in the form of additional shares instead of cash and is expressed as a percentage. For example, a 20 percent stock dividend means that shareholders receive one new share for every five shares owned. Therefore, an investor who owns 100 shares will now have 120 shares. The result is a 20 percent increase in the total number of outstanding shares. Shareholders do not gain value after a stock dividend or split because the price of the stock declines by the same percentage as the stock dividend or split.

Q 4:22   What is the effect of noncash dividends on the balance sheet?

Cash and stock dividends produce different results on the balance sheet, and stock splits have no effect on the capital structure of a firm. Cash dividends result in a reduction in cash and a corresponding reduction in retained earnings. Stock dividends increase the total number of outstanding shares, increase the total value of common stock par and paid-in-capital surplus, and reduce retained earnings. Please note that the par value of a stock is an arbitrary amount, and the paid-in capital surplus is the difference between what the firm originally sold the shares for and the par value. Stock splits reduce par value but do not change the common equity part of the balance sheet. The shares are increased but there is a counterbalancing decline in par value.The following explains the effect of a 10 percent stock dividend on the balance sheet. [Groppelli & Nikbakht, 2000]

	Before Stock Dividend	*After Stock Dividend*
Common stock ($1 par, 1,000,000 shares outstanding)	$ 1,000,000	
Common stock ($1 par, 1.1,000,000 shares outstanding)		$ 1,100,000
Capital in excess of par value	10,000,000	13,400,000
Retained earnings	6,000,000	2,500,000
Total stockholder's equity	$17,000,000	$17,000,000

Assume the market value of a share of stock is $35. The number of new shares is 100,000 (1,000,000 × .10), and the value of the new shares is $3.5 million (100,000 × $35). The $3.5 million is divided into $100,000 100,000 shares × $1 par value) added to common stock, with the remaining $3.4 million ($3,500,000 − $100,000) going to capital surplus. Additionally, $3.5 million comes out of retained earnings. Total shareholder equity is left unchanged because no cash has come in or out. The following explains the effect of a two-for-one stock split on the balance sheet.

	Before Stock Dividend	*After Stock Dividend*
Common stock ($1 par, 1,000,000 shares outstanding)	$ 1,000,000	
Common stock ($.50 par, 2,000,000 shares outstanding)		$ 1,000,000
Capital in excess of par value	10,000,000	10,000,000
Retained earnings	6,000,000	6,000,000
Total stockholder's equity	$17,000,000	$17,000,000

There is a reduction in the par value from $1 to $0.50, and the number of outstanding shares doubles to $2.0 million. However, there is no change in the capital structure of the firm. Total shareholder equity is left unchanged.

Q 4:23   How can a company increase shareholder value by buying back the company stock?

A firm with excess cash may decide to buy back some of its shares through a repurchase program. When a firm buys back shares it decreases the number of shares outstanding and increases the earnings per share because the earnings are spread over fewer shares. As a result of increasing earnings, the return on equity (ROE) will also increase. The return on equity is a component of growth.

$$\text{Growth rate(g)} = \text{ROE}^*(1 - \text{Payout ratio})$$

An increase in growth should cause a corresponding increase in the company's stock price.

To see how ownership interest increases, assume a company has 10.0 million shares outstanding and an investor owns 1.0 million shares, which equals a 10 percent ownership in the company. If the company decides to buyback 3.0 million shares over the next several years, shares outstanding will decease to 7.0 million. However, the stockholder's ownership increased from 10 percent to 14.2 percent without spending a single dime of new money. The company used its own capital to increase stockholder ownership interest. If the company had paid out cash dividends, the stockholder would be responsible for paying taxes on those dividends, resulting in less money to invest. The investor has secured a larger ownership interest by doing nothing.

Stock repurchase programs may also allow a firm to hide poor results. For example, assume a firm had net earnings of $100 million and 10.0 million shares outstanding, resulting in per share earning of $10 ($100 million ÷ 10 million). Over the next 10 years, the company implemented a $5 million buyback program, reducing the number of outstanding shares to 5 million. The company only reports net earnings of $75 million, resulting in per share earnings of $15 ($75 million ÷ 5 million). Therefore, in 10 years the company effectively increased per share earnings from $10 to $15 even though actual net earnings dropped from $100 million to $75 million.

To determine what is causing the increase in per share earnings, simply compare the company's actual net earnings against per share earnings, using an annual compounding growth rate. In the example, earnings per share increased 4.13 percent, but actual net earnings had a loss of 2.83 percent. Therefore, the conclusion is that the increase in earnings per share was not a result of increasing earnings but merely the result of a stock repurchase program.

The Efficient Market Hypothesis

Q 4:24 What is meant by capital markets being efficient?

Efficient capital markets are based on several assumptions including (1) a large number of competing participants are analyzing securities; (2) new information comes to the market in a random way; (3) investors adjust to new information rapidly in an unbiased way (not necessarily correctly); and (4) expected returns implicitly include risk.

Q 4:25 What is the efficient market hypothesis and what are its three forms?

The premise of the efficient market hypotheses (EMH) is that investors cannot consistently outperform the market on a risk-adjusted basis because security prices fully reflect all available information and are consistent with the risk involved. The EMH does not state that an individual cannot outperform the market. It states that an individual cannot outperform the market on a riskadjusted basis over an extended period of time.

EMH is divided into the weak-form EMH, semistrong-form EMH, and strong-form EMH. The weak-form EMH assumes that stock prices *fully reflect all available stock market information*. The weak-form EMH assumes that security returns are independent of each other and that correlation between stock prices over time is virtually nothing. The weak form can be explained by the random walk theory. Therefore, historical price behavior or technical indicators cannot produce superior returns. Information used in technical analysis has no predictive value. However, the weak-form EMH does state that using good research may produce superior returns, and fundamental analysis may have value.

The semistrong-form EMH states stock prices *fully reflect all public information*. This includes a company's past history and information learned from studying financial statements, the industry, and economic environment. Therefore, an investor cannot expect to achieve superior returns using fundamental analysis. The semistrong-form EMH does not assume that an individual cannot achieve superior returns; it only assumes that superior returns should not be expected.

The strong-form EMH states that stock *prices fully reflect all public and private information*. Therefore, not even access to inside information can produce superior returns. It assumes that inside information cannot be kept inside. As stated before, this does not assume an investor cannot be expected to achieve success; only that success should not be assumed. If investors have success using inside information in one situation, they most likely will fail in other situations. In the end, they are not expected to produce superior results using inside information. This being said, an investor who accepts both the semistrong-form and strong-form EMH will generally avoid all active managers because superior returns cannot be expected.

The Valuation of Common Stocks

Q 4:26   How is an asset valued?

The value of any asset is the present value of the asset's expected future cash inflows. Future cash inflows are discounted back to the present value at the required rate of return that reflects given levels of risk.

Price of an asset = Present value of its future cash inflows

The resulting valuation is compared to the stock's current price to determine if a stock is overvalued or undervalued. If present value is greater than market price, the stock is bought or held. If present value is less than market price, the stock is avoided or sold.

The cash inflow of a common stock is measured by its annual dividends and the change in its stock price. Cash inflows for a bond are the amount of interest received by the bondholder in a given year plus the change in the bond's price. Three conditions must exist for an asset to increase in value:

1. The asset must continuously produce cash inflows;
2. Cash inflows must have a positive rate of growth (increasing over time); and
3. Risk must be controlled.

Q 4:27   How does one value a stock with no dividend growth?

When a company pays a constant annual dividend, the price of a common stock can be determined by the following:

$$V_0 = \frac{D_1}{(1+k)^1} + \frac{D_2}{(1+k)^2} + \frac{D_3}{(1+k)^3} + \cdots + \frac{D_\infty}{(1+k)^\infty}$$

where V_0 denotes the value or price of a common stock, D is the constant annual dividend, and k is the required rate of return on the stock. The equation can be simplified further as

$$V = \frac{D_0}{k}$$

This model is the same equation as that used to value a preferred stock. The only difference is the required rate of return on the common stock, which tends to account for more risk than that of a preferred stock.

Q 4:28   How does one value a stock with constant dividend growth? (Mayo, 2000)

The constant growth dividend discount model assumes that dividends may increase at a fixed rate on an annual basis in the future. For example, if the latest dividend is $1 and dividends grow at an annual rate of 5 percent, the dividend next year is

$$\$1(1+.05)^1 = \$1.05$$

The dividend in the second year is

$$\$1(1+.05)^2 = \$1.10$$

The pattern of 5 percent growth is expected to continue into the future.

The value of a common stock with a constant rate of growth can be determined by discounting future dividends at the required rate of return as follows:

$$V_0 = \frac{D_0(1+g)^1}{(1+k)^1} + \frac{D_0(1+g)^2}{(1+k)^2} + \frac{D_0(1+g)^3}{(1+k)^3} + \cdots + \frac{D_0(1+g)^\infty}{(1+k)^\infty}$$

Fortunately, this equation can be simplified as

$$V = \frac{D_0(1+g)}{k-g} \quad \text{or} \quad \frac{D_1}{k-g}$$

where D_0 is the latest dividend paid per share, D_1 is the expected dividend per share for Year 1, k is the required rate of return on the stock, and g is the expected growth rate of dividends. The stock's present value is the current dividend multiplied by the growth rate in earnings and dividends divided by the required rate of return.

Example 4-2: What is the value of a stock that paid a $2 dividend last year and that is expected to grow annually at 5 percent? The risk-free rate is 4 percent and the expected return on the market is 10 percent. The stock's beta is 1.7. *See* Q 4:58 et seq.

$$k_{\text{stock}} = R_{\text{risk free}} + \text{Beta}_{\text{stock}}(R_{\text{market}} - R_{\text{risk free}})$$

$$k_{\text{stock}} = 4\% + 1.7(10\% - 4\%) = 14.2\%$$

Once k is determined, the value of a stock is found by applying the constant dividend discount model.

$$V = \frac{\$2(1+.05)}{.142 - .05} = \$22.82$$

Therefore, if the stock is bought at a lower price than $22.82, its expected return will exceed 14.2 percent. If the stock is bought at a higher price than $22.82, its expected return will not exceed 14.2 percent. For example, if the stock price is currently $25, the anticipated return is

$$E(r) = \frac{E(D)}{P} + E(g)$$

where $E(r)$ is the expected return (as a percentage); $E(D)$ is the expected dividend; P is the price of the asset; and $E(g)$ is the expected growth. The expected return on an investment in the stock is

$$E(r) = \frac{\$2}{\$25} + 0.05 = 13\%$$

Q 4:29 How does one value stock with unusual dividend growth? (Mayo, 2000)

There are situations where dividends are not always fixed or maintained. Dividends may increase or decrease over time, and the model summarized for solving a constant dividend stream cannot be used. In addition, supernormal growth companies tend to have very high growth rates in their early years before slowing down in later years. The supernormal growth in the beginning years often exceeds the required rate of return. Therefore, if $k < g$, the dividend discount model cannot be used. In such cases, the multiple growth discount model is used to value a stock. A numerical approach will clarify the procedure:

Example 4-3: The current dividend is $1.00 and is expected to grow at a higher rate of 15 percent for four years, after which time the new growth rate will be 7 percent a year. The required rate of return is 11 percent. The first step is to determine the dollar dividend in each year of super growth. This is found by compounding the beginning dividend by 15 percent for each of four years.

$$D_0 = \$1.00$$
$$D_1 = \$1.00(1.15) = \$1.15$$
$$D_2 = \$1.00(1.15)^2 = \$1.32$$
$$D_3 = \$1.00(1.15)^3 = \$1.52$$
$$D_4 = \$1.00(1.15)^4 = \$1.74$$

After the dividend stream is found, it must be discounted to the present using the required rate of return of 11 percent. The present value can easily be found using a calculator:

Calculator Solution

PV D_1: N = 1, i = 11, FV = \$1.15, PMT = 0 $\Rightarrow$CPT PV = \$1.04

PV D_2: N = 2, i = 11, FV = \$1.32, PMT = 0 $\Rightarrow$CPT PV = \$1.07

PV D_3: N = 3, i = 11, FV = \$1.52, PMT = 0 $\Rightarrow$CPT PV = \$1.11

PV D_4: N = 4, i = 11, FV = \$1.74, PMT = 0 $\Rightarrow$CPT PV = \$1.15

V_{1-4} = \$1.0+4 + \$1.07 + \$1.11 + \$1.15 = \$4.47

The dividend growth model applies from Year 5 on, when constant growth is expected, so the value of the stock during normal growth is

$$V_{5-\infty} = \frac{D_4(1+g)}{k-g} = \frac{\$1.74(1.05)}{.11 - .05} = \$30.63$$

The \$30.63 is the expected price of the stock at the beginning of Year 5 (end of Year 4); therefore, it must be discounted backwards to find the present value of a cash steam. The present value factor is four years and 11 percent. This solution is found using a calculator.

Calculator Solution

$$N = 4, i = 11, FV = \$30.63, PMT = 0 \Rightarrow CPT\ PV = \$-20.18$$

The value of the stock is the sum of all future cash flows.

$$V = V_{1-4} + V_{5-x} = \$4.47 + 20.18 = \$24.65$$

When using the dividend growth model, notice that g cannot be greater than k. In addition, it is important to note that if the gap between k and g widens, a stock's intrinsic value will fall. If the difference between k and g narrows, a stock's intrinsic value will grow. Small changes in k and g cause great changes in a stock's intrinsic value. However, if the growth rate increases, the valuation exceedingly increases until it becomes undefined (where growth rate equals required return).

By using the dividend discount model, the intrinsic value of a company can be found. Therefore, if the intrinsic value is greater than current market price, the stock is undervalued and should be bought or held if already owned. If the intrinsic value is less than current market value, the stock is overvalued and should be avoided, or sold if already owned. If intrinsic value equals current market price, then the stock is correctly priced.

The Required Return for Stock Valuation

Q 4:30   How is the required return (k) for a stock determined?

To value a common stock, the analyst will need to determine the required rate of return, which is made up of the real rate of interest, the inflation premium, and the risk premium. The following shows this relationship:

$$\text{Required rate of return}(k) = R_{\text{real rate}} + I_{\text{inflation rate}} + P_{\text{risk premium}}$$

The $R_{\text{real rate}}$ and $I_{\text{inflation rate}}$ are called the nominal risk-free rate of interest, known as $R_{\text{risk free}}$:

$$\text{Nominal } R_{\text{riskfree}} = (1 + R_{\text{real rate}})(1 + I_{\text{inflation premium}}) - 1$$

If the real rate is 5 percent and the expected inflation rate is 3 percent, then the nominal risk-free rate is

$$(1.05)(1.03) - 1 = 8.15\%$$

The nominal rate is usually estimated by adding the real rate to the inflation premium. The estimate of the nominal risk-free rate is

$$5\% + 3\% = 8\%$$

The risk premium is the added return that investors require over the nominal risk-free rate to compensate for a security's many uncertainties. There are many sources of uncertainties, including both systematic and unsystematic risk. Systematic risk is nondiversifiable risk such as market risk, interest rate risk, reinvestment rate risk, purchasing power risk, and exchange rate risk.

Unsystematic risk is diversifiable risk, which includes business risk and financial risk.

The required rate of return can also be found by using the capital asset pricing model (CAPM). *See* Q 4:17. The required return is comprised of the risk-free rate an investor can earn by investing in a riskless security such as a U.S. Treasury bill and the risk premium. According to the CAPM, the risk premium is both the additional return an investor earns above the risk-free rate and the volatility of a particular security to that of the market. Therefore, the required rate (k) of return is

$$K_{stock} = R_{risk\ free} + Beta_{stock}(R_{market} - R_{risk\ free})$$

If the difference between the market rate and risk-free rate widens, a stock's risk premium will grow. This is an important concept in stock valuation. The larger risk premium causes the stock's intrinsic value to decrease unless the stock can grow faster to keep up with the added risk. If growth cannot keep up with the high risk premium, the stock's current value may come crashing down.

Alternative Valuation Techniques for Common Stocks

Q 4:31   How is the P/E ratio or earnings multiplier used to value stocks? (Reilly & Brown, 2000)

The earnings multiplier, also referred to as the P/E ratio, is used by many investors to determine the value of a stock. The earnings multiplier tells an investor the price being paid for each $1 of earnings. For example, a stock earning $5 per share with a 15 P/E ratio means an investor is willing to pay $75 a share for the stock. The earnings multiplier is identified by:

$$P_0 = \text{Current market price} = \frac{E_0 \times P_0}{E_0}$$

The expected earnings multiplier is used to value a stock by estimating earnings for the next 12 months. The equation then becomes:

$$P_0 = \text{Current market price} = \frac{E_0 \times P_0}{E_0}$$

The P/E ratio is really just a restatement of the dividend discount model. The dividend discount model is

$$P_0 = \frac{D_1}{k - g}$$

where P_0 is the current price, D_1 is the dividend expected to be received at the end of Year 1, k is the required rate of return on the stock, and g is the expected growth rate of dividends. The firm's dividend is related to earnings and the portion distributed. When dividing both sides of the formula by expected earnings for the next 12 months, E_1, the result is

$$\frac{P_0}{E_1} = \frac{\dfrac{D_1}{E_1}}{k - g}$$

This equation indicates that a P/E ratio depends on the same factors to value a stock as that achieved through the use of the dividend discount model. The factors include: (1) the dividend payout ratio (dividend divided by earnings, D/E); (2) the required rate of return *(k)*; (3) the expected growth rate of dividends *(g)*.

The use of the P/E ratio instead of the dividend discount model has one major advantage and one major disadvantage. The advantage is that P/E ratios can be applied to stock that are not paying cash dividends. The dividend discount model assumes the firm is paying or going to pay a cash dividend. The disadvantage is that the P/E ratio does not tell if a stock is overvalued or undervalued to its market price. Investors are required to draw inferences to historical P/E ratios in determining if a ratio is high or low. The dividend discount model allows for comparison to determine if a stock is overvalued or undervalued to its actual price. However, the estimated value of a stock can be determined by using the P/E ratio and applying it to estimated earnings for the next year (E_1). Consider the following:

Example 4-4: A firm has an expected payout ratio of 50 percent, a required rate of return of 11 percent, and an expected dividend growth rate of 6 percent. Earnings for the current year (E_0) are $2.00.

The *future earnings multiplier* is computed as

$$P/E_{\text{future ratio}} = \frac{.50}{.11 - .06} = 10\times$$

Current earnings are $2.00 and g is 6 percent, so

$$EPS_{\text{estimate}} = 2.00(1.06) = \$2.12$$

The future value of the stock is estimated as

$$V_1 = (EPS_{\text{estimate}})^*(P/E_{\text{future}}) = \$2.12 \times 10 = \$21.20$$

Compare this estimated value (at the end of Year 1) of the stock to its market price to determine if the stock should be bought or sold. To accurately compare it to its current price, the price and ending dividend must be discounted by the required rate of return of 11 percent. If the present value of the future stock value and dividend payments are greater than the current market price, the stock is underpriced and should be bought. If the present value of the future stock value and dividend payments is less than the current market price, the stock is overpriced and should be avoided.

There is a relationship between the P/E ratio and all components of the dividend discount model. The higher the payout ratio, the higher the P/E. Second, the higher the expected growth rate, g, the higher the P/E. Finally, the higher the required rate of return, k, the lower the P/E. The spread between k and g is the main determinant of the P/E ratio, but the dividend payout ratio does have an impact. The expected (P_0/E_1) earnings multiplier is what should be used when valuing stocks, not the historical (P_0/E_0) ratio.

Q 4:32　How does one measure management's ability to use retained earnings?

To increase per share earnings, a company must have the capacity to retain earnings and invest those earnings in business ventures that can generate more earnings per share. For example, saving $10,000 each year will result in $100,000 after 10 years. However, investing $10,000 in a stock earning 10 percent compounded annually results in $159,000 after10 years. Retained earnings should add value to a company's net worth, as long as the company kept more than it paid out in dividends. However, most companies use their retained earnings for maintaining the status quo, such as applying the retained earnings to research and development or replacement of plant and equipment. If a company can use its retained earnings to produce above average returns, then it may be better off keeping those earnings instead of paying them out. We measure management's ability to use retained earnings by taking the earnings per share increase over a 10-year period and dividing by the per share amount of retained earnings over the same 10-year period.

> **Example 4-5:** If a company earns $0.25 a share and 10 years later earns $1.35 a share, then per share earnings rose by $1.10. Total earnings add up to $7.50 per share during the same 10-year period, in which $2.00 was paid out in dividends. The company retained earnings of $5.50 a share ($7.50 − $2.00 dividend), and the $5.50 in retained earnings produced $1.10 in additional income. The firm earned a return of 20 percent ($1.10 ÷ $5.50) on the $5.50 a share in retained earnings.

The higher return the better. Investors should compare firms within the same industry to get a sense of expected returns.

Q 4:33　How is the relative value to a Treasury bond used to value a stock?

All investments compete with each other. When bond yields go up, stock prices go down and vice versa. A way to value stocks is to divide the relative per share earnings by the yield on a 10-year Treasury bond. This compares the rate of return for a company to a Treasury bond. If a company earns $0.40 per share and the rate of return for a 10-year Treasury bond is 5.11 percent, then the relative value is $7.82 a share (.40 ÷ .0511). Therefore, paying $7.82 for a share of stock will give a return equal to a 10-year Treasury bond. Consequently, buying a stock for lower than its relative value yields an investment that is earning more than 5.11 percent. For a firm to equal a 5.11 percent bond yield, its P/E would have to be 19.5 (1 ÷ 5.11). If the P/E (19.5) is multiplied by forward earnings of $0.50 per share (instead of current earnings), the fair value for the stock is $9.75. Using forward earnings is preferable to current earnings if an analyst can accurately predict the forward earnings.

Q 4:34   What is price-to-book value?

The price-to-book value is defined as the firm's stock price divided by its per-share book value. The book value is the sum of stock, additional paid-in capital, and retained earnings on a firm's balance sheet. A low ratio suggests a stock is undervalued, and a high ratio suggests it is overvalued. What is considered high or low depends on the discretion of the analyst but should be used in comparison to other stocks. It has become an important measure of relative value among stocks.

Q 4:35   What is the price-to-sales ratio?

The price-to-sales (P/S) ratio is defined as the firm's stock price divided by its per share sales. This is often used in place of the P/E ratio for firms that have no earnings. However, it is a meaningful tool as well for firms that do have earnings, and should be used for comparison purposes. Earnings and cash flows are directly related to sales of a firm that makes this a useful ratio. A low P/S ratio indicates low valuation; whereas a high P/S ratio indicates high valuation.

Q 4:36   What is the price-to-cash flow ratio?

The price-to-cash flow ratio is defined as the market value of the firm dividend by its per share cash flow. The ratio is often used in conjunction with the P/E ratio because emphasis is placed on growth in cash flows versus earnings; earnings are often subject to accounting manipulation, whereas cash flows are often more stable. Cash flows are often used to predict financial strength and potential problems.

Technical Analysis

Q 4:37   What information do contrarians use in technical analysis? (Reilly & Brown, 2000)

Contrarians follow the rule of doing the opposite of what the general investor does. Therefore, contrarians believe the majority of traders, investors, and institutional advisors are wrong most of the time. The hard part is determining if these investors are bearish or bullish in order to take the opposite side. There are several tools used by contrarians that are covered in this heading.

Mutual Fund Cash Positions. Contrarian investors feel mutual fund cash positions are a good indicator to institutional investor behavior, which they feel is usually wrong at picking bottoms or tops in the market. The mutual fund ratio is

$$\text{Mutual Fund Ratio (MFR)} = \frac{\text{Mutual fund cash}}{\text{Total fund assets}}$$

In general, a higher ratio means mutual funds are holding cash and are bearish on the market. Contrary opinion investors would view this as a time to buy. Why? Because this implies that institutional investors have a lot of cash on the sideline ready to buy stocks.

A lower ratio implies mutual funds have very little in cash positions and are bullish on the market. Contrarian investors would consider this a time to sell. Why? Because institutional investors would have little cash left to continue buying in order to sustain an upward market cycle.

Investor Credit Balances in Brokerage Accounts. Contrary opinion technicians feel that individual investors are poor predictors of market movement. They feel that rising balances indicate that investors are very bearish, which they consider a bullish signal. The more cash left on the sidelines, the greater chance that it will be put to use to move the market higher. Falling balances means that investors are bullish, so contrarians will be bearish and sell into the market. The reason in this case is that investors have little cash to move the market higher.

Investment Advisory Opinion. This theory states that when most financial advisors become bearish on the market, that is the time to buy stocks. The time to sell stocks is when most financial advisors become bullish on the market. The index is calculated as

$$\text{Investment Advisor Ratio} = \frac{\text{Bearish Opinions}}{\text{Total Opinions}}$$

If the investment advisor ratio is high, it signals that advisors are bearish on the market. In this case, contrarians are bullish and buy. If the investment advisor ratio is low, it signals that most advisors are bullish. Therefore, contrary opinion technicians are bearish and sell. The reason as to why investment advisors are wrong is because they seem to react to trends rather than to forecast them. Therefore, they report on what is happening instead on what is going to happen.

OTC vs. NYSE Volume. Contrarians believe that OTC issues are more speculative than NYSE issues. High trading volume on the NYSE is a bullish signal; whereas high trading volume on the OTC is a bearish signal. The ratio is

$$\text{Volume Ratio} = \frac{\text{OTC Volume}}{\text{NYSE Volume}}$$

High volume ratio signals investors are bullish, and contrarians are bearish and sell. A high ratio generally indicates heavy speculative trading. If the volume ratio is low, then investors are bearish, and contrarians are bullish and buy. A low ratio indicates an oversold market and low speculative trading.

CBOE Put/Call Ratio. Contrarians believe that options are a speculative game and those that play in the option market are almost always consistent losers. Therefore, speculators tend to buy calls when they expect prices to rise and buy puts when they expect prices to fall. In general, option players are often more optimistic than pessimistic about the market, and the ratio is usually below 1.0; indicating that more calls than puts are bought. If the put/call ratio increases, investors are more bearish on the market. If the put/call ratio decreases, investors are more bullish on the market. The formula is

$$\text{Put/Call Ratio} = \frac{\text{Puts}}{\text{Calls}}$$

If the put/call ratio is equal to or greater than .50, option traders are bearish but contrarians are bullish and ready to buy. If the put/call ratio is equal to or less than .35, option traders are bullish but contrarians are bearish and ready to sell. However, these numbers are not always true if emotional sentiment is moving the market. In addition, investors tend to look at a five-day average for the put/call ratio before making a decision. Therefore, if the put/call ratio is equal to or greater than .50 for a five-day average, this may signal a time to buy. If it is equal to or less than .35 for a five-day average, this may signal a time to sell.

Q 4:38 What technical indicators do smart money technicians use? (Reilly & Brown, 2000)

Some technical analysts follow the money movement of what they consider to be sophisticated traders. Smart money traders follow a different logic than contrary opinion technicians. These investors have developed several tools to indicate where smart money is moving.

The Confidence Index. The confidence index is found in Barron's, and is the ratio of Barron's average yield on 10 top-grade corporate bonds to the yield on the Dow Jones average of 40 bonds. This is shown by

$$\text{Confidence Index (CI)} = \frac{\text{Barron's Average Yield on 10 Top Grade Corporate Bonds}}{\text{Dow} - \text{Jones Average 40 Bonds}}$$

The confidence index measures the difference between high-quality bonds and a large cross-section of bonds. It is also stated as

$$\text{CI} = \frac{\text{Quality Bond Yield}}{\text{Average Bond Yield}}$$

The spread on high-quality bonds is always lower than the spread on a large cross-section of bonds: this ratio should never exceed 100. The spreads between both sets of bonds get smaller as the ratio approaches 100. When investors are confident about the economic and market outlook, they sell high-quality bonds and buy lower-quality bonds. When high-quality bonds are sold, prices fall and yields rise. When lower-grade bonds are purchased, prices rise and yields drop. The confidence index then rises during periods of confidence as the yield spread narrows and drops during periods of pessimism as the yield spread widens. Therefore, the confidence index moves in the opposite direction of yield spreads. Spreads narrow when the confidence index gets bigger, and spreads widen when the confidence index drops.

T-Bill Yields and Eurodollar Rates. To determine investor attitude on a global front, technicians often look at T-bill yields and Eurodollar rates. Technicians believe the spread widens in times of international crisis because money flows into safe U.S. T-bills.

Short Sales by Specialists. Technical traders often watch what specialists do on exchanges to follow the movement of smart money. The information for total short sales on the NYSE appears in Barron's. Specialists often sell stocks short to manage markets, but they exercise discretion in areas when they feel strong about market movements. The ratio is

$$\text{Specialist Short Sales Ratio} = \frac{\text{Specialist Short Sales}}{\text{Total Short Sales on the NYSE}}$$

If the ratio is low, it is a bullish sign for a technical trader indicating that specialists are buying. If the ratio is high, it is a bearish sign indicating that specialists are selling. The ratio is very short-term-sided, and will not predict long-term movements in the market. In addition, this ratio has become very unreliable in recent years because of specialists using stock index futures and options to hedge positions.

Margin Debit Balances in Brokerage Accounts. Technicians believe that margin borrowing is an indicator of knowledgeable investors. A high margin balance is a bullish indicator, and a low margin balance is a bearish sign. Monthly data on margin debt are found in Barron's. A potential problem with using this information as an indicator of market movement is that it may be difficult to interpret because it is an absolute value.

Q 4:39   What market indicators are used in technical analysis? (Reilly & Brown, 2000)

Breadth of the Market. The breadth of market measures the number of advancing stocks to the number of decreasing stocks. Technical investors argue that indexes only provide a limited number of companies, which often influence the direction of the market. In other words, an index may move upward when in fact the broad market is moving downward because of many medium to small-sized companies. This often misleads the direction of the market.

The breadth of the market is determined by using the advance-decline line. The advance-decline line is a sum of advancing stocks to declining stocks on the NYSE. If the advance-decline line and the market index move together, then movement is broad-based across the market. To a technical trader, the broad-based move is interpreted as a strong sign of market direction. A divergence between the trend for the index and the advance-decline line would signal a market peak or bottom. For example, near a peak in the market, the Dow Jones industrial average (DJIA) continues to move up while the daily advancedecline ratio turns negative and the advance-decline series begins to flatten out and decline. In contrast, near a market bottom, the DJIA continues to move down while the daily advance-decline ratio turns positive and the advancedecline series begins to level off and turn upward before the market index. Technicians often believe a true bottom in a bear market is not reached until the daily advance-decline ratio becomes very negative, indicating that declining stocks far outnumber advancing stocks. It is at this point that investors toss in their towels and give up on the market. Only then can the market start to move back up.

Short Interest Ratio. The short interest ratio measures the cumulative number of shares sold short by investors and not divided by the daily volume of trading on an exchange. The formula is

$$\text{Short Interest Ratio} = \frac{\text{Outstanding Short Interest}}{\text{Average Daily Volume on Exchange}}$$

As an example, if the outstanding short interest of the NYSE was 750 million shares and the average daily volume on the exchange was 250 million, the short interest ratio is 3 (750 ÷ 250). The means that outstanding short interest is three days' trading volume.

Technicians often consider a high number as a bullish sign because there is potential demand to buy back the short positions. In contrast, a low number is a bearish sign because there is potential for short selling. The ratio has often increased over time.

Stocks Above Their 200-Day Moving Average. Computing the number of stocks above their 200-day moving average is often used by technicians to determine market movement. If more than 80 percent of stocks are trading above their 200-day moving average, the market is considered overbought and technicians will sell stocks. If less than 20 percent of stocks are trading above their 200-day moving average, the market is considered oversold and should be bought.

Blocking the Uptick-Downtick Ratio. Over the years, exchanges have become dominated by institutional investors who often trade large blocks. If the block trade is above the prior trade, it is an uptick. If the block trade is below the prior trade, it is a downtick. In general, it is thought that an uptick results from buying and a downtick from selling. *See* Q 4:6. The block uptickdowntick ratio is believed to reflect institutional investor sentiment, which indicates the flow of smart money. The ratio is calculated as

$$\text{Block Uptick} - \text{Downtick Ratio} = \frac{\text{\# of Block Uptick Transactions}}{\text{\# of Block Downtick Transactions}}$$

A low ratio is a bullish signal because it indicates an oversold condition. In contrast, a high ratio is a bearish signal because it indicates an overbought condition.

Q 4:40   What are the stock price and volume techniques used in technical analysis?

Dow Theory. The Dow theory is one of the oldest methods available for predicting what direction the market will take. It was founded by Charles Dow, who published The Wall Street Journal. Dow recognized three movements in security markets: major trends, intermediate trends, and short-term trends. Major trends are broad market movements lasting several years. Intermediate trends, occurring within the major trends, are influenced through current events and resemble waves lasting for several weeks or months. Short-term trends are daily ripples that have no significance.

It is up to the technician to properly calculate the direction of the major trend. The term *bull market* is used to indicate an upward major trend, and the term *bear market* is a downward major trend. Bull markets exist when upward trends rally past prior highs, whereas declines stay above previous lows. Therefore, a major decline occurs when successive rallies do not penetrate previous highs, and previous lows are penetrated. The intermediate trends give rise to *technical corrections*. This term is often used when markets are considered to be over-bought or oversold, and an adjustment to offset the excess occurs.

Dow theory employs the DJIA and the Dow Jones transportation average. If the averages are moving upward together, it signals a strong bull market. In contrast, if both are moving downward together, it suggests a bear market. If they are moving in opposite directions, there is uncertainty as to the direction of the market. A trend continues as long as the averages confirm each other.

Importance of Volume. Price movement in one direction shows the net effect on the price in that direction. However, price movement alone does not show how widespread the excess demand or supply is for a security. This is where volume comes into play. Low volume tells us nothing about market movement. High volume tells how widespread interest and demand are in a stock. Therefore, a price increase on high volume is a very bullish indicator, whereas a price decrease on strong volume is a very bearish indicator.

Technicians often use a ratio of upside-downside volume. The ratio is defined as

$$\text{Upside-Downside Volume Ratio} = \frac{\text{Volume of stocks that increased}}{\text{Volume of stocks that decreased}}$$

The data is reported in the Wall Street Journal and in Barron's. A value of 1.50 or more is a bearish signal indicating the market is overbought. If the ratio is 0.75 or lower, it is a bullish signal indicating the market is oversold. The ratio ranges between 0.50 and 2.00.

Support and Resistance Levels. Stocks generally trade in ranges. The lower limit is a stock's support level, and the higher limit is its resistance level. The support level is when technicians feel a stock should be purchased, whereas the resistance level is when a stock should be sold. Technicians state that if a stock is to break its support level, rapid decline will occur before another support level is defined. The previous support is now its resistance level. Alternatively, if a stock were to penetrate its resistance level, it would quickly move to the upside before reaching a new resistance level. The previous resistance level is now a support level.

Moving Average Lines. Moving averages allow technicians to find trends in stock prices. Stocks will trade above their moving average if the trend is up and will trade below the moving average if the trend is down. If the price of a security breaks through its moving average on heavy volume, this indicates a reversal of the long-term trend. The most often used average to determine long-term trends in a security or industry group is the 200-day moving average. Typically, the terms *overbought* and *oversold* are indicative of how far the price is from the 200-day moving average. Technicians believe that stocks will tend to gravitate back to their 200-day moving average when extended too far from the average.

Relative Strength Ratio. Technicians believe that once a trend begins, it must continue until an event happens to stop it. The relative strength indicator indicates if the trend is stock-specific or is caused by market movements. If the ratio increases over time, technicians expect superior performance to continue. The ratio works in declining markets too. If the price of the stock does not decline as much as the rest of the market, the stock's relative strength ratio will increase. Technicians believe if the ratio remains stable or rises in down markets, the stock should do very well in rising markets. It is defined as

$$\text{Relative Strength Ratio} = \frac{\text{Stock Price}}{\text{Market Price}}$$

Professional Asset Management

Investment Companies

Q 4:41 What is the difference between open-end and closed-end investment companies?

Closed-end investment companies. Closed-end investment companies issue a specified number of shares comprised of stock or a combination of stock and debt. The shares cannot be redeemed, and new shares are not issued after the initial offering. These shares trade on the open market.

A closed-end investment company may trade at a price that is greater or less than net asset value (NAV). If the price is less than NAV, it is selling at a discount. If it is greater than NAV, it is selling at a premium. The reason for the market price to be different from the NAV is because of supply and demand. However, some investors use market price relative to NAV as a guide for determining when to purchase or sell a closed-end fund. For example, if the shares are selling at a discount, an investor may view this as an opportune time to buy the fund. In contrast, an investor may sell the shares if they are trading at a premium.

Q 4:42   How do investors pay fees to a closed-end investment company?

Investors pay fees several ways in a closed-end investment company. They pay brokers'commissions when buying and selling shares, as with any other kind of stock. They pay management fees that are subtracted from the income earned by the assets. Finally, investment companies pay brokerage fees for buying and selling securities within the close-end fund, and these fees are passed on to the investors.

Open-End Investment Companies. In contrast to closed-end investment companies, open-end investment companies are not traded on the secondary markets. Open-end investment companies are also called mutual funds. Shares of a mutual fund are purchased directly from the fund at the net asset value plus any applicable sales charge. A no-load fund charges no sales fee when buying and selling shares. Conversely, a load fund charges a sales fee to the investor. The investor pays the offering price. The loading charge is stated as a percentage of the offering price. It is determined as

$$\text{Offering Price} = \frac{\text{NAV}}{(1 - \text{load})}$$

Example 4-6: Assume an investor is looking to purchase an open-end fund with a load of 5.5 percent and net asset value of $10. The offer price is

$$\frac{\$10}{(1 - .055)} = \$10.58 \text{ per share}$$

When the mutual fund receives money from an investor, it issues new shares and purchases additional assets. If an investor sells the shares, they are redeemed and the fund pays the investor from its cash holdings. In some instances, a fund may have to sell shares within the fund to pay the investor.

The sources of return are similar between a closed-end and open-end investment company except in one way. The market value of a closed-end fund may rise or drop relative to the net asset value. The price of a mutual fund is equal to and sometimes greater than the net asset value (*i.e.,* there may be a sales charge) but the price is never less than the net asset value. Therefore, an investor is able to use the open market to buy closed-end funds at a discount and sell them at a premium. This possibility does not exist with open-end investment companies.

Q 4:43   What is net asset value?

The NAV is the asset value of all shares owned by the investment company. It is total assets (stock, bonds, cash) minus total liabilities (accrued fees) divided by the number of shares outstanding.

Example 4-7: The NAV is calculated as:

Stock owned	$1,000,000
Debt owned	+ $ 800,000
Cash	+ $ 200,000
Total assets	$2,000,000
Liabilities	−100,000
Net Worth	$1,900,000
Number of shares outstanding	500,000
Net asset value per share	$ 3.80

Q 4:44   What is a unit investment trust (UIT)?

A unit investment trust represents a fixed portfolio of assets and is sold to investors in units of $1,000. The assets of a unit investment trust are frozen. That means no new securities are purchased. In addition, the securities already purchased are seldom sold. The trust is self-liquidating. After a period of time, the portfolio is sold and the funds are distributed to the stockholders. When funds are received, they are not reinvested into the trust. Unit investment trusts are designed to meet specific objectives, such as interest income. Expenses are lower than closed-end and open-end funds because the portfolio is fixed. This generally means that there is no management fee.

Q 4:45   How do fees and expenses affect returns for mutual funds?

There are many expenses that come with owning a mutual fund. One expense is a *load charge*, which is part of the offering price. The load charge is a one-time commission on mutual funds. It is applied when a fund is purchased, when it is sold, or a combination of both. A *no-load* fund sells at its net asset value. *No-load* does not mean that there are no expenses. There are other annual expenses such as 12b-1 fees, management fees, operating expenses, and transaction costs. All mutual funds pay annual fees. These fees are not always obvious to the investor. They are collected by mutual fund companies by reducing the per share price of a fund. However, there is no evidence that funds with loads perform better than no-load funds.

Expenses and fees differ among mutual funds and have a large impact on an investor's overall return. A considerable difference is evident when comparing an actively managed fund to an unmanaged stock index fund. The following table indicates the difference in portfolio value:

Assume $500 monthly investment at 11 percent annual return:

End of Year	Value of Managed fund with fees of 2.25%	Value of unmanaged stock index fund with fees of 0.25%	Lost dollars because of fees
1	$ 6292	$ 6361	$ 69
5	$ 37,738	$ 39,849	$ 2,111
10	$ 96,097	$ 107,897	$ 11,800
15	$186,340	$ 224,098	$ 37,758
20	$325,891	$ 422,527	$ 96,636
25	$541,688	$ 761,370	$219,682
30	$875,392	$1,339,988	$464,596

This indicates that over a 30-year period, the difference (or lost dollars) from investing in a mutual fund with higher expenses and fees is $464,596. Mutual fund expenses and fees can substantially reduce an investor's portfolio value. Investors should always consider these costs before purchasing a mutual fund. In addition, funds that have a high turnover ratio generate more transaction costs, which are assumed by the investor.

Q 4:46   What is a 12b-1 fee?

A 12b-1 fee is the marketing cost assigned to a mutual fund. These are common fees for no-load funds and have a large impact on a portfolio's value. For example, if the 12b-1 fee is 50 percent for a no-load fund, it takes eight years for the 12b-1 fee to exceed a 4 percent load fund. However, it's important to understand that load funds can also have 12b-1 fees.

Q 4:47   What tax considerations are there when buying mutual funds?

Investment companies receive favorable tax treatment: They do not pay federal income taxes. Earnings are passed through to the investors. Mutual fund distributions are subject to income and capital gains taxation. It is the investor who ultimately pays taxes. The investor pays all taxes on profits realized by a fund even if these profits are received in cash or reinvested into additional funds. In addition, the investor is responsible for taxes if the shares are sold.

Mutual funds contain hidden capital gains that an investor is responsible for even without receiving the capital gains as income. If a fund is initially offered at $10 and rises to $15 over a period of two years, no taxes are paid by its stockholders if the fund did not redeem shares. However, suppose an investor purchases the shares at the net asset value of $15. If the next day the fund sells its securities and distributes the capital gains, the investor who just purchased the shares must pay the necessary capital gains tax.. In addition, many funds indicate a date when capital gains and income are distributed to shareholders. Investors should be aware of this date. The majority of funds make two distributions. The first is a mid-year income distribution. The second distribution occurs at year-end and consists of income and capital gains. In the example above, assume the investor purchases the shares just prior to the distribution date. The investor is the holder of record and is responsible for paying any tax on income and capital gains even though the rise in price occurred much earlier. It then makes sense to delay the purchase and buy shares when the fund goes ex-dividend. *See* Q 4:19.

The net asset value adjusts according to the capital gain distribution. In the previous example, the net asset value declines to $10 per share ($15 − $5). The investor may offset capital gains by selling the shares. This results in a loss of $5. However, the investor still loses because of fees and expenses that are paid in the process.

Hidden capital gains result in unexpected taxes, but hidden capital losses offer tax-free gains. For example, if the fund's per share price drops from $10 to $5, the fund has an unrealized loss of $5. Assume an investor purchases the shares at the net asset value of $5. If the shares rise to $10 and are redeemed by the fund, the investor does not incur any capital gains tax as long as the shares continue to be held. However, unrealized losses are not always an opportunity if the price decline is a result of poor management.

The return of a mutual fund is stated before tax. However, the investor only gets to keep the after-tax return. Tax efficiency is defined as the ability to generate returns without generating large amounts of tax obligations. There is no tax obligation if a fund does not receive income or realize capital gains. Conversely, if a fund sells securities within its portfolio, each sale results in a taxable event. If these are short-term sales, then tax is paid at the stockholder's marginal federal income tax rate. If a fund rarely sells its investments, the likelihood of long-term gains is greater.

Tax efficiency is an index that converts before-tax returns to an after-tax return. It gives the after-tax return as a percentage of the before-tax return.

Example 4-8: Assume a net asset value of $30. The fund appreciates 10 percent and gains are distributed by the fund. The fund increases to $33 and after the $3 distribution, its price declines to $30. The shares are reinvested by the individual into 0.1 shares. The investor originally had 1 share, and now has 1.1 shares valued at $33. If the capital gain rate is 20 percent, then the individual pays $0.60 in taxes (.20 × $3.00). The before-tax return is 10 percent, whereas the after-tax return is 8 percent ($2.40/$3.00). Therefore, the tax efficiency index is 80 (8%/10%). This value is compared to other funds when determining which one is more tax-efficient.

The tax efficiency index has several flaws. First, it is difficult to find the composition of returns and the appropriate tax rates when the returns were earned. Second, a high ratio may imply more taxes in the future even though it indicates lower taxes in the past. A high tax efficiency index is achieved when capital gains are not paid. If a fund is ready to sell out of several positions, there may be tax consequences to the stockholders even though the fund had a high tax efficiency index.

A fund's turnover ratio is another measure of tax efficiency. In general, funds with a greater portfolio turnover ratio generate more tax consequences for their investors. The mutual fund turnover ratio identifies the amount of buying and selling happening in a specified mutual fund. A turnover ratio of 50 percent means that a fund is expected to replace 50 percent of its investments over a year. If a turnover ratio is 100 percent, then a fund replaces 100 percent of its investments over a year. If the entire portfolio is turned over in a year, any gains are most likely short-term.

Q 4:48   Does the size of the fund affect the return?

A fund grows over time by issuing new shares. As the fund gets larger, it becomes less efficient at selling and buying blocks of stock. For example, a smaller fund is able to quickly buy and sell smaller blocks. Larger funds need more time to establish or liquidate a position. The extra time needed may result in lower prices when selling and higher prices when buying, resulting in lower returns.

Another drawback to large funds is the inability to sustain growth. For example, a 15 percent increase in value for a $1 billion portfolio is more difficult than the same increase for a $1 million portfolio because of the shear size of the portfolio. If one of the stocks in the former generates above-average performance, it would have little impact on the overall portfolio. In contrast, the price of one stock in a smaller fund may have a substantial impact on the total value.

There are benefits that a large fund has over a small fund. Large funds have a proven track record, whereas small funds do not. An investor can determine how well management has performed. In most cases, management for a smaller fund has not been tested in bear and bull markets. Large fund managers generally have experienced up and down markets and have made it through them. However, investors should ask themselves if management can continue to sustain growth because past performance does not necessarily indicate future performance.

Q 4:49   What is a real estate investment trust?

A real estate investment trust (REIT) is a publicly traded closed-end investment company that invests in a managed, diversified portfolio of real estate or real estate mortgages and construction loans. Think of a REIT as a real estate mutual fund. REITs are traded on exchanges and can sell for premium or discounts to the NAV.

Investors must pay the tax on the REIT's earnings as they are distributed. Distributed income is taxed as ordinary income. Capital gains and losses from the sale of assets in the REIT portfolio retain their character and are taxed as gains and losses when distributed.The advantages of REITs include: (1) limited liability, (2) ability to leverage, (3) use as collateral, (4) liquidity, (5) diversification in the real estate portfolio, and (6) inflation hedge.

The disadvantages of REITs include: (1) loss of control, (2) lower potential returns, (3) management fees and administrative charges, and (4) no flow-through of tax benefits—losses cannot be passed through.

Q 4:50   What is an exchange-traded fund?

An exchange-traded fund (ETF) offers purchasers the ability to invest in a basket of stocks that mirror closely an underlying benchmark index. They trade daily on exchanges and are priced continuously by the marketplace throughout the day. The funds rely on an arbitrage mechanism to keep the prices at which they trade roughly in line with the net asset values of their underlying portfolios.

Measurements of Risk

Systematic and Unsystematic Risk

Q 4:51   What is systematic risk?

Systematic risk is risk that affects the entire market, such as market risk, interest rate risk, purchasing power risk, foreign currency risk, and reinvestment risk. Systematic risk cannot be eliminated through diversification because it affects the entire market. Beta is a measure by which systematic risk is determined. Beta is only an accurate measure of systematic risk when calculated for a diversified portfolio.

Q 4:52   What is unsystematic risk?

Unsystematic risk is unique to a single business or industry, such as operations and methods of financing. These risks include business risk and financial risk. Unlike systematic risk, unsystematic risk can be eliminated through diversification. Several studies have found that unsystematic risk has been significantly reduced with portfolios of 10 to 15 stocks. As more stocks are added to a portfolio, the fewer losses that one company in the portfolio will have to cause a negative impact on the total performance of the group of securities.

Risk Measurements

Q 4:53   Why is the price range of a stock not a good measure of risk?

The range in the price of a stock is really a measure of risk. A stock with a greater range tends to be more risky than a stock with a smaller range. However, two stocks with equal ranges may not have the same degree of risk. For example, a stock that trades from $20 to $40 has the same range as one that trades from $90 to $110. The percentage move from $20 to $40 is 100 percent, whereas the percentage move from $90 to $110 is only 22 percent. Therefore, the latter would dictate a more stable price but both securities have equal risk according to their ranges. Clearly, there is an inherent problem in the above scenario when considering range as a measure of risk.. This is resolved by analyzing dispersion around an average value. Dispersion considers all possible outcomes from the average. The greater dispersion around the average return implies that a stock carries more risk. Dispersion is measured by standard deviation.

Q 4:54   What is standard deviation?

Standard deviation measures how actual values differ from the expected values for a given series of values. It is a measure of variability of returns of an asset compared to its mean or expected value. The standard deviation measures total risk. The larger the dispersion around a mean value, the greater the risk and the larger the deviation for a security. Therefore, calculating standard deviation allows for more selectivity when choosing individual securities for a given level of risk. There is a direct relationship between standard deviation (σ, omega) and risk.

Observations will tend to cluster around the expected mean, and the bell-shaped curve is often used to represent the dispersion. The standard deviation is a measure of this dispersion or *variability*.

Approximately 68 percent of outcomes fall within ± 1 σ of the mean.

Approximately 95 percent of outcomes fall within ± 2 σ of the mean.

Approximately 99 percent of outcomes fall within ± 3 σ of the mean.

Example 4-9: The standard deviation for stock *A* is 1 and the standard deviation for *B* is 3. If Stock *A* has an average return of 15 percent, then 68 percent of all returns fall within 14 and 16 percent. For stock *B*, if its average return is also 15 percent, then 99 percent of all returns fall within 9 percent ($-2*3\sigma$ of the mean) and 21 percent ($+2*3\sigma$ of the mean). The larger standard deviation for *B* indicates more variability.

Standard deviation is an absolute measure of dispersion. That is, it can be influenced by the magnitude of the original numbers. If stock *A* and stock *B* have different returns, a comparison of standard deviation may not indicate that *B* is more diverse. Other measures of risk are useful complements to standard deviation.

The steps to calculating *historical* standard deviation are:

2. For each observation, take the difference between the individual observation and the average return.

3. Square the difference.

4. Total the squared differences.

5. For sample σ, divide this sum by one less than the number of observations. For population σ, divide this sum by the total number of observations (for CFP, assume sample unless stated differently).

6. Take the square root.

Example 4-10: Capital Assets, Inc., has an average return of 12 percent and the following individual returns for the corresponding time periods listed below. What is the standard deviation for Capital Assets, Inc.?

Year	Actual return	Average return	Difference	Difference squared
1	12%	6.8%	5.2	27.04
2	10	6.8	3.2	10.24
3	−5	6.8	11.8	139.24
4	7	6.8	.2	.04
5	10	6.8	3.2	10.24
Sum of squared differences =				186.80

The standard deviation is $(186.80 \div (5 - 1))^{1/2} = 6.83\%$

Q 4:55   What is the coefficient of variation?

To compare a series of very different values, the coefficient of variation is preferred to using only standard deviation. Where standard deviation is a measure of absolute dispersions, the coefficient of variation is a measure of relative dispersions. The coefficient of variation is defined as the ratio of the standard deviation divided by the mean. The larger value indicates greater dispersion relative to the arithmetic mean of the return.

Example 4-11: Stock A has standard deviation of 7 and an average rate of return of 5 percent. In contrast, stock B has a standard deviation of 10 and an average rate of return of 12 percent. The standard deviation expresses that stock B has greater risk than stock A because of a higher standard deviation. However, the relative dispersion is less for stock B than for A. Investment A has a 1.4 (7 ÷ 5) coefficient of variation, whereas investment B has only a .83 (10 ÷ 12) coefficient of variation. Considering the relative dispersion, investors seeking less risk would consider purchasing stock B instead of stock A.

Q 4:56   What is covariance?

Sometimes it is desirable to determine how a return varies from other returns instead of its own return. This variability is measured by the covariance.

A positive covariance indicates that variables move in the same direction, and a negative covariance indicates they move in opposite directions. Larger numbers indicate a stronger relationship and smaller numbers indicate a weaker relationship. However, covariance is an absolute number and can be difficult to interpret. It is often converted into the correlation coefficient, which is easier than covariance to interpret.

The covariance between the returns of securities 1 and 2 is

$$\text{cov}_{1,2} = (R_{1,2})(\sigma_1)(\sigma_2)$$

where

$R_{1,2}$ is the correlation coefficient.

σ_1 is the standard deviation of stock 1.

σ_2 is the standard deviation of stock 2.

Q 4:57 What is the correlation coefficient?

The correlation coefficient is a measure of how different returns vary for different stocks. The numerical values of the correlation coefficient range from +1 to −1. If two variables move exactly together, the value of the correlation coefficient is 1. This indicates perfect positive correlation. If two variables move exactly opposite to each other, the value of the correlation coefficient is −1. Low numerical values indicate little relationship between the two variables, such as −0.10 or +0.15.

The maximum amount of risk reduction is predetermined by the correlation coefficient. The correlation coefficient is the engine that drives the whole theory of portfolio diversification. There is an inverse relationship between correlation and diversification. The lower the correlation, the greater the diversification. If the correlation coefficient between securities is less than 1, then the risk of a portfolio will always be less than the simple weighted average of the individual risks of the stocks in the portfolio. Diversification requires that asset returns not be highly correlated. Risk is erased when returns are perfectly negatively correlated. However, the elimination of risk does not eliminate positive returns.

Example 4-12: If the return for *XYZ* yields 20 percent and *YYY* yields −10 percent, the net is 5 percent. If, in the next period, *XYZ* yields −5 percent and *YYY* yields 15 percent, the net is still 5 percent. The swing in return for *XYZ* is +20 to −5, while the swing in return for *YYY* is −10 to +15. The correlation coefficient is −1.0 because of negative correlation, but the return on a portfolio equally invested in the two securities is 5 percent. Risk is reduced by a lower positive correlation and a greater negative correlation among the returns.

An important concept comes into play: the individual asset's return and risk are important, but the asset's impact on the portfolio as a whole is even more important. The asset's return and variability should be looked at in the context of the portfolio. It is very likely that a highly positive asset will reduce the risk in a given portfolio because the asset has a return that is negatively correlated with the returns offered by the other assets of the portfolio. Therefore, failure of an investor to consider the relationship among the assets in a portfolio can prove to be counterproductive. Diversification reduces the investor's risk exposure without necessarily reducing a portfolio's average return.

The correlation coefficient between the returns of securities 1 and 2 is

$$R_{1,2} = (cov_{1,2})/\sigma_1\sigma_2$$

where

$Cov_{1,2}$ is the covariance between stocks.

σ_1 is the standard deviation of stock 1.

σ_2 is the standard deviation of stock 2.

Q 4:58 What is the beta coefficient?

The beta coefficient is a measure of systematic risk and should be used for a diversified portfolio. In the construction of a well-diversified portfolio, all unsystematic risk is removed. A diversified portfolio is a portfolio of systematic risk, and the beta coefficient is a measure of *volatility* for a diversified portfolio—that is, the volatility of some return relative to a benchmark. In many cases, the benchmark is the S&P 500 Index. In contrast, standard deviation is a measure of *variability*. Variability is the variation of returns from average return.

If the stock has a beta of 1.0, the implication is the stock moves exactly with the market. A beta of 1.2 is 20 percent riskier than the market and a beta of 0.8 is 20 percent less risky than the market. However, the investor must understand that the beta coefficient for an *individual security* may be unstable over time. Therefore, it is not an accurate predictor of future movements in stock prices. On the other hand, the beta coefficient for a *portfolio of securities* is fairly stable over time. For portfolios of securities, as one stock's beta increases, another tends to decrease, thus averaging each other out over time. Therefore, a portfolio's historical beta coefficient can be used as an indicator of future portfolio volatility. However, beta has little meaning if the returns between the fund and the market are weak. If there is a strong relationship between the return of a stock and the return of a market, the beta coefficient is significant. Therefore, the coefficient of determination is used to determine if beta is meaningful.

Q 4:59 What is the coefficient of determination?

The coefficient of determination is often referred to as R^2. It gives the variation in one variable explained by another and is an important statistic in investments. No causality is claimed by the coefficient of determination. It is the job of the investor to interpret it.

The beta coefficient reports the volatility of some return relative to the market (S&P 500). In the case of mutual funds, it is the return of a fund relative to the return of the market. The strength of the relationship is indicated by R2. Let's assume that R2 equals .15. An investor can assume that beta has little meaning because the variation in the return is caused by something other than the movement in the market. In other words, there is substantial unsystematic risk. If R2 equals .95, it can be concluded that the variability of the returns is primarily a result of variability of the market. Therefore, the portfolio's primary source of risk is systematic. In this case, the beta coefficient would be a good measure of risk.

The coefficient of variation is systematic risk. Unsystematic risk is $1 - R^2$. In order to compare mutual funds, it is necessary to use the appropriate benchmark. Assume the following:

	S&P 500		5-Year Schwab Small Cap Index		
	β	R^2	Return	β	R^2
XYZ small cap fund	.75	25	14.3%	1.15	89
ABC small cap fund	.81	19	17.9%	1.30	71

This indicates that the S&P 500 index is not the appropriate benchmark to use. It compares apples to oranges. To compare apples to apples, it is necessary to use an appropriate small cap index when evaluating these mutual funds. Therefore, the Schwab Small Cap Index is used. This information further explains that *ABC*'s larger return (and risk) is a result of the manager's willingness to allocate more to speculative small cap stocks. For an investor looking for less risk, the choice is *XYZ* because of a higher R^2.

The coefficient of determination is not a good or bad number. It indicates the strength of the relationship and is no greater than 100. As R^2 drops, the beta for a diversified portfolio becomes less significant. As a rule of thumb, a minimum R^2 of 75 should be used when evaluating the significance of measures for a diversified portfolio.

Measurements of Performance

The Rate of Return

Q 4:60   What is the holding period return?

The holding period return (HPR) is determined by taking the total return divided by the initial cost of the investment. It is the following:

$$HPR = \frac{P_1 - P_0 + D}{P_0}$$

Where, P_1 is the sale price, P_0 is the purchase price, and D is the dividend paid. For example, an individual buys a stock for $10 and collects a $2 dividend and later sells it for $15 dollars, the HPR is

$$\frac{\$15 - \$10 + \$2}{\$10} = 70\%$$

There is a major weakness in using the holding period. It does not consider how long it took to earn the return.

Q 4:61 What is the rate of return?

The correct way to calculate the return is to solve for the rate of return. The rate of return is commonly known as the time value of money. The equation that answers the previous question is

$$P_0(1+r)^n = P_n$$

where P_0 is the purchase price of the security, r is the rate of return for the period, n is the number of periods, and P_n is the price at which the security is sold. To find the rate of return, assume a stock was purchased at $50 and later sold at the end of the fifth year at $85. The rate of return is easily solved using a calculator:

Calculator Solution

$$PV = -\$50, \ FV = \$85, \ N = 5 \Rightarrow \text{Solve for } i = 11.19\%$$

The rate of return is 11.19 percent. The rate of return is superior to the holding period return.

Q 4:62 What is the geometric average?

Another way to determine the rate of return over a period of years is to use the geometric average. The standard formula for the geometric average is

$$G = \sqrt[n]{X1 \times X2 \times X3 \times \ldots \times Xn}$$

The geometric average can be calculated using the annual rate of returns:

Year	Rate of Return
1	10%
2	20
3	−10
4	−3
5	15

In this example, the returns are redefined to make them positive. This is done by adding 1.0 to the returns. The term $(1 + R_t)$ represents the year-end value relative to the initial investment at the beginning of the year.

$$[(1.10)(1.20)(0.90)(0.97)(1.15)]^{1/5} - 1 = .0579 \text{ or } 5.79\%$$

The arithmetic mean and the geometric mean produce very different results.

Example 4-13: A stock is bought at $100 and at the end of one year it is selling at $125, but then it is sold in the second year at $100. The rate of return is not what is expected when using the average rate of return. In the first year the stock indicates a gain of 25 percent ($25 ÷ $100). In the second year the stock indicates a loss of 20 percent (−$25 ÷ $125). The average rate of return is

$$(25\% - 20\%) \div 2 = 2.5\%$$

Using the arithmetic mean, the investor earned 2.5 percent even though the stock produced neither gain nor loss. The geometric average is

$$((1.25)^*(0.80))^{1/2} - 1 = 0\%$$

The geometric mean accurately reflects the ending value in Year 2 equal to the starting value in Year 1. The compounded rate of return is 1 percent.

Q 4:63   What is the internal rate of return?

The internal rate of return is the discounted rate that makes the present value of the cash outflows equal to initial cash inflows such that the net present value is equal to zero. Assume an investor bought a stock for $35, collected $4.00 in dividends for four years, and later sold the stock at $55. The return is found by solving for the internal rate of return (IRR).

$$PV = -\$35, FV = \$55, PMT = 1, N = 4 \Rightarrow \text{Solve for } i = 14.40\%$$

The IRR has two problems. First, it assumes all cash flows received during the period are reinvested at the IRR. If the investor receives a higher rate of return on the first-year dividend, the true return will exceed the IRR. In contrast, the true return will be less than the IRR if the first-year dividend was invested at a lower rate of return. Second, it is difficult to calculate the IRR with more than one purchase of the specified security.

Q 4:64   What is the dollar-weighted rate of return?

The dollar-weighted rate of return applies the concept of IRR to investment portfolios. The dollar-weighted rate of return is defined as the IRR of a portfolio, taking into account all cash inflows and outflows.

Example 4-14: An investor buys one share of stock for $50 at the beginning of the first year and buys another share for $55 at the end of the first year. The investor earns $1 in dividends in the first year and $2 in the second year. What is the IRR if the shares are sold at the end of the second year for $65 each?

There are two cash outflows: $50 at time period t = 0 and $55 at time period t = 1.There are also two cash inflows: $1 at time period t = 1 and $132 ($2 dividends plus $130 proceeds) at time period t = 2. The next step is to group net cash flow by time. The t = 0 net cash flow is −50, and t = 1 net cash flow is −54 (−$55 + 1), and the t = 2 net cash flow is $132 ($130 + $2). The net cash flows can be entered on the calculator to solve the IRR.

The IRR is 17.21 percent. This is also called the dollar-weighted rate of return because it weighs the amount of all dollars flowing into and out of a portfolio during each time period.

Q 4:65   What is the time-weighted rate of return?

The time-weighted rate of return method does not weigh the amount of all dollar flows during each time period. It computes the return for each period and takes the average of the results by finding the holding period for each period and averaging the returns. If the investment is for more than one year, the geometric mean of the annual returns should be computed to find the timeweighted rate of return for the measurement period.

From the previous example, the return for the first year is

$$(\$55 - \$50 + \$1) \div \$50 = 12\%$$

The return for the second year is

$$(\$130 - \$110 + \$2) \div \$110 = 20\%$$

The arithmetic average return is

$$((1.12)(1.20))^{1/2} - 1 = 15.9\%$$

In the investment management industry, the time-weighted return is the preferred method of performance measurement because it is not affected by the timing of cash flows. If a client adds funds to an investment portfolio at an unfavorable time, the dollar-weighted return will tend to be depressed. If funds are added at a favorable time, the dollar-weighted return will tend to be elevated. The time-weighted rate of return is less than the dollar-weighted rate of return because the stock performed better in the second year, when the investor owned more shares. In contrast, if the stock performed better in the first year, when the investor had fewer shares, the time-weighted return would have been more than the dollar-weighted return.

Q 4:66   What is the real return (inflation adjusted)?

The real return is the earnings from an investment that are above the inflation rate. For investors to achieve their financial goals, they must overcome the loss of purchasing power caused by inflation. The real return is determined by the following formula:

$$\frac{1 + \text{nominal rate}}{1 + \text{inflation rate}} - 1 \times 100$$

where the nominal rate is the absolute return, and the inflation rate is the rate of inflation for the period.

Example 4-15: An individual invests $1,000 at the beginning of the year and earns 10 percent. The resulting balance is $1,100. The inflation over the period is 3 percent. Therefore, the initial investment of $1,000 is equal to $1,030 at the end of the year. The real return is the difference between the earnings ($100) and increase in value as a result of inflation ($30). The difference of $70 is divided by the initial investment adjusted for inflation ($1,030). The real return equals 6.8 percent. It is also found by the following formula:

$$\frac{1.10}{1.03} - 1 \times 100 = 6.79\%$$

Q 4:67   What is the required rate of return?

The CAPM determines the required rate of return for any risky asset. It specifies that the return on an investment (r) depends on the return the individual earns on a risk-free asset and a risk premium. The return of a U.S. Treasury bill is used as the risk-free asset. The risk adjusted return is expressed as

$$r = r_f + (r_m - r_f) \text{ beta}$$

where r_f is the risk-free asset and r_m is the return on the market. The risk premium, which is the additional return of the market over the risk-free rate of return $(r_m - r_f)$ is adjusted by the systematic risk associated with that asset, the beta coefficient.

Q 4:68   What is the expected rate of return?

The expected return is the anticipated growth from an investment. It is the return that is expected to occur for the amount of risk undertaken. The expected return is calculated as

$$E(r) = \frac{E(D)}{P} + E(g)$$

where $E(r)$ is the expected return (as a percentage), $E(D)$ is the expected dividend (current dividend $\times$ (1+ expected growth rate)), P is the price of the asset, and $E(g)$ is the expected growth.

Example 4-16: If the stock is selling at $50 and is expected to pay a $3 dividend, which is expected to grow 5 percent per year, then the expected return is:

$$\frac{\$3}{\$50} + .05 = 11\%$$

Risk-Adjusted Return Using the Jensen Performance Index, the Treynor Performance Index, and the Sharpe Performance Index (Mayo, 2000)

Q 4:69   Why use the risk-adjusted return?

When determining the various returns earned by a portfolio, a higher return by itself is not necessarily indicative of superior performance. Alternatively, a lower return is not indicative of inferior performance. A return from a money market fund would be less than a return from a stock, because an investor takes on more risk with a stock. Essentially, money market returns should not be compared to stock returns. In addition, earning 10 percent from a low-risk portfolio is better than earning 10 percent from a high-risk portfolio. An investor does not standardize for differences in risk when comparing absolute returns and needs to adjust for risk to find the optimal return for a portfolio. Upon making the risk adjustment, an investor is able to determine if a given portfolio outperformed the market or another portfolio.

The expression "beat the market" is often misleading as it implies that a fund outperformed the market return. The expression does not specify what market or benchmark was used and the level of risk assumed. To really outperform the market, an investor must have superior market timing to sell when securities are considerably overvalued and to buy when securities are undervalued. Alternatively, portfolios need diversification to eliminate unsystematic risk because the market does not reward such risk. An investor can measure how well a fund is managed or diversified by correlating returns from a portfolio to those of an appropriate market benchmark. The benchmark often used for comparisons is the S&P 500 Index because it is a proxy for the market. However, it becomes difficult to quantify performance on a risk-adjusted basis.

Q 4:70   How is risk measured?

There are three major composite equity portfolio measures that combine risk and return to give a quantifiable risk-adjusted number. These composite performance measures are the Treynor index, the Sharpe index, and the Jensen index. Investors may use these measures together to determine if a portfolio or fund manager actually "beat the market." All three measures provide the actual risk-adjusted return. The differences among them rest with the measures of risk and the calculation process; however, all three are part of the CAPM.

The CAPM determines the required rate of return for any risky asset. It specifies that the return on an investment (r) depends on the return the individual earns on a risk-free asset and a risk premium. The return on a U.S. Treasury bill is used as the risk-free asset. The risk-adjusted return is expressed as

$$r = r_f + (r_m - r_f) \text{ beta}$$

where r_f is the risk-free asset and r_m is the return of the market. The risk premium, which is the additional return of the market over the risk-free rate of return ($r_m - r_f$) is adjusted by the systematic risk associated with that asset, the beta coefficient.

Q 4:71   What is the Treynor performance index?

The Treynor index uses a portfolio's beta to measure risk and is expressed as

$$T_i = \frac{r_p - r_f}{\text{beta}}$$

where r_p is the realized return of the portfolio and r_f is the risk-free rate. The extent to which the realized return exceeds the risk-free rate is divided by the portfolio's beta. The risk-variable beta measures systematic risk and indicates nothing about the diversification of a portfolio. It implicitly assumes a completely diversified portfolio. The Treynor index standardizes the return in excess of the risk-free rate by the volatility of the return. To understand how to interpret the Treynor index, consider the example below:

Example 4-17: The S&P 500 earns 10 percent when a government T-bill earns 7 percent. Portfolio X earns a 12 percent return with a beta of 1.2, and portfolio Y earns 14 percent with a beta of 1.9. Using that information, the Treynor index is calculated for the market portfolio and each portfolio as follows:

$$T_m = \frac{0.10 - 0.07}{1.00} = 0.030$$

$$T_x = \frac{0.12 - 0.07}{1.2} = 0.042$$

$$T_y = \frac{0.14 - 0.07}{1.9} = 0.037$$

This indicates that X and Y outperformed the market on a risk-adjusted basis, and portfolio X performed better than portfolio Y. The Treynor index must be computed for the market to determine if a particular portfolio outperformed the market. However, the results do not indicate by how much each portfolio outperformed the market.

Q 4:72   What is the Sharpe performance index?

Another measure of performance is the Sharpe index, which is the following equation:

$$S_i = \frac{r_p - r_f}{SD_p}$$

The new input is SD_p, which represents the standard deviation of the portfolio. The composite measure is similar to the Treynor index, but it measures the total risk of the portfolio by including standard deviation instead of only the systematic risk. It does not implicitly assume that a portfolio is well diversified. The Sharpe index standardizes the return in excess of the risk-free rate by the variability of the returns.

Example 4-18: Assume the previous examples are continued and portfolio X has a standard deviation of 30 percent and portfolio Y has a standard deviation of 20 percent. In this case, portfolio X equals 0.17 and portfolio Y equals 0.35. Because portfolio Y has a higher score, its performance is superior to that of portfolio X. It is safe to assume that the additional return (*i.e.*, 14 versus 12 percent) more than compensates for the additional risk.

In the example, the Sharpe index produces a ranking that is the opposite of the Treynor index. The difference in ranking occurs because the measure of risk is different. Consider a utility fund with an average return of 10 percent and a standard deviation of 15 percent. This means that 68 percent of the time, the return ranges from negative 5 percent to positive 25 percent. This represents a great amount of variability. However, the same fund may have a beta of 0.7, indicating less volatility than the market returns.

It is important to understand that variability and volatility mean different things. Variability refers to how much a return changes from year to year to its average return. Volatility compares a return relative to a benchmark, such as the S&P 500. The utility fund has a low beta. Therefore, its return does not change more than the market. However, there is a large variation from year to year in the fund's return, even though it is less volatile compared to the market. There is a large amount of unsystematic risk unique to the utility fund and only a slight amount of systematic risk.

The Treynor index gives a superior risk-adjusted return when a low beta is used, and the Sharpe index gives an inferior risk-adjusted return when there is excessive diversifiable risk. In comparison with the Treynor index, the Sharpe index does not indicate if a portfolio outperformed the market without calculating for the market. It does not tell how much a portfolio outperformed or underperformed the market.

Q 4:73   What is the Jensen performance index?

The Jensen measure is similar to the Treynor and Sharpe indexes because it is based on the CAPM. The Jensen index determines how much the realized return differs from the required return. The following formula is used to find alpha:

$$a = r_p - [r_f + (r_m - r_f) \text{ beta}]$$

In the equation, the a (referred to as alpha) value indicates whether a portfolio manager is superior or inferior in market timing and stock selection. A positive alpha indicates a superior manager, and a negative alpha indicates an inferior manager.

Example 4-19: Assume a return of 15 percent with a beta of 1.2 for manager X when the market return is 14.3 percent and the risk-free rate is 7 percent. The alpha is expressed as

$$a = 0.15 - [0.07 + (0.143 - 0.07)1.2] = -0.0076$$

The negative result indicates inferior performance. If portfolio manager Y earns a return of 12.5 percent with a beta of 0.7, the alpha is expressed as

$$a = 0.125 - [0.07 + (0.143 - 0.07)0.7] = 0.0039$$

This indicates superior performance because it is positive. The absolute return for manager X is higher, but the risk-adjusted return for manager Y

is greater, denoting superior performance. Therefore, manager Y not only outperformed manager X but also outperformed the market return on a riskadjusted basis.

In the example, portfolio X performed 0.76 percent worse than the market, while portfolio Y performed 0.39 percent better than the market. As shown in the above example, the Jensen index computes the absolute value. Conversely, the Treynor and Sharpe indexes compute a relative value.

Q 4:74   How do the different types of risk-adjusted measurements compare?

Like the Treynor index, the Jensen index does not evaluate the ability of a portfolio manager to diversify because it uses beta, which calculates risk premium in terms of systematic risk. These are usually safe measures to use when comparing a diversified portfolio of mutual funds. The Sharpe index uses the standard deviation of returns as a measure of risk. Therefore, the Sharpe index scores a portfolio manager on both rate of return and diversification. A completely diversified portfolio has identical rankings for Treynor and Sharpe measures because total variance is a result of systematic risk, indicating a completely diversified portfolio. Alternatively, a poorly diversified portfolio may have a high ranking using Treynor and Jensen measures and a low ranking using the Sharpe index. The differences in ranking are directly the result of diversification.

All three performance indicators are complementary to each other but provide different information. Each measure provides very similar rankings when dealing with a diversified portfolio of mutual funds. However, in a such a portfolio the Jensen or Treynor index is preferred. If such a portfolio existed, then each mutual fund would represent only part of an investor's total risk. Investors are more concerned with the nondiversifiable risk associated with the portfolio, so beta is an appropriate measure of risk. The Jensen and Treynor indicators are not good measures of performance for specialized sector funds. If the specific portfolio constitutes all of an individual's assets, then total risk is a more appropriate measure.

Analysis of Financial Ratios

Liquidity Ratios

Q 4:75   What are liquidity ratios?

Liquidity ratios measure how quickly a firm can convert assets into cash without incurring a loss. It is important to compare this ratio with the firm's industry and to determine if internal trends are developing.

Q 4:76   What is the current ratio?

The current ratio is

$$\frac{\text{Current Assets}}{\text{Current Liablities}}$$

It is desirable to have more current assets than current liabilities. A general rule of thumb is to have a ratio of 2:1. This means that a firm's current asset can decrease by half and still meet short-term obligations.

Q 4:77   What is the quick ratio?

The quick ratio is

$$\frac{\text{Cash} + \text{Marketable Securities} + \text{Receivables}}{\text{Current Liablities}}$$

This ratio indicates the amount of highly liquid assets available to meet current liabilities.

Q 4:78   What is the cash ratio?

The cash ratio is

$$\frac{\text{Cash and Marketable Securities}}{\text{Current Liablities}}$$

The cash ratio is the most conservative of all the liquidity ratios.

Activity Ratios

Q 4:79   What are activity ratios?

Activity ratios measure how quickly a firm is converting its inventory and accounts receivable into cash. The more rapidly it can do this, the quicker the firm receives cash. As with all ratios, activity ratios should be compared with competing firms and analyzed for internal trends.

Q 4:80   What is receivables turnover?

The receivable turnover ratio is

$$\frac{\text{Net Annual Sales}}{\text{Average Receivables}}$$

The ratio measures how fast account receivables are paid to get cash for paying off current liabilities. The ratio uses average receivables from beginning receivables plus ending receivables divided by two.

Example 4-20: The firm's receivables level was $50.5 in 2006 and $65.4 in 2005. The average for both years is $57.95 ($50.5 + $64.4/2). If net sales are $575.00, then the receivables turnover ratio is

$$\frac{\$575.00}{\$57.95} = 9.9$$

This means that annual sales are almost 10 times the level of receivables. Inventory turns over about every 37 days. The average receivable collection period is

$$\frac{365}{\text{Annual Receivables Turnover}} = \frac{365}{9.92} = 36.7 \text{days}$$

The receivables turnover ratio is a value that a firm does not want to sway too far from the norm for the industry.

Q 4:81   What is inventory turnover ratio?

The inventory turnover ratio is

$$\frac{\text{CGS}}{\text{Average Inventory}}$$

The inventory ratio uses average inventory for the year. It can be calculated using net sales instead of cost of goods sold (CGS), but the latter is the preferred way.

The average inventory processing time is

$$\frac{365}{\text{Annual Inventory Turnover}}$$

The inventory turnover ratio follows the same conclusions as those drawn from the receivables turnover ratio. A very low number and long processing time relative to the industry implies that capital is tied up in inventory far beyond the firm's needs. Conversely, a very high number and short processing time relative to the industry imply scarce inventory levels, which lead to back orders and sluggish delivery. The inventory turnover ratio is a value that should not deviate too far from the competition.

Operating Efficiency Ratios

Q 4:82   What are operating efficiency ratios?

Efficiency ratios measure how well a firm uses its capital and assets.

Q 4:83   What is total asset turnover?

The total asset turnover ratio is

$$\frac{\text{Net Sales}}{\text{Average Total Net Assets}}$$

An exceptionally high number relative to the industry implies lack of productivity to meet demand or assets that are fully depreciated and out of date. A very low number relative to the industry implies that capital is tied up in assets extending beyond the firm's needs.

Q 4:84   What is net fixed asset turnover?

The net fixed asset turnover is

$$\frac{\text{Net Sales}}{\text{Average Net Fixed Assets}}$$

An exceptionally high number relative to the industry implies lack of productivity to meet demand or the use of assets that are fully depreciated and out of date. A very low number relative to the industry implies that capital is tied up in excessive fixed assets.

Q 4:85   What is equity turnover?

The equity turnover ratio is

$$\frac{\text{Net Sales}}{\text{Average Equity}}$$

Equity includes common and preferred stock, paid-in capital, and retained earnings. The ratio is different from the total asset turnover ratio in that it does not include current liabilities and long-term debt. The equity turnover ratio is improved by increasing the proportion of debt capital in a firm's capital structure.

Operating Profitability Ratios

Q 4:86   What are operating profitability ratios?

Operating profitability ratios indicate profits as a percentage of sales and as a percentage of capital.

Q 4:87   What is gross profit margin?

The gross profit margin is

$$\frac{\text{Gross Profit}}{\text{Net Sales}}$$

Gross profit is net sales minus cost of goods sold. Therefore, gross profit margin measures the percentage earned on sales after deducting cost of goods sold. For example, if the gross margin is 25 percent, the firm earned $0.25 on every dollar of sales before deducting sales, general, and administrative (SG&A) expenses. The ratio indicates the firm's relative cost-price position when compared to other firms in the industry.

Q 4:88   What is operating profit margin?

The operating profit margin is

$$\frac{\text{Operating Profit}}{\text{Net Sales}}$$

Operating profit is gross profit minus SG&A expenses. Therefore, operating margin is the percentage earned on sales before adjusting for interest and taxes. In addition, some firms add back depreciation and amortization expenses to compute a profit margin consisting of earnings less interest, taxes, depreciation, and amortization (EBITDA). The operating margin then uses all controllable expenses. The variability of the ratio indicates the business risk for a firm.

Q 4:89   What is the net profit margin?

The net profit margin is

$$\frac{\text{Net Income}}{\text{Net Sales}}$$

The net income used is earnings after interest and taxes but before dividends. The ratio should use earnings from continuous operations, not discontinued operations.

Q 4:90   What is return on owner's equity?

The return on owner's equity is

$$\frac{\text{Net Income} - \text{Preferred Dividend}}{\text{Average Common Equity}}$$

The net income used is earnings after interest and taxes but before preferred dividends. The equity is the sum of common stock, additional paid-in capital, and retained earnings minus preferred stock. This identifies how much a firm is earning on the common shareholders' investment.

Q 4:91   What is return on equity?

If an investor is concerned with the firm's total equity, preferred dividends and equity are added back into return on owner's equity. This ratio for return on equity (ROE) is

$$\frac{\text{Net Income}}{\text{Equity}}$$

The return on shareholders' equity shows how efficiently a company can make money and profitably use retained earnings to make more money for its shareholders. Return on equity can be increased by employing more debt financing and less equity financing, because earnings are applied to a smaller equity base, which increases the return on equity. The result is a firm having a small return on assets but a large return on equity. A substantial difference between return on equity and return on assets indicates the firm's ability to successfully utilize financial leverage.

Q 4:92   What is return on assets?

Return on assets (ROA) is

$$\frac{\text{Net Income}}{\text{Total Assets}}$$

This is a measure that reveals what management is able to earn on all assets.

Business Risk (Brown & Reilly, 2000)

Q 4:93   What is business risk?

Business risk is the risk associated with the nature of the business. It is uncertainty of earnings caused by variability in the firm's sales. It is measured by the variability of the operating income over a period of time. The variability is determined by standard deviation using historical operating earnings. The standard deviation is an absolute figure. Therefore, the standard deviation of operating earnings is divided by the mean operating earnings to find the coefficient of variation. The coefficient of variation provides a relative figure used to compare firms of different sizes.

$$\text{Business Risk} = \frac{\text{Standard Deviation of Operating Earnings}}{\text{Mean Operating Earnings}} = f(\text{Coefficient of Variation of Operating Earnings})$$

A minimum series of 5 years to a maximum of 10 years is used to calculate the coefficient of variation from operating earnings. Operating earnings of less than 5 year is not meaningful, and a series of more than 10 years is out of date. Two factors contribute to the variability of earnings measured by business risk: sales variability and operating leverage.

Q 4:94   What is sales variability?

Sales variability greatly affects a firm's earnings. It is influenced by customers, products, and advertising. The nature of the business and the current economic environment also affect a firm's sales. The variability of a firm's sales is measured by the coefficient of variation for the past 5 to 10 years. It is the standard deviation of sales divided by the mean sales for a period.

$$\text{Sales Variability} = \frac{\text{Standard Deviation of Sales}}{\text{Mean Sales}} = f(\text{Coefficient of Variation of Sales})$$

Q 4:95   What is operating leverage?

Operating leverage is a comparison of variable costs to fixed costs. If a firm has a high operating leverage, a large percentage of the firm's costs are fixed. Fixed production costs cause more variation in operating income than sales. Operating leverage means that a small change in sales results in a large change in operating income. Profits decline by a greater percentage than sales during bad times. Conversely, profits increase by a greater percentage than sales during boom times.

$$\text{Operating Leverage} = \frac{\sum_{i=1}^{n} \left| \frac{\% \Delta OE}{\% \Delta S} \right|}{N}$$

The operating leverage is a percentage change in operating earnings (earnings before interest and taxes) relative to the percentage change in sales over a period of time.

The degree of operating leverage (DOL) is the percentage change in operating income that results from a percentage change in sales.

$$\text{Degree of Operating Leverage} = \frac{\text{Percentage Change in EBIT}}{\text{Percentage Changes in Sales}}$$

Financial Risk (Brown & Reilly, 2000)

Q 4:96   What is financial risk?

Financial risk is the risk related to a firm's sources of financing. It reflects the use of fixed income securities, including debt and preferred stock. An increase in financial leverage for a firm causes an increase in financial risk. The amount of financial risk that is acceptable for a firm depends on the business risk. A firm is receptive to more financial risk if the business risk is low. In contrast, a firm is unwilling to accept more financial risk if the business risk is high. The degree of financial leverage (DFL) is the percentage change in earnings per share that results from a percentage change in earnings before interest and taxes (EBIT).

$$\text{Degree of Financial Leverage} = \frac{\text{Percentage Change in EPS}}{\text{Percentage Change in EBIT}}$$

Q 4:97   What is the debt-equity ratio?

The debt-equity ratio is

$$\frac{\text{Total Long} - \text{Term Debt}}{\text{Total Equity}}$$

The numerator is composed of all long-term obligations, including convertible bonds. The denominator includes common stock, retained earnings, and preferred stock, although some analysts exclude preferred stock. The larger the debt figure, the more financial risk a firm has assumed. The higher the number gets, the increased likelihood of volatile earnings because of greater financial risk.

Q 4:98   What is long-term debt/total capital ratio?

The long-term debt/total capital ratio is

$$\frac{\text{Total Long} - \text{Term Debt}}{\text{Total Long} - \text{Term Capital}}$$

Long-term capital includes all long-term debt, total equity, and preferred stock.

Q 4:99   What is the interest coverage?

The interest coverage ratio is

$$\frac{\text{Income Before Interest and Taxes (EBIT)}}{\text{Debt Interest Charge}} \qquad \frac{\text{Net Income} + \text{ Income Taxes} + \text{ Interest Expense}}{\text{Interest Expense}}$$

This measures a firm's ability to service debt. It reveals how much a firm is earning relative to what is owed. For example, a ratio of 3 indicates that the firm has \$3 of operating income for every \$1 in interest expense.

The number 1 minus the reciprocal of the interest coverage reveals how low earnings can decline before a firm is unable to pay interest expenses. For example, if the coverage ratio is 3, then earnings can decline by 67 percent (1 minus 1/5), and the firm would still be able to pay interest expenses.

Cash Flow Ratios

Q 4:100   What is the cash flow coverage ratio?

The cash flow coverage ratio is

$$\frac{\text{Net Income} + \text{ Depreciation Expense} + \text{ Change in Deferred Taxes}}{N}$$

Cash flow coverage equals net income plus depreciation expense plus a change in deferred taxed (if there is an increase) for the period (N).

Q 4:101   What is the cash flow to long-term debt ratio?

The cash flow to long-term debt ratio is

$$\frac{\text{Net Income} + \text{Depreciation Expense} + \text{ Change in Deferred Taxes}}{\text{Book Value of Long} - \text{ Term Debt}}$$

Chapter 5

Fixed Income

Investment planning includes bonds, securities, and Treasury issues. This chapter discusses the various types of instruments available as well as the formulas necessary to provide the best information to clients.

Types of Bonds

Q5:1   What is a zero coupon bond?

Zero coupon bonds are sold with no coupon at a discount and redeemed for face value at maturity. Interest is accrued over the life of the bond. The accrued interest is taxed as if it were received. Therefore, there is no tax avoidance with buying zero coupon bonds. The interest is taxed even though it is not received until maturity. For example, a 10-year zero coupon bond is purchased with a face value of $1,000, priced to yield a 7.5% annual return. What is the interest paid over the life of the bond?

$$N = 20; \ I/Y = 3.75; \ PMT = 0; \ FV = 1,000; \ \text{solve } PV = \$485.19 = \text{Price}$$

The accrued interest that can be expected is

$$\$1,000 - \$485.19 = \$514.81$$

Interest is assumed to be distributed twice a year for zero coupon bonds even though it is not paid (i.e., $N = 20$, $I/Y = 3.75\%$).

The tax disadvantage of accrued interest can be circumvented in retirement accounts because tax is deferred until funds are withdrawn.

Zero coupon bonds are extremely volatile in periods of changing interest rates. In general, the price of a bond is more volatile the longer the term to maturity or the smaller the coupon payment. The reason for the increased price volatility relative to other bonds is that the entire return is in one single payment at maturity. The current price of a bond is the present value of interest and principal payments. The price of a bond is less volatile to interest rates when periodic interest payments are received before maturity. However, the price of a zero coupon is fully the result of the present value of a single payment received at maturity since no periodic interest payments are made. Zero coupon bonds should be bought when interest rates are expected to fall to take advantage of the increased bond price.

Q5:2   What is an accrual bond?

Accrual bonds are similar to zero coupon bonds except they are redeemed at par value plus any accrued interest. In other words, the payment of interest is deferred until maturity. For example, assume a five-year $1,000 par value accrual bond pays 7.5 percent interest compounded annually. The investor will receive how much cash at maturity? The accrued interest is calculated as

$$N = 5; I/Y = 7.5\%; PMT = \$75 \ (\text{i.e., } \$1,000 \times 7.5\%); PV = 0; \text{solve } FV = \$435.62$$

Therefore, at maturity, the investor will receive $1,000 face value plus $435.62 accrued interest, totaling 1,435.62.

Q 5:3   What is an investment grade bond?

Investment grade bonds are not a particular type of bond, but refer to any debt of high quality—rated triple B or higher.

Q 5:4   What are secured versus unsecured bonds?

Secured bonds have a claim to assets of a corporation in the event of default, insolvency, or liquidation. For example, a mortgage bond is secured by real property or buildings. Unsecured bonds are not backed by collateral.

Q 5:5   What are debentures?

Debentures are promissory notes that are not backed by collateral (they are unsecured) and supported by the creditworthiness of a firm or government agency. During bankruptcy, debentures are redeemed only after all secured debt has been paid off. Therefore, debentures pay a higher yield than secured debt because of the added risk. Additionally, some debentures are subordinated, and these are even more risky than other debt. During bankruptcy, subordinated debentures are paid off after all other unsecured debt is paid off. Investors are often attracted to subordinated debt because of higher yields and other embedded options, such as convertible provisions.

Debentures are often sold to the public by corporations to raise cash. Debentures are general obligations of a company so they do not tie up specific assets. Because assets are not tied up, a firm can get additional funds from a bank and use the assets as collateral. Banks are more often willing to loan funds when backed by other assets. However, there is always the risk that a firm may overextend itself by issuing too much debt. Default on a debenture generally means that all senior debt is also in default.

Q 5:6   What are high yield securities?

High yield securities are often referred to as "junk" bonds. These are bonds that are low quality, speculative grade, usually with ratings below triple B. The features are the same as investment grade debt. However, the poor quality means they offer higher yields than investment grade debt. Triple B or better is generally considered investment grade. High yield securities often have a call feature and sinking fund. They are usually debentures, and may be subordinated to the firm's other debt. However, some high yield securities have collateral (*i.e.*, mortgage bonds). These bonds are often issued to finance a takeover and merger, or help a start-up firm raise capital.

High yield securities are divided into two classes. The first are those companies that were initially investment grade, but have fallen to speculative grade because of financial problems. These are commonly known as *fallen angels*. The second are firms with less than investment grade ratings. This is common for start-up firms that have little credit history.

Floating Rate Securities

Q 5:7   What are floating (or variable) rate securities?

Floating rate securities are bonds with a coupon rate that varies with changes in short-term rates. The market price for floating rate securities changes less than fixed coupon bonds when interest rates increase or decrease. In general, bond prices and interest rates are inversely related. When interest rates increase (decrease), bond prices decrease (increase). However, because floating securities tend to fluctuate with short-term rates, the inverse relationship between bond prices and interest rates does not exist. Variable bonds are similar to floating bonds except in frequency and time. Floating rate bonds adjust more than once per year and use short-term reference rates. Variable bonds do not adjust more than once per year, and they use a long-term reference rate.

Q 5:8   What is a coupon formula floater?

The floating coupon security generally has a coupon that is determined by some reference rate and adds a stated margin rate. The floating coupon rate is generally a short-term interest rate index plus a fixed spread. The spread is usually expressed in basis points and is called the stated margin. For example, assume the London Interbank Offered Rate (LIBOR) is the index and the quoted spread is 150 basis points. If the LIBOR rate is currently 4.5 percent, than the floating coupon rate is 6 percent. The stated margin rate can be added to or subtracted from the reference rate. In general, the spread is larger the longer the maturity of the floating security. This is due to the upward rising yield curve and concern by investors over rate caps. A cap is a ceiling put on the bond that limits the maximum coupon paid by the issuer. The opposite is called a floor, which limits the minimum coupon received by the bondholder.

Q 5:9   What is a leveraged floater?

A leveraged floater security has a coupon that will increase or decrease by more than a one-to-one basis with the reference point. The formula is a reference point, usually a short-term interest rate index, *multiplied by* a multiplier *plus* a quoted margin. For example, assume the London Interbank Offered Rate (LIBOR) rate is the reference point. The LIBOR rate is 4.5 percent and the quoted margin is 70 basis points. The multiplier is usually a value expressed between 0 and 1. If the multiplier is .7, then the leverage floater is 3.85 (4.5% × .7 + .70%). It is clear that the leveraged floater security is moving more than the LIBOR rate because of the constant.

Q 5:10   What is an inverse floater?

These bonds have a coupon rate that moves inversely to the reference rate, with a leverage factor. The formula is the constant rate *minus* the multiplier *multiplied by* the reference rate. The constant and multiplier are included in the prospectus at the time the bond is issued and remain constant for the life of the bond. If the reference rate increases, a larger amount is subtracted from the constant, resulting in a lower coupon. For example, assume a bond is set equal to 25 percent − (2.5 × LIBOR), with a cap of 25 percent and a floor of 0. The cap limits the maximum amount that is paid by the issuer, whereas the floor limits the minimum amount received by the holder.

Different Ways to Retire Debt

Q5:11   What is bullet maturity?

Bullet maturity involves paying off the entire principal in one payment at the maturity date. These are non-amortizing securities.

Q5:12   What is a serial bond?

A bond issue in which specified bonds mature each year. Interest is paid off at different intervals. Serial bonds are common with state and local governments to finance capital improvements, but are not common with corporations. These are non-amortizing securities.

Q5:13   What are amortizing securities?

Amortizing securities make both interest and principal payments. For example, mortgage-backed and asset-backed securities pay both interest and principal payments each month until maturity when the entire principal is paid up.

Q5:14   What is a sinking fund?

Sinking funds are a series of periodic payments to retire a portion of the bond issue prior to maturity. One type of sinking funds allows the firm to deposit cash with a trustee who invests the funds to earn interest. The principal and accumulated interest is then used to retire a portion of the bonds, using a random selection process or lottery. The bonds would be retired at the call price which is usually par. The other type of sinking fund allows the issuer to purchase a portion of bonds to be retired in the open market if the price is below par. Sinking funds have several advantages: (1) it ensures the final payment at maturity will not be too large; (2) it enhances liquidity; (3) bonds prices are more stable because the issuer becomes an active participant when prices fall. The primary disadvantage to a sinking fund is the call feature, which can take an investor by surprise. Additionally, an *accelerated sinking fund provision* can exist. This allows the issuer to retire more bonds than the sinking fund calls for. This provision is used when interest rates are low and the bond price is higher than the call price, which is usually at par.

Q 5:15   What is the difference between refundable versus nonrefundable bonds?

The act of issuing new debt and using the proceeds to retire old debt is called *refunding*. This practice is common with bonds having high coupon rates during a time of low interest rates. It is advantageous for a firm to refinance the existing bonds at a lower coupon rate. Nonrefundable bonds contain restrictions that prevent them from using proceeds from new debt to retire old debt and the high coupons. However, a bond can be callable but nonrefundable, meaning the source of the funds to retire debt should not come from issuing new debt.

The Different Types of Embedded Options

Q 5:16   What is an embedded option?

An embedded option is a right of an issuer or bondholder as indicated in the bond indenture. Embedded options play an important role to the valuation of bonds. They affect the timing and magnitude of cash flows. They also affect the rate of performance for a bond over time. There are several embedded options that are granted to issuers and borrowers.

Q 5:17   What is a call provision?

A call provision allows a firm to buy back bonds at a specified price before maturity. It is often used after a period of high interest rates. If bonds were issued during high interest rates, it may make sense for a firm to refinance new debt at a lower interest rate. The proceeds from issuing new debt are then used to retire the older debt with the higher coupon rates. The act of issuing new debt and using the proceeds to retire old debt is called *refunding*. The call price is usually less than the market price. If the call price is higher than the market price, it would not be beneficial for the issuer to call the bonds. However, the call provision is set above par in order to protect investors from losing their higher yield bonds, and declines in later years. In general, bonds usually are not called until a period of time has passed.

Q 5:18   What is a prepayment provision?

Prepayment provisions are common with amortizing securities. It allows the borrower to prepay the loan balances before maturity. This is often common with home mortgages and car loans.

Q 5:19   What is an accelerated sinking fund provision?

The accelerated sinking fund option allows the issuer to retire more bonds than required under a sinking fund.

Q 5:20   What is a put provision?

The bondholder has the option to sell the bonds back to the issuer for a specified price. This is common when bonds are trading below par because of high interest rates. Bond owners would "put" the bonds back to the issuer and take the proceeds to invest in other bonds paying the current (higher) coupon rate. The put price is generally close to par. If an investor acquires a bond with a put provision, he or she must pay a price for it. The extra price is usually subtle but reflected in a lower coupon rate than a bond without the put provision. If interest rates remain below the coupon rate, then the issuer will benefit because it sold a bond at a lower coupon than would be required if it had no put provision. However, if interest rates increase, investors profit because they are not locked into a debt instrument with a lower yield than other competing bonds. Therefore, if an investor anticipates rising interest rates, or wants to hedge against rates increasing, a put option may be an attractive investment.

Q 5:21   What are conversion rights?

Conversion rights allow a bondholder to convert the bond into shares of common stock. The conversion feature acts as a benefit to induce investors to buy the bonds. It allows a corporation to have a debt instrument in its capital structure. However, the conversion feature usually comes at a cost. These bonds tend to trade at a lower coupon rate than other bonds, and are subordinate to other debt issued by the corporation. They often have a sinking fund provision, and are often called by corporations to force bondholders to convert to common stock. The true benefit to holding these bonds is the safety of debt with the potential for capital gains. Convertible bonds will increase in value as the underlying stock increases.

Convertible bonds are subject to investor risk. Their price often fluctuates with the market forces of supply and demand because they can be actively traded. Changes in the stock price result in changes to the value of the convertible security. In addition, as with any other bond, their prices are influenced by changes in interest rate. Therefore, both the underlying stock and interest rates cause variations in the price of convertibles. Furthermore, convertibles are in double jeopardy during periods of high interest rates and low stock prices. Their lower coupon rate causes their price to decline faster than other nonconvertible debt. Additionally, the lower stock price will pull the convertible bond price down with it. Both of these factors can cause a considerable decline in the price of convertible bonds.

The value of a convertible bond compared to common stock is based on its conversion value. The conversion value is a product of the face value of the bond, the conversion price, and the market price of the stock. The number of shares in which the bond is converted into is found by taking the face value of the bond and dividing it by the conversion price. This is called the conversion ratio and is listed in the indenture. For example, if the bond is priced at $1,000 and the conversion price is $25, the conversion ratio equals 40 shares

($1,000 ÷ $25). The number of shares a bond is converted into, times the market price of the stock, gives the value of the bond in terms of stock. If the bond is convertible into 40 shares, and the market price of the stock is $23, then the bond's value is worth $920 relative to stock ($23 × $40). The conversion value of a bond is expressed as

$$C_s = \frac{\text{Face value of bond}}{\text{Conversion price}} \times \text{Market price of stock}$$

The equation shows a relationship between the stock price and the conversion value. As the price of the stock increases, the conversion value of the bond also increases. If the value of the bond and the value of the stock were equal, the bond's value relative to stock would be par (the bond's face value). The market price of a convertible bond cannot be less than the conversion value, or an opportunity for arbitrage would exist.

Types of Risk Associated with Bond Investing

Q 5:22   What is interest rate risk?

A bond's price is inversely related to interest rates. When market interest rates increase, a bond's price goes down. When market interest rates drop, a bond's price goes up. Why does this relationship exist? Because the value of a bond is the present value of its cash flows discounted back at the appropriate current market discount rate. A higher interest rate discounted back will give a lower present value. A lower interest rate discounted back will give a higher present value. This inverse relationship between interest rates and price means that to make profits in the bond market, an investor simply needs to predict the direction of future interest rates. If an investor anticipates that interest rates will rise, then they are predicting that bond prices will fall. The reverse is true, if they predict interest rates will drop, they are anticipating that bond prices will rise. However, guessing the direction of interest rates can be a challenging event.

Q 5:23   What is the time to maturity effect on bond price?

The length of time to maturity affects the price of a bond. When interest rates fall, a bond's price increases, but the price of a bond with a longer maturity will rise more than the price of a bond with a shorter maturity. Investors who speculate with interest rates will choose a bond with a longer term to maturity, and investors who are concerned with safety of principal will choose a bond with a shorter term to maturity.

Q 5:24   What is the coupon rate effect on bond price?

A bond's price is also related to the coupon rate. The lower the coupon rate, the greater the interest rate risk. Bonds with higher coupon rates will be more sensitive to interest rate changes than bonds with lower coupon rates. Why?

Because bonds with higher coupon rates will deliver a greater amount of their cash flows during the earlier years. Zero coupon bonds are the most ratesensitive issues because they deliver their entire future cash flows at maturity.

Q 5:25   What is the market yield effect on bond price?

A bond price trades inversely to yields. If current interest rates increase, bond prices will fall. If current interest rates decrease, bond prices will rise. There is a deeper relationship between price and yield. As the yield increases, the price curve gets flatter. Changes in current yields have a smaller effect on the bond's price when yields increase. As yields drop, the price curve gets steeper. In this case, changes in current yields have a large impact on the bond's price. This relationship shows that yields affect price volatility. When yields are high, bond price volatility is low (flatter price curve). The reverse is true, when yields are low, bond price volatility is high (steeper price curve).

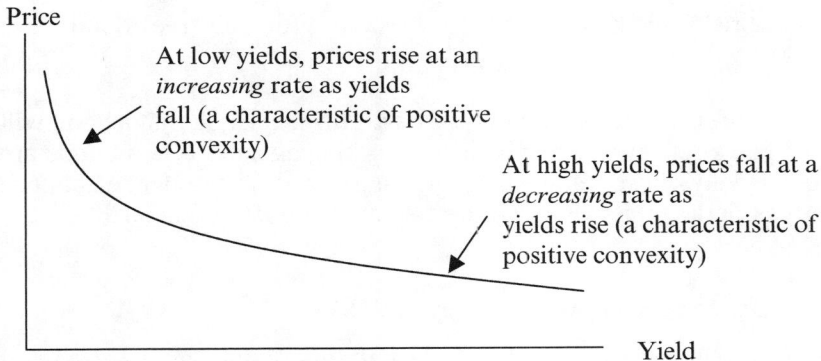

Price

At low yields, prices rise at an *increasing* rate as yields fall (a characteristic of positive convexity)

At high yields, prices fall at a *decreasing* rate as yields rise (a characteristic of positive convexity)

Yield

Q 5:26   What is call and prepayment risk?

The issuer calls a bond when interest rates drop, and the call price is below the theoretical market price. The issuer can issue new bonds at a lower coupon rate. If a bond is callable, the future cash flows are less predictable and a bond has greater interest rate risk because the life of a bond can be much shorter than its maturity date. Holders of callable bonds also have more risk of investing the proceeds at lower interest rate of return after the bond is called. This type of risk is called reinvestment risk. Additionally, the potential for capital appreciation is reduced because investors are unwilling to pay a price above the call price. Therefore, the call price acts like a ceiling in periods of falling interest rates and price appreciation is limited. This holds more value for the issuer. The price of a bond without a call provision will continue to rise as interest rates fall. However, an advantage that comes with callable bonds is that when interest rates rise, the price of a callable bond does not drop as much as the price of a straight bond because of the call provision.

In the case of mortgage and asset-backed securities, investors are exposed to the risk of prepayment of principal. Prepayment has the same underlying risks as explained above for callable bonds. In addition, there is contraction risk, the risk that homeowners pay all or most of their loans when interest rates decline. On the other hand, the reverse is also true—investors should benefit from extension risk, when prepayments slow down as interest rates rise.

Q5:27   What is credit risk?

There are three forms of credit risk. First, default risk is the failure of the issuer to meet the terms of the indenture (*i.e.*, maximum financial ratio for the firm). Therefore, default risk is not just limited to timely paying interest and principal payments. Second, credit spread risk is the extra return above a riskless security (*i.e.*, Treasury Bill) that investors demand to compensate for the added risk of the security. Credit spread risk is also known as the risk premium, and is explained by the following [Schweser 2000]:

$$\text{Yield on a risky security} = \text{yield on a risk-less (default free) bond} +$$
$$\text{risk premium}$$

The final type of credit risk is downgrade risk. This is the risk that a bond will be downgraded as a riskier security by a credit rating agency. When bonds are downgraded, its yield will simultaneously adjust upward. The opposite happens when a bond is upgraded, its yield will immediately adjust downward.

Q5:28   What are the different rating agencies?

To aid investors in determining the probability of default, there are several primary companies that have developed credit rating systems. The three largest companies are S&P, Moody, and Fitch. These three companies rate the degree of risk associated with most bonds. All three rating systems are very similar, where investment grade securities are rated triple B and higher. The highest among them is triple A, also called prime grade. Bonds below triple B are called junk bonds or high yield securities. Within each given rating, other degrees are used to rate bonds. For example, Moody's uses numbers 1 through 3 to indicate degrees of quality within a rating, with 1 being the highest rating and 3 being the lowest rating. S&P and Fitch use plus (+) and minus (−) to show relative strength and weakness within a rating category, with + representing a higher rating and − the lowest rating.

Q5:29   What is marketability and liquidity risk?

Marketability risk implies the ease to which a bond can be bought or sold. Liquidity risk represents the ease to which the bond can be sold at a fair price without risk of loss. A bond can be marketable but not necessarily liquid. The primary measure of liquidity is the size of the spread between the bid and ask. A larger spread signals an illiquid market. Investors want liquid markets to sell their securities quickly at a fair price. In general, liquidity improves when more participants are engaged in trading the security.

Q5:30   What is inflation and purchasing power risk?

Inflation risk, or purchasing power risk, arises from variations in cash flows from a security because of inflation, which reduces the purchasing power of money. For example, if the purchaser buys a bond paying a coupon rate of 5 percent but inflation later increases to 5.5 percent, then the purchasing power of the cash flow (*i.e.*, money) has declined. Bondholders must receive a coupon payment that is at least equal to the inflation rate to maintain their purchasing power. All bonds have inflation risk, but floating coupon bonds may have less because their coupon rates adjust to market conditions.

Q5:31   What is exchange rate risk or currency risk?

Exchange rate risk, or currency risk, occurs when bond payments are denominated in a foreign currency, and the value of the currency fluctuates relative to the value of the home currency. If the foreign currency increases against the home currency, each unit (*i.e.*, dollar) will be worth more. The reverse is true if a foreign currency decreases against the home currency—in such cases, each unit will be worth less.

Q5:32   What is volatility risk?

Volatility compares price change relative to something else. A volatile price implies that it fluctuates more than some base. To understand how volatility affects the price of a straight bond or embedded call/put option, it is important to understand the relationship between price and yield. When yields rise, the price curve flattens. When yields fall, the price curve gets steeper (also see interest rate risk). Consequently, when yield levels are low, bond price volatility is greater than when yield levels are high. Lower yield levels cause greater volatility in the price of a bond, and result in higher value for a call or put option. Therefore, when yield volatility levels increase (lower yields), the price of a callable bond will decrease because of the increased value of the embedded call option. The value of a callable bond is its straight bond price minus the value of an embedded call option. The reverse is true for an embedded put option. The value of a putable bond is its straight bond value plus the embedded put option. When yield volatility increases, the value of a putable bond increases because the embedded put option increases. Therefore, to sum it up, yield volatility affects callable and putable bonds in the opposite way.

Q 5:33 What is the risk premium when describing interest rates?

The risk premium is the added risk assumed when buying a non-Treasury security. Treasuries have no credit risk, and are viewed as the safest securities in the world. The interest rates on a Treasury are considered the benchmark for other securities. The minimum risk an investor is willing to take on is the equivalent rate earned on an *on-the-run* Treasury security.

The minimum risk is also called the *base interest rate*. All competing non-Treasury securities must earn this base interest rate plus a premium for the added risk of investing in a non-Treasury security. The spread is the difference between the yield of a non-Treasury security and the yield of a Treasury security. For example, if a 10-year corporate bond is yielding 8.5 percent and a Treasury is yielding 6.0 percent, then the spread is 150 basis points. The spread equals the additional risk assumed by an investor with buying a non-Treasury security. Therefore, the risk premium is the *base interest rate* plus the spread.

Different Types of Money Market Instruments

Q 5:34 What are money market mutual funds?

Money market mutual funds specialize in short-term securities. This is an alternative to other money market instruments. They are made up of many short-term instruments available in the open market (Treasury bills, commercial paper, bankers acceptance, certificates of deposit, repurchase agreements, etc.). As with most mutual funds, these instruments are managed by one or a team of investment professionals.

Q 5:35 What is a Treasury Bill?

U.S. Treasury Bills are issued by the federal government. These securities are in denominations of $1,000 to $100,000 and mature in 3 to 12 months. They are sold at a discount. Interest is subject to federal income tax but exempt from state and local tax.

Q 5:36 What is commercial paper?

Commercial paper is unsecured short-term promissory notes issued by corporations. Only firms with excellent credit ratings are able to sell commercial paper, so the risk of default is small. The maturity of commercial paper is usually less than 270 days. The minimum round lot transaction size is $100,000. However, some issuers will sell in denominations of $25,000. Commercial paper is sold at a discount. Interest is subject to federal and state taxation.

Q 5:37   What are bankers acceptances?

Bankers acceptances are short-term promissory notes guaranteed by a bank. The bank takes ultimate responsibility for repaying these loans to the holder. These acceptances are sold on a discounted basis just like Treasury bills and commercial paper, and are common with international trade. Acceptance finance is a way to facilitate trade.

Q 5:38   What are certificate of deposits?

A certificate of deposit, or CD, is a time deposit with a specified maturity. It is nonnegotiable or negotiable. A non-negotiable CD is one in which the initial depositor must wait until maturity to receive the funds. If funds are withdrawn prior to the maturity date, there is an early withdrawal penalty. In contrast, a negotiable CD allows the depositor to sell the CD in the open market any time before maturity. Depository institutions can sell negotiable CDs or jumbo CDs if an investor has $100,000 or more to invest. Maturities tend to be up to one year. CDs of less than $100,000 are generally nonnegotiable with a few exceptions. Eurodollar certificate of deposits are issued by branches of domestic banks located abroad or by foreign banks. They are similar to domestic CDs except that they are denominated in dollars instead of a foreign currency.

Q 5:39   What is a repurchase agreement?

A repurchase agreement or "repo" is the sale of a short-term security with the commitment by the seller to buy back the security at a specified price and date. The repurchase price is higher than the initial sale price. The difference between the sale price and the buy price is the dollar interest cost of the loan. The sale price and the buy price are specified in the agreement. A repurchase agreement is generally a collateralized loan. Banks are usually net sellers of collateral (net borrowers of funds). Money market funds, municipalities, and corporations are usually new buyers of collateral (providers of funds). If the term of the loan is one day, it is called an *overnight repo*; if the term is more than one day, it is called a *term repo*. The interest rate charged on a repo is usually less than other sources of financing, such as a bank loan.

Example: Suppose a government dealer needs to finance its long position by purchasing $10 million in Treasury securities. The dealer has several sources for financing this purchase. The dealer can use its own money or borrow from a bank. Instead, the dealer chooses to use the repo market to obtain the financing. The $10 million in Treasury securities is used as collateral for the loan. The repo rate (*i.e.*, interest rate) that the dealer agrees to pay is specified. In this case, the dealer has a customer with over $10 million. The dealer agrees to sell the $10 million in Treasury securities to the customer for an amount specified by the repo rate, and buy them back for $10 million the next day. From the customer's perspective, the agreement is a *reverse repo*. Therefore, a *reverse repo* is an agreement to buy securities and sell them back.

Dealers can also use the repo market to cover a short position. For example, if a dealer shorted $10 million in Treasury securities, and now needs to cover the position, the dealer can do a *reverse repo*. That is, buy the securities and sell them back.

Securities Issued by the U.S. Treasury

Q 5:40   What are Treasury bills?

Treasury bills are issued in denominations of $1,000 to $100,000 and mature in 3 to 12 months. They are sold at a discount and carry no coupon. Treasury bills are part of an auction process, so the discount price is not set. The highest bidder gets the bills. For example, if an investor bids $9,800 for the bill, he or she will receive $10,000 at maturity. The yield works out to 2 percent ($200 ÷ $9,800). Of course, the yield is lower if the bid price is higher. After the auction, a bill can be traded in the open market. The secondary market is active for bills, and they are quoted in terms of discount yield. The discount yield is different than the annualized yield on a bill or yield to maturity on a bond. The discount yield uses the face amount and a 360-day year, whereas the annualized yield uses the market price and a 365-day year. Treasury bills are the safest securities available in the market. Interest is subject to federal income tax but exempt from state and local tax.

Q 5:41   What are Treasury notes and bonds?

Treasury notes have maturities in two to ten years in denominations of $1,000 to more than $100,000. Treasury bonds are the government's long-term debt, and have maturities greater than ten years. Notes and bonds are issued as coupon securities. Treasury notes and bonds are the safest intermediate— and long-term investments available for purchase because they are backed by the government. This increased safety results in yields that are lower than high quality corporate debt. Interest is subject to federal income tax but exempt from state and local tax. The secondary market for note and bonds is active.

Treasury notes and bonds are quoted as a percent of face value, and quotes are in fractions of 32nds. For example, the bid and ask price of a 5 percent note due in 2010 is quoted at 90:10-90:11. The quote of 90 and 10/32 implies a price of $903.32 (90.3125% of $1,000) and 90 and 11/32 implies a price of 903.44 (90.3437% of $1,000). Even finer quotes are provided in 1/64, 1/128, and 1/256. A quote of 90:10 + implies a fraction of 1/64 has been added, and equals $901.56 (90.1562% of $1,000).

Q 5:42   What are inflation protected securities or TIPS?

TIPS are securities issued by the federal government that have coupon payments that periodically adjust to changes in the inflation rate. Changes in inflation are represented in the principal and not the coupon. The *inflationadjusted principal* is multiplied by the real rate to get the appropriate coupon payment. The real rate represents the fixed coupon rate net of inflation. For example, suppose a par value of $10,000 and a coupon rate of 4 percent. Annualized inflation for the next six months is 5 percent.

First, compute the *inflation-adjusted principal*. If the annual inflation rate is 5 percent, then the semi-annual rate is 2.5 percent (5% × 1/2). Apply this to the principal of $10,000 to get an inflation-adjusted principal of $10,250 ($10,000 × 1.025). Next, compute the *semi-annual coupon payment*. This is found by multiplying the inflation-adjusted principal amount with the semi-annual real rate. The semi-annual coupon rate equals $205 ($10,250 × 2%).

Inflation is measured by changes in the CPI-U index (an index that measures changes in the cost of living for urban consumers). If consumer prices drop, then there is risk that the principal will be reduced below the initial par value. However, at maturity, the Treasury pays the holder the greater of the par value or the inflation-adjusted principal, putting a floor on the value of these bonds.

Q 5:43   What are Treasury STRIPS?

In 1985, the Treasury introduced zero coupon bonds call STRIPS, standing for Separate Trading of Registered Interest and Principal Securities. STRIPS are direct obligations of the federal government. STRIPS do not pay a coupon, but interest is taxed as it is accrues. Therefore, it is appealing to purchase STRIPS in retirement accounts because tax in retirement accounts is deferred until funds are withdrawn. Thus the tax disadvantage on STRIPS can be avoided.

STRIPS are more volatile than other government bonds during periods of changing interest rates. The price of a bond is more volatile the longer the term to maturity or the smaller the coupon payment. The reason for the increased price volatility relative to other bonds is that the entire return is one single payment at maturity. The value of a bond is the present value of interest and principal payments. Interest payments made in early years helps reduce the volatility of a bond's price to changes in interest rates. However, the price of STRIPS is fully the result of the present value of a single payment received at maturity. To take advantage of the greater price volatility found in STRIPS, it is better to buy them when interest rates are expected to fall.

Q 5:44   How are Treasury securities issued and traded?

Primary Market Treasury securities are issued through an auction. Three-month and six-month treasuries are issued every Monday. One-year treasuries are issued every four weeks. Two- and five-year notes are auctioned every month. 10-year notes and 30-year bonds are auctioned quarterly. Treasury auctions are conducted on a competitive bid. The bid is sent on a yield basis. The lowest yield (highest price) bidder is awarded the securities. Noncompetitive bids can also be submitted for up to $1 million face value, and are based on quantity, not yield. The price paid for noncompetitive bids is based on the average price of all competitive bids.

All noncompetitive bids and nonpublic buys (purchases by the Federal Reserve) are added up and removed from the auction, temporarily. The competitive bids are made to successively higher yielding bidders until the total amount offered, including noncompetitive and nonpublic offers is awarded. The highest yield (lowest price) accepted by the Treasury is called the *stop yield*. The difference between the average yield of all bids accepted and the stop is called the *tail*.

Secondary Market The secondary market is an over-the-counter market consisting of U.S. government securities dealers that set the bid-and-ask price. The most recently auctioned Treasury securities are called *on-the-run* or *current coupon* issues. These new issues replace older Treasury issues called *off-the-run* issues, and issues replaced by several recent issues are called *well-of-the-run* issues. The bidask spread is larger for off-the-run issues than it is for on-the-run issues because they have less liquidity, and even worse for well-off-the run issues. The issue with less liquidity will have a lower yield because it suffers from liquidity risk. Therefore, off-the-run issues will have a higher yield than on-the-run issues. In addition, the lower liquidity with off-the-run issues causes an increased yield spread between the two issues. Another component of the secondary market is the when-issued market. When-issued Treasury bills and Treasury coupon issues are traded before they are issued by the Treasury. When-issued trading extends from the day the auction is announced to the day they are issued. All deliveries of whenissued trades occur on the issue day of the Treasury.

Federal Agency Debt

Q 5:45 What types of federal agency debt exist?

Bonds issued by federal agencies are not debts of the federal government. Therefore, their yields are higher than those yields available on U.S. Treasury debt. They are considered extremely safe because they have the backing of the federal government. However, in most cases this backing is only moral backing; in the case of default the federal government is not obligated to support the debt. Other agency debt has a legal backing. In this case, the Treasury is legally bound to assume any obligation contained in the debt's indenture.

Federal agency debt can be purchased by an individual investor, although this is usually not the case. Federal agency debt is usually traded among mutual funds or pension plans. Many investors are not aware of the advantages offered by this debt. However, investors should consider these issues as a source of income with capital preservation and higher yields.

Federal agencies issue debentures and mortgage-backed securities, and are classified as federally related institutions and government-sponsored entities. Federally related institutions include the Government National Mortgage

Association (Ginnie Mae), which is owned by the federal government and as such is backed by the full faith and credit of the U.S. government. These bonds have no credit risk because there is no chance of default. The other type of agency debt, government-sponsored entities, includes the Federal National Mortgage Association (Fannie Mae), the Federal Home Loan Bank Corporation (Freddie Mac), and the Student Loan Marketing Association (Sallie Mae). These are privately owned, publicly chartered, institutions that were created by the U.S. government to support a specific need. Investors are exposed to credit risk, but this risk is regarded as slight since the government provides a moral backing.

Q 5:46   What are mortgage-backed securities, mortgage pass-through securities, and collateralized mortgage obligations?

Mortgage Pass-Through Securities A mortgage pass-through security represents a self-amortizing pool of mortgages in which principal repayments and interest payments are "passed through" to the investor of the certificates, after subtracting servicing fees. Payments are made on a monthly basis and consist of scheduled principal and interest, and any unscheduled payments consisting of prepayments and defaults. The timing and amount of cash flows are largely dependent on prepayments. This means that payments vary from month to month, and the amount received by the investor also varies each month.

If no prepayments are made, each monthly cash flow will remain constant. It is only the composition of the cash flows between interest, principal, and servicing fees that change when a loan amortizes. Through amortization, as the loan balance drops for the mortgages, the amount of scheduled principal paid off increases and the amount of interest declines. The servicing fees are usually based on a percentage of interest. Therefore, the servicing fees will decrease as the loan amount declines.

Mortgage pass-through securities should be evaluated by fixed-income investors because they provide many benefits. Their yields can be as much as 200 basis points higher than comparable government and corporate fixed-income debt. They are considered to be a higher credit quality than AAA corporate bonds because mortgage pass-through securities are issued by federal agencies. In addition to being safe as investments, these securities prove to be very liquid in the marketplace. They are more liquid than corporate bonds and as liquid as Treasuries. Finally, they are a very good source for an investor interested in receiving a monthly income.

Like all investments, mortgage pass-through securities do also carry a degree of risk. The first type of risk is interest rate risk. The price of mortgage pass-through securities varies when interest rates change, as with any other fixed-income debt security. All pools have the same interest rates. If interest rates were to increase, the price of a mortgage pass-through security would drop. Investors would suffer a capital loss if they sold the security in the open market. However, the reverse is also true if interest rates were to drop. An investor selling the security when rates drop would benefit from a price increase.

In addition to interest rate risk, mortgage pass-through securities also suffer from reinvestment rate risk. The timing and amount of payments can often be uncertain. When interest rates decrease, homeowners will refinance mortgages at lower interest rates. The principal amount received from a mortgage pass-through security will be greater, but owners can only reinvest this amount at a lower rate of return. The overall return is reduced. The opposite is true with rising interest rates. Prepayments decrease because of less refinancing, and owners of pass-through securities receive lower payments.

The uncertainty in the monthly payments affects the valuation of a mortgage pass-through security. If mortgages are paid off sooner than expected, the realized return will be higher than the expected return. The opposite is true if mortgages are paid off later than expected; the realized return would then be smaller than the expected return. Therefore, it is possible for the same two securities with the same price to have different yields because of the anticipated rate in which the mortgage loans are paid off. A higher yield is anticipated if the mortgage loans are expected to be retired rapidly than if the same mortgage loans are expected to be retired slowly.

Collateralized Mortgage Obligations (CMOs) A Collateralized Mortgage Obligation is a derivative of a pass-through security held by a trust in which prepayment and reinvestment risk is reduced. The CMO is subdivided into different classes (called *tranches*), which receive different cash flow payments. The principal repayment is directed to the first tranche until it is retired, and then paid to the next tranche. Principal repayments are not made to the next tranche until the prior tranche is retired. The process is repeated until all tranches are retired. However, interest is paid off annually on the amount of loan in each tranche. From accepting a later repayment of principal, investors in the longer tranches accept a higher interest rate than investors in the early tranches.

CMOs reduce but do not eliminate prepayment and reinvestment rate risk, but this risk is less than that obtained from purchasing a mortgage passthrough security. With a mortgage pass-through security, prepayments are spread over the entire life of the security. In the case of a CMO, prepayments are spread over each tranche. The timing of principal repayment becomes slightly more known. For example, an investor in need of cash is better served by purchasing the first tranche, while an investor in little need of cash is better off with acquiring a later tranche.

Q 5:47 What is an asset-backed security?

An asset-backed security represents a pool of asset-linked debts in which principal repayments and interest payments are paid to the investors in the securities. Investors receive payments on a monthly basis, consisting of scheduled principal and interest, and any unscheduled payments consisting of prepayments. However, unlike mortgage-backed securities, prepayments are almost unaffected by changes in market interest rates, resulting in relatively predictable cash flows. All asset-backed securities have one or more credit enhancements that result in a higher credit rating. The credit enhancements take the form of corporate guarantees, letter of credit, insurance wraps, and internal enhancements built into the asset-backed security. They offer investors higher yield than corporate bonds of similar quality and maturity. The market for asset-backed securities is very liquid. Asset-backed securities are supported by collateral from installment loans or revolving lines of credit. Installment loans have defined amortization schedules. In contrast, revolving lines of credit do not have a specific amortization schedule.

Q 5:48 What is a medium-term note (MTN)?

Medium-term notes are investment-grade unsecured debt, issued by corporations, federal agencies, and countries. The term "medium" can be misleading because these securities have maturities from 9 months to greater than 30 years. The maturities match the financial needs of the borrower. Therefore, they are highly flexible instruments that are designed to respond to market changes. Their yields are usually quoted as a spread over a Treasury security of comparable maturity, and reflect the credit risk of the issuer. However, with the advent of structured MTNs, issuers can offer floating interest rates that meet the needs of the market. For example, a corporation can create an MTN with an interest rate that varies inversely with market interest rates by attaching an inverse floating rate. At the same time, the corporation can enter into a swap arrangement to protect itself against the risk of issuing an inverse floating rate MTN. The use of structured MTNs is increasing because of the flexibility and speed in which they can meet market changes.

Medium-term notes differ from corporate bonds in that they are offered on a *best-effort basis*. This means that the investment banker is not guaranteeing a specified amount of money from selling the securities, but only agrees to make a best effort to sell them. The risk of selling the securities resides with the issuing firm. In contrast, corporate bonds are done on a *firm commitment basis*, which means that the investment banker is guaranteeing the sale of the securities at a specified price. The investment banker purchases the bonds from the issuer and sells them to the public. The risk of selling the securities resides with the investment banker. The size and timing of the offerings are also different between corporate bonds and MTNs. Investment grade bonds are rarely offered in amounts less than $100 million. MTNs are generally issued in amounts of less than $25 million. MTNs are also sold on a discrete basis. Bonds are sold on a continuous basis. Therefore, MTNs offer the ability to raise a large amount of cash within a very short amount of time.

State and Local Government Securities

Q 5:49 What types of securities are issued by state and local governments?

State and local governments issue several types of bonds. *General obligation bonds* are backed by the full faith and credit of the taxing power of the issuing government. Bonds supported by the revenue of a project are called *revenue bonds*. General obligation bonds have less risk than revenue bonds because they are supported by taxes, whereas revenue bonds are supported only by the funds generated by a project. *Moral obligation* bonds are backed by states if the issuer is unable to make payments. States are not legally bound to make payments; they simply take on a "moral obligation."

Municipal bonds tend to lack marketability and liquidity. These issues are traded over the counter, and the market is thin, causing a large spread between bid and ask. Municipal bonds trade in denominations of $5,000 face value.

Most debt issued by state and local governments is a long-term serial issue. Serial bonds offer the benefit to the buyer of knowing when the bonds are going to mature. The bonds are purchased based on the investor's time horizon. However, not all state and local government debt is long term. Short-term debt is a tax or revenue anticipation note, and is issued on the anticipation of future expected revenue. The government anticipates receipts in the future and issues debt against these receipts.

Foreign Bonds

Q 5:50   What influences the price and yield of international bonds?

International bond prices and yields are vastly influenced by the currency denomination. The currency denomination has a greater influence on the price and yield of a bond than the country in which the bonds trade or the home of the issuer. Issues denominated in U.S. currency are affected by the direction of U.S. interest rates. Issues denominated in other currencies are affected by the direction of interest rates in the country of their currency.

Q 5:51   What are foreign bonds and Eurobonds?

Foreign bonds are issued in a country by a corporation that is not a resident of that country. For example, *Yankee bonds* are issued by non-U.S. corporations but are traded in the United States. *Yankee bonds* are registered with the SEC. Foreign bonds can be denominated in any currency. In contrast, Eurobonds are issued outside the legal system of a country. They are identified by their home currency (*i.e., Eurodollar* bonds). Eurobonds are unregistered and unsecured corporate debt. Specific to *Eurodollars*, they are not registered with the SEC; therefore, new issues cannot be sold to the U.S. public until the "seasoning" period has expired.

The Risk Structure of Interest Rates

Q 5:52   What affects spreads?

Differences in Issuers. The intermarket yield spread is the spread offered between two issues of the same maturity in different sectors. The *intermarket* *yield spread* is often used when comparing the Treasury sector to some other non-Treasury sector. In contrast, the *intramarket yield spread* is the spread between two securities in the same sector. The corporate sector consists of many issuers such as utilities, industrials, finance companies, and banks. Therefore, the *intramarket yield spread* for a utility bond earning 5.2 percent and a bank bond earning 5.5 percent is 30 basis points.

The U.S. bond market is divided up into several sectors based on the issuer of the bonds. These sectors include: the U.S. government sector, the agency sector, the municipal sector, the corporate sector, the mortgage sector, the asset-based sector, and the foreign sector.

Differences in Credit Quality or Risk of Default. In the majority of cases, lower quality bonds will give a higher yield than higher rated bonds. A credit spread is defined as the spread between Treasury securities and non-Treasury securities identical in all respects except for different credit ratings or quality. Credit spreads will widen during recessions and narrow during times of economic prosperity. In anticipation of a down market or recession, investors will sell low-grade securities and buy high-quality Treasuries, causing spreads to widen. The reverse is true if investors anticipate a strong economy: they buy low-grade securities, becoming more risk adverse, and sell high-grade securities. The result is a narrowing spread during times of economic prosperity.

Differences in Embedded Options. Call and put provisions are embedded options attached to bonds. The call provision allows an issuer to retire debt before maturity in order to issue new bonds at a lower interest rate. The put provision allows the bondholder to sell the bonds back to the issuer for a specified price. This is common when bonds are trading below par because of high interest rates. The existence of an embedded option affects the spread between a Treasury and a non-Treasury with an embedded option. The spread is larger for a security with a call provision (more risk) because it benefits the issuer. In contrast, the spread is smaller for a security with a put provision (less risk) because it benefits the investor.

Differences in Tax Treatment. Municipal bonds are attractive to highincome investors falling in the top tax brackets. These bonds provide tax protection from federal income tax. The tax protection results in yields that are less than Treasury securities. The yield of a municipal relative to a Treasury is expressed in percentage terms. The after-tax yield on a bond issue after paying taxes is computed as

the after-yield = pre-yield on an equivalent but fully taxable
bond × (1 − marginal tax rate)

Alternatively, high-income investors want a tax-exempt yield that equals the yield on a taxable bond. The *taxable equivalent yield* is calculated to determine what yield must be earned on a taxable bond to equal the same yield for a taxexempt municipal bond. It is calculated as

$$\text{Taxable equivalent yield} = \frac{\text{Tax exempt yield}}{1 - \text{marginal tax rate}}$$

For example, assume a municipal bond yields 4.3 percent. Assume a Treasury security is yielding 6.7 percent. The investor is in the 39 percent tax bracket. Which investment should be purchased? The tax equivalent yield is

$$4.3 \div (1 - .39) = 7.04\%$$

Since 7.04 percent is greater than 6.7 percent, the investor should choose the municipal bond because it earns a higher taxable equivalent yield.

$$\text{The after-yield} = 6.7\% \times (1 - .39) = 4.08\%$$

Here, 4.08 percent is less than 4.3 percent, so the choice again is to purchase the municipal bond. Both equations yield the same result.

Differences in Maturity. The longer the maturity, the more sensitive the price of bonds to interest rates. The spread between two maturity sectors of the market is called maturity spread. The relationship between yield and maturity is called the term structure of interest rates.

Differences in Liquidity. Investors are willing to accept lower yields on bond issues that are more liquid. In contrast, lower liquidity results in higher yields because there is more perceived risk. The spread between Treasuries relative to non-Treasuries partially reflects the difference in liquidity between the two issues. Within the Treasury market, on-the-run issues have more liquidity than off-the-run issues. Therefore, on-the-run issues have lower yields than offthe-run issues.

The Term Structure of Interest Rates

Q5:53   What is the term structure of interest rates? (Fabozzi, 1995)

Yield to maturity assumes all cash flows are discounted at the same interest rate and are reinvested at the yield-to-maturity rate. However, cash flows are not reinvested at the yield-to-maturity rate. The realized return does not equal the yield-to-maturity. In practice, interest rates exhibit a term structure. The term structure means that interest rates vary depending on when the cash flow is received. Therefore, bonds are really defined as packages of cash flows.

In explaining the concept of term structure, it is best to begin with the yield curve. The yield curve is a graphical representation of the relationship between bond yields of the same credit quality over different maturities. The yield curve is constructed using the Treasury market because: (1) the Treasury market is default risk free so credit quality does not affect yields, and (2) the Treasury market is highly active and escapes problems of illiquidity. The Treasury yield curve is upward sloping in normal economic conditions. During economic contractions, an inverted yield curve is common. An inverted yield curve happens when shortterm interest rates exceed long-term interest rates. The yield curve can also be flat.

The Treasury yield curve is often used as a benchmark for setting bond prices and determining yields in other bond sectors. However, using the yield curve to determine the relationship between required yield and maturity can be inadequate because bonds with the same maturity may have different yields. The problem results from different coupon rates attached to securities. It is often corrected by applying the yields of zero coupon bonds.

When using the yield curve to price bonds, it is important to know how a bond is valued. The price of a bond is the present value of cash flows, discounted back at the appropriate interest rate. The interest rate is determined using the yield of a Treasury security with the same maturity plus a risk premium. However, there is a problem with using the Treasury yield curve to determine the interest rate used to discount cash flows. For example, consider two 10-year Treasury bonds with different coupon rates to choose from:

10-year Bond A	6%
10-year Bond B	9%

The cash flows per $1,000 of par value for 10 six-month periods are $30 per periods 1-19 for Bond A and $45 per periods 1-19 for Bond B. The cash flows in period 20 are $1,030 and $1,045, respectively. The result is cash flows that are different for two 10-year Treasury securities of the same maturity. Thus, it is not appropriate to use the same interest rate to discount the cash flows; it is best to use a unique interest rate for each cash flow during the period in which the cash flow is received.

As previously mentioned, bonds are defined as packages of cash flows. Consequently, they are packages of zero coupon bonds from which the yield earned is the difference between the price paid and the maturity. For example, Bond A (same applies to Bond B) can be viewed as 20 zero coupon instruments each maturing in 6-month periods. The components consist of each coupon payment date and the maturity date. Therefore, the price of the bond is a component of all zero coupon packages.

The value of each zero coupon instrument is determined by using the yield of a zero coupon Treasury with a similar maturity. This yield is called the *spot rate*. The spot rate is defined as the interest rate used to discount a single cash flow. The relationship between spot rate and maturity can be graphically demonstrated on the *spot-rate curve*. Treasuries do not extend beyond one year, so the curve cannot be constructed from observation. Therefore, theoretical assumptions are used to find the yields, and the curve is called the *theoretical spot-rate curve*.

Q5:54   How are spot rates determined?

The theoretical price of a Treasury security equals the present value of each cash flow discounted back at the theoretical spot rate. It is important to remember that the value of a treasury security equals the value of a package of zero coupon securities with the same coupon cash flow. A Treasury bill sells at a discount and matures at par with no coupon payments. A treasury bill is really a zero coupon instrument. Therefore, the spot rate for a six-month Treasury bill is its yield to maturity. The same holds true for a one-year Treasury bill, the spot rate is equal to its yield to maturity. It is then possible to calculate the spot rate of a two-year Treasury bill. Take a look at the following table (assume annual compounding):

Maturity	Yield to Maturity	Coupon Rate	Price
1.00 years	0.04	0.00	96.15
2.00	0.06	0.05	98.16

Using $1,000 par, the cash flow for a two-year Treasury is

$$1 \text{ year } .05 \times \$1,000 = \$50$$

$$2 \text{ year } .05 \times \$1,000 + 1,000 = \$1,050$$

The present value of the cash flow is

$$\frac{50}{(1+Z_1)^1} + \frac{1050}{(1+Z_2)^2}$$

where Z_1 is the one-year theoretical spot rate and Z_2 is the two-year theoretical spot rate.

The one-year spot rate is equal to its yield to maturity (4 percent). The price of a two-year treasury is $98.16. Therefore, the theoretical spot rate of a two-year Treasury can be calculated as

$$98.16 = \frac{50}{(1+.04)^1} + \frac{1050}{(1+Z_2)^2}$$

Solving for Z_2:

$$98.16 = 48.07 + \frac{1050}{(1+Z_2)^2}$$

$$50.09 = \frac{1050}{(1+Z_2)^2}$$

$$(1+Z_2)^2 = 20.9623$$

$$Z_2 = (20.9623)^{1/2} - 1$$

$$Z_2 = 3.5785$$

If we double this yield, the yield for the theoretical two-year spot rate is 7.15 percent. It is easy to find the spot rate of a three-year Treasury by using the spot rate of the one-year and two-year Treasuries. The same steps outlined for a two-year spot rate are used to find the three-year spot rate. One last point, a yield spread is added to the spot rates when valuing a security with default risk.

Q 5:55   What are the different types of term structure theories?

Several theories have emerged to explain the shape and slope of the yield curve. The three most accepted theories are expectations theory, liquidity premium theory, preferred habitat theory, and market segmentation theory.

Expectations Theory. Expectations theory says that long-term interest rates are equal to an average of short-term interest rates that are expected to prevail in the future. The term structure is a combination of the current rate and *forward rates*. The forward rate is any unobservable rate that is expected over the long term. For example, the forward rate is the yield on a six-month Treasury six months from now. In addition, there is a relationship between spot rates and short-term forward rates. For example, the spot rate for a five-year Treasury is the six-month spot rate and the implied six-month forward rates.

Expectations theory states that any combination of bonds will produce the same expected return. For example, a five-year bond will have the same expected return as buying a two-year bond followed by a three-year bond. Therefore, expected future rates are equal to forward rates.

Liquidity Preference Theory. Another theory for the term structure of interest rates is liquidity preference theory. This theory shares the same assumption as expectation theory in that long-term rates are made up of an average of short-term rates that are expected in the future. However, liquidity theory adds liquidity risk premiums to the mix. Investors pay a liquidity premium (lower yields) for investing short term. In contrast, investors receive a liquidity premium (higher yields) for investing long term. The hypothesis believes that future interest rates are uncertain. Investors pay a premium for the uncertainty. Therefore, expected future rates do not equal forward rates because of liquidity premiums.

Habitat Theory. The third theory is preferred habitat theory. This theory is different to the liquidity preference theory in that it disputes that the risk premium must rise for securities with longer terms to maturity. It accepts the assertion that the term structure of interest rates is based on short-term interest rates expected to prevail in the future, plus a non-uniform risk premium. Thus, this theory asserts that investors have preferred sectors or habitats in which they invest but are willing to shift to other maturities if compensated for the appropriate risk premium.

Market Segmentation Theory. The final theory for the term structure of interest rates is market segmentation theory. The theory asserts that investors have specific maturity segments based on their liability needs. Regulatory or self-imposed management constraints and creditors can restrict their lending to specific maturities causing changes in the yield curve. Where preferred habitat theory says investors are willing to shift to other sectors, market segmentation theory assets that investors are unwilling to shift from one sector to another in order to take advantage of opportunities. The yield curve is based on supply and demand for securities within each maturity.

Q5:56　What are the different types of yield spreads?

There are three different types of spreads. First, the *nominal spread* is the difference between the yield to maturity of a bond minus the yield to maturity of a riskless security with a similar maturity. The *static spread* (also called Z spread) is the spread added to each spot rate for a riskless security. Finally, there is the *option-adjusted spread*, which is the difference between the static spread and the option cost.

There is an important relationship between the Z spread and the option-adjusted spread. The relationship is shown as

$$Z \text{ spread} - \text{option-adjusted spread} = \text{option cost}$$

For example, assume a callable bond has an option-adjusted spread of 125 basis points. A similar option-free bond has a Z spread of 150 basis points. The option cost is

$$150 - 125 = 25 \text{ basis points}$$

For callable bonds, an investor requires more yield for taking on the added risk than for an option-free bond. The option value is greater than zero. The option-adjusted spread is less than the Z spread.

For putable bonds, an investor requires a lower yield than for an option-free bond. The option value is less than zero. The option-adjusted spread is greater than the Z spread.

Bond Valuation

Q5:57　How is the value of a bond calculated, given the expected cash flows and discount rate?

The price of a bond is the present value of future cash flows discounted at the appropriate interest rate. It is important to know the features of a bond to find the value. The *coupon payment* is the amount of interest received by the bondholder. It is paid on an annual, semiannual, or quarterly basis. The *maturity date* is the date in which the principal must be paid by the issuer. At maturity, the bond is retired. The *face value* is the price of the bond at maturity.

To determine the value of a bond, the present value of interest payments and the present value of the face amount received at maturity are each calculated and then added together. That is, the present value of a bond equals the present value of interest payments plus the present value of the principal at maturity:

$$P_B = \frac{PMT}{(1+i)^1} + \frac{PMT}{(1+i)^2} + \ldots + \frac{PMT}{(1+i)^n} + \frac{FV}{(1+i)^n}$$

where P_B is the price of a bond; PMT is the coupon payment; i is the current interest rate; n is the number of years to maturity; FV is the face value at maturity. For example, firm A has issued a five-year bond with a 10 percent coupon and a face value of $1,000. The interest rate for competitive bonds with a similar length of time to maturity and credit risk is 7 percent. Interest is paid annually. The value of the bonds is determined by

$$P_B = \frac{\$100}{(1+0.07)^1} + \frac{\$100}{(1+0.07)^2} + \frac{\$100}{(1+.07)^3} + \frac{\$100}{(1+.07)^4} + \frac{\$100}{(1+.07)^5} + \frac{\$1000}{(1+.07)^5} = \text{Stop!}$$

There is no need to work this out by hand. It is best to perform the following steps on a financial calculator:

Calculator Solution

FV = $1,000, PMT = $100, N = 5, i = 7 ⇒ Solve for PV = −1123

The present value of the bond is $1,123, so it is selling at a premium (higher price than the face value) because the bond is paying a 10 percent interest rate where the current market interest rate is only 7 percent. The bond is attractive to investors and sells at a premium.

If other competitive bonds are paying a current interest rate of 12 percent, the 10 percent coupon is less attractive to bondholders. They are not willing to pay $1,000 for a bond that is paying a 10 percent interest rate when they can pay the same price for other competitive bonds yielding 12 percent. Therefore, the price of the bond must drop to yield 12 percent. The equation is expressed as

$$P_B = \frac{\$100}{(1+0.12)^1} + \frac{\$100}{(1+0.12)^2} + \frac{\$100}{(1+.12)^3} + \frac{\$100}{(1+.12)^4} + \frac{\$100}{(1+.12)^5} + \frac{\$1000}{(1+.12)^5} + \$927.90$$

Calculator Solution

FV = $1,000, PMT = $100, N = 5, i = 12 ⇒ Solve for PV = −927.90

The price of the bond is $927.90. The bond is said to be selling at a discount (lower price than face value). In this situation, an investor will be competitive with similar bonds and yield 12 percent on their investment.

The two calculations show that when current market interest rates rise, bond prices fall. The reverse is also true: when current market interest rates drop, bond prices rise. The relationship between market interest rates and bond prices presents an opportunity for investors to make money in the bond market if they can correctly anticipate the future direction of interest rates. If investors anticipate that interest rates will drop, they can purchase bonds to participate in capital appreciation. If they anticipate that interest rates will rise, they can sell bonds and lock into any capital gains before prices fall.

Semiannual Compounding. In the majority of cases, bonds pay interest twice a year (semi-annually) instead of once a year. The equation previously presented is modified slightly by adjusting the total number of periods and the amount of each payment. The total number of periods becomes 10 and the amount of payment is $50. The cash flows (interest and principal) are

CF Year 1	CF Year 2	CF Year 3	CF Year 4	CF Year 5
$50 $50	$50 $50	$50 $50	$50 $50	$50 $50 $1,000

The competitive market rate of a similar bond is 12 percent. The appropriate discount rate to use then becomes 6 percent if we divide the current market rate in half (semi-annual compounding). The equation for determining the value of a bond is

$$P_B = \frac{\$50}{(1+0.06)^1} + \frac{\$50}{(1+0.06)^2} + \frac{\$50}{(1+0.06)^3} + \frac{\$50}{(1+0.06)^4} \frac{\$50}{(1+0.06)^5} \frac{\$50}{(1+0.06)^6}$$

$$+ \frac{\$50}{(1+0.06)^7} + \frac{\$50}{(1+0.06)^8} + \frac{\$50}{(1+0.06)^9} + \frac{\$50}{(1+0.06)^{10}} + \frac{\$1,000}{(1+0.06)^{10}} = \$926.39$$

Calculator Solution

$$\text{FV} = \$1,000, \text{PMT} = \$50, \text{N} = 10, i = 6 \Rightarrow \text{Solve for PV} = -926.39$$

The value of a bond is somewhat lower with semi-annual compounding than it is for annual compounding because the price must decline more to compensate for the additional compounding. In contrast, if a bond sells at a premium, its price is slightly higher with semi-annual compounding than it is for annual compounding.

There is an interesting relationship between price and yield. As the yield of a bond rises, the price of the bond will fall at a decreasing rate. In contrast, as the yield of a bond falls, the price of the bond will rise at an increasing rate. The graph that represents this relationship is called a price-yield curve and it forms a convex shape. In addition, there are other fundamental price-yield properties. If the yield to maturity equals the stated coupon rate, the price of the bond is its par value. If the yield to maturity is greater than the coupon rate, the price of the bond is lower than par value. If the yield to maturity is less than the coupon rate, the price of the bond is greater than par value.

A fluctuation in bond prices is also dependent on the coupon rate and length of time to maturity. The prices of bonds with smaller coupons are more volatile to changing market interest rates. For example, the price of a bond with a 6 percent coupon is more volatile to current market interest rates than a bond with a 10 percent coupon. The length of maturity also affects the price of a bond. The price of a bond will be more volatile to current market interest rates the longer the term to maturity. For example, if Bond A matures in 5 years and Bond B matures in 15 years, then the price of Bond B will fall (rise) more to a rise (fall) in current market interest rates.

Valuing a Bond Between Coupon Payments

Q 5:58   What is accrued interest?

A bond generally pays interest semi-annually up until maturity. However, interest is earned every day. Therefore, when a bond is purchased, the buyer owes the seller accrued interest for the days the seller held the bond. The interest is added to the purchase price that the buyer must pay. The *dirty price* is the bonds value plus any interest earned but not yet received by the seller. The *clean price* is the price without accrued interest. Some bonds do not trade with accrued interest. These bonds are said to be *flat*, and are commonly in default and do not pay interest.

Q5:59 How many days are there between the last coupon payment and the next?

The day count depends on the fixed income security being evaluated. Treasury coupon securities use the convention of an actual/actual day count. This means that the actual number of days in a month is the actual number of days in the coupon period, and a non-leap year has 365 days. For example, a Treasury security whose last coupon payment was February 1 will have the next coupon payment on August 1 (6-months later). If the settlement date for the Treasury security is June 10, then the actual number of days from settlement to the next coupon payment is 52 days, shown as follows:

June 10 to June 30	20 days
July 1 to July 31	31 days
August 1	1 day
	52 days

In contrast to the actual/actual count convention, there is the day-count convention of 30/360 used by corporate, municipals, and agency securities. This means that each month has 30 days and each year has 360 days. For example, use the same information from the previous example, but assume the bond is a corporate rather than a Treasury security. The number of days between June 10 (the settlement date) and August 1(the next coupon payment) is 51 days, and is shown below:

What remains of June	20 days
July	30 days
August 1	1 day
	51 days

Q5:60 How is the present value of cash flows received during fractional periods calculated?

To answer this question, the first step is to compute the number of days between settlement and next coupon payment. The second step is to compute the number of days in the coupon period. The final step is to perform the following calculation:

$$w = \frac{\text{Number of days between settlement and next coupon payment}}{\text{Number of days in the coupon period}}$$

An example best explains this process in valuing bonds. Assume a three-year $1,000 par value corporate bond that has a 10 percent semiannual coupon payment and 12 percent yield to maturity. The bond works under a 30/360 counting convention. The bond matures August 1, 2005, and the bond is being valued for settlement on June 10, 2003. The number of days between settlement and the next coupon payment is 51 and the number of days in the coupon period is 180.

$$w = \frac{51}{180} = .2833$$

The number of coupon payments remaining is five. The semiannual interest rate is 6 percent. The semiannual coupon payment is $50. The value of the bond is calculated by using a financial calculator. To determine the bond value:

Calculator Solution

N = 0.2833, I/Y = 6, FV = 50, PMT = 0 ⇒ CPT PV = 49.16

N = 1.2833, I/Y = 6, FV = 50, PMT = 0 ⇒ CPT PV = 46.38

N = 2.2833, I/Y = 6, FV = 50, PMT = 0 ⇒ CPT PV = 43.75

N = 3.2833, I/Y = 6, FV = 50, PMT = 0 ⇒ CPT PV = 41.27

N = 4.2833, I/Y = 6, FV = 1,050, PMT = 0 ⇒ CPT PV = 817.79

The sum of all cash flows is $998.35 per $1,000 par value. The price of the bond is the dirty price because it includes the accrued interest.

Q 5:61   How much accrued interest must the buyer compensate the seller for?

The accrued interest depends on the number of days between the last coupon payment and the settlement date. In general, bond prices are quoted with the clean price (without accrued interest). In contrast, the dirty price includes accrued interest. Accrued interest is computed as

$$AI = \frac{\text{Number of days from last coupon payment to settlement date}}{\text{Number of days in coupon period}} \times \text{Coupon Payment}$$

Assume a $1,000 par value corporate security with a 10 percent coupon rate. The last coupon payment was February 1 and the next payment is August 1 (6 months later). If the settlement date for the Treasury security is June 10, then the actual number of days from settlement to the next coupon payment is 51 days (using the 30/360 day count convention). The number of days in the coupon period is 180 (360 ÷ 2). The accrued interest per $1,000 of par value is

$$AI = \frac{51}{180} \times \$50 = \$14.17$$

Yield Measures

Q5:62   What is the current yield?

The current yield only considers the coupon component of bonds. It does not include any reinvestment income and price appreciation or depreciation. The current yield is

$$\frac{\text{Annual coupon payment}}{\text{Price of bond}}$$

For example, assume a $1,000 par value bond priced at $950 with a 10 percent semiannual coupon rate. The current yield is

$$\frac{\$100}{\$950} = 10.5\%$$

The current yield is important to investors interested in income. Those investors that want high yearly income want bonds with a high current yield.

Q5:63   What is the yield to maturity?

The yield to maturity is the internal rate of return of a bond if held to maturity. It considers the current interest return and all price appreciation or depreciation. It is also a measure of risk and is the discount rate that equals the present value of all cash flows. From a firm perspective, it is the cost of borrowing by issuing new bonds. From an investor perspective, it is the rate of return that is received if the bond is held to maturity. It is calculated mathematically by

$$P_B = \frac{PMT}{(1+i)^1} + \frac{PMT}{(1+i)^2} + \cdots + \frac{PMT}{(1+i)^n} + \frac{FV}{(1+i)^n}$$

The i is the current rate of interest in the market for a competitive bond of similar risk and maturity.

Finding the yield to maturity by mathematical computation is a very difficult task. An investor would need to keep picking values for i until the right and left side of the equation are equal. This can take time and patience! The good news is that the yield to maturity can be easily solved using a financial calculator. For example, assume a $1,000 par bond is priced at $950 with a 10 percent semi-annual coupon payment. The bond matures in three years. The yield to maturity is found by

Calculator Solution

N = 6, PV = −$950, FV = $1,000, PMT = $50 ⇒ CPT YTM = 6.01 × 2 = 12.02%

The PV should be entered as a negative number because the calculator considers it a cash outflow, whereas interest and principal repayment are cash inflows.

The relationship between the current yield and yield to maturity is worth touching on. If a bond sells at a premium, the yield to maturity is less than the current yield because the investor suffers a loss when the bond matures at par value. In contrast, if the bond sells at a discount, the current yield is less than the yield to maturity because of price appreciation at maturity.

Yield to maturity is the most often used yield measure in the bond market. However, is does have a shortcoming. It assumes all cash flows are discounted at the same rate and are reinvested at the yield-to-maturity rate. Therefore, if cash flows are not reinvested at the yield-to-maturity rate, the realized return does not equal the yield to maturity. This is defined as reinvestment risk. The reinvestment risk is greater when the maturity date and the coupon payment increase.

Q 5:64   How does one compare the yield to maturity for bonds with different coupon frequencies?

Many times investors find themselves comparing yields of bonds with different coupon frequencies. In the United States, the majority of bonds pay interest semi-annually (known as the *bond equivalent basis*). Many international bonds pay interest annually. How are the yields compared? The comparison is made by converting the bond equivalent yield to an equivalent annual yield (or vice versa). For example, assume an IBM bond paying interest semi-annually trades in the U.S. with a 6.00 percent yield to maturity. It also trades in Europe paying an annual coupon with a 6.05 percent yield to maturity. To find the bond with the greater *true yield*, convert the semiannual yield to an equivalent annual yield by

$$\text{Equivalent annual yield} = \left(1 + \frac{\text{Nominal yield}}{\text{\# of payments in a year}}\right)^{\text{\#of payments in a year}} - 1$$

$$\text{Equivalent annual yield} = \left(1 + \frac{.06}{2}\right)^{2} - 1 = .0609 = 6.09\%$$

The equivalent annual yield for a 6 percent semiannual coupon bond is 6.09 percent. This means that the annual coupon bond has a slightly lower yield to maturity (6.09% > 6.05%).

Q 5:65   What is the yield to call?

Many bonds trade with a call provision. This means that the bonds are callable by the issuer before maturity. Bonds are often called when prevailing interest rates are less than the coupon rate. The yield to call is used to determine the internal rate of return earned by the bond until it is called or retired by the firm. The yield to call is calculated in a similar way as the yield to maturity except (1) the expected call date is used in place of the known maturity date and (2) the principal plus call penalty is used in place of principal only.

Suppose a bond matures after ten years and pays a 10 percent semiannual coupon rate and is selling for $925. The yield to maturity is 11.26 percent. An investor believes the bond will be called in five years at a penalty of $75 per $1,000 bond. The yield to call is calculated using a financial calculator.

Calculator Solution

N = 10, PV = −$925, FV = 1,075, PMT = $50 ⇒ CPT YTC = 6.60 × 2 = 13.2%

N is the 5-year call period multiplied by 2 (semiannual payments). The PV should be entered as a negative number because the calculator considers it a cash outflow, whereas interest and principal repayment are cash inflows.

The yield to call is 13.2 percent, which is greater than the yield to maturity (11.26 percent). The reason for this is that the bond is selling at a discount, and it takes a greater return to erase the discount sooner. In addition, the yield to call is higher because the investor receives a call penalty.

In contrast, if the bond were selling at a premium of $1,195, the yield to maturity is 7.22 percent. If the bond is called in five years, the yield to call is

Calculator Solution

N = 10, PV = −$1195, FV = 1075, PMT = $50 ⇒ CPT YTC = 3.32*2 = 6.64%

In this example, the yield to call is less than the yield to maturity. The yield is reduced because the premium is spread out over a smaller time horizon.

If a bond is selling at a discount, it may make sense for a firm to purchase bonds instead of calling them and paying the penalty. The reverse is true if a bond is selling at a premium; it may be more advantageous for the firm to call the bonds and pay the penalty. This is most certainly the preferred course if the bonds are selling for more than the call penalty.

Q 5:66   What is the yield to put?

The put provision allows the bondholder to sell back the bonds to the issuer at a put price. The put provision is advantageous to a bondholder and not the issuer. A put is likely when prevailing interest rates are significantly higher than the coupon rate attached to the bond. The yield to put is the rate of return if a bond is put to the issuer.

Suppose a bond matures after ten years and pays a 6 percent semiannual coupon rate and is selling for $870. The yield to maturity is 7.90 percent. The first put price is $975 in 3 years. The yield to put is calculated using a financial calculator.

Calculator Solution

N = 6, PV = −$870, FV = $975, PMT = $30 ⇒ (CPT YTP = 5.21*2 = 10.42%

where N is the 3-year put period multiplied by 2 (semiannual payments). The PV should be entered as a negative number because the calculator considers it a cash outflow, whereas interest and principal repayment are cash inflows.

The yield to put is 10.42 percent, which is greater than the yield to maturity (7.90 percent). Therefore, it is very likely that the investor will put this bond back to the issuer because the yield to put is extremely greater than the yield to maturity. Consequently, the current bond price is greatly lower than the put price. It takes a greater return to erase the discount sooner which is why a bond selling at a discount can be a positive to the bondholder.

In contrast, if the bond were selling at a $1095 (premium), the yield to maturity is 4.78 percent. The yield to put is

Calculator Solution

N = 6, PV = −$1095, FV = $975, PMT = $30 ⇒ (CPT YTP = 0.95*2 = 1.90%

In this example, the yield to put is extremely less than the yield to maturity. The yield is reduced because the premium is spread out over a smaller time horizon. Therefore, if a bond is selling at a premium, the bond will not be put back to the issuer. Of course, this is always the case when the bond price is higher than the put price because of reinvestment risk. The coupon rate of bonds with similar maturity and quality is less. The put provision is only beneficial when interest rates have increased above the coupon rate, allowing an investor to benefit from reinvesting proceeds at higher coupon rates.

Measurement of Interest Rate Risk

Q 5:67　What is duration and how is it calculated?

When comparing bonds with the same length to maturity but different coupons, the bond with the lower coupon is more volatile to changing interest rates. For comparing bonds with the same coupons but different maturities, the bond with the longer maturity is more volatile. But how are bonds with different maturities and coupons compared? The most often used technique is finding the duration of a bond (or portfolio). Duration is the average time it takes to capture interest and principal repayments. It seeks to compare bonds with different coupons and maturities by determining how sensitive the price of each bond is to interest rate changes. More specifically, duration measures a bond's sensitivity to a 100-basis-point change in interest rates.

To illustrate how duration is determined, consider a 10 percent semiannual 3-year bond. The current interest rate on similar bonds is 12 percent. Therefore, the bond is currently selling for $950.82. The cash flows are

Year	Payment
0.5	$ 50
1.0	$ 50
1.5	$ 50
2.0	$ 50
2.5	$ 50
3.0	$1,050

The duration of a bond is the sum of the present value of cash flows weighted by a time period (t) in which the payment is received. All individual present values are summed and then divided by the current price of the bond. The following demonstrates this relationship:

Period	Interest	Cash Flow	Solve Present Value	PV * t
1	6%	$ 50	$ 47.17	$ 47.17
2	6%	$ 50	$ 44.50	$ 89.00
3	6%	$ 50	$ 41.98	$ 125.94
4	6%	$ 50	$ 39.60	$ 158.40
5	6%	$ 50	$ 37.36	$ 186.81
6	6%	$ 1,050	$740.21	$4441.25
				$5048.57

$$\text{Duration} = \frac{\$5048.57}{\$950.82} = 5.30 \div 2 = 2.65 \text{ years}$$

Because of semiannual compounding, the annual payment and interest rate are divided by 2 and the number of payments is multiplied by 2. The duration of 5.30 is also divided by 2 to get 2.65 years.

The duration of 2.65 years means that the investor collects on average all interest and principal repayment within 2.65 years. Keep in mind that not all payments are received at 2.65 years. Duration represents the weighted average of all payments. Therefore, duration is not the sum of all present values (which is the price of the bond). The longer the term to maturity, the more weight put on the calculation.

The calculation just shown is known as Macaulay duration (named by Frederick Macaulay in 1938). The calculation tells us that bonds with similar duration will experience comparable changes in price. In most cases, bonds with longer durations are more volatile to changes in interest rate.

In general, bonds exhibit more price volatility the longer the term to maturity. If two bonds have the same coupon, the bond with the greater maturity will have the longer duration. Furthermore, low coupon bonds are generally more volatile than high coupon bonds. If two bonds have the same maturity, the bond with the lower coupon will have the longer duration. However, the process gets a little more complex for a bond with a shorter maturity and smaller coupon. The same problem exists for a bond with a longer maturity and larger coupon. For bonds with different maturities and coupon rates, duration is an excellent technique for determining which bond is more volatile to changes in interest rates. The bond with the longer duration will decline more in price in relation to an increase in interest rates. By contrast, the bond with the longer duration will increase more in price in relation to a decrease in interest rates.

Duration is used to determine how much the price of a bond will change to *small* changes in interest rates. The relationship is

$$\text{Percentage change in price} = -\frac{1}{1 + (\text{yield} \div k)} \times \text{Macaulay duration} \times \text{yield change} \times 100$$

The first two parts of the equation are combined into one expression and called *modified duration*. Modified duration is

$$\text{Modified duration} = \frac{\text{Macaulay duration}}{1 + (\text{yield} \div k)}$$

k is the number of payments per year ($k= 1$ for a annual bond, $k= 2$ for a semiannual bond, $k = 12$ for a monthly payment bond).

The relationship between price volatility and duration is

$$\text{Percentage change in price} = \text{modified duration} \times \text{yield change} \times 100$$

Consider a 10 percent semiannual 3-year bond. The current interest rate on similar bonds is 12 percent. Therefore, the bond is currently selling for $950.82. The Macaulay duration is 2.65. Therefore, the modified duration is

$$\text{Modified duration} = \frac{2.65}{1 + (.12 \div 2)} = 2.50$$

What is the percentage price change if yields rise or drop 50 basis points (a yield change of +0.005)?

$$-2.50 \times (0.005) \times 100 = -1.25\%$$

The percentage price change is 1.25 percent if yields increase or decrease by 50 basis points. It is important to note that duration does an excellent job estimating the percentage price change when there is a *small* change in yield. However, duration is not accurate when there are large changes in yield. This is a result of convexity. If convexity can be determined, the approximate price of a bond to large changes in interest rates can be improved.

The modified duration is also defined as the percentage change in price for a 100 basis-point change in yield. For the previous example, the modified duration is 2.50, so the price of a bond will change approximately 2.50 percent for a 100 basis-point change in yield. The mathematical computation is

$$-2.50 \times (.01) \times 100 = -2.50\%$$

Modified duration is used to determine the percentage price change. It does not calculate the dollar price change to a bond. The dollar price volatility is

Dollar price volatility = (modified duration) × (dollar price) × (yield change)

From the previous example, if the bond is currently selling for $950.82 and the modified duration is 2.50, the dollar price duration is for a 100 basis-point change in yield is

Dollar duration = 2.50 × 950.82 × .01 = 23.77

This means the price of a bond will change by $23.77 for a 100 basis-point change in yield.

Approximating Duration. Macaulay's duration is often misleading because some bonds have durations greater than their maturity. Duration is not the weighted average life of a bond. In fact, it is possible for a bond to have a duration that is greater than the length of maturity. This is common with collateralized mortgage obligation bonds.

Duration can precisely be defined as the approximate percentage change in the price of a bond to a small change in interest rates. More specifically, duration is the approximate percentage change in price to a 100 basis-point change in interest rates. Therefore, duration of 2.65 means that the price of a bond will change approximately 2.65 percent to a 100 basis-point change in interest rates. Additionally, the earlier calculation is not needed to find the duration of a bond.

The following formula for approximate duration is used:

$$\text{Approximate duration} = \frac{P_- - P_+}{2P_0(\Delta y)}$$

Where P. is the new price if the yield is decreased by y, P_+ is the new price if the yield is increased by Δy, P_0 is the current bond price, and y is the required yield (in decimals).

To illustrate how the approximate duration is found, consider the same 10 percent semiannual 3-year bond. The yield to maturity is 12 percent. The bond is currently selling for $950.82. Also assume a 50 basis-point change in the current yield. The estimated bond prices with a rise of 50 basis points is

Calculator Solution

N = 6, I = 6.25, PMT = 50, FV = 1,000, Solve PV ⇒ $939.01

N = 6, I = 5.75, PMT = 50, FV = 1,000, Solve PV ⇒ $962.83

The approximate duration is

$$\frac{962.83 - 939.01}{2(950.82)(0.005)} = 2.50$$

How good is this number? The modified duration calculated earlier is also 2.50. Therefore, this formula does a very good job in finding the modified duration.

Q 5:68   What is convexity?

There is a relationship between the prices of a bond to changes in interest rates. The price of a bond will increase as interest rates decrease. In contrast, the price of a bond will decrease as interest rates increase. To find how sensitive bond prices are to small changes in interest rates, duration is used.

The price-yield relationship can be represented by a tangent line. The tangent line shows the rate of change in price to changes in yield. The slope of the tangent line is one basis point. The tangent line is strongly related to duration. In fact, duration is used interchangeably with a tangent line because both estimate the rate of change in price. There is more duration the steeper the tangent line and less duration the flatter the tangent line.

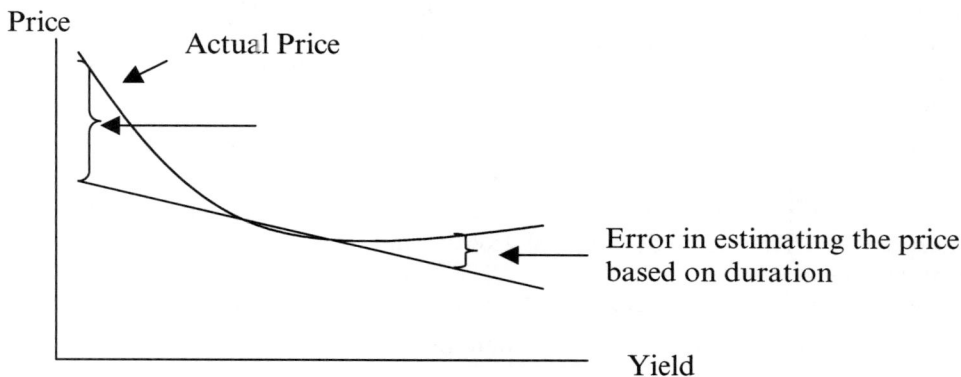

There is an interesting relationship between duration (tangent line) and the approximate change in price. The actual price change is greater than the estimated price change when yields decrease. By contrast, the actual price change is less than the estimated price change when yields increase.

However, duration becomes less exact with greater changes in yields because the price-yield relationship is curved rather than linear. How curved the path actually is depends on the degree of convexity. The distance between the tangent line (estimated price) and the curvature of the actual path (actual price) is the error in estimating price based on duration. If the degree of convexity is measured, the price of a bond can be estimated with more accuracy.

The convexity of an option-free bond is approximated using the following formula:

$$\text{Approximate convexity} = \frac{P_+ + P_- - 2P_0}{2P_0(\Delta y)^2}$$

where P_+ is the new price if the yield is increased by y, P_- is the new price if the yield is decreased by Δy, P_0 is the current bond price, and Δy is the required yield (in decimals).

Duration is used to approximate the first percentage change in price. Convexity is used to approximate the second, and is added to duration. The approximate percentage price change resulting solely from convexity is

$$\text{Convexity} \times (\text{yield change})^2 \times 100$$

This is the approximate percentage change not explained by duration. The formula used to find the approximate percentage price change of duration and convexity is

$$- (\text{duration})(\Delta y) + \text{convexity} \, (\Delta y)^2$$

Preferred Stock

Q 5:69   What is preferred stock?

Preferred stock usually pays a fixed dividend that is not guaranteed. It is expressed as a percentage to par or dollar amount. For example, a $5.00 preferred represents a $5 annual dividend per share. The dividends are paid from earnings and given preference over common stock dividends. *Cumulative preferred* is preferred stock in which dividends are accumulated rather than paid. The dividends are said to be in arrearage. This means they have not been paid but will be at some time in the future before dividends are paid to common stock holders. *Noncumulative preferred* is preferred stock in which dividends do not accumulate. In this case, any missed dividend payments are not paid in the future.

Preferred stock is perpetual. This means that a firm does not have to generate sufficient money to retire it. This is a big difference from issuing bonds. However, if a firm chooses to change its capital structure by replacing the preferred stock with debt financing, it would need to buy the shares back in the open market. This can cause a premium to be paid based on supply and demand principles.

There are some significant differences between preferred stock and bonds. Preferred stock is usually purchased by investors seeking a fixed stream of income, as are bonds. However, preferred stock is less risky than common stock but is more risky than debt. A firm has a legal obligation to make interest payments to bondholders. By contrast, a firm does not have to make dividend payments to preferred stockholders. In addition, preferred stock has greater market fluctuation than bonds. This can be explained by the longer term (perpetual) and uncertainty (risk) associated with dividend payments.

Even though preferred stock is more risky than bonds, it does not necessarily have higher yields. The reason is explained by the federal corporate income tax laws. The interest paid by bonds is fully taxable to the receiving firm, but not so for dividends. Corporations that receive dividends from other taxable domestic corporations are entitled to deductions. The percentage of deduction depends on the corporation's investment in the corporation paying the dividend. The dividend-received deduction is as follows:

- If a corporation owns less than 20 percent of the stock in the paying corporation, the deduction equals 70 percent of the dividend received and only 30 percent is taxed as income.

- If the corporation owns as least 20 percent but less than 80 percent of the stock in the paying corporation, the deduction equals 80 percent of the dividend paid and only 20 percent is taxed as income.

- If the corporation owns 80 percent or more of the stock in the paying corporation, the deduction equals 100 percent of the dividend received.

Tax laws may encourage firms from buying preferred stock, but they discourage firms from issuing it. Interest on bonds is a tax-deductible expense for the issuing corporation. This is not the case for dividends. Because preferred stock dividends are paid out of earnings, the result is lower earnings per share.

These tax laws may prove to be advantageous to corporations purchasing preferred stock, but no such tax benefit exists for the individual investor. Therefore, when purchasing preferred stock, an investor may experience inferior returns when adjusting for risk. Additionally, preferred stock is less marketable than many other securities. This can cause a large spread between the bid and ask, which may be unattractive to an investor.

Q5:70 How is preferred stock valued?

Preferred stock is a perpetual debt instrument. Its dividends continue indefinitely because there is no maturity on preferred stock. The value of preferred stock is the present value of its dividends discounted at the appropriate interest rate over an infinite period of time. The value of a preferred stock is

$$V_p = \frac{D}{(1+k)^1} + \frac{D}{(1+k)^2} + \frac{D}{(1+k)^3} + \cdots + \frac{D}{(1+k)^x}$$

where V_p is the price of the preferred stock, D is the dividend, and k is the discount rate. The formula is further reduced to

$$V_p = \frac{D}{k}$$

For example, assume a preferred stock pays an annual dividend of $2 per share. The discount rate for comparable preferred stock is 8 percent. The present value of a share is

$$V_p = \frac{\$2}{.08} = \$25$$

Therefore, an investor is paying too much if the preferred stock is purchased for over $25 per share. By contrast, the stock is relatively cheap if it is trading under $25 per share.

Derivatives

Option Fundamentals

Q 5:71   What is an option?

An option is a contract that gives the owner the right (but not a legal obligation) to trade an underlying asset at a predetermined future date and price. The value of an option depends on the value of an underlying asset. The price paid for the option contract is called the premium.

Options are classified as calls and puts. A call gives the holder the right to buy an asset at a predetermined price. A put gives the holder the right to sell the asset at a predetermined price. The seller of an option contract is called an option writer. The writer of a call must deliver the asset at a predetermined price. The writer of a put must purchase the asset at a predetermined price.

Q 5:72   What is the strike price and expiration date?

The strike price is the predetermined price for an option. If a call is exercised, the holder buys the asset at the strike price. If a put is exercised, the holder sells the asset at the strike price. If a call writer is assigned, the writer must deliver the asset at the strike price. If a put writer is assigned, the writer must purchase the asset at the strike price. The predetermined time when the option contract expires is called the expiration date.

One stock option contract generally represents 100 shares of the underlying stock. For example, a XYZ Dec 75 call priced at $2.50 represents an actual cost of $250 dollars (100 shares times $2.50 per share). The contract will expire in December and the stick price is $75.

Q 5:73   When do options expire?

Listed stock options expire on the Saturday following the third Friday of the expiration month. The only exceptions are when legal holidays fall on this Friday or Saturday. The Saturday is a result of allowing exchange members and brokerage houses to work out any errors that may exist.

Brokerage houses generally put forth procedure for handling exercises. First, the brokerage house may automatically exercise any option contract that is 75 cents above the strike price. This number can be less or more depending on the firm. The investor needs to give specific instructions for not exercising contracts above the strike price. Secondly, there is a notification deadline for exercises which is usually 4:00 PM EST on expiration Friday. This time can also vary depending on the firm.

Q 5:74   What is the definition of in-the-money, out-of-the-money, and at-the-money?

If the underlying stock price is greater than the strike price, a call option is said to be in-the-money. The call option is said to have value. If the underlying stock price is less than the strike price, a call option is said to be out-of-the-money. In this case, the call option has little to no value. If the underlying stock price is equal to the strike price, a call option is said to be at-the-money. Here again, the call option has minimal value.

The same can be said for put options. If the underlying stock price is less than the strike price, a put option is said to be in-the-money. The put option (as with a call option) has value when it is in-the-money. If the underlying stock price is greater than the strike price, a put option is said to be out-of-themoney. There is little to no value for the put option. If the underlying stock price is equal to the strike price, a put option is said to be at-the-money.

Q 5:75   What is the difference between American and European options?

American options allow the holder the right to exercise the option contract at some predetermined price any time before or at expiration. European options allow the holder to exercise the option only at expiration. The majority of options that are traded are American options. It is important to understand that the name of the option has nothing to do with the geography. Instead, the difference is when the option is exercised. In addition, American options have more theoretical value than European options because of the early exercise privilege.

Q 5:76   What makes up the value of an option?

Price and Strike Price. The price of a stock option is partially determined by the price of the underlying stock. For a call option, when the stock price is less than the strike price, the option is out-of-the money. In this case, the value of the call option approaches zero. As the price of the stock rises, the call option also rises. The price of the call option rises slowly at first and increases as the stock goes in-the-money. In-the-money is when the stock price is greater than the strike price for a call option. When the stock price rises, the option price increases at a slower rate than the stock price. There is a greater increase in the option price as the stock price continues to rise. As the call option goes significantly in-the-money, the change in option price approaches 100 percent of the change in stock price.

The reverse can be said about the relationship between the stock price and strike price for a put option. In the case of a put, there is a greater increase in the option price as the stock price drops. A put is in-the-money when the stock price is less than the strike price. The change in option price approaches 100 percent of the change in stock price as the stock price significantly drops below the strike price.

Time Decay. Options have an expiration date. The amount of time before expiration greatly affects the price of an option. The extent to which the price of an option exceeds its intrinsic value is called time premium. The effect of time on the price of option is often shown by a *time decay line*. The time decay line shows that an option's price does not decay in a straight line, but is determined by the square root of time. If a 30-day option is priced at $1, the 60-day option is priced at approximately $1 \times 2 = 1.414$. The square root is taken because the 60-day option has almost twice as much time before expiration. The following demonstrates this relationship [Chicago Board Option Exchange]:

If the 30-day option = $1, then the 60-day option $\approx 1 \times \sqrt{2} = 1.414$

If the 30-day option = $1, then the 90-day option $\approx 1 \times \sqrt{3} = 1.734$

If the 30-day option = $1, then the 120-day option $\approx 1 \times \sqrt{4} = 2.000$

If the 30-day option = $1, then the 150-day option $\approx 1 \times \sqrt{5} = 2.235$

If the 30-day option = $1, then the 180-day option $\approx 1 \times \sqrt{6} = 2.450$

This shows that an option loses less than one-third of its value from time decay during the first half of its life. However, the time premium quickly disappears as an option approaches the expiration date. All else being equal, this demonstrates that option buyers benefit from buying longer-term options. Conversely, option sellers benefit from selling shorter-term options.

In addition, the time premium for a call option declines when the price of the stock rises above the strike price. The reverse is true for a put option, the time premium declines when the price of the stock drops below the strike price.

Interest Rates.   Rising interest rates increase call prices but depress put prices. This is because higher interest rates increase the present value of funds used to exercise the call option. However, the overall effect of interest rate changes is small on an options price.

Volatility.   The more volatile the stock price, the higher the option price. The greater the standard deviation of a stock, the more likely there will be price swings commanding higher option prices. Increased volatility will put a higher premium on put and call prices because volatility is non-directional. If expected volatility increases, call and put prices also increase.

When expected volatility increases, in-the-money options move more in price than out-of-the-money options. This is a result of probability theory. For example, a $25 stock has a greater likelihood of moving $1 than $5. The same holds true for an option. The out-of-the money option has less of a chance of going in-the-money than an option already in-the-money.

Option models require the input of several variables to find the option price. These input variables include: stock price, exercise price, time, interest rate, stock dividend, and expected volatility. Of these, only expected volatility is an unknown factor. Expected volatility is found by using the price of the option as an input variable and solving for the volatility assumption. The resulting variable is called implied volatility. Implied volatility is the volatility percentage that makes up the price of an option. It is the volatility that the current option price "implies" that the underlying stock must have in order for the option price to be right. It is the resulting number found by running the price of an option back-wards and solving for volatility instead of the option price.

Implied volatility is very important to a trader of options. Options with expensive prices reflect a high volatility estimate built in by the market. In this case, the market expects large price swings in the underlying stock before expiration. The more implied volatility, the greater the percentage move in the underlying stock needed for an option to double in price. For example, assume implied volatility increases from 20 to 30 percent for an option. In order for the price of the option to double, the underlying stock has to have a greater price increase than before.

The price of an option is really dependent on the future volatility of the stock, but ultimately the process of predicting future volatility is subjective. There are mathematical calculations done by computers that estimate future volatility based on historical volatility.

Q 5:77   What is intrinsic value and time value?

The price of an option is based on intrinsic value and time value. The intrinsic value is the minimum price an option can command. For call options, it is the stock price minus the strike price for an in-the-money option. Conver-sely, for put options, it is the strike price minus the stock price since a put is in-the-money when the stock price drops below the strike price. The time value is the premium minus the intrinsic value. For example, a $50 XYZ Call is priced at $5. The underlying stock is trading at $53. The intrinsic value is $3 and the time value is $2. An out-of-the-money option consists entirely of time value because there is no intrinsic value.

Parity exists when an option trades with no time value, but only intrinsic value. This exists only when a stock is in-the-money. For example, a $50 call option priced at $3 when the stock is at $53 is trading at parity. Parity is common when an option is significantly in-the-money with only a short time before expiration. In this case, there is no time premium because the option is certain to be exercised. The option then trades like a stock.

Q 5:78   How much will the price of an option change for a $1 move in the stock price? (Chicago Board Option Exchange)

There is a relationship between the price of a stock and the strike price. For a call option, the option price rises when the stock price increases. The option price increases at a slower rate than the stock price for out-of-the-money calls. There is a greater increase in the option price as the stock price continues to rise. The option price moves dollar for dollar to the stock price when the stock price is significantly above the strike price.

How much the option price changes to a $1 move in the stock price is known as the *delta*. For example, a delta of .50 means that the option moves 50 cents for a $1 move in the stock price. If an option is out-of-the-money, then the option price changes much slower to a stock price change. If the option is at-the-money, the option price changes by approximately 50 percent of a change in the stock price. For options that are significantly in-the-money, the option moves dollar for dollar with the stock price. In this case, the delta is 1.00, indicating that a $1 move in stock price equals a $1 move in the option price.

Delta changes over time. It changes based on where the option price is relative to the stock price. It is important to understand that the delta only gives current estimates of the expected value of an option price relative to the stock price.

Call options have a positive delta because they increase in value as the stock increases in price. The delta for a $50 call is slightly positive if a stock moves from $44 to $45. The delta is much more positive if a stock moves from $54 to $55. Conversely, put options have a negative delta because they increase in value as the stock decreases in price. The delta for a $50 put is slightly negative if a stock moves from $55 to $54. The delta is much more negative if a stock moves from $45 to $44.

Q 5:79   How does an option price erode per unit of time? (Chicago Board Option Exchange)

Theta is the rate at which an option price erodes over a period of time. As an option approaches its expiration date, the price decays at an increasing rate. A time decay line demonstrates that an option loses less than one third of its value from time decay during the first half of its life. The largest impact of time decay happens during the last weeks up until expiration.

Q 5:80   How much does the option price change for a one percent change in volatility? (Chicago Board Option Exchange)

Increased volatility will put a higher value on put and call prices. If expected volatility increases, call and put prices rise. In contrast, option prices fall when expected volatility decreases. The amount of change is measured by *vega*.

The vega is a measure of change in the price of an option caused by a change in volatility. A vega of .50 means that a one percent change in implied volatility causes a 50-cent change in the price of an option. In-the-money options have a higher vega than out-of-the-money options. Therefore, when expected volatility increases, in-the-money options move more in price than out-of-the-money options.

Q 5:81   What is put-call parity?

Put-call parity means that a relationship exists between the prices of puts and calls and the underlying stock. It keeps the prices in check so an opportunity for arbitrage does not happen. Arbitrage is the opportunity to make money without making an investment. Put-call parity makes certain the price of a call and put change with each other and the underlying stock. The put and call can be considered too expensive or cheap but one cannot be more expensive or cheaper than the other. Put-call parity says the price of the call plus the present value of the strike price minus the price of the put equals the price of the stock:

$$P_s = P_c + \frac{P_e}{(1+i)^n} - P_p$$

where P_s is the price of the stock, P_c is the price of the call, P_e is the strike price, i is the interest rate, n is the option period (three month expiration is 0.25, six month expiration is 0.50, etc.), and P_p is the price of the put.

The equation can be changed to have the price of the stock plus the price of the put minus the price of the call minus the present value of the strike price equals zero:

$$0 = P_s + P_p - P_c - \frac{P_e}{(1+i)^n}$$

This must happen for arbitrage not to exist. Arbitrage holds true if the right side of the equation equals a value other than zero.

Option Strategies

Q 5:82   What strategy is used when buying calls?

A call is an option to buy a specified amount of shares (usually 100) at a specified price (strike price) within a specified time period (expiration date). Investors should buy calls when they expect the underlying stock or index to rise. A long call position can be used in a speculative way through leverage, or conservatively as an insurance policy. The percentage increase in a call often exceeds that of the stock in a rising market. Conversely, when the price of the underlying stock decreases, the percentage loss in the call is often greater than the stock. This is the effect of leverage. However, the absolute gain or loss on the call is less than owning the stock because options are less expensive. The maximum gain is unlimited. The maximum loss is the premium paid for the options. The breakeven equals the strike price plus the premium.

Time decay accelerates as the option approaches expiration. This is an important point when buying out-of-the-money calls that are close to expiration. In this case, a call buyer needs a rapid rise in the underlying stock price to neutralize the effects of accelerating time premium decay.

Purchasing call options is more speculative the greater they are out-of-the-money. This is another result of time decay. The out-of-the-money or at-the-money calls lose 100 percent of time premium at expiration. These call options have no intrinsic value. The underlying stock needs to go above the strike price at expiration for the call buyer to make money. The in-the-money calls also experience time decay but at less than 100 percent of the premium. In-the-money calls have intrinsic value, which does not decay. The underlying stock needs to trade below the strike price at expiration for an investor to lose the entire premium.

The price move of an in-the-money call is almost similar to the price move of the underlying stock. The premium becomes more sensitive to price changes in the underlying stock. When purchasing out-of-the-money or at-the-money calls, a call buyer find opportunity by using leverage. This is accomplished by purchasing a larger number of contracts.

The speculative behavior of a call buyer is supported by delta. The delta is higher the more a call is in-the-money, and becomes lower the further a call is out-of-the-money. Therefore, a speculative buyer purchases a larger amount of contracts to benefit from leverage. For example, assume a trader has $500 to spend on buying calls. The price of the stock is $49. The cost of a 50 call is $3.75 and the cost of a 45 call is $2.00. The delta for the 50 call is .79, which means a $1 price move in the stock causes a 79 cents price move in the call premium. If the delta for the 45 call is .57, then a $1 price move in the stock results in a 57-cent price move in the call premium. The trader can afford to purchase one in-the-money call or two out-of-the-money calls. The out-of-themoney calls result in a delta of 1.14 (2 × .57) versus the in-the-money call having a delta of .79. The amount of leverage is clear. By purchasing two out-of-the-money calls, a $1 increase in the stock price results in a $1.14 increase in value of the calls. However, greater leverage comes with added risk of the options expiring worthless. Conversely, in-the-money calls have less leverage but also less risk of expiring worthless.

Speculative call buyers should also understand that volatility is priced into the option before expected events, given an inflated price to the call. For example, if a company expects to release earnings in a week, the price of the option may be inflated because of a higher volatility factor. The higher premium is often referred to on the street as "juice." After earnings are released, the premium would lose this "juice" quickly and possibly cause an unexpected loss for the call buyer even if the price of the stock rises after earnings.

However, there is a difference between speculating and investing in calls. Speculators are concerned with delta, time decay, and intrinsic value. An investor is more concerned with purchasing a call as an insurance policy. For example, an investor interested in purchasing 1,000 shares of XYZ at $50 may consider purchasing 10 contracts of XYZ at-the-money calls. This is an investment decision because the options protect against a $50,000 commitment. This is a type of insurance. In effect, the call investor pays a premium for the calls, which are similar to the cost for insurance. The investor participates in an upward rally without risking a large sum of cash.

Which approach is better, speculation or insurance? The answer is that neither approach is better than the other. Each offers its own advantages and disadvantages. It is important to understand each approach to better match the investment strategy being used.

Q 5:83　What strategy is used when buying puts?

A put is an option to sell a specified number of shares (usually 100) at a specified price (strike price) within a specified time period. Put buying is a speculative strategy using leverage or a conservative strategy of insurance. The strategy for buying puts is for a trader to profit from or protect against a price decline in the underlying stock. The maximum gain increases as the stock price decreases, and is only limited by the stock going to $0. The maximum loss is the premium paid for the options. The breakeven equals the strike price minus the premium.

The decay of premium accelerates as expiration nears. The rate of decay for put options is slower than that for call options. But the difference is slight. The rate of erosion also catches up to puts. Another difference between calls and puts is how time premium decays for in-the-money options: The in-the-money put loses time premium faster than an in-the-money call. But again, this rate of decay is only slightly noticeable.

Out-of-the-money calls are often the favorite to a put speculator because of leverage. In general, a speculator wants to purchase more options at a cheaper price with a limited amount of money. This is done by purchasing out-of-the-money puts because these are cheaper than in-the-money puts. The delta is higher the more a put is in-the-money, and becomes lower the further a put is out-of-the-money. Therefore, the out-of-the-money puts offer a greater potential for large percentage gains to a speculative put buyer. For example, assume a trader has $500 to spend on buying puts. The price of the stock is $49. The cost of a 50 put is $3.75 and the cost of a 45 put is $2.00. If the delta for the 50 put is .77, then a $1 price move in the stock causes a 77-cent price move in the put premium. If the delta for a 45 put is .55, then a $1 price move in the stock results in a 55-cent price move in the put premium. The trader can afford to purchase one in-the-money put or two out-of-the-money puts with the $500. The out-of-the-money puts result in a delta of 1.10 (2 × .55) versus the in-themoney put having a delta of .77. In the purchase of two out-of-the-money puts, a $1 decrease in the price of the stock results in a $1.14 increase in value of the puts. However, greater leverage comes with more risk of the options expiring worthless. In contrast, in-the-money puts have less leverage but also less risk of expiring worthless.

Buying puts are not just a speculative strategy. For an investor wanting to protect against downside loss without selling his or her stock position, puts are insurance against falling stock prices. This is known as *protective puts*. An investor has an option to buy a low-cost insurance policy by purchasing low premium, out-of-the-money puts. By contrast, an investor can purchase in-the-money puts to provide more protection but at a higher cost. For example, if a stock is selling at $49, then a 50 put is going to cost more than a 45 put, but the 50 put provides complete protection on the downside. The 45 put allows for a $4 decline in the stock before the insurance kicks in.

Another benefit of puts is their advantageous over selling stock short. When selling short, an investor sells the stock high and buys it back at a lower price.

The difference is the profit to the investor. However, selling short requires that stock be borrowed, so an investor is exposed to unlimited risk if the stock continues to increase in price. Conversely, by purchasing a put, an investor profits when the stock declines and the maximum loss is the amount paid for the option. This strategy is similar to short selling when buying in-the-money puts because these are more sensitive to price changes in the underlying stock than out-of-the-money puts.

A speculator is more concerned with leverage and delta. The speculator often buys puts out-of-the-money. The investor is purchasing puts as insurance against a position in stock. An investor may also purchase puts to short the stock while the risk is limited to the premium paid for the option. However, buying puts as insurance is not necessarily a true indication of bearishness. If an investor is really bearish on the market, it makes more sense simply to sell the stock.

An interesting point to note is that purchasing puts against a long position is the same as buying calls outright. Both strategies have limited loss (the premium paid) with unlimited gain. Therefore, if puts are bought as insurance on a stock, it turns the position into a call option. Obviously, this can only exist for the life of the option.

Q 5:84   What is naked call selling?

The act of selling an option is known as *writing*. Therefore, investors may *write naked calls*. Selling naked calls exposes an investor to considerable risk. If the call is exercised because the price of the stock rises, the option writer is obligated to buy the stock back and deliver it to the buyer. The price of the stock can be significantly higher than when the call was originally sold. It is important to understand that the strategy for naked call writing does not involve ownership of the underlying stock (a strategy known as covered call writing). The maximum gain with this strategy is the premium received. The maximum loss is unlimited. The breakeven is the strike price plus the premium.

Call selling is considered a very risky strategy because of the possibility of large losses with little gains. The motivation to selling calls is to take advantage of volatility and time decay. If expected volatility is high, the premium for the call is larger, resulting in more money coming in for the seller. The seller hopes that volatility diminishes over time or is exhausted upon expiration to benefit from the trade. Therefore, the seller of a call believes that expected volatility will not be greater than implied volatility in the premium. A call seller also takes advantage of time decay by selling an option in the final weeks before expiration. This is when time decay accelerates.

In-the-money calls have higher premiums than at-the-money and out-of-the-money calls, but also greater risk. The amount of time premium for in-the-money calls is less than at-the-money and out-of-the-money calls. As a result, in-the-money calls are more sensitive to price movements when the underlying stock price rises. The seller of a call cannot take advantage of time decay when a stock goes deep in-the-money. There is less room for error and more risk of loss.

If the underlying stock moves higher, the losses can really begin to grow. In contrast, an out-of-the-money call has more cushion against a rising stock price because most of the premium is time value that quickly diminishes as expiration approaches.

A trader should understand that the delta drops as the stock price declines for call options. This is not a good outcome for a seller of calls! The call becomes less sensitive to the underlying stock. This means that the option drops in price but loses less and less with each price decline in the underlying stock price. In effect, the in-the-money call begins to look more like an at-themoney call. The call seller wants the premium to erode in order to buy it back at a cheaper price than originally sold, or expire worthless at expiration.

Q 5:85   What is naked put selling?

The act of selling an option is known as *writing*. Therefore, investors may *write naked puts*. Naked put selling is a strategy in which the option trader assumes the risk of the underlying security in exchange for the premium. In other words, the risk is the stock being assigned to the owner of the call. The writer puts an emphasis in the underlying stock's price not declining. The maximum gain is the premium received. The maximum loss is the cost of buying the stock at the strike price. The loss continues to grow as the underlying stock declines below the strike price. The breakeven is the strike price minus the premium.

An option trader sells puts for several reasons. First, the goal of a put seller might be to earn the premium. Premiums are large when implied volatility is high. Additionally, time decay is positive for put selling. The decay of the premium accelerates as expiration nears. The put seller benefits from selling puts in the weeks close to expiration because of accelerating time decay. Second, the put seller may have the goal of purchasing the stock at a lower rate. For example, assume the 50 XYZ put is trading at $3 when the stock is $52. If the put drops to $48 and is assigned to the put holder, the stock is acquired at $50 less the $3 premium. Therefore, the investor really owns the stock at $47 when it is now trading at $48.

There can be opportunity loss if the stock trades above the breakeven price at expiration. In the previous example, the breakeven price is $50 (strike) plus $3 (premium). Therefore, any price above $53 is opportunity loss for the investor. If the put was purchased with the sole intention of owning the stock, the investor should have only bought the stock and not sold the put.

Selling puts with the willingness of owning the underlying stock is investing. If the seller of a put does not have the funds necessary to purchase the underlying stock if assigned, then investing becomes speculation.

Q 5:86   What is covered call selling?

The act of selling an option is known as *writing*. Covered call selling (or writing) is taking a short call with a long stock position in the underlying stock.

If the option is exercised, the seller supplies the stock at the strike price. The call seller limits the gain on the stock by the premium received plus the strike price minus the price paid for the underlying stock. For example, assume a seller receives $5 for selling a 50 XYZ call and pays $52 for 100 shares of XYZ stock. The maximum gain is $3. Therefore, the maximum gain is made when the stock trades above the strike price at expiration. The maximum loss is the price paid for the security minus the premium received from selling the call. That means that by selling calls to receive a premium, an investor partially hedges against his or her stock position. The breakeven is also the price paid for the underlying security minus the premium received.

Covered Writing. Covered writing is also known as *buy-writing*. It is when an investor simultaneously sells calls and buys an equal amount of shares in the underlying security. This strategy reflects varying opinions of investors. At-the-money buy-writes are neutral and out-of-the-money buy-writes are bullish. This is because at-the-money buy-writes generate more income than out-of-the-money buy-writes but realize most of the income from the premium and not the price appreciation of the stock. The out-of-the-money buy-writes participate in a rising stock price. The out-of-the-money buy-writes cost less but provide less protection against a price decline when compared to at-the-money buy-writes.

This raises an interesting point about purchasing in-the-money calls for a greater premium. High premium levels are directly related to volatility. However, the option with more volatility (higher premium) is not always the superior choice because the underlying stock can have more risk from a wider price range. This can result in the investor missing out on a price rise or suffering large losses from a price drop. The choice of what calls to write should be the investor's opinion of the underlying stock. If the investor does not want to own the underlying stock if it is not called away, then writing calls with large premiums is not the answer. The investor is better off selling the stock.

Overwriting. The investor already owns the underlying stock and now sells calls to generate income. The call writer is not expecting the stock to make a big move up or down. The investor does not sell calls if the stock price is expected to rise. Conversely, if a price decline in the underlying stock is expected, the investor sells the stock or buys puts.

It is evident that this strategy limits the amount of upside potential. There is an opportunity loss. The premium is being received at the cost of a rising stock price. Therefore, the investor is expecting the underlying stock to trade relatively flat while maintaining the short position in the call. In general, the covered call writer is mostly neutral and slightly bullish.

Q 5:87　What is covered put selling?

The investor sells the stock short and sells the put in order to construct the covered put. If the put is exercised, the investor buys the shares and uses this to cover the short position. This is the opposite of covered calls in which the investor sells existing shares if the call is exercised.

As with a covered call position, this strategy is used if an investor expects a stable stock price. The investor is neutral to slightly bearish. For example, assume a stock trades at $53 and the strike price of a put is $55 with a premium of $5. An investor sells short the stock and sells the put. If the stock stays below $58, the investor makes a profit. The maximum profit is $3 (the time premium). The maximum loss is unlimited if the stock price rises.

Q 5:88 What is a protective call?

The *protective call* strategy is constructed by combining an underlying short stock position with a long call position. This is the opposite of a *protective put* strategy in which the investor purchases the underlying stock and a put.

This strategy limits the loss on the short position by purchasing a call. If the price of the underlying stock keeps rising, the amount of loss is limited by the call. This safety comes at the cost of paying for the call. For example, assume a stock trades at $52. The strike price of the call is $55 and the price of the call is $2. An investor sells short the stock and buys the call. The maximum possible loss is limited to $5. The position is profitable if the stock trades below $50. Therefore, the potential for profit is very large if the underlying price declines.

Warrants

Q 5:89 What are warrants?

Warrants are equity call options directly issued by a corporation to buy the underlying stock at a specified price over a specified time period. The distinguishing difference of a warrant from an ordinary call option is that, if exercised, the company issues more common stock shares to give to the holder of the warrant. Therefore, when warrants are exercised, the total number of outstanding shares increases. The increase in shares is dilutive to the firm's earnings.

An ordinary call option gives the holder the right to buy 100 shares of the underlying stock upon exercise. In contrast, a warrant specifies the number of shares a holder can purchase at time of issue. Warrants usually give the right to buy one common share. They are not limited to this. Some warrants give the option to buy more or less than one share. Sometimes this conversion term is the result of mergers or stock splits. Therefore, the theoretical value of a warrant is equal to the terms of exchange (N) multiplied by the difference between the market price of the common stock (P_s) and the exercise price of the warrant (E_p):

$$TV_w = N_x(P_s - E_p)$$

For example, assume a warrant that gives the right to buy 0.5 shares at the exercise price of $55. The market price of the stock is $70. The theoretical price of the warrant is

$$TV_w = .5(\$70 - \$55) = \$7.5$$

Consequently, $7.50 is the lowest price the warrant can sell for. This is what is meant by theoretical price. However, warrants trade on stock exchanges like other stocks. Their price is usually higher than the theoretical price because investors put a premium on warrants in anticipation that the underlying stock price will rise above the exercise price.

If the stock price is less than the exercise price, the theoretical value is zero. Conversely, if the stock price is greater than the exercise price, the theoretical value is greater than one. However, the market value of the warrant is positive even when the stock price is less than the exercise price. This is because of the premium put on the warrant. When the price of the stock continues to increase in value, the likelihood of further increase vanishes. At this point, the market value slowly resembles the theoretical value.

Warrants exhibit more percentage change in price relative to the underlying stock. This is because of leverage effect. The leverage of a warrant is

$$\text{Leverage of a warrant} = \frac{\% \,\Delta \,\text{price of warrants}}{\% \,\Delta \,\text{price of stock}}$$

For example, the theoretical price of the warrant is $7.50. Assume the stock increases to $75, the theoretical value of the warrant increases to $10 [.5 ($75 − $55)]. Therefore, the stock increases 7 percent and the warrant increases 33 percent. The leverage effect is

$$33\% \div 7\% = 4.7 \text{ times the price appreciation in the stock}$$

The fair value of a warrant is usually determined by the same techniques used to value an option. The value is the result of five factors: current stock price, exercise price, time to expiration, risk-free rate, and standard deviation. The fair value is

$$FV_w = P_s \times (Nd_1) - \left[\frac{X_p}{e^{rt}} \times (Nd_2) \right]$$

where Nd_1 is the probability that the option pays off, Nd_2 is the probability of exercising the option, P_s is the price of the stock, X_p is the exercise price, r is the risk-free rate; and t is the time to expiration. The Nd_1 and Nd_2 probability factors are found using the five factors that determine the price of an option. Assume the following factors are given:

$$P_s = \$70$$
$$Nd_1 = .60$$
$$X_p = \$55$$
$$Nd_2 = .65$$
$$R_f = 4\%$$

Expiration = 1 year

Solving the equation:

$$FV_w = \$70 \times (.60) - \left[\frac{\$55}{e^{.04 \times 1}} \times (.65) \right] = \$7.65$$

The fair value of the warrant equals $7.65. Therefore, the market price equals the fair value in order to prevent arbitrage from happening.

As previously explained, the market value starts out higher than the theoretical value (minimum price). This is because the premium investors are willing to pay in expectation of continued stock price increases. However, the stock reaches a point of becoming overvalued and the probability of more increases in the price of the stock is improbable. At that point, the market and theoretical price become equal.

Chapter 6

Income Tax Planning

The financial planner must deal with tax issues in every part of the client's personal life and business. This chapter explores the tax issues that arise with a client's home and children; investments and retirement; employees, tax credits and other business functions; and dealing with the IRS.

x Issues When Planning for Children

1 What is the "kiddie" tax?

a child under the age of 14 has unearned income above a specified nt, the excess is taxed at the parent's marginal tax rate, not at the child's marginal tax rate. This tax is in place to keep parents from shifting income-producing assets to their children in order to minimize the overall tax bill.

For 2006, the first $850 of the child's unearned income is not taxable; the next $850 is taxable at the child's tax rate; and anything over $1,700 is taxable at the parent's marginal rate. Children who are 18 and older at the end of the tax year are not subject to this rule. For children 18 and older, the first $850 of unearned income is not taxable, and anything over $850 is taxable at the child's rate.

Q6:2   What is the dependent care tax credit?

The dependent care tax credit applies to expenses paid by individual tax-payers for the care of their dependents if the expenses are necessary to allow the taxpayer to be gainfully employed. The expenses must be paid by a taxpayer who maintains a household in which one or more "qualifying individuals" reside either for household services or specifically for the care of a qualifying individual. Household services include ordinary domestic services in the home, such as laundry, cleaning, and cooking that are partly for the care of the qualifying person. Outside of the home, care expenses for a child under age 13 include costs of day care facilities, day camp, nursery school, or for a babysitter in the home. Expenses for schooling for the first grade and above do not qualify.

A "qualifying individual" is a person under the age of 13 whom the taxpayer can claim as a dependent, a dependent who is physically or mentally incapable of self-care, or a taxpayer's spouse who is physically or mentally incapable of self-care.

Depending on the taxpayer's income, a credit of 21 to 35 percent applies to the expenses to the limit of $3,000 for one dependent or $6,000 for two or more dependents. For 2006, the limits are phased out for adjusted gross incomes between $15,000 and $43,000. The credit percentage is reduced by 1 percent for each $2,000 of adjusted gross income over $15,000.

Tax-free reimbursements under an employer's dependent care program will reduce the $3,000 or $6,000 credit base. For example, if an employee has one child and receives a $1,000 reimbursement of child-care costs from the employer's plan, the amount eligible for the tax credit is reduced to $1,000 ($3,000 − $2,000). A reimbursement over $3,000 would remove the availability of the credit. The $6,000 credit limit is similarly affected. Form 2441 must be filed with Form 1040 to claim the dependent care tax credit.

Q6:3   What is the child tax credit?

The tax law provides an annual tax credit that may be claimed against an individual's tax liability for each qualifying child of the taxpayer. The amount of the tax credit is $1,000 in 2006. The credit amount applies for each qualify-ing child. A "qualifying child" is someone who is under 17 at the end of the tax year who can be claimed as a dependent by the taxpayer. The child must be a son, daughter, stepson, stepdaughter, adopted child, or eligible foster child of the taxpayer, and must be a U.S. citizen or resident alien.

The credit is phased out for upper income taxpayers. The phaseout occurs when the taxpayer's adjusted gross income with certain minor modifications exceeds the following levels:

Filing Status	Beginning Phaseout Amount
Married filing jointly	$ 110,000
Head of household	$ 75,000
Single	$ 75,000
Qualifying widow(er)	$ 75,000
Married filing separately	$ 55,000

Use the Child Tax Credit Worksheet in the IRS instruction booklet or in Publication 972 to figure the credit. The credit is $1,000 multiplied by the number of qualifying children. The credit is reduced by $50 for each $1,000 (or fraction of $1,000) of modified adjusted gross income (AGI) that exceeds the phaseout threshold for filing status.

Example: Mary is single and has two dependent children under 17. Mary's modified AGI is $78,500 for 2006. She files her tax return as head of household. Because her modified AGI exceeds $75,000 (her phaseout value) by $3,500, she must figure a reduced credit amount. For each $1,000 (or fraction of $1,000) that exceeds the phaseout value, $50 of credit is reduced. In this case, the credit is reduced by $200 ($50 × 4) to $1,000. Mary may claim a $1,000 tax credit as long as her tax liability is at least that much.

If the full amount of the credit cannot be claimed because of the tax liability limitation, the taxpayer may be able to obtain a refund for the balance on Form 8812, Additional Tax Credit. All taxpayers with one or more qualifying children who have more than $10,000 of earned income must complete Form 8812 to compute the refundable portion of the credit.

Q 6:4   What is the adoption expense credit?

Adoptive parents may be able to take an adoption expense tax credit for qualified expenses paid in the course of adopting a child. The tax credit is up to $10,960 and is phased out for adjusted gross incomes are in excess of $164,410. The credit is completely phased out when AGI reaches $204,410. Both the credit and phaseout numbers are indexed for inflation.

Qualified adoption expenses include legal fees, court costs, attorney fees, and other related costs that have the principal purpose of a taxpayer's legal adoption of an eligible child. Costs associated with adopting the child of the taxpayer's spouse or costs for surrogate parenting arrangements are not considered qualified expenses for the purpose of this credit.

A child eligible for adoption is either under the age of 18 or is physically or mentally incapable of self-care. An eligible special needs child must be a citizen or resident of the United States. The State must first determine that the child cannot or should not be returned to either parent's home, and unless adoption assistance is provided to the adoptive parents, the child will probably not be adopted.

The adoption credit is allowed to taxpayers who adopt a special needs child regardless of the amount of qualified expenses paid by the taxpayer. Therefore, even if the adoptive parents do not incur $10,960 in expenses, they can take the full $10,960 tax credit.

In the tax year when the adoption becomes final, the taxpayer is allowed to claim the credit for expenses paid during that year. For tax years in which the expenses are paid but the adoption does not become final, the taxpayer must claim the credit in the year after which the expenses were paid. If the expenses are paid in a year following the year in which the adoption becomes final, the expenses may be claimed for the year in which they were made.

The adoption of a foreign child or of a child with special needs qualifies for the credit only if and when the adoption becomes final. The credit must be claimed in that same year even if the credit was paid in a prior year. For those taxpayers whose credit exceeds their tax liability, there is a five-year carryover period available.

Tax Issues When Planning for Employment

Q 6:5   What job search costs can be deducted?

Subject to the 2 percent AGI floor for miscellaneous deductions, expenses of looking for a new job in the same line of work may be deducted, whether or not a new job is found. If the individual is unemployed when seeking a new job and the period of unemployment has been substantial, the IRS may disallow the deduction. Expenses of seeking a first job are not deductible even if a job is obtained. In addition, expenses of looking for a job in a different line of work are not deductible.

Employment and outplacement agency fees paid in looking for a new job may be deducted if they are in the same field as one's present occupation. Money spent for creating, printing, and mailing of resumes to prospective employers also may be deducted.

If looking for a new job in a present occupation, travel expenses to and from the area of the employment search may be deducted. The amount of time spent on personal activities compared to the amount of time spent in looking for work is important in determining whether the trip is primarily personal or primarily to look for a new job. Even if travel expenses themselves are not deductible, the expenses of looking for a job may be.

Q6:6   What job-related expenses can be deducted?

If an employee incurs work-related education expenses, all or part of the cost of the education may be deductible as a business expense deduction. These expenses are deductible only to the extent that they exceed 2 percent of adjusted gross income. If the education is required by an employer or by law for the employee to keep his or her present salary, status or job, that education qualifies for the deduction. In addition, if the studies are used to maintain or improve skills for the current position, these studies also qualify for the deduction. However, if the education is needed to meet the minimum education requirements of the employee's present trade or business, it does not qualify for the deduction. This is also true if the education is part of a program of study that will qualify an employee for a new trade or business.

If the field of study qualifies, transportation costs of going directly from work to school are deductible if attendance at school is realistically expected to last for one year or less. In addition, expenses for overnight travel, including meals and lodging, are deductible if the main purpose of the trip is to attend a work-related course or seminar.

Q6:7   How should unreimbursed employment expenses be handled?

Unreimbursed employment expenses can be deducted that are paid or incurred during the current tax year and that are part of carrying out a trade or business as an employee. The expenses must also be ordinary and necessary. An expense is *ordinary* if it is common and accepted in the particular type of trade or business, and *necessary* if it is appropriate and helpful to the trade or business.

Examples of unreimbursed employee expenses are:

- Bad business debt of an employee;
- Education that is work-related (*see* Q 6:6);
- Legal fees related to the job;
- Malpractice insurance premiums;
- Occupational taxes;
- Passport for a business trip; and
- Subscriptions to professional journals and trade magazines related to the type of work.

These expenses can be included as miscellaneous itemized deductions on Schedule A if they total more than 2 percent of adjusted gross income.

Q6:8   How are employer-provided education expenses handled?

If an employee receives education assistance benefits from an employer under an education assistance program, up to $5,250 of those benefits can be excluded each year. This means the employer should not include this benefit in wages, tips, and other compensation shown in box 1 of the W-2 form. It also means that this benefit does not have to be listed on the employee's income tax return. However, if the education expenses exceed the amount of the benefit received from the employer, the excess can be deducted as a miscellaneous itemized deduction. Also, if the employer-provided educational benefit exceeds more than $5,250, the excess will be included as wages on the employee's W-2 form.

Education assistance benefits include payments for tuition, fees, books, supplies and equipment for both undergraduate and graduate-level courses. Items that are not covered are meals, lodging, transportation, and any supplies that an employee keeps after completing the education except for textbooks.

Tax Issues When Planning in Divorce Situations

Q 6:9   What are the tax issues with property settlements?

If property is transferred in settlement of marital rights, the spouse making the transfer does not recognize either gain or loss on the transfer, whether the property has appreciated or declined in value. The transfer is treated like a gift, and the spouse receiving the property takes the basis in the property that the transferring spouse had. The receiving spouse also assumes the transferor spouse's holding period for the property. The transfer will receive this treatment if it is "incident to a divorce," which means that it occurs within one year after the divorce or is related to the ending of the marriage. The transfer is related to the ending of the marriage if it is made pursuant to a divorce or separation agreement and occurs within six years after the date on which the marriage ends.

When doing tax planning for a divorce, the tax basis must be considered when dividing the assets. A spouse who receives a low-basis asset should negotiate the appropriate offset factor to the asset's fair market value.

Q 6:10   What are the rules for community income of separated spouses?

Code Section 66 provides the rules for community income: the section applies when the spouses have lived apart for an entire calendar year and do not file a joint return for the year. When Section 66 applies, if one or both spouses have earned income for the year, no portion of that which is transferred between spouses applies to the other spouse. The only exceptions are payments for support of children or de minimis amounts. This rule applies to situations when one or both spouses claim that they knew nothing of the other's community income.

If the couple qualifies for Code Section 66, earned income is treated as income of the spouse who earned it. Business income is treated as income of the individual who owns the business unless the other spouse actively manages the business. The distributive share of partnership profits is income taxed to the spouse who has the distributive share.

Q6:11   What are joint tax return considerations in divorce planning?

The financial planner should consider an indemnity agreement, especially when there is a likelihood that income will be understated or deductions will be overstated. When filing joint returns, both spouses will be jointly and severally liable and must make up any deficiencies that are assessed. In most cases when divorce is eminent, couples should file separate returns.

When a joint tax return is filed, the spouse earning a higher income will want the other spouse to sign the return. However, the spouse cannot be made to sign the return. United States Tax Court cases have considered such returns as joint returns, even when neither spouse has signed them: the returns contained only the typed names of the filers.

Q6:12   May the costs of getting a divorce be deducted?

Legal fees and court costs of getting a divorce are not deductible; nor are expenses paid in arranging child custody and support payments. Also, expenses paid in arriving at a financial settlement are not deductible.

However, several costs of a divorce are deductible: The fees paid for tax advice relating to a divorce are deductible, along with fees paid to determine or collect alimony or to determine the estate tax consequences of a property settlement. It is important to remember that when working with financial advisors, it is necessary to get a breakdown of the amount charged for each service.

Q6:13   What are the tax issues regarding alimony?

The term "alimony" refers to the legal obligation imposed on one spouse to make monetary payments to the other spouse. Other terms such as "maintenance and support" and "spousal support" are used interchangeably with "alimony." Payments that qualify as alimony are deductible by the payer spouse and are taxable to the payee spouse as ordinary income.

To qualify as alimony:

1. The payment must be required in a written divorce or separation agreement.
2. The payment must be in cash, which includes checks and money orders.
3. The payer and recipient spouse do not file a joint tax return.
4. The payment must not be designated as "not alimony" in the divorce or separation agreement.
5. The payment cannot be designated as child support.
6. The payments are not required after the death of the recipient spouse.
7. Spouses who are legally separated under a decree of divorce or separate maintenance may not be members of the same household.

Payments that do not qualify as alimony:

- Payments that are designated as child support.
- Payments that are noncash property settlements.
- Payments that are a part of community property income.
- Payments used to keep up the payer's property.
- Payments that are not required by a divorce or separation agreement.

There are two situations where payments that would otherwise qualify as alimony will be treated as child support: (1) if the payments are reduced six months before or after the child turns 18, 21, or the local age of majority; (2) if the payments are reduced on two ore more occasions that occur not more than one year before or after a another one of the spouses' children reaches a certain age from 18 to 24. In either of these cases the amount the alimony is reduced is not considered alimony; it is considered child support and is not deductible to the payer or considered income to the payee.

If a spouse is obligated to pay both alimony and child support under a decree but pays less than the full amount due, the payment made is first applied to satisfy the child support obligation. This means that the child support obligation must be met before any amount of alimony is deductible.

The spouse who makes the alimony payment is allowed to deduct the amount on his or her tax return. However, he or she must file Form 1040, not Form 1040A or 1040EZ. The spouse who receives the alimony must report it on line 11 of Form 1040. He or she is not allowed to use Form 1040A OR 1040EZ.

Q 6:14 What is the "recapture" of alimony?

If alimony payments decrease or terminate during the first three calendar years of payment, the alimony recapture rule may apply. This means that the payer of the alimony must add to income a portion of the previously deducted alimony, and the recipient of the alimony may deduct amounts previously reported as income. The recaptured amounts are reported on the third-year tax return only.

The recapture rule applies if the alimony paid in the second or third year of the three-year period is more than $15,000 less than in the prior year. The threeyear period starts with the first calendar year in which an alimony payment is made. See IRS Publication 504, titled Worksheet for Recapture of Alimony.

If either spouse dies or remarries before the end of the third year and payments cease as a result of that event, then the alimony recapture rule does not apply.

Q 6:15 Are child support payments deductible?

Because child support payments are not treated as alimony, they are not deductible by the payer spouse and not considered income to the receiving spouse. A payment is considered child support if the divorce or separation agreement specifies it as such or if the payment is reduced either on a contingency relating to the child or at a time that can clearly be associated with the contingency. Examples of a contingency are when the child reaches a specific age (such as 18 or 21), gets married, dies, leaves school, leaves the household, or is gainfully employed. The amount that is reduced due to a contingency is considered child support.

If a spouse is obligated to pay both alimony and child support under a decree but pays less than the full amount due, the payment made is first applied to satisfy the child support obligation. This means that the child support must be met before any amount of alimony is deductible.

Q6:16   Who claims children as dependents?

Generally, the parent who has physical custody of the child is entitled to the dependency exemption regardless of how much support was provided by each parent. Custody is determined by the most recent divorce or separation agreement or a court decree. If physical custody is joint or the agreement does not establish custody, then custody will be with the parent who has physical custody of the child for the greater portion of the year.

However, there is an exception to this general rule. The noncustodial parent may claim the exemption if the parent who has custody signs a written declaration that he or she will not claim the exemption for the child for the tax year, which can be done through Form 8332 (Release of Claim to Exemption for Child of Divorced or Separated Parents). If the decree unconditionally allows the noncustodial parent to claim the exemption, that parent can attach a copy of the applicable language from the decree or agreement instead of using Form 8332.

Q6:17   What are the tax issues regarding retirement or pension plans and a divorce?

A state court can allocate an interest in a qualified retirement plan to a former spouse in a qualified domestic relations order (QDRO). Payments that are made as the result of a QDRO to the former spouse will not affect the participant in the pension plan. The benefits are taxed to the former spouse when he or she receives them and are not subject to the 10 percent early withdrawal penalty. They may be rolled over tax-free into an IRA or a qualified retirement plan. To avoid the 20 percent withholding rule on a distribution, a direct transfer from one trustee to another may be preferred over a rollover. In order for the distributions made to a former spouse to be considered a nontaxable event, the funds must be distributed to the spouse directly from the plan.

Q6:18   What is a QDRO?

A QDRO is a qualified domestic relations order, which is an order by the court that tells the administrator or trustee of a qualified retirement plan how much to pay out to the non-owner spouse pursuant to a divorce. Without a

QDRO, a withdrawal by an owner spouse from a qualified plan to pay a property settlement to a non-owner spouse may trigger income and penalty taxes even though the owner does not receive the proceeds.

Some pension plans may not accept QDROs. If the plan does not, the plan documents themselves will govern any payout due to the divorce.

QDRO rules do not apply to IRAs. The transfer of an individual's interest in an IRA to his or her spouse or former spouse under a divorce or separation agreement is not considered a taxable transfer made by the individual; thereafter, the IRA is treated as maintained for the benefit of the spouse or former spouse.

Also, QDRO rules do not apply to nonqualified plans. However, there have been rulings that life insurance benefits under an employer-sponsored nonqualified plan and an ERISA welfare benefit plan are subject to QDRO rules if the divorce decree specifies how the life insurance benefits must be distributed.

Q6:19   What are the tax issues regarding IRAs and a divorce?

Under the terms of a divorce agreement, if a spouse transfers his or her interest in an IRA to the former spouse, there is no taxable transfer. Starting from the date of the transfer, the spouse that receives the IRA is treated as the owner. IRAs do not require a QDRO in order to roll over assets to the former spouse.

All taxable alimony received under the divorce agreement is treated as compensation for purposes of the IRA contribution and deduction limits. The rules for deducting contributions to a traditional IRA apply.

Q6:20   How does a married couple plan for community property interests?

Community property is all property that has been acquired by the efforts of either spouse during their marriage while living in a community property state. It does not include property acquired by only one of the spouses by gift, devise, bequest, inheritance or property acquired by either spouse prior to their marriage. Both spouses own community property equally. The traditional community property states are Arizona, California, Idaho, Louisiana, Nevada, New Mexico, Texas, and Washington. Wisconsin is also a community property state, which adopted the Uniform Marital Property Act. This Act presumes that property owned by the spouses is property of the marriage; it does not belong to just one spouse. However, the rule can be overcome by evidence that sufficiently establishes otherwise.

When it comes to classifying income, most of the community property states follow what is referred to as the California rule. Under this rule, income from community property is community property, as is anything bought with that income. In contrast, income from separate property is separate property, as is anything bought with that income. Three community property states (Texas, Idaho, and Louisiana) follow what is called the Texas rule. This rule treats income earned from separate property during the marriage as community property. The Texas rule is similar to the California rule in that any gain on separate property that is sold as separate property is treated as separate property. In addition, anything bought with the proceeds of the sale is separate property.

Arizona, California, Idaho, Washington, and Wisconsin have a concept called *quasi-community property*, which is defined as property that has been acquired by a resident while domiciled in a noncommunity property state that would have been community property had the resident been domiciled in a community property state at the time of acquisition. For example, if a married couple move to California owning common stock acquired with a salary earned during the marriage while the couple were residents of Colorado, the stock is quasi-community property. Quasi-community property is treated as separate property of the acquiring spouse until divorce or death. If the parties divorce, the property is divided in a manner similar to community property.

In general, assets included in a taxable estate of a decedent receive a stepup basis. The receivers of the bequests receive a basis in those assets equal to the fair market value at date of death or, alternatively, six months after death. The step-up in basis is only available to those assets in the taxable estate. If assets are kept out of the estate, such as gifts, they will not enjoy the step-up in basis. Community property states have a full step-up in basis. For tax purposes, the new cost basis is the fair market value (FMV) at the date of death for both halves of the community property even though only one-half is included in the decedent spouse's estate. In contrast, common law states have a step-up basis for half of the assets—a step-up in basis for the decedent's share of ownership, not the survivor's share.

Community property states have a decided advantage over common law states with regard to basis adjustments at death. Couples residing in community property states should hold appreciated property as community property. On the other hand, if property has decreased in value, community property will receive a full step-down in basis at the first death. In that case, some other form of title might be preferred.

Tax Issues When Planning on Selling a Home

Q 6:21   What is the treatment of capital gains on selling a home?

After May 6, 1997, a homeowner who sells a personal residence may exclude from income up to $250,000 of gain, and a married couple may exclude up to $500,000 of gain realized on the sale. The previous deferral-of-gain rules under Section 1034 and the age 55 lifetime exclusion of $125,000 have both been repealed. Individuals must have owned and lived in the home as a principal residence for at least two out of the five years prior to the sale of the home. The two years do not have to be consecutive. This exclusion applies to only one sale every two years.

To get the full $500,000 exclusion, married couples must meet several conditions:

1. They must file a joint return.
2. Either or both spouses must have owned the residence for at least two of the five years prior to the sale.
3. Both spouses must have used the residence as their principal residence for at least two out of the five years prior to the sale.
4. Neither spouse may have sold a home more than once every two years (sales before May 7, 1997 are not taken into account).

If only one of the spouses meets the use test, then the couple will be able to exclude only $250,000 in gain.

If the home is sold when it has not be owned or used for two out of the five previous years, then the gain on the house is taxable. However, if the home is sold due to a job relocation, for health reasons, or due to unforeseen cicumstances, the homeowner(s) may qualify for a reduced exclusion which is prorated based on the number of days the owners met the two-year ownership and use requirements. For example, if a married couple owned and used the house for 13 months (or 395 days), they would be allowed a maximum exclusion of $270,000 (395 days divided by 730 days times $500,000).

Q 6:22   What is the treatment of a capital loss when selling a home?

A loss on the sale of a personal residence may not be deducted.

Q 6:23   What is the treatment for moving expenses?

Moving expenses can usually be deducted if the move is because of a change in job. The expenses are deducted from gross income in arriving at AGI. This can be advantageous because expenses do not have to be itemized to receive the benefit of the deduction.

There are several tests that must be met in order to deduct the moving expenses. First, the moving expenses must have been incurred within one year from date an employee first started to work. If the employee does not move within one year of beginning to work, he or she ordinarily cannot deduct the expense unless evidence of circumstances existed that prevented the move within that time. For example, it took more than a year to sell the former home.

Second, the move will meet the distance test if the location of the new job is at least 50 miles farther from the former home than the old job was from the former home. For example, if the former job was five miles from the former residence, a new job must be more than 55 miles from the former house.

Finally, the move must meet a time test to deduct moving expenses. The employee must work full time for at least 39 weeks during the first 12 months after arriving in the general area of the new job location. If the employee leaves the first job without meeting the time requirements and gets a second job in the same general location, time spent on the two jobs may be combined to meet the 39-week rule.

If self-employed, the individual must work full time for at least 39 weeks during the first 12 months, and for a total of at least 78 weeks during the first 24 months after arriving in the new job location. Any full time work can be counted either as an employee or as a self-employed person. However, the employee need not need work for the same employer or be self-employed in the same trade or business for the full 78 weeks; the rule requires only that the employee work within the same general commuting area.

The costs of moving household goods and personal effects (including intransit or foreign-move storage expenses) and travel expenses (including lodging but not meals) for one trip can be deducted by the taxpayer and by every member of the household. Household members do not have to travel together or at the same time.

Form 3903, Moving Expenses, is filed to deduct qualified moving expenses that were not reimbursed by an employer or to deduct qualified expenses in excess of any amount reimbursed. The deduction is taken as an adjustment to income on line 26, Form 1040.

Q 6:24   What mortgage interest may be deducted?

Generally, home mortgage interest is deductible provided the loan is secured by the homeowner (of either a main residence or a second residence). The loan may be a mortgage to buy the home, a second mortgage, a line of credit, or a home equity loan.

The home mortgage interest may be deducted provided the holder of the mortgage files Form 1040 and itemizes deductions on Schedule A. The person must be the one who is legally liable for the loan, and the mortgage must be a secured debt on the qualified home (primary residence or second home). Payments made for someone may not deduct them if the payer is not legally liable to make the payments.

In most cases, all home mortgage interest is deductible depending on the date the mortgage was taken out. If the mortgage was taken out prior to October 14, 1987, the full interest amount from debt secured by a primary residence or a second home is deductible. For indebtedness assumed after October 13, 1987, a taxpayer may claim itemized deductions for "qualified residence interest" on (1) up to $1 million of acquisition debt ($500,000 if married filing separately) and (2) up to $100,000 of home equity debt. The $1 million debt amount includes any mortgages taken out prior to October 14, 1987.

Home equity debt taken out after October 13, 1987, may have the interest deducted up to a limit of $100,000 ($50,000 if filing married filing separately). The deduction is limited to the *lesser* of the interest on:

- The fair market value of the home minus the total acquisition indebtedness; or
- $100,000 for the main and second homes combined.

    Example: The FMV of Mary's home is $100,000, and the current balance on the original mortgage (home acquisition cost) is $90,000. The bank offers a home mortgage loan of 125 percent of the FMV of the home less any outstanding mortgages or other liens. To consolidate any other debts, Mary should take out the full $35,000 home loan mortgage with the bank [(125% × 100,000) – 90,000]. Mary's home equity debt deduction is limited to $10,000, the lesser of:

- The $100,000 maximum limit; or
- The amount that the FMV of $100,000 exceeds the home acquisition debt of $90,000.

    Example: John acquires a qualified residence for $270,000 with a $200,000 mortgage. The full $200,000 debt is deductible as qualified residence interest. John pays the mortgage down to $59,000, making the house now worth $425,000. John takes advantage of the appreciation and refinances a new $200,000 mortgage. Only $59,000 of the new debt is acquisition indebtedness. An additional $100,000 may qualify as home equity indebtedness.

If AGI is greater than $150,500, the taxpayer will be limited in the amount of itemized deductions taken. (These numbers are for the 2006 tax year.)

Q 6:25   May real estate taxes be deducted?

Real estate taxes are deductible for all property owned by a taxpayer, unlike the mortgage interest deduction, which can only be taken on two homes. These taxes are deductible in the year they are paid to the taxing authority. Real estate taxes are any state, local, or foreign taxes on real property levied for the general public welfare. The taxes must be based on the assessed value of the property and must be charged uniformly against all property within the jurisdiction of the taxing authority. Taxes placed in escrow are not deductible; nor are penalties and interest on any late payments.

Q 6:26   May points from a mortgage loan be deducted?

Points from a mortgage loan are deductible in full in the year paid if all of the following requirements are met. First, the settlement statement must clearly identify the amount of the points (often referred to as "loan origination fees," or "discount points"). Second, the points must be computed as a percentage of the loan principal amount. Third, the points must be paid on a loan to purchase or build the taxpayer's principal residence, and the loan must be secured by the residence. Fourth, the amount paid as points must not exceed the normal rate charged in the local area. Fifth, the points must be paid from the taxpayer's own funds, not from the mortgage loan proceeds. Finally, the taxpayer must use the cash method of accounting.

Taxpayers who refinance to obtain a lower interest rate must amortize points over the life of the loan unless the loan proceeds are used to substantially improve the main residence. If only a portion of the proceeds is used to improve the home, only that portion is deductible in the year paid. The remaining portion may be amortized over the life of the loan. If points are paid on a home improvement loan where the proceeds are used to improve the principal residence, they are fully deductible in the year paid.

Tax Issues When Planning for Higher Education

Q 6:27   Is student loan interest deductible?

Generally, student loan interest is deductible. A maximum of $2,500 in interest charges may be deducted. For the interest to be deductible, the loans must be used for tuition, fees, room and board, books, equipment, and transportation. The loan must be for a student who is taking at least one-half the normal full-time load in a degree, certificate, or other qualified program at an eligible institution. Eligible institutions include colleges, vocational schools, or other post-secondary institutions that qualify to participate in department of education student aid programs. There are several restrictions to deducting the student loan interest:

- The deduction is not available to any taxpayer who is claimed as a dependent on another tax return.
- The deduction is not available to married taxpayers filing separately.
- The taxpayer must have the primary obligation to repay the loan.
- Interest on a loan from a related person does not qualify for the deduction.
- Loans made under a qualified employer plan do not qualify for the deduction.

Q 6:28   How are scholarships taxed?

Amounts received from scholarships, fellowships, and grants are not included in gross income provided the student is a degree candidate and the money is used for tuition, enrollment fees, books, supplies, and equipment that are required by the educational institution.

If the student receives any payment for services required as a condition of receiving a scholarship or fellowship grant, it must be included in the student's income. Amounts received for room and board do not qualify for the income exclusion.

Q 6:29   What is the Hope Scholarship credit?

The Hope Scholarship credit is a nonrefundable tax credit of 100 percent of the first $1,100 and 50 percent of the next $1,100 of the student's qualified expenses. The credit is available for each of the first two years of attendance at a post-secondary school. The maximum annual credit is $1,650 for each eligible student, and a family may have more than one eligible student per year.

Qualified expenses include tuition and fees required for the enrollment and attendance of a student at an eligible education institution. Fees are included only if the fees must be paid to the institution as a condition of enrollment or attendance. The expenses qualify in the tax year they are paid and must be for education that begins either in the same tax year or in the first three months of the following tax year.

Expenses that do not qualify are personal expenses such as room and board, insurance, medical expenses, and transportation. Books, supplies, and equipment are not qualified expenses unless they are required to be purchased from the educational institution for the enrollment or attendance of the student.

To take the credit, the student must be taking one-half of the normal full-time workload for at least one academic period beginning during the tax year. The student must also be enrolled in a degree program or receiving a certificate or other recognized education credential. The credit can be claimed for only two tax years for any one student. To qualify, the student must not have completed the first two years of post-secondary education as of the beginning of the taxable year. The credit is not available to married taxpayers filing separate returns.

The 2006 phaseout for the credit is for modified AGIs between $45,000 and $55,000 for single and head-of-household filers. The 2006 phaseout for married filing jointly is $90,000 to $110,000.

The credit is allowed for an "eligible student." The student may be the taxpayer, the taxpayer's spouse, or a dependent for whom the taxpayer may claim a dependency exemption and for whom the taxpayer is deemed to have paid all expenses.

Q 6:30   What is the lifetime learning credit?

The lifetime learning credit is a nonrefundable tax credit of 20 percent of up to $10,000 of qualified expenses. The maximum credit is $2,000 for 2006 (20 percent of up to $10,000 in expenses). Unlike the Hope credit, the lifetime learning credit has no limit on the number of years for which the credit can be claimed.

Qualified expenses include tuition and fees required for the enrollment and attendance of a student at an eligible education institution. Fees are included only if they must be paid to the institution as a condition of enrollment or attendance. The expenses qualify in the tax year the fees are paid and must be for education that begins either in the same tax year or in the first three months of the following tax year.

Expenses that do not qualify are personal expenses such as room and board, insurance, medical expenses, and transportation. Books, supplies, and equipment are not qualified expenses unless they are required to be purchased from the educational institution for the enrollment or attendance of the student.

This credit is not based on a workload, so it is available even if the student is only taking one course. The credit is also available for undergraduate, graduate, and professional degree students, and students acquiring or improving their job skills. The credit is not available to married taxpayers filing separate returns.

The 2006 phaseout for the credit is modified AGIs between $45,000 and $55,000 for single and head-of-household filers. The 2006 phaseout for married filing jointly is $90,000 to $110,000.

A taxpayer may claim the credit once annually for the combined expenses paid by the taxpayer for all eligible students who include the taxpayer, the taxpayer's spouse, and individuals claimed as dependents.

Q 6:31   What is the Education Savings Bond program?

A taxpayer may be able to exclude from income all or part of the interest he or she receives on the redemption of qualified U.S. savings bonds during the year if the proceeds are used to pay for qualified higher education expenses during the same year. Series EE bonds issued after 1989 and series I bonds qualify for the interest exclusion. The bonds must be registered either in the name of the taxpayer or in the names of the taxpayer and spouse, but not in the name of a dependent child. In addition, the taxpayer must be at least 24 years old before the bond's issue date.

Qualified higher education expenses include tuition and fees required for the taxpayer, the taxpayer's spouse, or the taxpayer's dependent. They also include any contribution made to a qualified state tuition program or to a Coverdell Education Savings Account (ESA). Qualified expenses do not include expenses for room and board.

The qualified education institutions include most public, private, and nonprofit universities, colleges, and vocational schools that are accredited and are eligible to participate in student aid programs run by the federal Department of Education. The qualified expenses must be reduced by the Hope Scholarship credit, the Lifetime Learning credit, 529 Plan payments, Coverdell ESA payments, scholarships and fellowships, veteran's benefits, and other tax-exempt educational benefits.

If the total proceeds from the qualified U.S. savings bonds do not exceed the qualified expenses for the year, all of the interest may be excluded from income. However, if the proceeds are more than the expenses, only part of the interest may be excluded.

Q 6:32   How are savings bonds and CDs used to pay education expenses?

Savings bonds are sold at a discount and pay no annual interest. In this way they are similar to zero coupon bonds. Interest earned is not taxable at the state and local level, but is taxable at the federal level. Interest is excluded from federal income tax if used for higher education expenses in the same calendar year the bonds are redeemed. The following criteria must also be satisfied: (1) A person has to be at least 24 years old at time of issuance; (2) the bonds must be registered in the name of the purchaser or the child if intended for the child's education; (3) and only savings bonds issued after December 21, 1989, qualify.

Bondholders do not have to indicate that they intend to use the bonds for education purposes when they buy them. Qualified education expenses include tuition and fees. The cost of books and room and board are not qualified expenses. Qualified education expenses also include contributions to qualified tuition programs and Coverdell ESAs.

The amount of interest exclusion is phased out with high modified adjusted gross income (MAGI). For joint filers in 2006, a the phaseout range is between $94,700 and $124,700. For single filers, the interest rate exclusion is phased out between $63,100 and $78,100. The exclusion is not available for married tax-payers filing separately.

CollegeSure CDs are another alternative for funding education costs. They are sold in whole units and fractional units. One unit pays for one year of tuition, room, board, and fees at an average private college; 0.40 units pays for one year at an average in-state public college. This product is purchased from the College Savings Bank. Individuals do not have to buy CollegeSure CDs in one lump sum. They may invest small amounts of cash that slowly build up into a full unit or more.

The annual interest on a CD is calculated on the basis of the Independent College 500 Index. There is no limit on how much a CD can earn. The CD is guaranteed to keep up with college costs and guaranteed to earn a minimum of 4 percent even if college costs do not increase in a given year. They are FDIC-insured up to $100,000, and investors pay no fees or commissions. If the student earns a scholarship, the parents get back all the money they have invested plus the accumulated interest.

Q 6:33 What are Coverdell Education Savings Accounts?

The Coverdell Education Savings Account (ESA), formerly known as an Education IRA, is a trust established to pay qualified education expenses of a designated beneficiary. Contributions to a Coverdell ESA are nondeductible, and earnings in the account are tax-deferred. Subsequent distributions are tax-free if used for qualified education expenses.

The total contribution limit to all Coverdell ESAs set up for one beneficiary is $2,000 per year. Any individual, including the beneficiary, may contribute $2,000 for the beneficiary each year until the beneficiary reaches the age of 18. However, contributions can be made for a special needs beneficiary age 18 or over who has a physical, mental, or emotional condition that requires additional time to complete his or her education. The contributions for any given year must be made before April 15 of the following year.

The modified phaseout ranges for contributions are: those married filing jointly, $190,000 to $220,000; all others, $95,000 to $110,000. The phaseout ranges apply to the person making the contribution, not to the beneficiary. If a parent is above the AGI limits, the parent can gift the $2,000 to a child who has less income and who then makes the contribution to the ESA.

There is a 6 percent excise tax imposed on contributions over $2,000. The excise tax does not apply if any excess contributions and related earnings are withdrawn by June 1st of the following year.

Qualified expenses include tuition and fees, books, supplies, and other necessary equipment. Room and board are also included, as are academic tutoring and uniforms. These expenses are available for elementary and secondary educational institutions along with post-secondary institutions.

Withdrawals from the Coverdell ESA are generally tax-free up to the amount of the beneficiary's qualified education expenses. Withdrawals more than the beneficiary's expenses are included in income for the beneficiary and are subject to a 10 percent penalty. If there is a balance in the Coverdell ESA that is not used for education expenses, the funds must be distributed within 30 days after a beneficiary reaches the age of 30. The beneficiary is then taxed on the earnings portion of the distribution.

The tax can be avoided if the ESA is rolled over to another family member who is under the age of 30. The rollover must be within 60 days of the distribution, and only one distribution can take place within a 12-month period. The family member can be the beneficiary's child, a brother or sister, a stepchild, a stepbrother or stepsister, a niece or nephew, and all in-laws and spouses of any of the above.

Upon the death of the beneficiary, if the Coverdell ESA is transferred to a surviving spouse or a family member, as defined above, the recipient treats the ESA as though he or she is the designated beneficiary. If the transfer is to someone else, the distribution is taxable to the transferee at the date-of-death fair market value.

Q 6:34   May a withdrawal from a regular IRA or Roth IRA be used for education expenses?

Withdrawals from a traditional IRA or Roth IRA that are used for qualified education expenses at a post-secondary school are not subject to the 10 percent penalty for early withdrawals. Qualified education expenses include tuition, fees, books, supplies, and room and board (provided the student is at least a half-time student). The expenses may be incurred by the taxpayer, the taxpayer's spouse, or any child or stepchild of the taxpayer or taxpayer's spouse. In addition, the child or stepchild is required to be a dependent of the taxpayer.

Q 6:35   What are qualified tuition programs?

Qualified tuition programs are also known as 529 Plans. Due to the changes in the laws related to IRC Section 529 in 2001, all plans under IRC section 529 have had their names changed to qualified tuition programs (QTPs). QTP plans are individually designed by sponsoring states or institutions; they are *not* federal plans. As a result, there is a tremendous amount of variety in the programs offered.

QTPs are offered in two varieties. First, there are prepaid tuition programs that allow the taxpayer to prepay some or all tuition costs on behalf of a designated beneficiary (the student). Second, there are the savings account plans that are established for paying all qualified higher education expenses on behalf of the beneficiary.

The contributor of funds to a QTP is not subject to an AGI limit. There is an election available that allows contributions larger than the annual gift exclusion ($12,000 in 2006) to be taken into account ratably over five years. Example: An individual can contribute $60,000 to a QTP in 2006 without gift tax consequences as long as no further gifts are made to the same person within five years. Contributions may be made to a QTP and a Coverdell ESA for the same beneficiary during the same year. Some states also provide an additional benefit of a state tax deduction or credit for contributions to the state QTP.

Any distribution from a state-sponsored QTP is excluded from income (income of both contributor and beneficiary) if used for qualified higher education expenses. However, distributions that are not used for qualified higher education expenses are subject to a 10 percent penalty.

To exclude a QTP distribution from income, the coordination rules require that qualified expenses be reduced in the following order: (1) amounts excluded from income (such as employer-provided education assistance or scholarships), then (2) amounts used to claim education credits, such as the Hope and Lifetime Learning credits.

Qualified educational expenses include tuition, fees, books, supplies, and room and board (provided the student is at least a half-time student).

Q 6:36   What are the different types of grants?

There are two primary types of grants: (1) Pell grants and (2) federal supplemental education opportunity grants (FSEOGs). Both types of grants are distributed on the basis of financial need and availability of federal funds and do not have to be repaid by the student.

Pell grants are given in amounts up to $3,750 per year and are available only for undergraduates. Full- and half-time students are eligible to receive Pell grants, but the amount is reduced for half-time students. Students may receive only one Pell grant in an award year. How much a student receives will depend not only on his or her expected family contribution (EFC) but also on cost of attendance and whether the student attends full-time or part-time. Students may not receive Pell Grant funds from more than one school at a time. The receipt of other grants and loans is sometimes contingent upon applying for or receiving Pell funds.

An FSCEOG is for undergraduates with exceptional financial need. These are students with the lowest EFC, and this loan gives priority to students who receive federal Pell grants. The maximum amount of the loan is $4,000. The loans are also only available to undergraduate students, both half-time and full-time.

Q 6:37   What are the different types of federal student loans?

Federal student loans are generally Perkins loans, Stafford loans, parent loans to undergraduate students (PLUS), and supplemental loans to students (SLS). College work study programs are also considered loans.

Perkins Loans. Perkins loans are funded mostly by the federal government, with a share contributed by the school. The school is the lender, and the student must repay the loan to his or her school. The loans are available to graduates and undergraduates, both half-time and full-time and are based on exceptional financial need. They come with a very low interest rate of 5 percent. The maximum amount given to undergraduate students is $4,000 for each year of undergraduate study (the total amount that can be borrowed as an undergraduate is $20,000 if the student has completed two years of under-graduate work; otherwise, the total is $8,000). The maximum amount given to a graduate student is $6,000 for each year of graduate or professional study (the total amount that can be borrowed as a graduate/professional student is $40,000, including any federal Perkins loans that were borrowed as an under-graduate). These loans allow for a grace period of nine months after graduation before loan payments are due. The repayment for the Perkins loan is usually ten years.

Stafford Loans. Stafford loans were formerly known as guaranteed student loans. They are available to graduates and undergraduates, but not to less than half-time students. They are based on financial need with limits applying as to the amount of funds that may be received, both in any one year and cumula-tively. Interest rates fluctuate with the 90-day Treasury bill plus 3.1 percent, capped at 9 percent for the first four years of repayment. They come as either subsidized or unsubsidized loans. A subsidized loan is awarded on the basis of financial need. Students will not be charged any interest before they begin repayment or during authorized periods of deferment. The federal government "subsidizes" the interest during these periods. An unsubsidized loan charges interest at loan inception until the loan is fully paid. The loan origination and insurance fees are frequently charged by lenders.

PLUS and SLS. These loans are available to parents of undergraduate stu-dents. The parents are allowed to borrow up to 100 percent of the cost of college less the amount the student received from Stafford and Perkins loans and any other aid sources. SLSs are available to students themselves who have applied for both a Pell grant and Stafford loan for graduate and undergraduate studies. PLUS and SLS are not available to half-time students. The loans are made by private lenders and come with a 9 percent maximum interest, varying interest based on the 52-week Treasury bill plus 3.1 percent beginning within 60 days of the loan. Repayment may be delayed until the student is out of school. PLUS and SLS are not needs-based loans.

Federal Work Study. Federal work study is funded by the federal government and administered by individual schools. Eligibility is based on financial need. Federal work study is available to graduates and undergraduates, both part-time and full-time. Eligible students are provided with employment while attending school to earn maximum amounts as set by the federal government.

Q 6:38   What is the benefit of a consolidation loan?

A consolidation loan is designed to help students and parents simplify loan repayments by allowing them to consolidate several types of federal student loans with various repayment schedules into one loan. If a student has more than one loan, a consolidation loan simplifies the repayment process because the student makes only one payment a month. There can also be the added benefit of a lower interest rate on the consolidation loan than what is currently being paid by the student on other loans. A consolidation loan is available even for students who may be in default on a federal education loan.

Both the direct loan program and the Federal Family Education Loan (FFEL) program offer consolidation loans. Direct consolidation loans are available from the U.S. Department of Education. FFEL consolidation loans are available from participating lenders such as banks, credit unions, and savings and loan associations. The interest rate for both direct consolidation loans and FFEL consolidation loans is fixed for the entire time the student is repaying the loan at the weighted average of the interest rates on the loans being consolidated, rounded up to the nearest one-eighth of a percent. As a result of law, the interest rate cannot exceed 8.25 percent.

Tax Issues When Planning Investments

Q 6:39   How is interest income handled?

Interest received from various sources is taxable as ordinary income. Taxable interest may come from savings accounts at banks or credit unions, from Treasury bills, Treasury notes, Treasury bonds, installment sales, and other sources. If interest income is received from any of these sources, or others, the taxpayer will receive a 1099-INT form. This form shows the interest received during the year. The taxpayers should keep this form in their tax records.

Q 6:40   How is dividend income handled?

Ordinary dividends are paid out of the earnings and profits of a corporation and are considered ordinary income to the taxpayer. This means that they are not capital gains. Most corporations use Form 1099-DIV to show the distributions the investor received from the corporations during the year. Taxpayers should keep this form with their records.

If an individual is involved in a dividend reinvestment plan and chooses to have the dividends used to purchase more shares of stock in the corporation instead of receiving cash, the dividends are still considered ordinary income and are taxable.

If the investor owns money market funds or mutual funds, he or she will receive a 1099-DIV form that will identify the amount of dividends received during the year, which will need to be reported as taxable income on Form 1040.

Q 6:41 How are capital gains handled?

In order to achieve the desired goal of paying the least amount of income tax on capital gains, the investor must determine which capital gains and losses to take before the end of the tax year. To do this, one must have at least a fundamental understanding of how the tax law requires investors to offset various types of capital gains and losses.

First, short-term losses (losses from property held 12 months or less) are applied against short-term gains. Next, the taxpayer investor applies long-term losses (losses from property held 12 months or more) against long-term gains. If the investor taxpayer has a short-term gain he or she can apply it against the net long-term losses. If the taxpayer investor has a short-term loss it can be applied against net long-term gains.

Following this procedure, if the taxpayer investor ends up with a short-term gain it will be taxed at his or her marginal tax rate, and if he or she ends up with a short-term loss, up to $3,000 of the loss may be applied against income. The remainder can be carried over to next year's taxes.

The procedure works the same way with a long-term gain. The gain would be taxed at the 20 percent capital gains rate (if the taxpayer's marginal tax rate is 27 percent or higher for 2006), or at the 10 percent rate if the taxpayer is in the 15 percent marginal tax bracket. If the taxpayer ends up with a net longterm loss, up to $3,000 of it could be applied against income with the remainder carried over to next year's income taxes.

Q 6:42 What are "wash sales"?

A "wash sale" occurs if a taxpayer sells stock or securities at a loss and within 30 days before or after the sale buys substantially identical stock or securities. If the taxpayer acquires the stock in a fully taxable trade or enters into a contract or takes an option to acquire substantially identical stock or securities, this is considered a wash sale.

When a wash sale occurs, the taxpayer is not allowed a deduction for the loss, and the basis of the substantially identical property is increased by the amount of the disallowed loss. In addition, the holding period of the new stock includes the holding period of the old stock. For example, an investor buys 100 shares of Z stock for $1,000 and at a later date sells if for $750, Then, within 30 days of the sale he or she purchases 100 shares of the same stock for $800. This is considered a wash sale, and the $250 loss is not deductible. The $250 loss is added to the cost of the new stock to get the basis in the new stock of $1,050 ($800 + $250).

Q 6:43 May an investor deduct investment interest costs?

If an individual borrows money to buy property to hold as an investment, the interest paid on the borrowed money is investment interest. That interest is subject to a limit in the amount of the net investment income (investment income minus investment expenses other than investment interest). The amount of the investment interest that was not deductible because of the limit for the tax year can be carried over to the next tax year.

Investment interest does not include any qualified home mortgage interest or any interest taken into account in computing income or loss from a passive activity.

Tax Issues When Planning for Retirement

Q 6:44 When are IRA contributions deductible?

Contributions made to a traditional IRA may be deductible. If an employee is an active participant in an employer-sponsored pension plan the employee's contribution may not be deductible. The deductibility of an IRA contribution is based on an individual's AGI modified to remove several deductions. If neither spouse is an active participant in an employer-sponsored pension plan, either spouse may take a full deduction of any IRA contributions. For 2006, the contribution limit is $4,000 ($5,000 if over age 50).

If one spouse is covered by an employer-sponsored pension plan, and the other spouse is not, then as long as the modified AGI of each is less than $150,000 the couple may take the full deduction.

If an employee is covered by an employer-sponsored pension plan, the employee may take the full deduction if the employee's modified AGI is less than $50,000 (single and head-of-household) and $75,000 (married filing jointly). When the employee's modified AGI exceeds $60,000 (single) and $85,000 (married filing jointly) then no deduction is allowed. When the modified AGI is between these ranges, a partial deduction is allowed. These numbers are for the year 2006.

If an employer-sponsored pension plan is a defined *contribution* plan, the employees are covered by the plan if amounts are contributed or allocated to their accounts for the plan year that ends with or within that tax year. If the employer-sponsored pension plan is a defined *benefit* plan, and the employee is eligible to participate in the employer's plan, then the employee is covered by the plan even if he or she declined to participate in the plan.

Q 6:45   When should an IRA plan be set up?

Both a traditional IRA and a Roth IRA can be set up at any time. Contributions to either plan must be in the form of money (cash, check, or money order). Contributions can be made to an IRA for a year at any time during the year or by the due date for filing the tax return for that year, *not* including extensions. For most people, this means that contributions for 2006 must be made by April 15, 2007.

Q 6:46   What is the tax impact of retirement distributions?

Determining cost basis. When determining the tax impact on any distribution, the participant's cost basis must be determined. The participant's cost basis includes:

- All after-tax contributions made by the employee to the plan.
- The cost of life insurance protection that was reported as taxable income by the participant, if the plan distribution is received under the same agreement that provides the life insurance protection. For a self-employed individual, the cost of life insurance protection is not included in the basis.
- All employer contributions that were taxable to the employee.
- Certain employer contributions attributable to foreign services performed before 1963.
- Plan loans that are included in income as a taxable distribution.

In-service distributions. If a participant takes an in-service (partial) distribution before termination of employment, the distribution will include both non-taxable and taxable amounts. The nontaxable amount is

$$\text{Distribution} \times \frac{\text{employee's cost basis}}{\text{total account balance}}$$

However, there is a pre-1987 "grandfathered" rule in which an individual may withdraw after-tax money first (*i.e.*, first-in first-out). If a distribution from the plan is made that is less than the total amount of pre-1987 after-tax contributions, the full distribution is received tax-free. Once all distributions from pre-1987 contributions are received, the regular rule applies. The taxable in-service distribution may be subject to an early distribution penalty and a mandatory withholding at 20 percent, unless the distribution is transferred to an eligible retirement plan as a direct rollover.

Taxation of annuity payments. The taxation of annuity payments includes a taxable portion and a nontaxable portion. If an employee has no cost basis in a plan, the entire amount of each annuity payment is subject to ordinary income. If an employee has a cost basis, one of two tables is used to determine the excludable portion of each monthly payment.

1. For a single-life annuity, based on the age of the annuitant:

Age of Participant	Number of Monthly Payments
Not more than 55	360
55-60	310
60-65	260
65-70	210
More than 70	160

2. For a joint and survivor annuity, based on the ages of both annuitants:

Combined Ages of Both Participants	Number of Monthly Payments
Not more than 110	410
111-120	360
121-130	310
131-140	260
More than 140	210

Once the cost basis is fully recovered, payments received subsequently are fully taxable. If the participant dies before the cost basis is fully recovered, an income tax deduction for the unrecovered basis is allowed on the participant's final income tax return.

Taxation of lump-sum distributions. Lump-sum distributions are taxed as ordinary income and may be subject to a 10 percent early distribution penalty. Lump-sum distributions generally are subject to a mandatory withholding at 20 percent. Tax is deferred on lump-sum distributions if rolled over to another qualified retirement plan or IRA account. Lump-sum distributions may be eligible for tax breaks. This includes ten-year averaging and capital gains.

The distribution qualifies for ten-year forward-averaging tax treatment if the participant was born before January 1, 1936 (*i.e.*, he or she was age 50 by January 1, 1986) and four conditions are met: (1) the participant must be at least age 59½; (2) the forward-averaging must be applied to all lump-sum distributions received during the year; (3) the employee must have been a plan participant for at least five years (with a waiver if distribution is due to death); and (4) only one forward-averaging election is allowed in a lifetime.

A plan participant who has attained age 50 by January 1, 1986, may also elect to treat pre-1974 plan accruals as long-term capital gains. Any amount taxed as capital gain is taxed at a rate no greater than 20 percent. However, this election may have little effect since under the post-Tax Reform Act of 1997 law, most long-term gains are taxed at 20 percent.

Taxation of death benefit. The same tax benefits apply to the death benefits paid to a surviving spouse. The surviving spouse can roll over the death benefit received from the participant to an IRA or other eligible retirement plan. However, the benefit of rolling over the plan does not extend to a nonspouse beneficiary.

Q 6:47 What is the penalty tax for premature withdrawal?

Premature distributions are generally subject to a 10 percent penalty and taxed as ordinary income. A distribution from a SIMPLE IRA (Savings Incentive Match Plan for Employees of Small Employers IRA) within two years of the opening of the SIMPLE IRA is subject to a 25 percent penalty tax. Premature distributions are generally distributions taken before age 59½ or that do not fall under Code Section 72(t) for qualified plans. The participant always has 60 days from the date of the distribution to avoid a penalty by placing the funds back into the account.

Q 6:48 What is a hardship withdrawal and what are its tax consequences?

Hardship withdrawals are available for qualified plans and 403(b) plans. The participant must have a triggering event to qualify for a hardship withdrawal. The triggering event has occurred when the participant has demonstrated to the plan administrator an "immediate and heavy financial need." The IRS has issued safe harbor guidelines that define what constitutes an "immediate and heavy financial need" in order to give the employer guidance. The following is a list of safe harbor triggering events:

- Medical care for the participant, spouse, and any dependents of the participant;
- Purchase of principal residence (applies only toward the purchase, not the mortgage payments);
- Tuition and related education fees (must be for post-secondary education of participant, spouse, or children); and
- Preventing eviction or foreclosure.

There is still a 10 percent penalty for hardship withdrawals, and the full distribution will be taxed as ordinary income. In addition, a six-month blackout exists on elective deferrals after a hardship withdrawal. The participant must exhaust all other options before taking out a hardship withdrawal.

Q 6:49 What are allowable distributions under Code Section 72(t) for qualified plans?

The following is a list of allowable distributions that will exclude an individual from paying the 10 percent penalty tax under Code Section 72(t) for qualified plans only:

1. Distributions made on or after the date on which the participant attains age 59½.

2. Distributions made to a beneficiary on or after the death of the participant.

3. Distributions attributable to the participant's becoming disabled.

4. Distributions that are part of a series of substantially equal periodic payments (not less frequently than annually) made for life (or life expectancy) of the participant or for the joint lives of the participant and his or her designated beneficiary. Distributions under this exception generally cannot be modified for five years unless another exception applied to the distribution when it initially commenced.

5. Made to an employee after severance from service after attainment of age 55.

6. A payment to an alternate payee pursuant to a QDRO.

7. Distributions used to pay qualified higher education expenses (including graduate education expenses) for the individual, the individual's spouse, or any child or grandchild of either.

8. Distributions made on account of an IRS levy.

9. A dividend paid with respect to certain stock held by an Employee Stock Option Plan (ESOP).

10. Amounts transferred to an IRA of a spouse or former spouse under a divorce or separation instrument.

11. Corrective distributions.

Q 6:50   What are allowable distributions under Code Section 72(t) for tax-advantaged, nonqualified retirement plans?

Tax-advantaged plans (*i.e.*, IRA, Roth IRA, SEP, and SIMPLE) do not need a triggering event for the owner to remove funds. The owner can remove funds at any time but is subject to a 10 percent penalty tax in addition to the balance being taxed as ordinary income. The following is a list of allowable distributions that will exclude an individual from paying the 10 percent penalty tax under Code Section 72(t) for tax-advantaged retirement plans only:

1. Distributions made on or after the date on which the participant attains age 59½.

2. Distributions made to a beneficiary on or after the death of the participant.

3. Distributions attributable to the participant's becoming disabled.

4. Distributions that are part of a series of substantially equal periodic payments (not less frequently than annually) made for life (or life expectancy) of the participant or the joint lives of the participant and his or her designated beneficiary. Distributions under this exception generally may not be modified for five years unless another exception applied to the distribution when it initially commenced.

5. Distributions for medical expenses in excess of 7½ percent of AGI.

6. Distributions for health insurance premiums made to an unemployed individual after separation from employment if the individual has received unemployment compensation for 12 consecutive weeks under any federal or state unemployment compensation law.

7. Distributions used to pay qualified higher education expenses (including graduate education expenses) for the individual, the individual's spouse, or any child or grandchild of either.

8. Distributions made for a first-time homebuyer's expenses. There is a lifetime maximum of $10,000. The distribution must be used within 120 days to buy, build, or rebuild the principal residence of the individual, his or her spouse, or any child, grandchild, or ancestor of either. A person qualifies as a first-time homebuyer is he or she had no present ownership interest in a principal residence during the preceding two years.

9. Distributions made on account of an IRS levy.

10. Amounts transferred to an IRA of a spouse or former spouse under a divorce or separation instrument.

11. Corrective distributions.

Q 6:51 What are the differences when comparing qualified plans to IRAs under Code Section 72(t)?

The following exceptions fall under IRAs but not qualified plans under Code Section 72(t):

1. IRAs allow distributions for health insurance premiums made to an unemployed individual after separation from employment if the individual has received unemployment compensation for 12 consecutive weeks under any federal or state unemployment compensation law.

2. IRAs allow distributions made for a first-time homebuyer. There is a lifetime maximum of $10,000.

3. IRAs allow distributions used to pay qualified higher education expenses (including graduate education expenses) for the individual, the individual's spouse, or any child or grandchild of either. See Q 6:49.

The following exceptions fall under qualified plans but not IRAs under Code Section 72(t):

1. Distributions made to an employee after severance from service after attaining age 55;

2. A payment to an alternate payee pursuant to a QDRO;

3. A dividend paid with respect to certain stock held by an ESOP.

Q 6:52 What are the required minimum distributions from an IRA?

The purpose of an IRA is to provide retirement income. Therefore, when a person reaches the age of 70½, he or she is expected to begin withdrawing the proceeds in an IRA rather than continue to let the funds accumulate and use the

IRA as a tool to build an estate. If the minimum amounts are not withdrawn yearly, a 50 percent nondeductible tax is levied on the amount of the minimum payment left in the IRA.

The required minimum payments must be withdrawn from the IRA by April 1 of the year following the year the person turns 70½. If an election is made to delay the first distribution until April 1 of the year following the year the person reaches 70½, the second distribution must be made by December 31 of the same year. This means there will be two distributions in that year.

The minimum distribution is based on the joint life expectancy of both the owner of the IRA and a survivor, who is assumed to be no more than ten years younger than the owner. If the spouse is more than ten years younger, the minimum distribution is based on the two spouses' joint expectancy. Once distributions are required, a minimum distribution must be made each year based on the age of the IRA owner and on the appropriate life expectancy table. However, the IRA owner is always permitted to take more out of the owner's IRA than the minimum required amount.

Note: These minimum distribution rules do not apply to Roth IRAs.

Q 6:53   What are the tax consequences to rollovers?

A "rollover" is the ability to transfer retirement plan assets from one plan to another plan. This can be done through a trustee-to-trustee transfer, where the assets are moved from one custodian directly to another, or through a rollover where the funds are distributed to the owner and then the owner rolls them over to another plan.

The trustee-to-trustee transfer has no tax consequences because there is no distribution to the taxpayer owner. In addition, there is no limit to the number of transfers the trustee or the owner can make in one year.

When a rollover is made and the funds are paid directly to the owner, a mandatory 20 percent federal income tax withholding is imposed on the funds. In addition, the owner has 60 days to take the received funds and roll them over to the new plan. If the owner fails to make the rollover in the 60-day period, an additional 10 percent tax is imposed on the portion withheld. Due to these penalties, it is generally better to do a trustee-to-trustee transfer instead of a rollover.

If the owner makes a tax-free rollover from a traditional IRA, he or she may not, within a one-year period, make another tax-free rollover of any amount from the same IRA. The IRA's owner also may not make a tax-free rollover from the account into which the first tax-free rollover was made.

Prior to 2002, an IRA owner was only allowed to make a rollover or transfer from one IRA into another IRA, from an employer's plan into an IRA, and from one employer's plan into another employer's plan. The current tax law greatly expands the flexibility to roll over retirement accounts from one form of account to another. In addition to the above list an IRA owner is now able to transfer:

- From a traditional IRA to a qualified retirement plan;
- From a SIMPLE IRA to a qualified retirement plan;
- From a 457 plan to a qualified retirement plan; and
- From a 403(b) plan to a qualified retirement plan.

Q6:54 What are the contribution limits?

The following table shows the contribution limits:

Calendar Year	Traditional IRA or Roth IRA	401(k), 403(b), 457 plans	SIMPLE
2006	$4,000	$15,000	$10,000*
2007	$4,000	$15,000*	$10,000*
2008	$5,000	$15,000*	$10,000*

* These numbers will be adjusted for inflation from this point forward.

Q6:55 What are the catch-up contribution limits?

Since 2002, additional "catch-up" contributions can be made if the IRA owner is at least 50 years old by the end of the plan year. The following table shows how the catch-up limits are phased in:

Calendar Year	Traditional IRA or Roth IRA	401(k), 403(b), 457 plans	SIMPLE
2006 and later	$1,000	$5,000	$2,500

The catch-up amounts are in addition to the limits imposed for each year. For example, in 2006, if the IRA owner is 50 years old or older the maximum contribution to a 401(k) plan would be $20,000 ($15,000 + $5,000).

Q6:56 What is the saver's tax credit?

Since 2002, a taxpayer meeting applicable income requirements could qualify for a tax credit of up to $1,000 for contributions or deferrals to retirement savings plans. The maximum credit is 50 percent of the first $2,000 contributed to a retirement plan. If the taxpayer files a joint return, he or she qualifies for the credit if AGI does not exceed $50,000 ($37,500 for head of household and $25,000 for all others). The phaseout ranges are:

Married Filing Jointly	Single	Credit Amount
$0 — $30,000	$0 — $15,000	50% of contribution
$30,001 — $32,500	$15,001 — $16,250	20% of contribution
$32,501 — $50,000	$16,251 — $25,000	10% of contribution
Over $50,000	Over $25,000	Not Available

Q 6:57   Are the distributions from a Roth IRA taxable?

Possibly. Qualified distributions or distributions that are a return of regular contributions from a Roth IRA are not included. A "qualified" distribution is considered one made after the five-year taxable period beginning with the first taxable year for which a contribution was made to a Roth IRA, and the distribution is for one of these reasons:

- It is made on or after reaching age 59½.
- It is because the IRA owner is disabled.
- It is made to a beneficiary or to the owner's estate after death.
- It is made to pay certain qualified first-time homebuyer amounts.

Withdrawals from a Roth IRA are deemed to come from contributions first and then from earnings, without regard to the five-year rule. Therefore, no income tax or 10 percent penalty applies to any withdrawal until total withdrawals exceed total contributions.

When the earnings are withdrawn and they do not meet the requirements for a qualified distribution, they are fully taxable and subject to the 10 percent withdrawal penalty. However, the 10 percent penalty does not apply if any of the following exceptions apply:

- The participant has made a series of substantially equal payments over his or her lifetime.
- The participant has incurred qualified college expenses.
- The participant has incurred qualified medical expenses that exceed 7.5 percent AGI.
- The distribution is to pay for health insurance premiums for certain unemployed individuals.

Tax Issues When Planning for Employee Benefits

Q 6:58   What are the tax issues related to incentive stock options?

Incentive stock options (ISOs) are options to buy shares of company stock at a stated price for a period of ten years from the date the option is granted. At the time the options are granted, there are no tax consequences because no income is reported. Also, there is no regular income tax due at the time the option is exercised. However, the bargain element (the difference between the fair market value at the time of exercise and the option price) is a tax preference item for alternative minimum tax purposes.

If the shares are held for at least one year after the option is exercised and two years after the grant of the option, the sale will result in long-term capital gain on the appreciation in value from the option price. If the holding periods are not met, the bargain element will be taxed as ordinary income, and any additional gain will be taxed as a capital gain.

Q 6:59   What are the tax issues related to nonqualified stock options?

Nonqualified stock options are options to buy company stock at a stated price and can be exercised over a specified period. When the option is exercised and the stock is purchased, the bargain element (the difference between the fair market value at the time of exercise and the option price) is treated as ordinary income. The employee will recognize capital gains or losses on any appreciation or depreciation in the stock value from the day of exercise until the day the stock is sold.

Q 6:60   How are employer-provided education expenses handled?

If an employee receives education assistance benefits from an employer under an education assistance program, up to $5,250 of those benefits each year may be excluded. This means that the employer should not include this benefit with wages, tips, and other compensation shown in box 1 of the W-2 form. This also means that this benefit does not have to be included on the recipient's income tax return. However, if the education expenses exceed the amount of the benefit received from the employer, the excess can be deducted as a miscellaneous itemized deduction. Also, if a benefit of more than $5,250 is received from the employer, the excess will be included as wages on the W-2 form.

Education assistance benefits include payments for tuition, fees, books, supplies and equipment. Since 2002, this benefit has been expanded to include both undergraduate and graduate-level courses. Prior to 2002, only undergraduate-level courses were covered. Items that are not covered expenses include meals, lodging, transportation, and supplies that an employee is allowed to keep after completing the education, except for textbooks.

Q 6:61   Are there tax consequences for group-term life insurance?

Generally, the cost of up to $50,000 of group-term life insurance coverage provided by an employer is not included in income. Amounts in excess of $50,000 are included as income at a rate per thousand dollars of coverage. The cost factor is taken from the government "I" table. Its rates are level for each five years of attained age and increase even into retirement. For example, if an individual is 40 years of age and has $100,000 of group-term life insurance, $50,000 of coverage would be included in income. At age 40, every $1,000 of coverage over $50,000 costs $0.10 per month. This means that $5.00 would be added to income each month (50 times $0.10).

Q 6:62   Are there tax consequences for child or dependent care plans?

Employees are allowed to receive up to $5,000 of tax-free dependent care benefits when the expenses are the same type that qualifies for the dependent care tax credit. The limit is $2,500 if filing separately. If the employee is married and a spouse earns less than the employee, the tax-free benefit is limited to the spouse's earned income. If the spouse does not work, all of the employee's benefits are taxable unless he or she is a full-time student or is disabled, in which case the spouse is treated as if he or she earned $200 per month if the dependent care expenses are for one dependent, or $400 per month for two or more dependents. Any benefits over $5,000 will be included as taxable wages.

Q 6:63   Are there tax consequences for adoption benefits?

If an employer pays or reimburses the employee for qualifying adoption expenses under a written, nondiscriminatory plan, up to $10,960 may be tax-free. There is a phaseout when the employee's modified AGI is between $164,410 and $204,410. The exclusion from income limit is not an annual limit: it applies to each effort to adopt an eligible child even if the effort lasts longer than one year.

Qualified adoption expenses include legal fees, court costs, attorney fees, and other related costs that have the principal purpose of paying the expenses of a taxpayer's legal adoption of an eligible child. Costs associated with adopting the child of the taxpayer's spouse or costs for surrogate parenting arrangements are not considered qualified expenses for the purpose of this credit.

If the child to be adopted is not a U.S. citizen or resident when the adoption effort begins, the exclusion is available only in the year the adoption becomes final. Payments from the employer in previous years (for the same adoption) will be included in wage income for that year, and then the employee is allowed to take the full exclusion in the year the adoption is final.

Q 6:64   Are there tax consequences for health plan benefits?

Specific reimbursements of medical expenses for the taxpayer, the taxpayer's spouse, or any dependent are tax-free. The payment does not have to come directly to taxpayer; it may go directly to the medical care providers. Taxfree treatment applies only to reimbursed expenses, not to amounts an employee would have received anyway, such as sick leave.

Reimbursements for dependents' medical expenses are tax-free, even if the employee does not claim the dependents as personal exemptions because the dependents' gross incomes exceed the annual ceiling for dependents. Furthermore, if the employee is divorced and his or her children have health coverage under the employee's plan, reimbursements of their expenses are not taxable to the employee even if his or her ex-spouse claims the children as dependents.

Reimbursements for cosmetic surgery do not qualify for tax-free treatment, unless the surgery is for disfigurement related to congenital deformity, disease, or accidental injury.

Q 6:65 What are the tax consequences for an employee winning an achievement award?

Achievement awards are taxable unless they meet special rules for awards of tangible personal property (such as a watch, television, or golf clubs) given to the employee in recognition of length of service or safety achievement. Cash awards, gift certificates, and similar items are taxable. As a general rule, if an employer is allowed to deduct the cost of a tangible personal property award, the employee is not taxed. The employer's deduction limit, and therefore the excludable limit for the employee, is $400 for awards from nonqualified plans and $1,600 for awards from qualified plans.

If the employer's deduction is less than the item's cost, the employee is taxed on the greater of (1) the difference between the cost and the employer's deduction but no more than the award's fair market value; or (2) the excess of the item's fair market value over the employer's deduction. The employer must tell the employee if the award qualifies for full or partial tax-free treatment.

Q 6:66 What are the tax consequences for the use of company vehicles, for parking, and for transit passes?

The costs of commuting to a regular job site are not deductible, but employees who receive transit passes or travel to work in an employer-financed van get a tax break by not having to pay tax on some or all of the benefit. If a company vehicle is provided, the value of the user's personal use is generally taxable. Regardless of personal use, the car's user is not subject to tax for a company vehicle that the IRS considers to be of limited personal value, This includes ambulances, flatbed trucks, garbage or dump trucks, one-passenger delivery trucks, tractors, school buses, passenger buses that seat at least 20, and police and fire vehicles.

For regular employees, up to $100 a month is tax-free for the combined value of employer-provided transit passes plus commuting on an employer's van or bus. If the cost of the transit pass is more than $100 per month, the excess is treated as taxable wages. Qualifying transit passes include tokens, fare cards, or vouchers for mass transit or private transportation businesses that use vehicles seating at least six passengers.

For regular employees, the value of employer-provided parking spaces or subsidized parking is tax-free up to a limit of $185 per month. The parking must be on or near the employer's premises, or at a mass transit facility such as a train station or a "park-and-ride" facility. If the value of the parking benefits exceeds $185 per month, the excess is taxable.

Q 6:67   What are the tax consequences of flexible spending plans?

A flexible spending plan reimburses employees for medical or dependent care expenses from an account set up with pre-tax dollars. Under a typical plan, the employee agrees to a salary reduction that is deducted from each paycheck and deposited in a separate account. As expenses are incurred, the employee is reimbursed from this account. The salary reduction contributions are not included in taxable wages. The downside to a typical flexible spending plan is that any unused account balance at the end of the plan year is forfeited; it may not be carried over to the next year. However, there usually is a grace period after the end of the year to submit reimbursement claims for expenses incurred in the previous year.

Q 6:68   What are the tax consequences for meals provided by an employer?

The value of employer-furnished meals is not taxable if the meals are provided on the employer's business premises for the employer's convenience. The IRS generally defines "business premises" as the place of employment, such as a company cafeteria. The employer-convenience test requires proof that an employer provides the free meals for a business purpose other than providing extra pay. If more than half of the employees are furnished the meals for the employer's convenience, then all of the on-premises meals are treated as being for the employer's convenience.

For example, a hospital maintains a cafeteria on its premises where all of its employees may eat during their working hours, and there is no charge for the meals. The hospital furnishes the meals in order to have its employees available for emergencies. Because the hospital provides the meals so that the employees are available for emergency calls during mealtimes, the meals are not income to any of the hospital employees who eat their meals at the hospital cafeteria.

An employer may furnish unprepared food, such as groceries, rather than prepared meals. Courts are divided on whether the value of the groceries is excludable from income.

Cash allowances for meals are taxable.

Tax Issues When Choosing a Type of Business Organization

Q 6:69   What are some of the tax issues with a C corporation?

A C corporation is a separate legal entity with its own tax status and tax rates. Only corporations pay income tax at the entity level. Corporations report taxable income on Form 1120 and are not subject to the passive activity loss rules. Taxable income paid and net income reported on financial statements is usually not the same. Corporations generally enjoy tax rates that are more favorable than rates for individuals.

If a corporation receives dividends from another corporation, it is entitled to a deduction. If the recipient corporation owns less than 20 percent of the stock of the paying corporation, the deduction is 70 percent of the dividends received. If the recipient corporation owns at least 20 percent but less than 80 percent of the stock of the paying corporation, the deduction is 80 percent of dividends received. If the recipient corporation owns 80 percent or more of the stock of the paying corporation, the deduction is 100 percent of dividends received.

Capital gains and losses recognized by corporations are taxed at the same rate as ordinary income and are not subject to the reduced capital gains rate. Deductions for capital losses may only offset capital gains, and no amount may be used to offset ordinary income. Net capital losses can be carried back three years and carried forward five years to offset capital gains.

If corporations accumulate earnings that exceed a certain level, they may be subject to the accumulated earnings tax. The accumulated earnings tax is a penalty tax designed to prevent tax avoidance through the accumulation of earnings within the corporation beyond expected needs of the business. A corporation is allowed to accumulate up to a minimum credit of $250,000 of earnings and profits without encountering any problem with the accumulated earnings tax. If the corporation accumulates more than this amount, the corporation must demonstrate to the IRS that the accumulation is for reasonable needs of the business. If it cannot demonstrate this need, the IRS imposes the accumulated earnings tax at a rate of 35 percent (in 2006) on all accumulated taxable income.

Regular corporations may also enjoy tax-favored fringe benefits that are not available or are only available on a limited basis for other types of taxpayers. Benefits that are nontaxable to the employee and immediately deductible by the corporation include: (1) health and accident plan exclusion from income; (2) employer payments to health and accident plan exclusion from income; (3) group-term life insurance exclusion from income; (4) travel and entertainment; and (5) meals and lodging for convenience of employees.

Benefits that are tax-deferred to the employee and immediately deductible by the corporation includes qualified pension and profit-sharing plans. Benefits that are immediately taxable to employee and immediately deductible by the corporation include; (1) group-term insurance greater than $50,000; (2) additional cash salary; and (3) group legal services

Q6:70 What are some of the tax issues with an S corporation?

S corporations are categorized as pass-through entities. This means that income from the business is passed through to the shareholders of the corporation, where they are taxed at the individual's tax rate. Losses by S corporation are also passed through to the shareholders.

Shareholders receive a Schedule K-1 (the same as partnerships) to incorporate into their individual tax returns. The cash flow from the S corporation is irrelevant to the computation of the shareholder's tax liability. Shareholders may also be employees of the corporation. The employee and the corporation pay FICA payroll taxes, and the corporation withholds federal income tax. The corporation issues a W-2 to any shareholder/employee together with a K-1. Shareholders are not subject to self-employment (SE) tax.

Shareholders *increase* the basis of stock by their share of the corporation's income and gain and decrease the basis of stock by their shares of the corporation's losses. The cash distribution is considered a nontaxable return of investment that reduces the shareholder's stock basis. Thus, cash distributions are generally nontaxable for pass-through entities. Losses are deductible to the extent of the owner's equity investment and debt obligation. In both cases, the basis may not be reduced below zero.

Q 6:71   What are some of the tax issues with a partnership or LLP?

Partnerships and LLPs are categorized as pass-through entities, which means that income from the business is passed through to the partners of the partnership, where they are taxed at the individual's tax rate. Losses by partnerships and LLPs are also passed through to the partners.

Each partner receives a Schedule K-1 that details information about the partner's distributive share of the partnership's income or loss from business items and separately stated items, such as dividend income, capital gains, and charitable donations. The cash flow from the business is irrelevant to the computation of the partner's tax liability. Thus, the partner is taxed on his or her distributive share of the partnership income whether or not the amount is actually distributed. General partners are required to pay self-employment (SE) tax on their distributive share of ordinary business income. Limited partners are not considered self-employed and are not required to pay SE tax on their distributive share of ordinary income.

The basis in a partnership *increases* through ordinary business income, capital gains, and dividend income and *decreases* from ordinary business loss, capital loss, and cash distributions. If a partner is allocated income (which is taxable) but receives no cash distribution of that income, the partner is making an additional investment in the partnership. The cash distribution in future years is considered a nontaxable return of investment. Thus, cash distributions are generally nontaxable for pass- through entities. Partners may deduct their distributive share of partnership losses for the year. However, this results in a reduction of their cost basis in the partnership interest, which cannot be reduced below zero. If a partner's share of loss exceeds the basis, the excess may not be deducted in the current year. It may be carried forward to future years, but the basis must be restored in order to deduct the carryforward.

Q 6:72   What are some of the tax issues with a sole proprietorship?

In a sole proprietorship, all income is taxed to the owner as self-employment income. The business is not a separate entity and does not file its own tax return. Sole proprietors file a schedule C form in addition to their personal tax forms.

Expenses incurred from the business are deductible from the owner's gross income. A sole proprietor may use its business structure to employ other family members and thus shift income, which could result in lower taxes.

Tax Issues When Planning for Dealing with the IRS

Q 6:73   What records should be kept and for how long?

The taxpayer should keep records that support an item of income or a deduction that are reported on a return until the period of limitations for the return runs out. (This is the period of time after which no legal action can be brought against the taxpayer.) For an assessment of tax owed, the time period is generally three years from the date the return was filed. For filing a claim for a credit or refund, the time period is generally three years from the date the return was filed or two years from the date the tax was paid, whichever is later. When a return is filed before its due date, it is treated as though it was filed on the due date. If the taxpayer did not report income that he or she should have reported and it is more than 25 percent of the income shown on the return, the period of limitations does not run out until six years after the return was filed.

If the taxpayer files a return that is false or fraudulent with the intent to evade taxes, there is no period of limitations. The taxing authority may bring an action at any time. This also true when the would-be taxpayer has never filed a return.

The taxpayer should keep a copy of the filed income tax returns—if possible, indefinitely, as the space required is minimal. It is especially important that the taxpayer keep documentation from brokers and mutual fund companies that will help determine the basis of the stocks and mutual funds the taxpayer owns. These records should be kept as long as the asset is owned and until the period of limitations for the associated tax return runs out.

The taxpayer should also keep records relating to the basis of property as long as the records are important in determining the basis of the original or replacement property. Generally, this means for as long as the taxpayer owns the property and, after it is disposed of, for the period of limitations that applies to the property.

Q 6:74   How does the taxpayer prepare for an audit?

After an audit has been scheduled (either at the IRS office or at the taxpayer's business or home), the first thing the taxpayer should do is examine the applicable return to refresh his or her memory. The items the IRS questioned in the notice of audit should be examined, and tax records should be organized accordingly. In addition, the rest of the return should be checked, and any items the taxpayer is unsure about should be substantiated.

Before the actual IRS examination begins, possible settlement terms should be considered. The taxpayer should assume that the IRS agent will assess additional tax, so the taxpayer should establish the range of reasonable amounts that might have to be paid. Giving some thought to this before the examination will help later when settlements are actually discussed.

The taxpayer may want to authorize an attorney, a CPA, an enrolled agent, or other individual recognized to practice before the IRS to represent the taxpayer at the audit so the taxpayer can avoid being at the audit. The taxpayer should provide the representative with authorization to represent him or her by filling out Form 2848. The representative will then be able to perform any acts the taxpayer could, including entering into a binding settlement agreement.

If the taxpayer does attend the audit, he or she should take only the records related to the items questioned in the IRS notice. No other records should be volunteered, because if the agent sees them, he or she might suggest new areas for investigation.

The key to handling the audit is advanced preparation. The taxpayer should be prepared to produce the tax records quickly. The records should be organized by topic so that time is not wasted leafing through pages for a receipt or other document. If the agent decides to question an item not mentioned in the notice of audit, the taxpayer should politely but firmly refuse to answer the question. The taxpayer should tell the agent that the taxpayer must first review the pertinent tax records. If the agent insists on following up, the taxpayer should instead schedule another meeting so that the records can first be reviewed and the necessary documentation can be made available. The agent might decide the matter is not worth the time and drop the issue.

Audits conducted at IRS offices may conclude quickly because they usually involve only a few specific issues. In some cases, the audit may take less than one hour. If the taxpayer is interested in recording the examination he or she can make an audio recording of the interview. Video recordings are not allowed. To make the audio recording, the taxpayer must first give written notice to the IRS agent conducting the interview no later than ten calendar days before the interview.

If the IRS has scheduled a field audit (one at the taxpayer's office or other place of business), the taxpayer should ask that the examination be held at the chosen representative's office instead. If the examination takes place at the taxpayer's place of business, the IRS agent should not be allowed to have free run of the office. The taxpayer should provide the agent with a comfortable work area and, if possible, find a place that is isolated so the agent is not distracted by the taxpayer's business operations. Any of the taxpayer's employees should be told not to answer questions about the business or engage in small talk that could arouse further questions by the agent.

Tax Issues When Planning for Installment Sales

Q6:75 How is gain calculated for each installment payment?

When using the installment method of payment, a portion of each payment other than interest represents part of the gain and is taxable. This taxable gain amount is based on the gross profit percentage, which is figured by dividing the gross profit by the selling price or contract price. Then, for each payment received, the gross profit percentage is multiplied by the payment amount to determine what portion of the payment is considered gain, and therefore is taxable.

The gross profit is typically the selling price less any selling expenses, such as brokers' commissions and legal fees, and less the adjusted basis in the property. The contract price is the same as the selling price unless an adjustment is made for an existing mortgage assumed by the buyer. If the buyer does assume a mortgage, then the contract price does not include the buyer's assumption of the existing mortgage. By following the line-by-line instructions to Form 6252, the gross profit percentage for the property can be calculated.

Example: In 2006 John sells a piece of real property for $120,000. The property has an adjusted basis of $56,000 and selling expenses are $4,000. John is to receive installment payments of $30,000 in 2006, 2007, 2008, and 2009. The gross profit percentage is figured as follows:

Selling price (contract price)	$120,000
Less: adjusted basis and selling expenses	60,000
Gross profit	$ 60,000
Gross profit percentage =	$ 60,000 = 50%
	$120,000

Therefore, in 2006 the homeowner will report a profit of $15,000 (50% of $30,000). In addition, he or she will report a profit of $15,000 for each of the following years, so that by the end of four years, the entire $60,000 profit will have been reported.

Q6:76   What is the minimum interest that must be charged?

The tax law requires that a minimum amount of interest be charged on deferred payment sales. The interest amount must be equal to the lesser of 100 percent of the applicable federal rate and 9 percent compounded semiannually. Otherwise, the IRS treats part of the sale price as interest. For tax purposes, the interest amount, either imputed or separately stated from the selling price, is taxable as income to the seller and deductible by the buyer if the property is business or investment property.

Q6:77   How are losses treated?

Losses may not be deferred under the installment method.

Q6:78   How may gains be spread out over several years?

By using the installment sale method the seller may spread out the gain over several years and may result in a lower total tax on the gain. By taking only a portion of the gain into income each year, the seller may avoid reaching a higher marginal tax bracket. Even if the seller is already in the highest bracket, the installment sale method may still be beneficial because the taxes are deferred to later years.

Tax Issues When Planning for Like-Kind Exchanges

Q 6:79   What is a "like-kind" exchange?

If an individual trades business or investment property for other business or investment property of like kind, he or she do not pay taxes on any gain or deduct any loss until the property is sold or disposed of. In this case, the gains are deferred until a later date. To be nontaxable, a trade must meet all six of the following conditions:

1. The property must be business or investment property. Both the traded and received property must be held for productive use in a trade or business. Neither property may be used for personal purposes.

2. The property, such as merchandise or inventory, must not be held primarily for sale to customers.

3. The property cannot be stocks, bonds, notes, certificates of trust or beneficial interest, or other securities, including partnership interests.

4. There must be a trade of like property. For example, the trade of real estate for real estate or personal property for similar personal property is a trade of like kind. The trade of an apartment house for a store building, or a panel truck for a pickup truck is also a trade of like kind. A trade of a piece of machinery for a store building is not considered a trade of like kind. Also, real property located outside the United States and real property located inside the United States is not considered like-kind property.

5. The property to be received must be identified within 45 days after the date of transfer of the property given up in the trade.

6. The property to be received must be received by the 180th day after the date on which the transfer takes place of the property given up in the trade or by the due date, including extensions for the tax return for the year in which the transfer of the property given up occurs.

If cash or unlike property is received in addition to like property and the above six conditions are met, it is considered a partially nontaxable trade. There will be a tax on any gain realized but only up to the amount of the cash and the fair market value of the unlike property received. In addition, a loss may not be deducted.

Q 6:80   How is the new basis calculated?

The basis of property received is generally the same as the basis in the property given up. If property is traded in a like-kind exchange and money is also paid, the basis of the property received is the basis of the property given up but is increased by the amount of money paid.

Example: George, a businessman, trades in a truck used in his business with an adjusted basis of $2,500 for a new one costing $20,000. The dealer allows a trade-in value of $4,000 on the old truck, and so George pays $16,000 for the new truck. The basis of the new truck is $18,500 (the adjusted basis of the old truck, $2,500, plus the amount paid on the new one, $16,000).

When unlike property or money is received in addition to like property in a partially nontaxable exchange, the basis of the property received is the basis of the property given up with the following adjustments:

1. The basis should be decreased by any money received or the fair market value of the unlike property received, and for any loss recognized on the exchange.
2. The basis should be increased by any additional costs incurred and by any gain recognized on the exchange.

Q6:81   How is the gain calculated?

If the amount realized from the trade is more than the adjusted basis of the property transferred, the difference is a gain. The adjusted basis in the property is the original cost, or the original basis, adjusted for certain items such as improvements made to the property and selling costs. Any gain realized is taxed, but only up to the amount of the cash and the fair market value of the unlike property received.

Example: Mary exchanges real estate that has an adjusted basis of $8,000 for property that has a fair market value of $10,000. In addition Mary receives $1,000 in cash. Although she realizes a gain of $3,000 ($11,000 of property received minus $8,000 of property transferred), Mary is taxed on only $1,000 of the gain (the gain recognized).

Q6:82   How is "boot" that is received handled?

If cash or other property of unlike kind is received in addition to like-kind property, the cash or unlike-kind property is considered *boot*. If mortgaged property is transferred, the amount of the mortgage is part of the boot. If both parties to the transaction transfer mortgages to each other, the party giving up the larger debt treats the excess as taxable boot. If one party pays cash to the other party, this is added to the mortgage received in figuring which party has given up the larger debt. The computation of boot, gain or loss, and basis of the property received is made on Form 8824. The example below illustrates the easiest way to understand the process.

Example: John owns an apartment house with a fair market value of $220,000 subject to an $80,000 mortgage. His adjusted basis is $100,000. John exchanges the property for Mary's apartment building, which has a value of $250,000, subject to a mortgage of $150,000. John also receives $40,000 in cash. Mary's adjusted basis in the property she trades is $175,000.

Calculation of Boot	Mary	John
Mortgage transferred	$150,000	$ 80,000
Less mortgage assumed	(80,000)	(150,000)
Cash paid or received	(40,000)	40,000
Boot	$ 30,000	$ (30,000)

In this example John receives a boot of $40,000 (cash received), and Mary's boot value is $30,000.

Calculation of their new basis for John:

Adjusted basis in building traded:	$ 100,000
Plus net mortgage assumed ($150,000 − $80,000):	$ 70,000
New adjusted basis:	$170,000

Calculation of the new basis for Mary:

Adjusted basis in building traded:	$175,000
Plus net amount paid ($80,000 + $40,000 − $150,000):	0
[This number cannot be negative.]	
New adjusted basis:	$175,000

Tax Issues When Planning for Capital Assets

Q6:83   What are "capital assets"?

In general, capital assets are property held for personal or investment purposes, rather than those assets that are held for business purposes. Almost all assets owned are considered capital assets and are subject to capital gain or loss treatment. Typical assets include real property, stocks, bonds, mutual funds, jewelry, household furnishings, and automobiles used for pleasure or commuting.

Q6:84   What is a short-term capital gain or loss?

Capital gain or loss on the sale or trade of investment property held one year or less is a short-term capital gain or loss. Short-term capital gains and losses are reported in Part I of Schedule D.

Q 6:85   What is a long-term capital gain or loss?

Capital gain or loss on the sale or trade of investment property held for more than one year is a long-term capital gain or loss. The shortest length of time that qualifies for long-term status is one year plus one day. The holding period starts on the day after the owner purchases the property and includes the day the owner sells it. Long-term capital gains or losses are reported in Part II of Schedule D.

Q 6:86   What are capital loss carryovers?

If capital losses exceed capital gains, a capital loss deduction can be claimed. The limit on capital losses in a single tax year is $3,000 ($1,500 if married filing separately). If there is a total net loss that is more than the yearly limit on capital loss deductions, the unused part may be carried over to the next year and may be treated as though it occurred in that year. If part of the loss is still unused, it may be carried over to later years until it is completely used up.

When a loss is carried over, it remains either a long-term loss or a shortterm loss. A long-term capital loss carried over to the next tax year will reduce that year's long-term capital gains before the loss reduces that year's shortterm capital gains.

For example, if George sells securities in 2006 that result in a capital loss of $7,000 and his income is sufficient to allow a capital loss; George can deduct $3,000 from his income for the capital loss and then carryover the remainder of $4,000 to the next year.

Q 6:87   What are capital gains distributions?

Capital gains distributions are paid out or credited to the recipient's account by companies who deal in regulated investments (commonly called mutual funds) and real estate investment trusts (REITs). These distributions are frequently composed of a combination of long-term capital gains and ordinary income. The nature of the gain is determined by how long the mutual fund or REIT has held the underlying property, not how long the owner has held the mutual fund shares. Consequently, the owner may have a long-term capital gain even though he or she has held the mutual fund shares for less than one year.

Q 6:88   What is cost basis?

The cost basis of property is usually its cost at purchase, the amount paid in cash or a debt obligation or other property or services. The cost also includes amounts paid for sales tax, installation and testing, shipping costs, legal and accounting fees, and recording fees.

The cost basis for real estate includes settlement fees and closing costs the purchaser pays for buying the property. Fees and costs for acquiring a loan on the property are not included. However, legal fees (including the title search), recording fees, surveys, transfer taxes and the owner's title insurance fees are included in the cost basis. In addition, if there are improvements made by the property's owner, this increases the owner's cost basis in the property. Improvements include replacing the roof, installing a new heating or air conditioning system, restoring a run-down house, and construction of a swimming pool, patios, decks, or a driveway. If the property is purchased as an investment and a deduction is taken for depreciation, then this amount decreases the basis in the property.

The basis of stocks or bonds generally is the buyer's purchase price plus any costs of purchase, such as commissions and recording or transfer fees. The basis of stocks must be adjusted for stock splits. For example, if John purchases 100 shares of ABC stock at $20, and then a 2-for-1 stock split occurs, his new basis in all 200 shares would be $10 ($20 divided by 2).

The basis for mutual funds generally is the purchase price plus any costs of purchase, such as commissions or load charges.

Q 6:89   How are shares that are sold identified?

Shares of stock or bonds that are sold can be identified using their basis when determining the gain or loss. Even if purchased in different lots at various prices and times, the shares can be adequately identified if the owner specifies to his or her broker the particular shares to be sold. The seller should receive a confirmation in writing of the specifics from the broker.

If the shares were acquired at different times or at different prices and cannot be identified individually, the basis of the shares acquired first should be used as the basis of the shares sold. Therefore, the oldest shares still available are considered sold first. This is known as the first-in first-out (FIFO) method.

A shareholder or bondholder may choose to use an average basis to figure any gain or loss when all or part of mutual fund shares are sold if the shares were acquired at various times and prices and were left on deposit in an account handled by a custodian. Once an average basis is used, it must continue to be used for all accounts in the same fund.

To figure average basis either the single-category or the double-category method may be used. In the single-category method, all shares are included in a single category. The adjusted basis of each share is the total adjusted basis of all shares in the category at the time of disposition divided by the number of shares in the category. In determining the holding period, the shares disposed of are considered to be those shares acquired first. For example, if John has bought the following shares of ABC fund, purchasing 100 shares in 2004 at $10 per share, 100 shares in 2005 at $12 per share, and 100 shares in 2006 at $17 per share and the 300 shares cost a total of $3900, the average basis per share is $13 ($3900 divided by 300).

In the double-category method, all shares in an account at the time of each disposition are divided into two categories: short-term and long-term. The adjusted basis of each share in a category is the total adjusted basis of all shares in that category at the time of disposition divided by the total shares in the category. The customer may direct the custodian handling the customer's account from which category the shares are to be sold. The custodian must confirm the specification in writing.. If confirmation is not received or specified, the shares sold against the long-term category must be charged first and then any remaining shares sold against the short-term category are charged.

Tax Credits That Are Appropriate for a Business

Q 6:90   What are business tax credits?

There are many different business tax credits, including the following:

- The investment credit, consisting of the rehabilitation property credit, the energy credit, and the reforestation credit (Form 3468);
- The work opportunity credit (Form 5884);
- The alcohol fuels credit (Form 6478);
- The research credit (Form 6765);
- The low-income housing credit (Form 8586);
- The orphan drug credit (Form 8820);
- The disabled access credit (Form 8826);
- The enhanced oil recovery credit (Form 8830);
- The renewable electricity production credit (Form 8835);
- The credit for wages paid in an empowerment zone (Form 8844);
- The Indian employment credit (Form 8845);
- The credit for employer-paid Social Security and Medicare taxes on certain tips received by employees of food and beverage establishments (Form 8846);
- The credit for contributions to certain community development corporations (Form 8847); and
- The welfare-to-work credit (Form 8861).

Each credit can be computed separately on the indicated tax form. If only one credit is claimed, that credit is considered a general business credit. The credit is subject to a limitation based on tax liability that is figured on the form used to compute a particular credit. If more than one credit is claimed, the credits are combined into one general business credit on Form 3800, except for the empowerment zone wages credit, which is figured on Form 8844 and is not carried to Form 3800. The combined credit is subject to a limitation based on tax liability.

If a full general business credit may not be claimed because of the tax liability limitation, the excess one year probably can be carried back one year, and any remaining credit can be carried forward for 20 years until the credit is used up. For credits arising in tax years before 1998, the carryback period is three years, and the carryforward period is 15 years.

Q6:91   What is the credit for excess Social Security tax?

If an employee worked for two or more employers in 2006, he or she may have had too much Social Security tax withheld from a paycheck. The excess can be claimed as a credit against the employee's income tax. For 2006, the maximum wages subject to Social Security tax was $94,200.

If an employer withheld Social Security tax that exceeded the tax limit for that year, the employee may not claim the extra amount withheld by that employer as a credit. Instead, the employer must adjust this for the employee.

If an employee is married and is filing a joint return, the employee may not add the Social Security tax withheld from the spouse's wages to the amount withheld from the employee's wages. The employee must figure the credit separately for each spouse to determine if either has excess withholding. If the employee files Form 1040, the credit should be entered on line 62. If Form 1040A is filed, the credit should be included in the total on line 41. The employee should write "Excess SST" and the amount of the credit in the space to the left of the line.

Tax Issues When Planning for Passive Activities

Q6:92   What is a passive activity?

A passive activity involves the conduct of any trade or business in which the taxpayer does not materially participate. He or she is treated as a material participant only if actively involved in the trade or business operations on a regular, continuous, and substantial basis. If not a material participant in the activity but the taxpayer's spouse is, the taxpayer is treated as being a material participant and the activity is not considered passive.

The IRS has seven tests that must be met for the taxpayer to be considered a material participant. If one of these tests is satisfied, the taxpayer will be considered a material participant in the activity. If not, then the activity is considered a passive activity. The IRS tests for whether one is an active participant are:

1. Participation for more than 500 hours per taxable year.
2. Participation during the taxable year that constitutes substantially all of the participation of all individuals involved.
3. Participation for more than 100 hours during the taxable year and no one else participates more than the particular taxpayer does.
4. The activity is a significant participation activity (SPA) for the taxable year, and the individual's participation in all SPAs during the taxable year exceed 500 hours. An SPA is an activity in which an individual participates for more than 100 hours but does not meet a material participation test.
5. Material participation in any five of the ten preceding taxable years.
6. The activity is a personal service activity, and the taxpayers materially participated for any three preceding taxable years. A personal service

activity involves performance of personal services in the fields of health, law, engineering, architecture, accounting, actuarial sciences, performing arts, consulting, or any other business in which capital is not a material income-producing factor.

7. Based on all the facts and circumstances, the taxpayer's participation is regular, continuous, and substantial during the taxable year.

Q 6:93   What are at-risk limits?

The purpose of at-risk rules is to keep a taxpayer from deducting losses from investments in which he or she has little cash invested and no personal liabilities for debts. The taxpayer is considered at risk for the amount of cash invested in the venture and the basis of property invested plus certain amounts borrowed for use in the activity. Borrowed amounts that are considered at risk are loans for which the taxpayer is personally liable for repayment or loans secured by property other than that used in the activity.

Q 6:94   What rental activities are considered passive?

Rental income and losses are automatically treated as passive income or loss unless earned or incurred by a real estate professional or the rentals are considered by law to be business activity. Rental activities that are not considered passive include short-term rentals, such as a hotel room; rentals that include significant services, such as hospitals; and rentals that are for nonexclusive use, such a golf course used for a round of golf.. Real estate professionals may also treat rental real estate activities as active income if they spend at least 750 hours in a real estate trade or business and more than 50 percent of their personal services are provided to those types of business.

Q 6:95   May passive activity losses be carried over?

Passive activity losses generally may not be deducted against other income, such as wages, portfolio income, or business income not derived from passive activities. However, a loss disallowed in the current year by the at-risk limitation may be carried over and deducted in the next taxable year, provided it does not fall within the at-risk limits or the passive loss limits in that year. The loss is subject to an unlimited carryover period until there is an at-risk basis to support the deduction. This may occur when additional contributions are made to the business or when the activity has income that has not been distributed.

Tax Issues When Planning for Net Operating Losses

Q 6:96   What is a net operating loss?

A net operating loss is generally a deductible business expense that exceeds business income. A net operating loss may also include the following losses and deductions:

- Casualty and theft losses, even if the property was used for personal purposes.
- Expenses of moving to a new job location.
- Deductible job expenses such as union dues, work clothes, and travel expenses.
- A share of a partnership or S corporation operating loss.
- The loss on the sale of small business investment company stock.
- The loss incurred on Section 1244 stock.

An operating loss may not include any of the following:

- Net operating loss carryback or carryover from any year.
- Capital losses that exceed capital gains.
- Deductions for personal exemptions.
- An IRA deduction.
- A self-employed person's contribution to a Keogh plan.
- The excess nonbusiness deductions over nonbusiness income plus non-business capital gain.

Form 1045 is used to compute net operating loss deduction.

Q 6:97   What happens when the taxpayer has a net operating loss?

When a net operating loss (NOL) is incurred, this loss can be carried back to offset past income to produce a refund of tax paid, and/or it can be carried forward to offset future income. The general rule is that an NOL can be carried back two years and forward 20 years. However, the carryback provision is extended to three years for NOLs that arise from casualties, that occur in a presidentially declared disaster area or that are incurred by businesses with less than $5 million in gross receipts. Farmers are allowed to carry back their NOLs five years.

> **Example:** In 2006, John, the sole proprietor of a small business, had a net operating loss of $60,000. In past years, John had reported the following amounts of taxable income: 2003:$80,000; 2004:$12,000; 2005:$5,000. The NOL can be carried back two years to 2004 and 2005 and can offset $17,000 ($12,000 − $5,000) of taxable income for those years. The remaining NOL of $43,000 can be carried forward for 20 years.

Tax Issues When Planning by the Small Business Owner

Q 6:98   What travel and entertainment expenses are deductible?

Almost every business routinely incurs travel and entertainment expenses. For some businesses this can be a substantial expense, and ensuring the maximum write-offs for these expenses becomes an important strategy for a business owner. There are many different expenses that fall into the travel and entertainment expenses category, including the following:

- **Airfare.** The cost for business travel is deductible. When travel is combined with personal pursuits, the fare may be partially deductible.
- **Limousine or taxicab.** The cost of transportation between an airport or station and the hotel or between business locations is deductible.
- **Baggage and shipping.** The cost of sending baggage and samples to temporary work locations, such as trade shows, is deductible.
- **Automobile expenses.** Expenses when using a car for business purposes are deductible.
- **Cleaning.** The cost of dry cleaning and laundering clothing while on the road is deductible.
- **Lodging.** The cost of overnight lodging is deductible.
- **Faxing and other services.** Hotel charges for sending faxes or providing other such services are deductible.
- **Meals.** The cost of meals incurred while away from home on business is deductible. The cost of meals when not away from home on business is deductible if the meal is shared with a business associate or client and business is discussed or goodwill is created. The cost of meals is deductible only up to 50 percent.
- **Tips.** Tips related to any deductible travel expense (taxi driver, hotel personnel) are deductible.
- **Gifts.** Regardless of the nature of the gift, only $25 per gift per person is allowed annually, regardless of whether the gift is for an individual or for a mass mailing.

Generally, fees for memberships in organizations for recreation, pleasure, or other social purposes are not deductible. This prevents a deduction for dues paid to airline clubs, golf and tennis clubs, athletic clubs, and other similar organizations. However, this does not apply to business, professional, or civic organizations. The dues for these organizations are deductible.

Q 6:99   What is a Section 179 deduction?

In general, a taxpayer may not deduct the cost of fixed assets such as furniture, equipment, and buildings used for business purchased during the year. The cost of these assets in not an ordinary expense; it must be recovered through depreciation. Taxpayers generally recover the cost of fixed assets acquired after 1986 using the modified accelerated cost recovery system (MACRS). MACRS specifies that assets are classified as 3, 5, 7, 10, 15, 20, 27.5, or 39-year-old property according to the useful life of the property.

Even though MACRS accelerates the depreciation of most assets into the early years of use, even greater acceleration is available to small businesses as provided in Section 179 of the Internal Revenue Code. A business acquiring assets other than real estate may expense $108,000 of business-use tangible personal property in the same year as the property is placed in service. Light trucks and trucks with gross vehicle weight of 6,000 pounds or more are limited to $25,000 of depreciation per year.

A business may only deduct Section 179 depreciation to the extent of the business's income for the year the asset was acquired. No loss may be created or increased under Section 179. Any of the depreciation that is not allowed due to insufficient income can be carried forward to future years.

Section 179 depreciation is not available for rental property or for automobiles. In addition, assets must be used at least 50 percent of the time for the trade or business.

For partnerships and S Corporations, the Section 179 deduction passes through to the owners. However, at the individual level, the deduction is limited to $108,000 for 2006 regardless of how many businesses an individual owns. If an individual has an excess Section 179 deduction, it can also be carried forward to future years.

Q6:100   Is a taxpayer allowed to write off start-up expenses?

Start-up costs are amounts a taxpayer incurs investigating the start of a new business or in acquiring an existing business. The investigation process may include a general search for a business or close scrutiny of an active trade or business. Start-up costs are those costs that would normally be deductible as ordinary and necessary business expenses. However, because the taxpayer is not in an active trade or business, the taxpayer must capitalize the start-up costs. If the taxpayer makes the proper election, he or she may amortize the start-up costs over a period of at least 60 months. If he or she fails to make the election, the start-up costs cannot be recovered until the business is sold.

To amortize the start-up costs, the taxpayer must make an election by the due date of the tax return, including extensions, for the tax year in which the business began. The taxpayer makes the election by attaching a detailed statement to his or her income tax return for the first year in which he or she begins the active conduct of the business. The statement should describe each startup cost incurred and state the specific number of months (60 or more) over which the start-up costs will be amortized. In addition, the trade or business should be described.

Tax Issues When Including Gross Income

Q6:101   What is gross income?

The federal income tax system begins with the premise that all income is subject to taxation unless specifically excluded. Income is generally in the form of money, property, and services. Gross income is derived from (but is not limited to) the following sources:

1. Compensation for services;

2. Gross income from business, after reasonable and necessary business expenses are deducted;

3. Gains from dealings in property;

4. Interest;

5. Rents, after reasonable and necessary expenses incurred to produce the rental income;

6. Royalties;

7. Dividends;

8. Alimony and separate maintenance payments;

9. Annuities;

10. Income from life insurance and endowment contracts;

11. Pensions;

12. Income from the discharge of a debt;

13. A partner's share of partnership income;

14. Income in respect of a decedent; and

15. Income from an interest in an estate or trust.

The Internal Revenue Code excludes the following classes or items from income in most cases:

1. Proceeds of life insurance paid because of death or terminal/chronic illness of the insured;

2. Amounts received under state worker's compensation acts;

3. Payments received under accident, health, and long-term care insurance policies;

4. Damages resulting from personal physical injuries or sickness;

5. Interest on qualified state or municipal bonds;

6. Property that is received as a bequest or a gift;

7. Scholarships and fellowships;

8. Return of an original investment in annuities and sales of property;

9. Contributions by an employer to provide accident or health benefits if part of a properly designed plan;

10. Amounts contributed by employees or employers to a cafeteria plan provided the employee chooses a benefit other than cash;

11. Amounts contributed by employers to medical savings accounts;

12. Employer-provided child or dependent care services;

13. Educational assistance provided by an employer up to $5,250 per year;

14. Noncash fringe benefits such as qualified employee discounts, reimbursement of qualified moving expenses, parking or bus passes used to get to work, and use of a company car for business;

15. Meals and lodging provided for the convenience of the employer to the employee;

16. Employer reimbursements of employment-related expenses incurred by employees if received under an accountable plan;

17. Employer-paid group life insurance up to $50,000 of face value; and

18. Withdrawals from prepaid tuition plans and state-sponsored college savings accounts if used to pay qualified education expenses.

Year-End Tax Planning Issues

Q 6:102   How can postponing income help?

Shifting income from one year to another is one of the most effective techniques an individual can use to reduce a tax bill. If tax planning shows that the person will be in the same or a lower tax bracket next year, he or she will probably want to delay the receipt of year-end income until early in the next year, provide the delay does not jeopardize any prospects for collecting the income. Listed below are a few techniques that may be used to achieve this goal:

1. **Delaying collections.** If the person is self-employed, he or she should delay year-end billings until late enough in the year so payment on them won't be received until early in the next year.

2. **Year-end bonuses.** Year-end bonuses don't have to be paid by the end of the year, so an employee should try to persuade the employer to pay the year-end bonus in January. Generally, the employer will not lose his or her deduction for the current year by delaying payment of the employee's bonus until next year.

3. **Interest income.** Interest on T-bills and bank certificates having a term of one year or less is not paid until maturity. Therefore, if funds can be transferred from an interest-bearing account to a certificate that has a maturity date in the next year, the interest can be deferred until the next year.

4. **Maximizing retirement plan contributions.** Increasing retirement plan contributions lowers taxable income for the year. If aged 50 or over, the taxpayer can make additional catch-up contributions to an IRA or 401(k) plan.

Q 6:103   How may accelerating income help?

There are certain situations where accelerating income into the current year may be beneficial. First, if a filing status can be changed due to an upcoming marriage or divorce, and this will put the taxpayer into a higher tax bracket next year, accelerating some income can reduce taxes over both years. Other reasons include an anticipated increase in income next year through changes in employment or selling of assets. In addition, if itemized deductions exceed taxable income this year, accelerating enough income into the current year to cover the excess deductions will allow the taxpayer to not lose them this year.

Here are several ideas on how to accelerate income:

1. **Collecting receivables.** If self-employed, the taxpayer should make sure to do all of the billing possible, and then collect the amounts due before the end of the year. If the taxpayer is using the cash method of accounting, income is not taken into account until it is received.

2. **Year-end bonuses.** If an employer pays bonuses after the end of the year, the employee should try to negotiate with the employer to pay out the bonus before the end of the year.

3. **Capital gains.** If the taxpayer has assets that have appreciated in value, a sale before the end of the year can provide the income needed to meet any tax planning goals.

4. **Dividends.** If the taxpayer has control over a corporation that pays a dividend, arrange for the dividend to be paid before the end of the year.

5. **IRA or retirement plan distributions.** If the taxpayer is over 59½ and either has a traditional IRA or is covered by an employer's retirement plan, he or she may increase this year's income by making withdrawals. In the case of the retirement plan, the right to make withdrawals is determined by the plan.

Q6:104   How can the taxpayer plan for deductions?

The taxpayer should decide whether to itemize deductions or claim the standard deduction. For those who are on the borderline, deductions can be pushed into one year to itemize and claim the standard deduction in the following year. Taxpayers can use this bunching strategy every other year for tax advantages. Because there are only a few expenses that are within an individual's control, one way to do the bunching is make more charitable contributions in the years in which deductions will be itemized.

Preparing for a Visit with an Accountant During Tax Time

Q6:105   What forms should the taxpayer provide for the accountant?

In general, the taxpayer should have documentation that supports all income, deductions, and credits that will appear on his or her tax return. In addition, if using a new accountant, the taxpayer should also bring a copy of the prior year's returns. If the tax preparer provides the taxpayer with a tax questionnaire or checklist, the taxpayer should fill it out as thoroughly as possible prior to the visit to the accountant.

Supporting documentation comes in many forms, the most common of which are listed below:

Item	*Documentation*
1. Wages and salaries	W-2 forms; usually provided by an employer
2. Dividends and interest	Form 1099-DIV and 1099-INT; usually provided by the bank or company paying the dividend or interest
3. Capital gains and losses	Broker's statements for purchase and sale of assets disposed of during the year and Form 1099-B
4. Business income from sole proprietorships and rents and royalties	Books and records from these activities. Might include 1099-MISC from payor of income.
5. Income from partnerships, estates, trusts, and S corporations	Form K-1: provided by the entity
6. Unemployment income	Form 1099-G; usually provided by the agency paying the compensation
7. Social Security benefits	Form SSA-1099
8. State and local income tax refunds	Form 1099-G
9. Original issue discount	Form 1099-OID; usually provided by the issuer of the long-term debt obligation
10. All distributions from annuities, insurance contracts, pensions, retirement plans, and IRAs	Form 1099-R; usually provided by the trustee of the plan
11. Sale of a residence	Form 1099-S; usually provided by the person responsible for closing the real estate transaction
12. IRA contributions	Form 5498; provided by the trustee of the IRA
13. Moving and employee business expenses	Receipts, canceled checks, and Form 4782 if moving expenses reimbursed by employer
14. Medical expenses	Receipts and canceled checks
15. Mortgage interest, and points paid on the purchase of a principal residence	Form 1098 or mortgage company statement
16. Real estate taxes	Mortgage company statement, receipts, or canceled checks
17. Charitable contributions	Receipts, canceled checks, and statements from charitable organizations

Q 6:106 What information should not be provided to the accountant?

If the taxpayer provides the accountant with a summary of dividends or charitable contributions, there is no need to provide all of the original documentation with the summary. However, the taxpayer should make sure in the case of dividends or capital gains that the summary numbers add up to the amounts on the 1099 forms.

If the taxpayer provides all of the original documentation along with a summary report to the accountant, the accountant will probably feel obligated to verify the accuracy of the numbers in the summary. This can be a time-consuming process, and therefore costly as well. The taxpayer should make sure he or she is able to provide full documentation if the accountant requests it.

Chapter 7

Estate Planning

Estate planning comprises a large part of the financial planner's job. This chapter explores property ownership and transfer, gifts to minors, transfer of business interests, and the basics of estates and trusts.

Q 7:1   What is estate planning?

Estate planning is defined as the art of accumulating and conserving one's property for transfer during an individual's lifetime or after death in a manner that minimizes taxes and probate costs while preserving the individual's wishes for disposition of assets. The driving force behind estate planning is to carry out the client's objectives. The planner's task is to carry out the client's objectives in a manner that helps the client achieve maximum tax efficiency. Estate planning requires the combined skills and expertise of qualified legal and tax professionals, along with an experienced personal financial planner, to obtain the delicate balance needed to achieve sophisticated estate planning objectives.

Q 7:2   What is a will?

A will is a written document directing the disposal of the decedent's property upon his or her death. Often the document is referred to as a "last will and testament." Historically, land was the most valuable asset in any estate. Wills were used to transfer title to real property, whereas "testaments" conveyed title to personal property, which was often of little or no value (*e.g.*, farming tools, clothes, etc.). Today, the distinction is virtually meaningless.

Q 7:3   What does "testate" mean?

A person who dies after writing a will is said to die testate, and the court distributes the decedent's property pursuant to the terms of the will. A testate decedent can disinherit children or favor certain relatives or nonrelatives. Many people want to leave money to charity at their passing. This objective is impossible without a valid will.

Q 7:4   What does "intestate" mean?

A person who dies without a valid will is said to die intestate. This is not to say that the decedent has no plans for distribution of his or her property. Instead of carrying out the decedent's wishes as stated in a will, the decedent's property is distributed in accordance with a state's intestacy statute. For example, if a widow dies without a will, her property will be divided equally among her children.

Charities will never receive a penny of the decedent's estate without a valid will. By dying intestate, the decedent effectively disinherits any charity from his or her estate plan.

Q 7:5   What is a holographic will?

A holographic will is a handwritten will. Some states recognize handwritten wills as valid and may be admitted to probate. However, even states that recognize holographic wills as valid often require that the standard formalities of will execution be observed. For example, if a state statute requires the signatures of two witnesses on a will for the will to be valid, a holographic will also requires two signatures to be valid. Consequently, there really is no substitute for drafting a will with an attorney to make certain that all of the will execution formalities are observed.

Q 7:6   What is a "nuncupative" will?

A nuncupative will is an oral will. For example, someone mortally wounded in an automobile accident may tell a bystander "I leave all of my earthly possessions to my daughter." Most states do not recognize nuncupative wills as being valid because of the potential abuse for fraud. It is too difficult to prove the veracity of the statements heard by a witness. Consequently, makers of nuncupative wills are considered to have died intestate in the vast majority of jurisdictions.

Q 7:7   Who may draft a will?

Usually an attorney will draft a client's will and is the recommended option. But a self-created will is also an enforceable instrument used to direct the distribution of one's own assets after death. Typically, individuals may draft their own wills either by hand (the holographic will) or through an oral instruction (the nuncupative will). While holographic wills tend to easily satisfy legal validity requirements, in many jurisdictions nuncupative wills are no longer recognized due to the difficulty of proof and the potential for fraud. (*See* Q 7:6.)

Q 7:8   What is a beneficiary?

A beneficiary is a person who receives either real or personal property in a will. In the old common law interpretation, "heirs" received real property and "next of kin" received personal property.

Q 7:9　What is the difference between an heir and a beneficiary?

Heirs are individuals entitled to receive, or inherit, possession of property from an individual who dies intestate (without a will). An "heir" contrasts with a "beneficiary," who receives possession of property from a testator (one who has executed a will) as a result of being named in a will. Living individuals do not have heirs because the term is applicable only after the death of the decedent. Those who would be heirs upon death may are termed "presumptive heirs" or "heirs apparent."

Q 7:10　What happens when an individual dies without a will?

Upon an individual's death, the state government applies a set of statutes, usually called intestacy statutes, to govern the manner in which the estate is distributed. In the event that one dies without a will, the state's intestacy statutes apply to an estate in order to determine how the property should be allocated. Typically, the statutory hierarchy followed begins with a living spouse and then proceeds to nearest relatives. If no relatives can be located, the entire estate is then "escheated" or remitted to the state. Without a valid will in place, property may not be left to charity or to a non-relative.

Q 7:11　Do all state laws treat intestacy in the same manner?

No. Some states have adopted the Uniform Probate Code (UPC). This is a model statute drafted by the National Conference of Commission on Uniform State Laws (NCCUSL). However, even in UPC jurisdictions, most state legislatures have enacted changes to the UPC. Consequently, every state will have a different approach to dealing with intestacy. Keep in mind that the end result is that the state acquires the property if a living relative within the degree of relationship mandated in the state statute is not located.

Q 7:12　What is probate?

Probate is generally referred to as the process by which an individual's estate is administered upon his or her death. It is intended to properly apportion the deceased individual's assets according to his or her intentions. In cases that the deceased has executed a valid will, this process is much more efficient. When no will exists, the state must apply its own provisions to determine a proper distribution of assets.

While state law governs probate rules, many states have adopted standard probate provisions in an attempt to promote uniformity amongst the states, thus avoiding "forum shopping" for a more sympathetic state jurisdiction. The UPC has been adopted in eighteen states, and many other states have adopted one or more UPC provisions on an ad hoc basis.

One of the advantages of creating a trust is that it generally avoids probate. However, certain trust regulations apply. The Uniform Trust Code (UTC) was approved in 2000 by the NCCUSL. Since that time it has been introduced in several state legislatures.

Q 7:13   What is the process of probating a will?

In addition to the more general definition of "probate" above, the word is also referred to as the act or process of proving a will. The process begins when the original will is deposited in the probate court of the county where the decedent resided. Once the will is validated as the genuine last will and testament of the deceased, the executor or administrator is then formally appointed to begin final distribution of the deceased's property and assets according to the specified terms of the will.

The process itself can be very difficult and time-consuming, depending on the complexity of the estate, any will disputes, and the adherence to state statutes. Probate can also generate a variety of expenses, including attorney fees, an executor's commission, court supervision costs, and applicable estate and inheritance taxes. As a result, several estate planning techniques have been established to avoid passing through probate, particularly in the case of jointly owned property.

Q 7:14   What is ancillary probate?

Ancillary probate is a process whereby a decedent's assets are admitted to probate in a secondary jurisdiction rather than the jurisdiction in which the decedent passed away. Normally this process occurs where the decedent owned real estate in several states at death. For example, assume a client resides and is domiciled in Florida but owns a condominium in Santa Barbara, California. When the client dies, the primary administration of the estate will be in Florida, but an ancillary probate of the California condominium will occur in California.

Ancillary probate can be quite time-consuming and expensive. Also, keep in mind that a Florida-licensed attorney may not probate the property in California unless the attorney is also licensed to practice in California. Often attorneys are subject to charges of unauthorized practice of law by attempting to handle both matters for clients.

Q 7:15   What is an alternative to probate?

Property either passes from a decedent to another through probate (whether the decedent dies testate or intestate), by operation of law (*e.g.*, joint tenancy), or by operation of contract (*e.g.*, an insurance beneficiary designation). Some clients attempt to place all of their assets into a revocable living trust to bypass probate entirely. The problem is that almost inevitably the client will have some technical violation of state statutes. For example, if a client changes the contents of a personal tangible personal property list under a trust, state law may require the signatures of two witnesses, which the grantor forgot to obtain.

Q 7:16   What are the advantages of probate?

Contrary to popular opinion, probate is not a threat to democracy and the American way of life. Probate is costly, but used in moderation, it is a very valuable planning tool. For example, rather than probating the totality of a client's estate, the planner should suggest to the client's attorney that only a small amount of tangible personal property (*e.g.*, the decedent's sock drawer) be probated. Under some state laws, the period for creditor claims is greatly reduced even if only a small portion of the estate is admitted to probate. For example, creditor claims against a trust could extend for one year versus 90 days for an estate admitted to probate.

Q 7:17   Can a person die intestate even with a will?

Yes, assuming there are valid grounds for challenging the validity of a will, a will may be found to be invalid and hence the individual dies intestate. Each state has its own rules for determining the validity of will execution. For example, some jurisdictions require that both the testator (*i.e.*, person whose will is being executed) and the witnesses sign in each other's presence. Consequently, if one of the witnesses leaves the room to take a phone call while the testator is signing, the will may not be valid, and the decedent dies intestate.

Q 7:18   What should a financial planner do to avoid a client dying intestate?

First and foremost, the planner needs to develop a referral relationship with several estate and trust attorneys in the planner's jurisdiction. The goal of the planner is to find the best-suited attorney to provide estate planning document-drafting for clients. One common mistake financial planners make is to have a relationship whereby the attorney refers business back to the planner. While this is possible, it is not likely, especially during the initial stage of the relationship.

Q 7:19   What other professionals are involved in an estate planning engagement?

Estate planning involves a team of financial professionals. As a general rule, the following professionals are involved:

- Attorney—Drafting the legal documents. Only the attorney is authorized to practice law.
- CPA—Preparing tax returns and fiduciary accountings for the estate and trust(s). Accountings are a vital component of fiduciary administration and are required to be presented to the court in order to conclude the estate administration process.
- Banker—Trust company acts in capacity of trustee for the decedent's trust. Based on changes to the banking laws, the bank may now perform virtually all services to the estate except for legal services. Therefore, the planner's

assistance in recommending a trustee could determine if it is the bank or the planner who ultimately directs the investment of the trust assets.

- Trustee—This role will likely be performed by the bank or trust company. However, often the decedent believes that a family member should serve in his or her individual capacity. This has both positive and negative aspects.

- Insurance planner—Use of this specialized expert is required whenever there is a policy of life insurance owned by the trust. It is very important to monitor the fiscal health of the cash value in the policy and to understand the contractual guarantees of the policy so that the trustee can determine if and when additional premium payments should be made.

- Investment planner—This is a critical player on the estate planning team. Without setting investment policy guidelines, the entire estate planning process may be for nothing. Academic studies have repeatedly shown the importance of asset allocation. The investment planner must determine realistic asset allocation models to balance the needs of the income and remainder beneficiaries. Also, the investment planner must work closely with the attorney to determine what fiduciary investment guidelines the planner must operate within either pursuant to the terms of the trust instrument or pursuant to state law.

- Estate planning quarterback—This position is the most important on any estate planning team. However, the individual planner must be equal to the task to optimally perform this role. Because of the combined expertise necessary to facilitate an effective estate plan, one professional needs to coordinate the various elements to assure harmony. Given the massive commitment of time this role entails, a planner almost certainly needs to charge fees to be fairly compensated for this undertaking.

Q 7:20   How should a planner go about recommending an attorney?

The planner should perform standard due diligence procedures to determine the attorney's background and qualifications. The planner should ask questions concerning the services to be performed to determine if the attorney is generally familiar with state law regarding estate administration.

Even after performing this process, it is still recommended that the planner develop a list of at least three attorneys that the planner refers to so as to avoid liability for a poor referral choice. Competent professionals believe that they can win the business despite the competition, so there should not be any hurt feelings in this process. Planners who have played the game of single-source referrals have often found themselves liable as codefendants for their own negligence in recommending legal counsel.

Q 7:21   What is the unauthorized practice of law?

The American Bar Association (ABA) has a broad interpretation of what does and does not constitute the unauthorized practice of law. Basically, the

ABA's position is that the practice of law consists of the rendition of services for others that call for the professional judgment of a lawyer. These services are not limited to legal drafting; it can also be interpreted to providing advice on an unsettled area of the law. Penalties for violation include both civil and criminal sanctions.

Besides the specific prohibition on the drafting of legal documents, what the financial professional can take from this rather vague interpretation is to involve the services of a competent attorney early in the estate planning process to avoid making a costly mistake.

One mistake that a novice planner may make is to share sample documents directly with a client. Many clients have sued planners believing (falsely) that the planner was recommending that the client "fill-in-the-blanks" on these legal forms without consulting an attorney. The financial planner should offer to present these documents directly to the client's attorney. This will facilitate communication with the client's attorney and keep the planner out of danger from a potential unauthorized practice of law lawsuit. If the client informs the planner that the client is not represented by an attorney, then the planner can make a referral from a list of qualified attorneys on whom the planner has performed due diligence.

Q 7:22   How often should a client's will be revised?

This is a decision that should be made in consultation with the client's estate planning attorney. Generally, every time there is a change in federal estate tax law, a client's estate plan should be reevaluated to take advantage of the new law. The challenge for financial planners is to stay alert through their estates and trusts attorney network to be aware of major revisions in state law that would signal a need to revise existing client estate planning documents.

The planner should ask prospective estate planning attorneys what practices and procedures they have in place to monitor changes in the tax law as well as the systems in place to notify clients that changes to federal tax law or state estate statutes necessitate a review of a client's estate planning documents. Remember that although these attorneys likely charge more, the additional cost is well worth the price in seeing that the client's estate plan stands the test of time and numerous changes to the applicable law of the jurisdiction.

Q 7:23   What is an obstacle to effective estate planning?

The ability of the client to face mortality is the most difficult obstacle to overcome in the estate planning process. There is a little known presumption in the financial planning community that is well known to almost every client: Soon after making a will the testator will die. Many clients avoid making a will for this very reason.

If the financial planning practice is more relationship-focused, the planner should consider bringing up estate planning during quarterly reviews of investment performance. It takes most clients an extended period of time to grapple with the emotional side of estate planning so patience is required of the planner. The planner should also consider referring the client to a psychologist who specializes in the issues of family wealth or family businesses if there are dysfunctional elements in a client's attitude or a client's family's attitude toward estate planning. Remember that there is always a plan in place for every estate known as the state's intestacy statute. At issue is whether the client wants to change this plan for the client's specific situation.

Property Ownership

Q 7:24   What types of property are considered in an estate?

When we speak in terms of property, we typically think of what technically constitutes a subset of property—real property. Real property encompasses items such as one's house, the land, the trees, or anything affixed to one's land. Property in an estate also includes personal property, which is divided into two types: tangible and intangible property.

Q 7:25   What is tangible personal property?

Tangible property implies some element of physicality (*e.g.*, home furnishings, art, china, crystal). That property has value itself.

Q 7:26   What is intangible personal property?

Intangible property is symbolic (*e.g.*, stocks, bonds, and cash). While these items do not seem symbolic, currency itself is literally only paper, and as such has no intrinsic value. Its value arises only in the meaning our society applies to the printing on the paper indicating its monetary value and its backing by gold or, in the case of stock, ownership shares in a corporation, etc.

Q 7:27   How is property owned by a single person titled?

Individual property ownership is referred to as "fee simple" or "fee simple absolute." Ownership in fee is often assumed and therefore is unstated. For example, a brokerage account will be titled "John Smith," not "John Smith, fee simple absolute."

Ownership in fee simple is not as powerful as it may appear on first impression. For example, a client may own a home in fee simple. Yet the home is subject to zoning laws (*i.e.*, if zoned as residential property, the client may not build a commercial office building on the property). The property is also subject to easements (the city owns the curb, and the utility company can dig in the front lawn to put down cable wiring) despite ownership of the property in fee simple.

Q 7:28   What is a joint tenancy?

Often property is not owned outright by one single individual. In these cases, the property is considered to be jointly owned and is subject to additional complexities upon the death of one of the owners. Joint tenancy is a type of concurrent property ownership by two or more individuals. In order to establish joint tenancy, co-owners must meet the following four criteria, called the "four unities":

2. **Unity of Time.** All joint tenants must take their interests at the same time. An owner may not convey a portion of his or her own interest in Property A to another owner in a joint tenancy. To establish a joint tenancy, both owners would take their interests in Property A at the same time.

3. **Unity of Title.** All joint tenants must obtain their interests from the same instrument (*e.g.,* the same deed or will).

4. **Unity of Interest.** All joint tenants must have an equal share in the property. An equal share includes both the same equal portion of the property and the same duration of interest (*e.g.*, life estate, fee simple).

5. **Unity of Possession.** All joint tenants must have an equal right to occupy the property, and no joint tenant may interfere with the rights of the other tenants to enjoy the property.

Joint tenancy typically contained a presumption of survivorship. If property is owned by joint tenants with the right of survivorship it means that when a joint tenant dies, the deceased's share passes directly through to the surviving tenants and is divided equally among them. Due to the survivorship feature, these tenancies in common do not need to go through probate.

In many states courts are now reluctant to apply the survivorship feature automatically. Unless it is specifically stated in the design instrument, many courts presume no survivorship and thus treat the joint ownership more like a tenancy in common.

Q 7:29   What are tenants in common?

In many jurisdictions a tenancy in common is a default type of concurrent property ownership where joint ownership is not specified. Upon the death of a tenant in common his or her shares of the property rights pass through the deceased's will to specific heirs or beneficiaries. The surviving tenants in common do not automatically receive the shares belonging to the deceased. Due to the lack of the survivorship feature, tenancies in common must go through probate.

Q 7:30   What is a tenancy by the entirety?

Tenancy by the entirety is a special type of joint tenancy enjoyed by married couples only. Tenancies by the entirety add a fifth unity to the joint tenancy criteria above, the unity of marriage. Tenancies by the entirety included the survivorship feature (*i.e.,* they pass by operation of law) and could thus avoid probate. Most states no longer make a current distinction between tenancy by the entirety and joint tenancy.

A major advantage of this form of ownership is that creditors of one spouse may not force, through a judicial sale, the liquidation of property owned by tenants by the entirety. For example, a husband and wife own a home in a tenancy by the entirety. If the husband is involved in an automobile accident and is subsequently held to be negligent in the amount of $50 million in damages, the creditor could not force the sale of the home in order to recover damages. However, if a creditor were a creditor of both the husband and wife, the creditor most likely would be able to recover against the property owned in tenancy by the entirety.

Q 7:31   When should a planner choose tenancy by the entirety versus sole ownership of assets?

Planners have read at one time or another that individuals in a high liability field often have their spouses own all of the significant marital assets. For example, the husband is a surgeon and is frequently sued due to the nature of his practice. The wife has sole title to the couple's home. Although likely the creditors of the husband may not be able to attach the home, the creditors of the wife could possibly force the sale of the property, such as if the wife is found negligent in an automobile accident. In a tenancy by the entirety, the creditors of one spouse may not force the sale of the home.

Planners should keep in mind that sole ownership of an asset is no protection from seizure by creditors. As with any kind of hazardous activity, even if the spouse does not engage in a high liability occupation such as surgery or financial services may still be subject to massive legal judgments in the daily activities of life.

Q 7:32   What are other types of property ownership rights?

Not all property ownership must be jointly owned. Most often, property is owned by a single owner for his or her exclusive use, or temporary use rights can be given to another for the life of the tenant only. The most commonly held ownership interest in property is held in a fee simple absolute estate. A fee simple estate property interest belongs absolutely to the estate owner, heirs, and assigns forever without condition or limitation. Fee simple ownership can be potentially infinite. The owner in a fee simple estate may sell or give the property away in his or her lifetime. In addition, a fee simple owner may direct its disposal in a will. *See* Q 7:27.

Another commonly seen property interest is a life estate. In a life estate the property interest is only maintained for the life of an estate owner with certain limitations on the life tenant's use of the property. The tenant in a life estate may use and enjoy the property only for the span of the measuring life, at which time all interest in the property reverts to the estate owner. The tenant may not assign or bequeath this property interest to others. (*See* Q 7:34.)

Common Law and Community Property

Q 7:33 What happens to property owned by married couples when one spouse dies?

If the decedent was married at the time of death it is crucial for the courts to determine which property was owned by the decedent and which property belongs to the surviving spouse. States use one of the following two types of marital property systems to make this determination: common law and community property.

Common Law	*Community Property*
• Used by the majority of the 50 states.	• Used by the following nine states— Arizona, California, Idaho, Louisiana, Nevada, New Mexico, Texas, Washington, and Wisconsin.
• Each spouse owns his or her entire income.	• Each spouse owns only ½ of his or her income. The other ½ vests in the other spouse as soon as it is earned.
• Each spouse owns any property brought into the marriage or acquired during the marriage by gift.	• Each spouse owns any property brought into the marriage or acquired during the marriage by gift.

Q 7:34 What is a life estate?

A life estate is a present possessory interest in property. This entitles the life tenant to use the property for as long as the person who is the measuring life remains alive. The measuring life could either be the life tenant himself or be a third party. For example, John could convey to Jim the right to use Whiteacre for the life of his sister, Sue. As long as Sue lives, Jim has the right to use Whiteacre. However, when Sue dies, the title to the property reverts to John, and Jim no longer has a right to use Whiteacre. In addition, in this example Jim could sell the right to use Whiteacre to a third party for the remainder of Sue's life. Furthermore, if Jim dies, Jim will pass his interest in Whiteacre on to his beneficiaries either through his will or in accordance with the intestacy laws of his jurisdiction.

The name for a life estate measured by the life of another (in our example, Sister Sue's estate) is called a life estate pur autre vie, which is French for the "life of another." One may ask how a French term invaded English common law. Remember that in 1066 the Normans under William the Conqueror invaded England and defeated Anglo-Saxon King Harold. In order to rule their massive conquest, the Normans redivided the property in England and developed many of the estate planning devices we use today.

Life estates were widely used in the past because English common law was rooted in the concept of primogeniture, which conveyed title to all property to the eldest male heir. Even the eldest son had limitations on his ability because he took title to his father's property as a life estate, which automatically passed title to his eldest male heir when the father died. Consequently, the only way to provide for mothers, siblings, etc., was to grant them a life estate pur autre vie in some of the property. And should the owner of the life estate be tragically short, as was usually the case until the twentieth century, then the eldest son would decide if grandmother would be granted a life estate and thereby still be able to put a roof over her head.

Q 7:35   What is an estate for a term of years?

An estate for a term of years is a more finite ownership than a life estate. The owner of the property can convey an interest in the underlying property for a term of five years, for example. The recipient of this interest now has the right to possess and enjoy the property for a term of five years. At the end of this time, the property reverts to the original owner. Estates for a term of years are far more predictable than life estates because the mortality of a measuring life does not have to be estimated.

Q 7:36   What is a remainder interest?

A remainder interest in property is a present interest but not a possessory interest. The remainder person acquires title to the property at the expiration of the possessory interest, including a life estate or an estate for a term of years. For example, if a trust established by Grandfather read "All income for life to Child and the remainder to Grandchild" the grandchild is a remainder beneficiary, and child has a life estate in the property.

Remainder interests may be vested or contingent. In the previous example, the remainder interest is vested, given that Grandchild will absolutely possess the property at Child's death. However, if the trust read "If the Jets win the Superbowl during the life of Child, then to Grandchild, otherwise to United Way" then we know the remainder is contingent to Grandchild upon the Jets winning the Superbowl. (In this instance, we can already determine that the remainder will go to the United Way!)

Q 7:37   What is the difference between legal ownership and equitable ownership?

Legal ownership determines who holds title to the property. For example, a trustee of a trust holds legal title to the property. Yet the trustee is under a beneficiaries of the trust. So even though an individual holds title to the property does not mean that control of the property is within his or her absolute discretion.

Beneficial ownership determines who should benefit, meaning who should possess or enjoy the property. For example, in a trust the beneficiaries do not hold legal title to the property. This is advantageous especially in a spendthrift trust whereby a creditor of the beneficiary may not attach trust corpus in satisfaction of an individual debt of the beneficiary. Yet the trust beneficiaries are entitled to receive income from the trust assets invested for the benefit of the beneficiaries.

If an individual holds legal and equitable title to an asset, that person is said to be an absolute owner of the property. This system of separating title to property is unique to English common law, although many legal systems, including countries in Europe, have adopted similar provisions. Many scholars of jurisprudence have referred to the concept of separating legal and equitable ownership as the English common law's greatest contribution.

Q 7:38   What is "situs"?

Situs is a concept that determines where property is located. The term "situs" is used for many purposes, including determining jurisdiction for the imposition of taxes. For example, Georgia may not tax Florida property unless the property also has contact or situs with respect to Georgia. This only makes sense because as a state resident of Y a property owner would not want to receive an unsolicited tax bill from the State of X.

In general, real property has situs where it is physically located and is taxable only in that jurisdiction. The taxing of tangible personal property is more complicated: it is generally taxed by the state where the property is located. Intangible personal property is generally taxed in the jurisdiction where the owner resides. For example, despite using a broker in Nevada, a Florida resident would be deemed to have situs in the portfolio in Florida. The question of law for an attorney would be if Nevada could also tax the same property to the owner given the business connection to the state.

Q 7:39   What are domicile and residency?

Domicile is where a person intends to return at some future date. For example, an individual born in New York who lives and works in California may be a New York domiciliary if the individual intends to return to New York. Residency is effectively where a person is located for tax purposes. For example, an individual who lives in New Jersey but works in New York may be considered a resident of New York if the individual owns residential property in New York despite the fact that the person is a domiciliary of New Jersey and owns a principal residence in New Jersey.

The problem for planners is determining where an individual will be located for imposition of taxes, including estate tax. This is a question of law that should be referred to an attorney licensed in the jurisdiction at issue.

The problem is that there is a strong possibility that multiple states may lay claim to the residency of an affluent client, especially if the client spends a substantial amount of time and owns real estate in the jurisdiction. The Supreme Court has held that access to the federal courts is denied until the amount of tax levied by two states exceeds the total value of the estate. Financial planners and their clients should beware and take notice that residency issues should not be taken lightly.

Inter Vivos Transfers

Gifts

Q 7:40   What is a gift?

"Gift" is defined in the common law as a voluntary transfer without consideration. Gifts can include sales, exchanges, or other types of property transfers from a donor (giver) to a donee (recipient) as long as the present value of the property is greater than the amount of consideration (if any) received. While not stated explicitly in the Internal Revenue Code or Regulations, for federal transfer tax purposes, a gift that is transferred for less than adequate and full consideration is subject to the following valuation formula:

> The value of the property transferred — consideration received
>   = the value of the gift

For example, using the above formula, if Grandfather makes a gift of a family heirloom valued at $60,000 to Granddaughter, the value of the heirloom for gift tax purposes would be as follows:

> $ 60,000 fair market value — $ 12,000 = $48,000 taxable gift.

Thus, Grandfather would owe gift taxes on the $50,000. To avoid paying taxes on the gift, Granddaughter would have had to pay $60,000 to Grandfather for the cabin. The $60,000 would be considered full and adequate consideration, hence would not qualify as a gift.

Q 7:41   What type of business transaction does not constitute a gift?

A bad business bargain is not a gift. For example, a Kentucky colonel sells his restaurant business to an attorney businessman for $1 million. The next year the attorney sells the same restaurant business to an investor for $400 million. Did the colonel make a gift of $399 million?

The answer is quite obviously no. The colonel was not under any duress to sell a business that he reasonably believed was worth $1 million. The fact that a more astute businessperson pocketed a windfall profit is simply a bad business bargain but does not constitute a taxable gift.

Q 7:42   What constitutes a gift under state law?

A gift under state law generally requires the following three elements

1. Intent of the donor to make the gift
2. Delivery of the gift to the donee
3. Acceptance by the donee of the gift

State law generally requires that the intent element exist. For federal transfer tax purposes intent is not required to create a taxable gift; rather it is considered a transfer for less than full and adequate consideration.

The reason for not requiring any intent of the donor for federal gift tax purposes involves the evidentiary issue in proving exactly what the donor intended at the time of the transfer. One can only imagine the reams of litigation that would ensue by donors litigating a subjective state of mind. Fortunately, Congress did not require intent on behalf of the donor to make a taxable gift.

Q 7:43   What date is used for gift valuation?

The date the gift is made. No other alternate valuation date is allowed.

Q 7:44   Why is gifting a superior transfer tax planning technique?

Technically, the federal gift tax is a tax-exclusive tax while the federal estate tax is a tax-inclusive tax. Stated differently, if a donor makes a gift and pays the gift tax and lives three years, the amount of the gift tax is removed from the estate. If the donor dies with both the gift and gift tax property in the estate, the decedent would have to pay estate tax on both amounts (*i.e.*, the decedent would pay tax on the tax).

The following chart highlights the distinction. For simplicity, no unified credit is assumed and the tax rate is a flat 50 percent.

	Estate	*Gift*	*Recapture*	*Net Gift*
FMV of Assets	$ 3,000,000	$ 3,000,000	$ 1,000,000	$ 2,000,000
Transfer Tax	(1,500,000)	(1,000,000)	(500,000)	(500,000)
Net to Beneficiaries	$ 1,500,000	$ 2,000,000	$ 500,000	$ 1,500,000

In the chart above, the donor is able to transfer $2 million in assets and save $500,000 in transfer taxes if the donor survives three years after making the gift. If the donor dies within the three-year period after making the gift, the amount of gift tax paid (*e.g.*, $1 million) is recaptured in the estate and estate tax is due on the gift taxes previously paid, resulting in an additional $500,000 liability to the estate. Should the estate have insufficient assets to pay the tax, the IRS will pursue the donees to collect the tax.

Q 7:45   Why would someone make a gift?

In addition to its use as a valuable estate planning tool, gifts are often made within a social context, including the donor's anticipation of demise or to observe the donee's enjoyment of the gift firsthand during life.

In the estate planning context, gift transfers are typically recommended to clients when at least one of the following conditions is present:

- When the asset to be given is likely to appreciate in value over time and the donor is interested in saving the estate tax on the potential appreciation.
- When the donor is interested in reducing his or her overall tax bracket. This is done by shifting income from the donor to the donee. See Chapter 5 for more information on the Assignment of Income Doctrine including the "fruit and the tree" metaphor.
- When the donor wants to achieve privacy about the transfer. Gifts are not subject to disclosure in a public proceeding like probate.

Q 7:46   When should clients start a gifting program?

As soon as possible. Clients tend to have an inaccurate view as to what will happen at their passing. Gifting currently will help to reduce the client's estate and save transfer taxes. However, seeing how the beneficiaries use the money is an excellent indication of what will happen to the estate assets.

Implementing a gifting program for clients is an excellent method for making clients serious about their estate planning decisions. Many clients have revisited their early estate planning decisions and have adopted more extensive estate planning strategies, including trusts with spendthrift provisions after viewing how the children handle the gifted assets.

Q 7:47   When do most clients want to implement a gifting program?

Shortly after death. Many clients do not want to give up control of their assets during their lifetimes. The financial planner should expect that most clients will likely only gift the $12,000 annual exclusion amount. Taxable gifts applied against the unified credit are often difficult to convince a client to undertake. Sound financial planning advice for a client is to undertake a regular, systematic gifting program initially and then develop a more extensive planning framework in subsequent years.

Q 7:48   What is the annual gift tax exemption?

The federal gift tax exemption is $12,000 per person per year. This means that a donor may make an annual property transfer of up to $12,000 each year for the same donee. Alternatively, the donor could also make an $12,000 tax-exempt gift to multiple donees in a single given year. The only limit is the $12,000 limit per single donee.

Q 7:49   May a spouse combine the annual tax-exempt contribution?

Yes. Using a transfer method called "gift splitting," donors can combine their $12,000 annual exemption to provide a tax-free $24,000 gift to a single donee. For example, parents can give a $24,000 stock certificate to their adult child and not pay any gift tax on the transfer.

In community property states, because income is already combined between spouses once it is earned, gifts are automatically split on transfers of community property assets. However, in common law states, gift splitting is elective if the other spouse provides written consent.

Q 7:50   What are the types of gifts that can be subject to tax?

The following are examples of the types of gifts that can be subject to gift tax:

- Cash
- Tangible personal property
- Real property
- Income that will be earned in the future (*e.g.*, royalties)
- Forgiveness of a debt
- Interest forgone by participation in an interest-free or below-market loan
- Payment of another's expenses (*e.g.*, a mortgage or car payment)
- Creation of a family partnership
- Stock or retirement plan interests
- Assignment of the benefits of an insurance policy
- Transfer of property to a trust

Q 7:51   What types of transfers are not considered taxable gifts?

Some types of gratuitous transfers are statutorily exempted from gift taxation, according to Section 2503(e) of the Internal Revenue Code. Some examples of exempt gifts include:

- Educational expenses such as tuition or training fees
- Medical expenses
- Charitable contributions
- Political contributions
- Property transfers at divorce

Note that in order to take advantage of these gift tax credits, the check or donation must be made payable directly to the institution (*e.g.*, the hospital, the educational institution, etc.).

Q 7:52   What types of transfers are not considered gifts?

Payment of a donor's liability is never considered to be a taxable gift. For example, when the monthly mortgage bill is paid, the money provided to the lender is not considered a gift. Failure to pay the mortgage would constitute a default under the loan agreement and eventual foreclosure on the property.

Similarly, parents have a legal obligation to support their children. Consequently, any payments made by a parent on behalf of a dependent child will not be considered gifts when used to provide support, including food, clothing, and shelter, for the child. However, a gift of a $90,000 luxury sports car upon graduation from law school would constitute a taxable gift from parent to child.

Q 7:53   What is the sufficiency-of-consideration test?

The sufficiency-of-consideration test is used to determine if consideration received by the transferor is equal in value to the property transferred in order to determine if the gift is exempt from gift tax. If the consideration provided for the gift is not found to be adequate and full consideration equal to the value of the property being transferred then the excess value is subject to gift tax.

Q 7:54   What are the transfer requirements for a completed gift?

A valid inter vivos transfer (a gift given during life) is one where the transferor has irrevocably parted with dominion or control over the gift. Each of the following conditions must be met for a gift to be considered a completed transfer:

1. Intent to make a gift.
2. Actual or constructive delivery of the gift.
3. Acceptance of the gift by the donee.

Q 7:55   What is a gift *causa mortis*?

A gift *causa mortis* is a gift given by a donor in anticipation of his or her own imminent death. These types of gifts are seen especially when the donor is suffering from the complications of a terminal illness. Gifts given in the anticipation of death are typically viewed as conditional gifts, which are only transferred upon the death of the donor.

Gifts *causa mortis* are considered completed transfers only following the death of the donor. If the donor does not die, most states allow the donor to actually reclaim the property from the donee. This is possible because the condition subsequent to constitute a completed gift under state law is the death of the donor, which did not occur given that the donor remained alive.

A gift *causa mortis* can be contrasted with an inter vivos transfer when all of the donor's ownership rights are relinquished to the donee during the donor's lifetime.

Q 7:56   What is a disclaimer?

If the intended beneficiary does not accept a post-mortem gift, the gift is considered to be "disclaimed" and is treated as if the intended donee has predeceased the decedent. Refusal of the gift must be in writing and, for federal estate tax purposes, must be made within nine months of the gifting. Transfers made after nine months are considered subsequent transfers of current ownership, which are then subject to federal gift taxation to the intended beneficiary who is disclaiming the gift.

Q 7:57   When should a financial planner use disclaimers?

Disclaimers are generally used when proper planning was not possible or unforeseen circumstances arose that have frustrated the original planning. For example, assume that Grandmother made a gift *causa mortis* to her daughter of the $1 million cash under her mattress. Daughter is independently wealthy in her own right and does not need the money. Daughter disclaims the gift, which likely reverts to Grandmother's estate. Let's assume Grandmother dies intestate, that Grandfather died years before, and that Daughter is the only child of Grandmother. Daughter can now disclaim the inheritance for a second time. Under the intestacy statutes, the cash passes to Granddaughter.

Without the disclaimer, the transfer would be taxed to Daughter and would subsequently be taxed again when transferred from Daughter to Granddaughter. Use of a qualified disclaimer results in substantial transfer tax savings in this circumstance.

Securities

Q 7:58   How are jointly owned securities treated for federal gift tax purposes?

The issue as to determining whether a gift has occurred is whether the account is in certificate form or titled in street name. "Street name" refers to securities held in the name of a broker rather than the owner(s). It is very unusual to see certificate shares in the securities industry in recent years.

Jointly owned securities are subject to gift tax when transferred in certificate form. This is because the signatures of both joint owners are required to transfer the securities, thus creating rights in the donee that previously did not exist when the account was in street name.

If a signature of one or more of the owners is required for a transfer, the addition of the donee/joint owner generates gift tax consequences. When securities are registered in street name, however, no signatures are required for transfer and no gift tax is triggered when the donee/joint owner is added to the account.

Financial planners should be careful of this tax trap: if the securities in street name are subsequently transferred in certificate form to the joint owners, a taxable gift has been made. If the certificate is subsequently retitled in the donor's sole individual name, a second taxable transfer has been made.

Gifts to Minors

Q 7:59   What is a UGMA?

UGMA stands for the Uniform Gift to Minors Act. The provisions of this act allow an adult to make a lifetime gift transfers of certain types of property to a minor who does not have a guardian. In nearly all states, the UGMA has been replaced by the more flexible allowances of an UTMA (Uniform Transfers to Minors Act).

Q 7:60   What is a UTMA?

UTMA stands for the Uniform Transfers to Minors Act. Like the UGMA, the provisions of this act also allow an adult to make a lifetime gift transfer to a minor who does not have a conservator. However, unlike the UGMA, which the UTMA has largely replaced, the UTMA provisions are more flexible in allowing nearly any kind of property to be the subject of a custodial gift.

UTMAs have also been termed "the poor man's trust" due to the fact that it provides the average investor with the ability to make a gift to a minor and avoid the problems and expense involved in drafting a formal trust arrangement. The property (typically an investment vehicle, like an annuity or securities) is then given to the minor and held by a custodian for the minor's behalf until the minor reaches the age specified by statute (usually 18 or 21).

Q 7:61   Is a custodial gift made under UTMA subject to federal gift tax?

No, gifts made under an UTMA provision qualify for the annual gift tax exclusion. However, state gift tax may apply to a custodial gift.

Q 7:62   How are UTMA accounts taxed for income tax purposes?

One complication of an UTMA is that this kind of account is subject to the "kiddie tax" rules for federal income tax. Please see the Kiddie Tax rules in Chapter 6 for more information. (*See* Q 6:1.)

Q 7:63   May a UTMA account be revoked?

No. Once the custodial gift has been made it is irrevocable.

Q 7:64   May gifts to more than one child be combined in the same account?

No. A separate custodial account must be established for each child.

Crummey Gifts

Q 7:65   What is the *Crummey* gifting technique?

A *Crummey* gifting technique (named for the 1968 *Crummey* Tax Court case) provides a way to qualify a future interest gift with the present interest annual gift tax exclusion of $12,000 per donee per year. Typically, gifts held in trust do not become immediately available for the present use and enjoyment of the beneficiaries. As such, these gifts are considered gifts of future rather than present interests and do not qualify for the present interest annual gift tax exclusion.

To preserve this valuable tax exclusion while still providing a future gift for beneficiaries, which may be funded in $12,000 tax-free annual increments per donee to a trust account, each of the beneficiaries must be given the right to demand immediate transfer of the gift each year. Notice of the annual donations to the fund must be provided to each of the beneficiaries using a "*Crummey* letter" informing the beneficiary of the gift of his or her right to withdraw the amount contributed to the trust on his or her behalf.

Q 7:66   How should financial planners discuss *Crummey* powers with clients?

The first piece of advice in this regard is not to call this a "crummy planning technique." The financial planner should discuss the benefits of using this technique with clients but only refer to this technique as a *Crummey* power around other professionals.

Gift Loans

Q 7:67   How are interest-free and below-market-rate loans treated?

In the event that an individual makes an interest-free or below-market-rate loan to a borrower, the lender is taxed based on the IRS applicable interest rate tables (typically the lender will be taxed at market rate). For example, if Uncle makes a loan to Niece at a 1 percent interest rate and the applicable IRS interest rate is 5 percent, then Uncle is taxed the additional 4 percent as taxable interest income on his 1040.

In addition to the added taxes on the interest income, the lender is deemed to have made a gift to the borrower of the amount of the interest income every year.

Q 7:68   How are loans under $12,000 treated?

Generally, loans under $12,000 are considered to be exempt from the gift tax and income tax rules described above.

Insurance Gifts

Q 7:69   How is life insurance valued for a gift transfer?

Life insurance (specifically whole life insurance) is valued for transfer tax purposes at the interpolated terminal reserve (as determined by the insurance company) plus the unearned premium. For example, if Insured Jones pays $10,000 for an annual insurance premium on January 1, on July 1 there would be approximately $5,000 in an unearned annual premium. A planner should obtain the interpolated terminal reserve by consulting the insurance company directly.

529 Planned Gifting

Q 7:70   What planning technique may be used for gifting college funding?

The donor (*e.g.*, parent or grandparent) may in effect fund a family education bank by placing funds into a 529 plan. A 529 plan is essentially a statesponsored trust specifically intended for the purpose of funding the expenses of higher education.

A single donor may contribute up to $60,000 (remember that a grandmother and grandfather would be allowed to contribute $120,000 to a § 529 plan) in a single year. Assuming the donor survives for five years, no taxable gift occurs. Technically, a gift of a future interest has been made, but the gift is treated as a gift of a present interest under the applicable federal tax law.

Q 7:71   What is the advantage of 529 plan funding?

One of the principal advantages of 529 plans is essentially flexibility. If the intended beneficiary does not decide to pursue higher education or if the grantor experiences financial hardship, the grantor is able to take back the plan funding, subject to a 10 percent penalty tax.

In cases of where multiple beneficiaries may exist, 529 plan funds not used for one beneficiary (who may decide to backpack through Europe rather than attend college) can be rolled over to another beneficiary plan without penalty.

In addition to its flexibility, 529 plan funding provides a valuable tax advantage as plan funds grow tax-deferred until distributed. Under current law, amounts withdrawn to pay higher educational expenses are tax-free.

Q 7:72   What is the maximum contribution per beneficiary of a 529 plan?

Plan maximums vary from state to state. Some states permit contributions of up to $300,000 per beneficiary. Expect funding maximums to increase as states vie with each other for funding dollars.

Joint Bank Accounts

Q 7:73   When does a completed gift occur in a joint bank account?

A completed gift does not occur until funds are withdrawn. For example, Mother names Daughter on a bank account and funds the account with $50,000. The gift is not deemed to have been transferred to Daughter until Daughter withdraws funds from the account.

Q 7:74   Are gifts between spouses taxed for federal gift tax purposes?

No, spouses who are both U.S. citizens are entitled to an unlimited gift tax exemption. If a spouse is a resident alien but not a U.S. citizen, then the spouse is limited to an annual transfer of $100,000 between the spouses.

Estate and Gift Tax Credits and Deductions

Marital Deduction

Q 7:75   What is the marital deduction?

The marital deduction allows an individual to pass an entire estate to a spouse free of both federal gift and estate taxes. The marital deduction may appear on the surface to provide a simple and inexpensive means of avoiding federal taxation in an estate. However, financial planners should be aware that this method of tax avoidance on the death of a spouse may prove to be a far more expensive option on the death of the surviving spouse (providing the surviving spouse does not remarry). When the surviving spouse dies, the combined taxes on the two estates may be greater than if the marital deduction had not been used when the first spouse died. Thus, like any other estate planning tax minimization technique, the marital deduction should not be carelessly applied.

Q 7:76 Is there a maximum limit on the marital deduction?

No. The marital deduction is unlimited.

Unified Credit

Q 7:77 What is the unified credit?

The unified credit is a tax credit that can be applied against either gift taxes or estate taxes. Each individual receives a $1 million dollar lifetime exemption for both estate and gift tax. For example, if an individual receives a $500,000 exemption for gifts given during his lifetime, then an additional $500,000 credit for estate taxes is available upon his death.

Charitable Contributions

Q 7:78 What are the tax ramifications of a charitable contribution?

Charitable contributions are exempted from both gift and estate taxes. So, assuming that a client makes a charitable contribution during her lifetime, she receives an income tax deduction and is not subject to gift taxes. If this contribution takes place after death, the estate receives an estate tax deduction. The charity also is not subject to tax on either lifetime transfers or bequests after death. Generally, the charity is also exempt from paying income tax on income earned from the donated property.

Q 7:79 What types of organizations are considered qualified charities?

To qualify as a charity an organization must be operated exclusively for charitable, religious, scientific, literary, or educational purposes; or to foster national or international amateur sporting competition; or for the prevention of cruelty to children or animals. In addition, certain activities are not permitted, including attempting to influence legislation or participating in a political campaign. A specific list of qualified charities can be obtained on the IRS web site at *http://www.irs.gov/bus_info/eo/eosearch*.

Q 7:80 When does a qualified appraisal for a donation need to be obtained?

A qualified appraisal (on Form 8283) must be obtained along with the donor's annual tax return for all donations of property valued at over $5,000. This appraisal must be made by an independent qualified appraiser. The appraisal may not be made by the donor, the donee, any person from whom the property was acquired, or certain related individuals or entities. The appraisal requirement does not apply to gifts of publicly traded securities. However, it does apply to gifts of nonpublicly traded securities valued at over $10,000.

Q 7:81   When is a written receipt required for a donation?

While it is recommended that a donor keep a detailed accounting of all donations, the donor must provide a detailed written receipt for all contributions, including cash, of $250 or more. Canceled checks do not function as an adequate receipt.

Q 7:82   How is life insurance used to make charitable contributions?

Life insurance is one of the favorite means by which individuals provide charitable contributions without reducing the overall size of the estate for potential heirs. An individual may assign the death benefit on his or her own life insurance policy to the charity, thus providing the charity with the security of a fixed-value contribution amount. Likewise, an individual may be able to provide the charity with a much larger ultimate contribution amount by means of relatively small annual premium payments.

An added feature of life insurance funding is that the death proceeds, unlike gifts or estate bequests, are free of administrative fees and taxes, such as federal income and estate tax, probate costs, brokerage fees, and other transfer costs. Upon the individual's death, the charity can immediately receive funds and avoid the often extensive delays of probate. In addition, the premiums paid during the individual's lifetime are deductible as a charitable contribution each and every year that premiums are paid.

Q 7:83   If a person dies intestate, may a charitable deduction be made from the estate?

No. Without a valid will in force, the estate of the deceased is unable to direct deductible contributions to charity.

Business Interests

Buy-Sell Agreements

Q 7:84   How may an owner's business interests be transferred?

An owner's business interests can be more easily transferred as part of the assets in one's estate if the business has implemented a formal buy-sell agreement. A buy-sell agreement arranges for the disposition of an owner's business interests in the event of the owner's death, disability, retirement, or early withdrawal. In addition, qualifying events could be specified in the event of an owner losing a professional license or becoming financially dissolute.

The requirements of a valid buy-sell agreement include a written contractual agreement specifying the purchase price, the terms of the agreement, and the funding arrangements. Note that the purchase price need not be a specified dollar figure, but it must include an agreed-upon method for valuation.

Q 7:85 What valuation methods of an owner's interests are used to structure a buy-sell agreement?

An owner's business interests may be valued in a variety of ways, including book value (assets minus liabilities), asset value, formula value, or fixed price (which may be adjusted every year). At least one valuation method must be selected and specified in the agreement.

Q 7:86 How can buy-sell agreements be structured?

Buy-sell agreements are typically structured in one of two ways: through an entity redemption plan or a cross-purchase plan. In an entity redemption plan, the owner's shares are bought back by the corporation, while in a cross-purchase plan the owner's shares are bought by another shareholder or partner in the business.

Q 7:87 What is the appropriate type of life insurance to use in a buy-sell agreement?

Generally, the type of insurance used in this arrangement is a single-life policy on the life of the "business parent." For example, the owner of the business funds an insurance policy, which is set up in an irrevocable life insurance trust. On the death of the owner, the spouse, who may be named as executor of the estate, is then paid by the death benefit of the insurance, and the beneficiaries, who may be the children, take back the stock in the trust.

In this way the business interest of an appreciating business is transferred immediately to the children instead of being included in the surviving spouse's estate, which is more likely to occur in a shorter interim, thus deferring taxes on any intervening appreciation until its inclusion in the estate of the children upon their deaths.

Taxation of Business Interests

Q 7:88 What are the tax implications when an individual dies with a closely held business interest?

The general rule is that all of the estate tax due on an individual's estate is payable in full within nine months of the date of death. However, in certain circumstances the IRS does allow an executor to defer payment in full, and instead spread out the payment of federal estate taxes that are attributable to the decedent's business interest over a period of years. In order to qualify for this deferral, the estate must meet certain specified requirements under federal statute.

Q 7:89   What is a Section 6166 business interest estate tax deferral?

IRC Section 6166 allows a four-year deferral of the payment of federal estate taxes for a business interest. During the first four years of the deferral, the executor pays only the interest due on the unpaid tax. This deferral period must be followed by a maximum ten-year principal payout of the tax due. This deferral applies on the first $2 million in business value. This deduction amount cannot apply, for example, to the first $2 million of tax due on the overall estate; it only applies to the first $2 million of the business's value, which may only comprise a portion of the overall estate.

Q 7:90   What percentage of the overall estate must include a business interest in order to qualify for a Section 6166 deferral?

The value of the business interest must exceed 35 percent of the adjusted gross estate in order to qualify for a Section 6166 deferral. In addition, the business must be classified as a closely held business (generally, a business with 45 or fewer owners).

Q 7:91   How is interest calculated on the Section 6166 deferral?

Interest on the deferral is allocated using the following formula:

- The first $1.12 million—nondeductible 2 percent interest rate.
- The balance (of the $2 million maximum)—nondeductible 45 percent of the applicable federal rate.

Q 7:92   What are the risks associated with using a Section 6166 deferral?

The risk of using a Section 6166 deferral is that the while the beneficiaries are running the business in place of the decedent, the tax owed on the business is still out there waiting to be paid. If in the meantime, somewhere before the end of the estimated total payout (a period of up to 14 years), the beneficiaries are unable to properly manage business operations or the business ceases operations, the taxes are still payable on a business of little or no value as an asset. The IRS will not waive payment on these deferred taxes even in the event of interim business failure.

Family Limited Partnerships

Q 7:93   What is a family limited partnership?

A family limited partnership is a partnership limited to members of a family as defined by the IRS to be an individual's spouse, ancestors, and lineal descendants. It is generally used as an income-shifting device.

Q 7:94   What are the advantages of setting up a family limited partnership?

Family limited partnerships are generally set up for the following two advantages:

1. *The taxpayer receives a discount, potentially, for federal transfer tax purposes.* The reason for this discount is that a potential buyer would generally pay less for an owner's interest in a family limited partnership rather than for shares of stock in, for example, a publicly traded corporation. As a general rule, valuation discounts are between 10 and 20 percent. Qualification for these discounts can be obtained by proving lack of marketability or through minority interest discounts.

2. *Creditor protection.* Most state laws mandate that only the partners may admit a new partner. Assignees only receive an "assignment" of the partnership profits (also called an assignee interest).

For example, if an assignee is pursued by a judicial lien, then only those assets that are distributed as income can be attached by the creditor. The family could opt not to receive any income out of the partnership for several years, allowing profits to accumulate. In the interim the creditor receives K-1s for taxable income each year. The creditor will then in effect have the IRS as a creditor and may as a result settle the dispute after a few years for payment of the outstanding tax liability due.

Self-Canceling Installment Notes

Q 7:95   How are self-canceling installment notes used in installment sales?

Installment sales are typically used as a means of breaking up the total payment of a business interest. For example, if Owner *A* wants to sell his business interest to Buyer *B* for $1million dollars, Owner *A* and Buyer *B* may work out a separate payment arrangement whereby Buyer *B* can make four payments of $270,000 each. The additional $20,000 may be added as interest or additional compensation for the benefit of paying in four installments.

In the example above, a self-canceling installment note may be used by a family limited partnership, for example, to agree to pay $300,000 for each installment payment. The agreement put in place for the additional compensation is that if the Owner *A* dies before the last payment is made, then the subsequent payments are canceled and Buyer *B* receives the property. (*See* Q 6:75–Q 6:78.)

Q 7:96   What are the mortality qualifications of the seller in a self-canceling installment sale?

In order to qualify for this type of planning technique, the seller must show that at the time he or she entered into the transaction, he or she had at least

50/50 odds of living for the next year or more. For example, if the owner was recently diagnosed with a terminal disease, the medical opinion may not show that the owner was 80 percent likely to die within three months.

Q 7:97   What are the income tax consequences of a self-canceling installment sale?

In the event that the seller dies before the last installment is made, the amount of money left unpaid is taxable as cancellation of indebtedness income. These amounts are typically allocated to the seller (usually the parent). Once the seller dies, payment of the taxes due on cancellation of indebtedness income is then charged to the buyer (typically the child).

This technique is actually tax-beneficial to the buyer/child as the tax rate on cancellation of indebtedness income is a reduced rate compared to the much higher rate on estate tax. In this way the property is transferred from the seller/parent to the buyer/child without becoming subject to heavy estate taxes.

Private Annuities

Q 7:98   What is a private annuity?

A private annuity is a personal arrangement between two individuals in which the transferor (the property owner or annuitant) conveys complete ownership of a property (typically a business interest) to a transferee (also known as the obligor) on the condition that the transferee makes periodic payments to the transferor.

In return for this valuable property transfer, the transferee is "obliged" to make regular periodic payments to the transferor, typically for the lifetime of the transferor or, in addition, the life of the transferor's spouse as well. The inclusion of the transferor spouse is called a joint and last survivor annuity under which payments continue until the death of the last survivor (until the death of both the husband and wife).

In a private annuity arrangement, the risk of mortality rests with the buyer. As a result the buyer typically pays less compared to the overall value of the property to help manage the risk that these payments might last over an extended lifespan.

Q 7:99   What are the risks associated with private annuities?

The primary risk of this arrangement is that the surviving annuitant has a longer lifespan than anticipated and the obligor may want to discontinue further annuity payments after a reasonable period of time. The biggest risk of discontinuing lifetime payments as specified in the agreement is that the IRS could then treat the arrangement as a sham transaction and consequently recapture the full amount of the property. Alternately, the IRS could allege fraud in the transaction. There is no statute of limitation consideration on prosecution for fraud. As a result, the best advice that planners can give to clients interested in entering into a private annuity is to be fully prepared to honor all the commitments promised at the beginning of the arrangement.

S Corporations

Q 7:100   What is an S corporation?

An S corporation is a business entity that has made an "S" election to have its income, deductions, capital gains and losses, charitable contributions, and credits passed through to its shareholders. It offers the shareholder(s) asset protection from individual creditors while at the same time allowing the shareholder(s) to personally deduct business losses on the individual's tax return. (*See* Q 6:70.)

Q 7:101   Who may own S corporation stock?

S corporation stock may be owned by the following trusts:

- **Grantor Trusts.** A risk of this ownership is that if the grantor dies the grantor trust expires upon the death of the grantor.
- **Electing Small Business Trusts.** A risk of this ownership is that the trust income on this trust is taxable at the highest marginal individual income tax rate.
- **Qualified Subchapter S Trusts.** In these trusts, there is a limitation on the length of time that stock can be held in trust (typically only 90 days). This limitation could be detrimental to making alternative planning arrangements.

Q 7:102   What is a planning technique to transfer S corporation stock?

As a result of these potentially negative trust treatments, a planning technique is to make arrangements for the transfer of S corporation stock well prior to the death of the transferor. An example of this planning would be to integrate S corporation stock into a buy-sell agreement, which would transfer ownership outright to a third party or on the death of the transferor. For income tax purposes, the tax laws generally do not favor trust ownership of S corporation stock for any extended length of time.

Section 303 Stock Redemption

Q 7:103   What is a Section 303 stock redemption?

IRC Section 303 allows the corporation to redeem stock in a post-mortem transfer. In the event that a stockholder dies, the executor of the estate can then sell the stock back to the corporation. The stock can be sold back at total cost of the administrative expenses (*e.g.*, attorney fees, accounting fees, funeral expenses, etc.) plus the estate taxes due and payable on the amount of stock being sold.

Q 7:104 What estate conditions must be met in order to qualify for a Section 303 stock redemption?

In order to take advantage of this redemption feature, the value of the stock must exceed 35 percent of the value of the other assets in the estate.

Q 7:105 May the corporation accumulate cash for the purpose of redeeming stock?

No. The corporation may not accumulate cash for the purpose of the redemption. The corporation is able to use available cash or life insurance proceeds to buy back the stock.

Q 7:106 What are the advantages of using a Section 303 stock redemption?

For the corporation, the redemption feature allows a closely held business to retake control of outstanding shares. For the estate of the decedent shareholder, the estate is provided with cash, which can be used to pay estate taxes and administrative fees without resulting in taxable dividend treatment. The amount paid to the estate is treated as an exchange price for the stock, resulting in no taxable gain because the stock is "stepped up" in basis (from the original price paid by the shareholder to the stock's current fair market value) on the death of the shareholder pursuant to Section 1014.

Retirement Plans

Income in Respect of a Decedent

Q 7:107 What is income in respect of a decedent?

Income in respect of a decedent refers to property received by the beneficiary that the beneficiary must pay income tax on in addition to estate taxes. An illustration of this concept is when the decedent had invested money in a qualified plan or as nonqualified deferred compensation. These retirement plan amounts that were not taxed during the lifetime of the decedent (*e.g.*, IRAs, 401(k)s, etc.) are taxable post-mortem to the beneficiaries receiving the property. Because these tax-free investments would be taxable to the investor when withdrawn during his or her lifetime, logically these amounts would still generate tax when withdrawn by the investor's beneficiary. After the death of the decedent these amounts may be subject to both income tax and estate tax simultaneously.

Q 7:108   What are deductions in respect of a decedent?

When the property being transferred to a beneficiary constitutes income in respect of a decedent, the beneficiary is entitled to an income tax deduction for estate taxes paid on the property. The beneficiary is entitled to itemize the deductions in respect of a decedent on Schedule A as a miscellaneous itemized deduction not subject to the 2 percent floor.

Q 7:109   Where does the beneficiary claim deductions in respect of a decedent on a federal income tax return?

The beneficiary must itemize his or her deductions on a federal income tax return in order to receive a benefit. These deduction amounts must be claimed on a Schedule A as a miscellaneous itemized deduction not subject to the 2 percent floor.

Nonqualified Deferred Compensation

Q 7:110   What happens to the proceeds of a nonqualified deferred compensation account after the death of the participant?

The proceeds of the account are passed directly to the designated beneficiary after the death of the decedent. Remember that this is the rule even if the decedent had forgotten to update this information and had previously named a beneficiary (an ex-spouse, for example) that was not the intended beneficiary at death. Because these plans are under the control of ERISA regulations, the decedent's will has no control over plan beneficiary designation after death.

Estates and Trusts

Durable Power of Attorney

Q 7:111   What is a durable power of attorney?

An integral element of estate planning is making arrangements to deal the potential incapacity of the estate owner (commonly referred to as the principal). A durable power of attorney (DPOA) can be executed to provide for the effective management of the estate in the event that the principal is unable to conduct business on his or her own behalf. Often this is a result of illness or mental incapacity but can also include a temporary lack of availability due to travel plans or a mutual understanding of the boundaries of the agent's discretionary authority to conduct business on the principal's behalf.

In the event of an emergency situation—for example a severe storm that causes damage to the roof of the principal's home, the agent who holds the DPOA (also referred to as the attorney in fact) can make immediate arrangements for the roof repairs without the need to wait for approval from the principal. Contrary to popular belief, a DPOA is typically used to perform the mundane daily tasks of managing the estate.

A DPOA is only in effect during the principal's lifetime. The death of the principal revokes power to the agent.

Q 7:112   What are the risks involved in providing an individual with a durable power of attorney on the principal's behalf?

The risk of providing another individual with a DPOA is that the person is able to conduct any type of business on someone else's behalf, even activities that might be considered outrageous or foolish. DPOAs are very broad and allencompassing. As a result, great care must be exercised in deciding on a suitable candidate when making this election.

Q 7:113   What is a "springing" durable power of attorney?

A "springing" durable power of attorney is a type of power of attorney that has more limitations on the execution of its powers. In a springing DPOA the agent is only permitted to exercise its authority when the principal is incapacitated. Typically, this "springing" is not triggered until the opinions of two authorized medical practitioners conclude that the principal is unable to render competent decisions on his or her own behalf.

Q 7:114   Does one need to be an attorney in order to receive a durable power of attorney?

No. An individual who receives a DPOA is considered to be the attorney-infact, meaning one who is authorized (or receives delegation powers) to represent an individual. There is no additional state requirement that one be an attorney-at-law in order to receive a durable power of attorney.

Q 7:115   Does the death of the principal terminate a durable power of attorney?

Yes. After the death of the principal the will must be probated, and an estate executor is named to complete final estate administration. Most states have a good faith exception for actions performed under a DPOA assuming in good faith that the principal was still alive. Without such an exception, the agent could be liable for any actions carried out after the actual death of the principal. For example, a trade placed in the account of the principal under a DPOA could be set aside by the executor of the estate, especially if the stock had gone down in value.

Q 7:116   Why may an inter vivos trust be a superior planning alternative to a durable power of attorney?

Investment portfolios require flexibility to manage and maintain. If the financial planner has only a DPOA, the death of the account holder renders the DPOA useless. The investment accounts are frozen by the brokerage firm until an executor is appointed and is able to act on the portfolio.

During this transition timeframe, significant changes could occur in the investment market, and the financial planner would be unable to react to changes by making any buy or sell transactions. Under an inter vivos trust, upon the death of the grantor, who likely was the first trustee, a successor trustee takes over the trust and can immediately make decisions concerning the portfolio.

The financial planner should carefully analyze the investment planning aspects involved in a specific client's situation so that the appropriate estate planning decisions can be made. A client may intelligently participate in the futures market, but how many planners want to be locked out of the futures market for an extended period of time due to the death of the client?

Fiduciaries

Q 7:117   What is a fiduciary?

A fiduciary is a person who holds or manages property for the express benefit of another. By definition the fiduciary owes the highest duty of good faith to the principal. Common examples of fiduciaries include trustees, guardians, executors, and estate administrators.

A fiduciary is not obligated to accept appointment as a fiduciary. However, once the position is accepted, the fiduciary must fulfill all of the obligations entailed in the appointment until the fiduciary resigns or is relieved from duties.

Q 7:118   What are the different types of fiduciaries?

In the estate planning context, there are three primary types of fiduciaries—the trustee, the executor, and the custodian. These fiduciaries each have differing levels of responsibility in the estate planning context.

The trustee is held to the highest standard of all of the fiduciaries. The trustee has a duty to make the trust property productive. A trustee may not sit idly by and simply invest the trust assets in a money market account. The trustee needs to determine the investment objectives of the trust, establish the asset allocation, and invest the trust assets accordingly. For example, a successor trustee to a decedent's revocable trust would need to immediately determine, in consultation with the estate's executor, how much, if any, estate tax is due on the trust assets. The trustee would then invest these assets in short-term investments (the estate tax liability must be paid within nine months of death). The trustee will then invest the balance of the assets for the benefit of the trust beneficiaries consistent with the terms of the trust document.

The executor is held to a lesser standard than a trustee. The primary duty of the executor is to safeguard the assets of the estate and ensure that all of the assets are accounted for. However, the executor generally does not have an obligation to invest assets for the long term given that most estate administrations (*i.e.*, probate) are expected to be concluded within one year's time. For example, an executor would most likely immediately liquidate a decedent's stock portfolio. The executor would be required to invest the estate's moneys into short-term investments, including money market funds. The executor would be liable if he or she invested the assets in a FDIC-insured checking account that yields less than a noninsured money market fund.

The custodian is held to a lesser standard than an executor. A custodian has no responsibility for earning a particular rate of return on assets. Rather, the function of the custodian is to safeguard assets. For example, a custodian collects the valuable assets in the inventory of the decedent's small business and transports these assets to a secure facility to prevent their theft.

Even in the world of fiduciaries, everything is relative. The financial planner should determine the type of fiduciary the planner is assisting. The planner's strategy should be consistent with the duties that the fiduciary is charged with performing.

Q 7:119   What is the source of authority for the fiduciary?

The source of a fiduciary's authority is dependent upon the type of fiduciary. A trustee derives his powers from a trust document. The trustee may be given customized duties and powers depending on how the trust document is drafted. Generally, a trustee provides annual accountings to the trust beneficiaries detailing the activities of the trust. A trustee who resigns must continue to serve until a successor is chosen or appointed by the court.

An executor derives his or her power from the court after being appointed by the testator under the testator's will. The executor's powers can be drawn both from the will and, where the will is silent, from state law. An executor must render an accounting of the estate administration to the court and must be formally discharged by the court.

Q 7:120   What are the duties of the fiduciary?

Fiduciaries are typically held to strict standards of professional conduct. A professional fiduciary in particular is held to a higher standard than that of a lay fiduciary (typically a family member), who is nevertheless still held to the standard of a person of ordinary prudence, care, and skill in performing fiduciary duties.

The following are commonly held principles governing fiduciary conduct:

- Loyalty to the beneficiaries.
- Duty to not delegate fiduciary responsibility to others if these tasks can be performed by the fiduciary.
- Accountability regarding the accounts and records of the estate.
- Full disclosure of information to the beneficiaries.
- Administration of the trusts or estates with reasonable care, skill, and diligence.

Trusts Overview

Q 7:121 What is a trust?

A trust is created when the owner of a property creates a property transfer whereby the ownership of the property is split between a trustee and one or more beneficiaries. The trustee holds the legal title to the property, and the beneficiary receives the equitable ownership in the property. The trust imposes a fiduciary relationship on the trustee to act for the behalf of the beneficiary. A trust is often created for the following purposes:

- **To save on estate taxes.** Trusts may be structured so that the beneficiaries have significant access to income and principal from the trust, when the principal (or corpus) of the estate is not included in the taxable estates of the individual beneficiaries.
- **To ensure income and asset protection.** Trusts are often set up to protect beneficiaries from themselves, whether due to a spendthrift nature or lack of financial sophistication. A trust also serves as a valuable to tool to protect assets from the beneficiaries' creditors.
- **To obtain competent and professional management of assets.** Trustees are typically selected for their financial expertise and for their fiscal responsibility to carefully manage assets for the beneficiaries in the manner intended by the donor.
- **To handle and consolidate wealth.** Trusts are typically enacted to manage sizable estates. By consolidating individual properties within a single trust, wealth may be more effectively managed and invested in order to maximize its future growth potential.

Q 7:122 Who are the parties to a trust?

The trust has numerous parties, each of which has a unique part to play in the creation and operation of a trust.

- Grantor—This is the person who creates the trust by executing a trust contract with the trustee and contributing the initial property to the trust. Depending on the circumstances under which the trust is created, there are different terms used to describe the grantor. For example, if the trust was created under a will, the term "trustor" would be the proper term of art to use. Other terms include "settler" and "creator."

- Corpus—This is the property that the trustee manages for the benefit of the beneficiaries. "Corpus" may also be referred to as the "principal" or the "res."

- Trustee—This is the fiduciary who accepts appointment to complete the objectives established under the trust document. The trustee holds legal title to the trust assets.

- Beneficiary—These are the recipients of the income and growth of the trust assets. Beneficiaries may be further divided into income and remainder beneficiaries. The trustee owes all beneficiaries under the trust an equal duty of loyalty and must balance investment decisions to treat the beneficiaries equally. While the trustee has legal title to the assets, the beneficiaries continue to hold equitable title to the assets.

Q 7:123   What are the typical tasks performed by a trustee?

The following is a general list of the tasks performed by a trustee:

- Gathering and accumulating control over all of the property.
- Segregating the trust property from his own and others' property.
- Enforcing claims and defending actions against the property.
- Preserving the property and making it productive.
- Paying income to the beneficiaries.
- Dealing impartially with multiple beneficiaries.
- Communicating with other trustees, if applicable, and acting in concert with them.
- Filing any and all applicable tax returns for the trust.

Q 7:124   What is the trustee's duty to make the property productive?

A trustee must not only keep trust property safe from loss but must also make the property productive even if that involves undertaking a reasonable level of risk in order to produce a higher return. Often, a grantor of a trust becomes emotionally involved with a specific asset during the grantor's lifetime, the retention of which defies logic and flies in the face of proper asset allocation. For example, the grantor may have a large undiversified position in one stock or a large tract of raw land that the grantor is determined will be the next great location for real estate development. The grantor decides to contribute this property to a trust under his or her will.

Once the property is in the trust, the trustee's responsibility to make the property productive controls. The trustee will most likely sell the grantor's asset immediately and take steps to properly diversify the sale proceeds. This action by the trustee may take many clients by surprise. A client who may be a grantor of a trust may think that the trustee will obviously agree with the grantor's wish to hold the asset during the grantor's lifetime and that the trustee will automatically retain the asset in the trust after the grantor's death. In fact, the trustee must take steps to immediately sell any unproductive property.

If the grantor wants to keep the specific asset, the trust document needs to specify that the trustee has the power to retain the asset. However, a professional trustee will also require that the trust document release the trustee from all liability relating to the requirement that the trustee retain the asset. The planner should discuss with the grantor client whether the client wants to insist on tying the trustee's hands in determining which assets the trustee should hold. If the trustee, who as an investment professional is charged with the fiduciary duty of investing assets for the benefit of the trust beneficiaries, does not want to retain the asset, then why would the grantor wish to retain the asset in the first place?

Q 7:125   What is the standard of care the trustee is held to in investing trust assets?

The standard of care a trustee must maintain in investing trusts assets depends on two factors. First, the trustee looks to the trust document to determine the trust powers conveyed under the trust. If the trust is silent with regard to powers, as often is the case, then the trustee refers to the applicable state statutes. States generally apply either a prudent person (man) rule or the newer (applying a higher standard) prudent investor rule. (As an aside, the first iteration of law was the "legal list" statute, which made the trustee liable for losses for any investment made that was not specifically "listed" in the statute.)

The prudent person rule requires the trustee to exercise the care that an ordinarily prudent person would exercise in the management of his or her own affairs. As a general rule, this standard is far less demanding than the prudent investor rule. However, many states, while not adopting a prudent investor rule, have substantially raised the bar on their existing prudent person rule by requiring the trustee to exercise care in diversifying assets and balancing risk and return.

The prudent investor rule is the latest iteration in the standard of care that a trustee must exercise in the management of investment decisions. Under this standard, the trustee must follow formal investment consulting procedures in investing trust assets. Preferably, these procedures should be documented in writing. Knowledge of modern portfolio theory (MPT) is required to successfully discharge the trustee's duties. (See Q 7:135.)

One substantive change in the standard of care under prudent investor rule is that, unlike under the prudent person rule, delegation of the investment powers to a more skilled advisor is encouraged. Consequently, although financial planners are held to a higher standard of care under the prudent investor rule, the planner has ample opportunities to solicit business from trustees, especially in assisting trustees in formalizing their investment policy decisions.

Q 7:126   How is a trustee replaced?

The first source of authority on replacing a trustee may be found in the trust document itself. Often, the grantor will have established standards for permitting the trust beneficiaries to remove a trustee and appoint a successor trustee to the trust. For example, the trust document may allow a majority of the beneficiaries to terminate Trustee X in favor of another trustee.

If the trust document is silent regarding a trustee's replacement, then state law can be invoked. Often, the law is heavily weighted in favor of the trustee. Typical grounds for removal may include the gross negligence. This is not surprising: a beneficiary may not appreciate a trustee denying demands for additional funds, contrary to the purpose of the trust, which is to retain and protect wealth. The beneficiary may consequently allege that a trustee is incompetent in an effort to replace the conservative trustee with one more willing to distribute funds to an insistent beneficiary.

The problem with attempting to dislodge a trustee who does not want to leave is that the trustee is entitled to use trust funds to pay attorney fees to defend against the lawsuit by the beneficiary. This is tantamount to having the trustee shoot at the beneficiary with the beneficiary's own bullets. Many beneficiaries have seen the trustee spend the last dollar of the trust in an effort to prevent his or her removal. It should be borne in mind that the grantor named a trustee in the first place; otherwise the grantor would have left the assets outright to the beneficiaries. The trustee is supposed to defend the castle walls of the trust even against the trust's own beneficiaries.

Q 7:127   Are there any adverse consequences of empowering the grantor or the beneficiaries to remove the trustee?

The degree of power that either a grantor or a beneficiary has to remove a trustee may create unintended estate tax consequences. At issue is whether the successor trustee would be subordinate to the grantor or the beneficiary. In essence, if the trustee is the night janitor in grantor's employ who makes $20,000 per year and the annual trustee's fees would be $100,000, there is an excellent chance that the janitor/trustee is subordinate to the grantor.

If the trustee is subordinate to the grantor or beneficiary, the assets of the trust will likely be included in the grantor's or beneficiary's estate on the basis that the subordinate trustee is the puppet and the controlling grantor or beneficiary is the puppet master. Therefore, the exercise of powers by the trustee is the equivalent of the exercise of the powers by the grantor or beneficiary. If any of these powers are sufficient to trigger inclusion in the taxable estate of the grantor or beneficiary, then the grantor or beneficiary must pay the full price for de facto control—and be taxed in their respective estates at death.

Q 7:128   What is the impact of the *Wahl* decision?

What is the effect of removing one nonsubservient trustee in favor of a second nonsubservient trustee? The IRS argued unsuccessfully for years that the power of a trustee or beneficiary to remove one trustee in favor of another trustee still caused the taxable inclusion in the estate of the grantor or beneficiary exercising the power. In the *Wahl* decision, the IRS finally acquiesced (*i.e.*, the IRS declared the taxpayers victorious and refused to pursue further litigation against other taxpayers on the issue). Shortly after *Wahl* was decided, the IRS issued a Revenue Ruling proclaiming that one corporate trustee can be removed in favor of another corporate trustee without risking possible inclusion in the estate of the grantor or beneficiary in possession of the power of removal.

Interestingly, the court in *Wahl* did not specifically limit its holding to corporate trustees; instead the opinion focused on nonsubservient trustees, both corporate and individual. This highlights the importance of a financial planner working with a competent team of professionals so that no planning opportunities or strategies are overlooked.

Q 7:129   What is a "spendthrift" clause in a trust?

A spendthrift clause prohibits a trust beneficiary from assigning (*e.g.*, selling or pledging) the beneficiary's interest in the trust. Without this provision, a trust beneficiary could assign his or her lifetime income interest (which could easily be for more than 40 years for a 40-year-old beneficiary) to a third party for a lump sum payment.

A grantor includes a spendthrift clause in the trust document for two primary reasons. First, the grantor believes that the trust beneficiaries may not be capable or responsible enough to manage the money by themselves without the supervision and professional assistance of a trustee. Often, beneficiaries who suddenly inherit wealth squander large sums in very short periods of time. The spendthrift clause eliminates this concern. Second, this provision shields the beneficiary against creditors. For example, a beneficiary of a trust is a well-respected physician. However, as a physician, the beneficiary is in a high liability field and may lose his personal assets through a lawsuit for medical negligence.

Assume that as a beneficiary of the trust the physician is entitled to a life income from the trust with the remainder interest in the trust already vested in the physician's children. While the physician's creditors may be able to perfect a judgment against the physician's income interest in the trust, the remainder interest will pass on to the physician's children free from the creditor's claims. The value of this liability protection should not be underestimated. Without the spendthrift clause, the creditor would likely be able to take everything.

Q 7:130   What is the situs of a trust?

The situs of a trust is the state in which the trust instrument is established. A trust may be established in any jurisdiction regardless of where the grantor resides. However, the requirements of a particular state's laws must be fulfilled, which usually involves appointing a trustee who is a resident in the given state.

Presumably, the tax laws of the state where the trust has situs apply, so where a grantor wants to locate a trust—in a high tax jurisdiction versus a low tax jurisdiction—should be taken into consideration.

Q 7:131   What is the advantage to establishing a trust in Alaska?

Alaska has recently established itself as a trust-friendly jurisdiction. Previously, to obtain the benefits now promised in Alaska, grantors had to move money to offshore jurisdictions, which posed their own unique set of problems, including possible increased IRS scrutiny. The Alaska trust statutes are drafted to convey the following benefits:

- **Protection from creditors.** Alaska is currently the only state that allows creditor protection on a self-settled trust, which is a trust where the grantor establishes a trust for his or her own benefit. Typically, a creditor may be able to attach funds in a self-settled trust arrangement. The Alaska statute purportedly protects these assets from seizure by the grantor's creditors. The effectiveness of this statute is not likely to be determined until the U.S. Supreme Court rules on this constitutional issue, specifically concerning the full faith and credit clause. It will be interesting to see how this case turns out (probably a decade or more from now).

- **No rule against perpetuities.** Alaska has statutorily repealed the common law rules against perpetuities. A trust with situs in Alaska may now continue into perpetuity. Care should be taken in drafting this type of trust, given that the perpetual existence of the trust may present its own unique problems. At the very least, a dissolution clause should be inserted in the trust so that the trust can be terminated should it become too cumbersome to administer effectively. This is quite foreseeable for a vehicle that could be in existence for several hundred years or even longer.

- **Titling of assets as community property.** Alaska permits assets to be titled as community property by statute even if the spouses have never lived in a community property state. The primary advantage is that jointly titled property (*e.g.*, property owned by joint tenants with rights of survivorship or tenants by the entirety property) owned by spouses will receive only a onehalf income tax basis step-up on the death of the first spouse. Community property in community property states receives a full and total step-up for income tax purposes on the death of the first spouse. This one aspect of Alaska law could result in potentially millions of dollars in income tax savings for clients with low basis stock positions. The surviving spouse could sell the stock and diversify the position immediately after the death of the other spouse rather than having to wait until the second spouse dies to sell the position without income tax consequences.

- **No state income taxation.** Given that a trust located in Alaska can continue on into perpetuity, it is an excellent idea to use a state such as Alaska as situs when the fact of no state income tax is important.

Planners should remember that the Alaska trust statutes have not yet been tested in court. Therefore there is not a high degree of certainty with which to craft sophisticated estate and asset protection planning strategies. However, the risk of transferring assets to an Alaska trust is substantially less than undertaking employment of a foreign trustee.

Q 7:132   What is a "total return unitrust"?

A total return unitrust (TRU) is a trust concept that embraces modern portfolio theory. Rather than focusing on traditional fiduciary accounting standards, which define income based on dividends and interest, the TRU pays out a fixed percentage of trust assets during the year to the trust income beneficiaries. The TRU technique effectively allocates a proportionate share of interest, dividends, and capital gains to the trust income beneficiaries. In the extreme a TRU may invest entirely in equities rather than in a more balanced allocation between stocks and bonds.

Estate Taxes

Q 7:133   What is the general rule regarding payment of estate taxes?

The general rule regarding the payment of estate taxes is that all amounts are payable within nine months of the date of death. The biggest problem with payment in this time frame is that the estate may contain illiquid assets that cannot be sold in time to supply sufficient consideration to pay all of the estate taxes due.

Q 7:134   May alternate valuation dates be used for the payment of estate taxes?

Yes, if assets have depreciated in value within six months after the date of death, the estate may pay the taxes due on the lesser value of the estate. The only way the estate may elect the alternate valuation date (AVD) is when less tax is due. Consequently, a nontaxable estate may never elect the AVD.

Q 7:135   How are assets valued for AVD?

One of the principal methods of valuing assets for AVD is fair market value when sold within the six-month period after death. The assets are then valued at date of sale rather than date of death. If the assets are considered "wasting assets"(*e.g.*, the principal balance on a mortgage receivable or an annuity) then those assets are valued on the date of death. Other assets (stocks, bonds, etc.) that may have depreciated in value after the date of death may be valued at the date of sale for AVD purposes.

Q 7:136   What is the three-year rule for estate taxation purposes?

Simply put, the three-year rule states that even if an individual transfers a property interest during lifetime, that interest is includable in the transferor's estate if the transferor dies within three years following the date of the transfer.

Q 7:137   To what situations does the three-year rule apply?

The three-year rule applies only to the following five situations:

1. Section 2036—Gratuitous lifetime transfers where the decedent retained the income or control over the income.
2. Section 2037—Gratuitous lifetime transfers conditioned on surviving the decedent.
3. Section 2038—Gratuitous lifetime transfers in which the decedent retained the right to alter, amend, or revoke the gift.
4. Section 2042—Life insurance in which the decedent possessed incidents of ownership or that was payable to or for the benefit of the decedent's estate
5. Gift taxes paid within three years of death.

Basis Step-up Issues in Estate Planning

Q 7:138   What is the income tax basis for assets received from the estate of a decedent?

The income tax basis for assets received from the estate of a decedent varies according following conditions:

- *Under community property law,* when one spouse dies, the assets of the surviving spouse receive a 100 percent basis step-up in all of the underlying assets.

- *In a joint tenancy created under common law,* when one spouse dies, the assets received by the surviving spouse receive a 50 percent basis step-up under Section 1014.

- *In a nonspousal joint tenancy,* if one joint tenant dies, there is a rebuttable presumption that on the death of the first co-tenant, all of the property is included in the decedent's estate, thus entitling the surviving tenant to a 100 percent basis step-up. If the decedent's estate rebuts this presumption, then the only portion includable in decedent's estate is equal to the consideration provided in purchasing the property. Consequently, the amount of basis step-up is equal to the amount of property includable in decedent's estate.

Property Valuation

Q 7:139   What is fair market value?

Fair market value is the price at which property would change hands between a willing buyer and a willing seller, neither being under any compulsion either to buy or to sell and both having reasonable knowledge of relevant facts.

Q 7:140   How are stocks valued in an estate?

Stocks are valued at the average of the high and the low trading prices on an established stock exchange on the decedent's date of death. The stocks are not valued on the closing price of the trading day. If the decedent dies on a nontrading day (Saturday or Sunday), the stock price is valued at the average of the high and low trading price on the last trading date preceding the death and the next opening trading date following the death.

Q 7:141   How are bonds valued in an estate?

Bonds are valued at their fair market value on the decedent's date of death. Remember that part of a bond is accrued interest at the decedent's date of death and the interest portion is interest in respect of a decedent. Interest in respect of a decedent does not receive a basis step-up at death.

Q 7:142   How are household goods valued in an estate?

There is a presumption in the Internal Revenue Code that all household assets belong to the husband and hence are taxable in the husband's estate upon his death. This issue can be controlled through use of an affidavit specifying which spouse owns which property in the home. For example, the wife owns a diamond ring, and the husband owns an antique pocket watch.

Powers of Appointment

Q 7:143   What is a power of appointment?

A power of appointment is a right provided in a will to allow the donee to name the recipient (also known as the appointee) of the donor's property at a future point in time. This power of appointment is really the authority given to another party to dispose of one's property. This measure is generally undertaken when the estate owner would like to put the responsibility of managing the estate and making appropriate decisions on the estate's disposal in the hands of an objective third party. It is often used as a means of obtaining professional objective advice and avoiding internal family conflict.

Q 7:144   What if an individual does not appoint an independent trustee?

If an individual appoints a trustee who is seen to be under that individual's direct control (*e.g.*, an employee or other subordinate), the entire amount of the assets are recaptured in the individual's estate, and the benefits of the trust are forgone.

Q 7:145   What is a general power of appointment?

A general power of appointment provides the individual with the ability to appoint assets to the individual himself or herself, to the individual's estate, to the individual's creditors, or to creditors of the individual's estate. If one or all of the four of these individuals may be appointed, 100 percent of the assets over which that power is held will be includable in the individual's estate at death.

Q 7:146   What is a special power of appointment?

A special or limited power of appointment provides the ability to withdraw each year the greater of 5 percent of the trust corpus or $5,000 without any adverse tax consequences.

Q 7:147   What happens when an individual dies with an unexercised power of appointment?

The position that the IRS takes on this issue is that the amounts that were not withdrawn (*e.g.*, $5,000 or 5 percent of the trust corpus) are treated as a gift to the trust and are hence includable in the estate of the decedent.

Q 7:148   What is a planning technique to avoid negative tax consequences of unexercised powers of appointment?

One way to avoid this possibility is to specify a particular date per year (*e.g.*, every January 5) to withdraw the 5 percent or $5,000 from the trust. The date setting makes it easier for the individual to remember to withdraw the funds annually. In addition, if the individual dies on any date other than the withdrawal date (January 5 in our example) the funds are not includable in the estate of the decedent.

QTIP Trusts

Q 7:149   What is a terminable interest property?

A terminable interest property is a property interest that terminates at the death of the donee.

Q 7:150   What is a qualified terminable interest property (QTIP) election?

QTIP is a type of tax election that affords terminable interest property with an unlimited marital deduction. Normally, terminable interest property would not be eligible for an unlimited marital deduction. For example, without the QTIP election, if a husband leaves his wife a life estate (*i.e.*, "all income to my wife for life") the husband's estate would pay estate taxes on the full amount of the transfer. With a QTIP election no estate taxes would be due at the death of the husband; they would be due on the death of the wife.

Q 7:151 What is a QTIP trust?

QTIP trusts are marital trusts that use the QTIP election. QTIP trusts are designed for married couples to provide the surviving spouse with the right to income for life. However, one of the provisions of a QTIP trust allows the first spouse to die to control how the property will be distributed on the death of the other spouse. In a QTIP trust the estate pays no estate tax on the first death; the estate elects to pay estate tax on the second death.

Q 7:152 Why would an individual use a QTIP trust?

Following the death of a spouse, property passes to a remainder person. Normally in estate planning the decedent spouse names his or her children as the remainder beneficiaries. This ensures that the surviving spouse cannot disinherit the decedent's intended beneficiaries through inter vivos transfers.

Q 7:153 When would an individual not want to use a QTIP trust?

A person may wish to avoid the use of a QTIP trust as an estate planning technique when at least one of the following conditions exists:

- **When the other spouse is likely to die very soon after the first spouse to die.** In this situation the estate taxes on the combined estates are likely to exceed the taxes due if each estate has been taxed separately.
- **If there are assets in the first estate that are likely to experience significant appreciation in value.** In this situation it may be more cost-effective to pay estate tax on the death of the first spouse and transfer any subsequent appreciation to the next generation rather than allowing the appreciation to accumulate in the estate of the spouse.
- **If the surviving spouse does not need the income following the death of the first spouse.** In this situation it would be advantageous to pass the estate directly on to younger beneficiaries, who would then delay paying additional estate taxes on the property until their deaths, which would likely occur many more years in the future.

Q 7:154 What is a reverse QTIP election?

Reverse QTIP elections are becoming an increasingly popular means of maximizing the generation-skipping transfer (GST) tax exemption ($2,000,000 for 2006). The GST is the highest marginal tax rate in the Tax Code for estate tax transfers. As a result, it is an essential estate planning technique to maximize all possible GST exemption options.

A reverse QTIP is the reversionary interest. It is reversionary because the estate is picking up the GST exemption on the first spouse. In this way there is a reversion to the first spouse's original GST exemption. The estate is thus treated (solely for GST purposes) as if it were still a part of the decedent's taxable estate. As a result, the estate is able to claim both the marital deduction and the GST exemption, maximizing tax savings.

In order to take advantage of the reversionary QTIP election it may be necessary to create two separate QTIP trusts, as the law mandates that reverse QTIP elections may only be made to a separate trust. One trust is set up to take advantage of the marital deduction, and the other to take advantage of the GST exemption.

Marital and Bypass Trusts

Q 7:155   What is a marital trust?

A marital trust is a type of trust that qualifies for the unlimited marital deduction, typically through use of the QTIP election.

Q 7:156   What is a bypass trust?

A bypass trust, also known as a nonmarital trust, is a type of trust that does not qualify for the unlimited marital deduction. The intended purpose of a bypass trust is to make full use of a decedent spouse's $2 million unified credit.

Q 7:157   When would someone use a bypass trust versus a marital trust?

In a well-rounded estate plan an individual would typically use both trust options for estates greater than $2 million. The first million dollars of the estate is typically placed in a bypass trust to make full use of the unified credit, and the remainder of the estate is placed in a marital trust to qualify for the unlimited marital deduction through use of a QTIP election.

Life Insurance Trusts

Q 7:158   What is an ILIT?

An ILIT (irrevocable life insurance trust) is a type of irrevocable (one that may not be changed) trust that owns life insurance that typically insures the life of the grantor. Generally, there will be no income tax returns to file on the trust, given that all earnings on the life insurance policy are tax-deferred for federal income tax purposes.

Q 7:159   What are the advantages to establishing an ILIT?

Because in an ILIT trust, the trust, not the grantor, possess all incidents of ownership in the life insurance policy, the death benefit is not included in the taxable estate of the decedent grantor. Consequently, an irrevocable life insurance trust may serve as a valuable estate planning tool as a means of avoiding estate tax.

Q 7:160 May Crummey powers be used with an ILIT?

Yes. Use of Crummey powers with an ILIT is a common planning technique. (*See* Q 7:66.)

Grantor-Retained Trusts

Q 7:161 What is an estate-freezing technique?

An estate-freezing technique is used to freeze the present value of an estate in order to shift the growth in the estate to beneficiaries, typically the next generation. Currently, there are no more freezing techniques per se available to a property owner. However, excess appreciation may be transferred out of the estate. A grantor-retained annuity trust may be used as an acceptable method of freezing the estate.

Q 7:162 What is a grantor-retained trust?

A grantor-retained trust is a type of irrevocable trust into which the grantor places assets. The grantor then retains an interest in these assets for a fixed period of years. At the end of this time, the principal of the trust then passes to a noncharitable beneficiary.

A grantor-retained trust is often referred to as a "defective trust" because the trust itself does not exist for federal income tax purposes. It does, however, exist for federal estate and gift tax purposes. All income on the trust, if any, is taxable personally to the grantor. This method is the opposite of the general rule in trusts where the trust itself pays income tax. The following three types of trusts are examples of grantor-retained trusts: GRAT, GRUT, and GRIT. (*See* Q 7:172.)

Q 7:163 What is a GRAT?

A GRAT or grantor-retained annuity trust is a type of grantor-retained trust that makes a fixed dollar payment annually to the grantor for the number of years specified in the trust. For example, if the original trust contribution was $100,000 and the fixed annual payment rate is 6 percent of that original amount, then the grantor will receive a payment of $6,000 annually regardless of the rate that the principal may have appreciated or depreciated in value.

Q 7:164 What is a GRUT?

A GRUT, or grantor-retained unitrust, is a type of grantor-retained trust that makes a variable percentage payout to the grantor for the number of years specified in the trust. Unlike a GRAT, which makes annual fixed periodic payments, GRUTs base their annual payouts on the actual value of the principal as determined annually.

If the principal of the trust increased over the year, then the payout for that year is greater than that of the previous year. Conversely, if the value of the principal fell over the year, then that year's annual payout would be reduced. For example, using the previous illustration, if the original trust contribution was $100,000 and the fixed annual payment rate was 6 percent of the current value of the trust as determined annually, then the grantor may receive a $6,000 payment in Year 1. However, in Year 2, the trust is valued at $150,000. The payout for Year 2 would then be increased to $9,000.

Q 7:165   What is a GRIT?

A GRIT, or grantor-retained income trust, is a type of trust in which the grantor payout is based on the income generated by the trust. Because some types of assets in the trust may never generate "income," these types of trusts have now been greatly limited by IRC Section 2702. GRITS may no longer be used in lineal family transfers (*e.g.*, from grandparent to grandchild) with certain exceptions, but may still currently be used in nonlineal family transfers (*e.g.*, aunt and uncle to their niece or nephew).

Q 7:166   What is the reciprocal trust doctrine?

The reciprocal trust doctrine is an attempt to close up a loophole in GRITs that could effectively allow lineal transfers. Under one possible scenario, before the Section 2702 ruling a parent who wanted to transfer a gift to her child could pair up with a brother who also wanted to transfer a gift to his child. Together they would then transfer gifts to each other's children. In essence, each would in effect be making an equal lineal transfer under a GRIT, which prohibits lineal transfers.

The reciprocal trust doctrine states that to the extent that the consideration on the transfers is mutual, it is treated as if it were a lineal transfer, hence disqualifying the transfers under a GRIT.

QPRTs

Q 7:167   What is a QPRT?

A QPRT, or qualified personal residence trust, is a type of GRIT in which lineal transfers are allowed. Often referred to as a "house GRIT," QPRTs are limited to transfers of personal residences. The limit on funding is one residence per grantor. Married couples are allowed a total of three residences, one per individual and one per couple.

Q 7:168   May the grantor in a QPRT buy back the residence?

No. The grantor is unable to buy back the residence from the trust. However, the grantor may pay rent to the trust.

Q 7:169   What is the advantage of a rental agreement under a QPRT?

While the rent is personal and nondeductible to the tenants (typically the parents) and treated as taxable income to the landlord (typically the children), the children are then able to depreciate the home. The upkeep and maintenance on the property is also deductible as a business expense under IRC Section 212 if the property is being kept as an investment. If the property is being kept as a trade or business Section 162 deductions apply. The income tax rates on the rent received by the children as a whole are lower than estate or gift tax, thus making a rental agreement a tax-advantageous transaction in estate planning.

Defective Trusts

Q 7:170   What is a defective trust?

Defective trusts (also known as grantor trusts) are trusts that are created through the intentional violation of the grantor trust rules for favorable income tax treatment found in Sections 671–677 of the Internal Revenue Code. The term "defective" in this context refers to a trust that is defective for income tax purposes only, not for estate and gift tax purposes. Defective trusts are treated as grantor trusts so long as the grantor is still alive. (*See* Q 7:164.)

Q 7:171   What rules are most commonly violated in defective trusts?

IRC Section 677, the rule that the income of the trust may not be used to pay life insurance premiums on a policy covering the life of the grantor, is a common example of a violation of trust treatment for income tax purposes. Consequently, virtually all ILITs are treated as defective trusts. IRC Sections 672–676 concern certain powers retained by the grantor, some of which also cause estate tax inclusion. These violations are less common.

Living Trusts

Q 7:172   What is a revocable living trust?

An *inter vivos* or living trust is a revocable trust created during the lifetime of the grantor. The grantor places his or her property into a trust to be managed by a trustee for a specified period of time or until the death of the grantor.

Q 7:173   What are the advantages of creating a living trust?

Living trusts are commonly used for the purpose of bypassing probate. However, the creation of a living trust may also be indicated to protect against the legal incompetency or incapacity of the grantor or the beneficiaries.

Q 7:174   May a revocable trust become irrevocable?

Yes, a revocable trust becomes irrevocable on the death or incapacity of the grantor or on the grantor's relinquishment of all property rights and title during lifetime.

Q 7:175   Is there any income tax advantage to establishing a living trust?

No. For federal income tax purposes all income from the trust is taxed to the grantor at the grantor's individual income tax rate, because the grantor is considered to be the owner of the trust corpus pursuant to Sections 672–676 of the Internal Revenue Code.

Q 7:176   What is the doctrine of merger?

The doctrine of merger states that if the same individual serves as the grantor, trustee, and remainder beneficiary, the trust does not exist.

Charitable Trusts

Q 7:177   How are charitable trusts generally structured?

Charitable trusts, also known as charitable split interests trusts, are generally structured to split the funds between both charitable and noncharitable beneficiaries. Depending on how the trust is structured, annual payments for a specified term are received by either the charitable or noncharitable beneficiary, with the corpus (or remainder) of the value of the trust then transferred to the other beneficiary at the end of the term.

Q 7:178   What is a charitable remainder trust?

A charitable remainder trust is a type of charitable split interest trust in which the charity receives the remainder interest of the trust fund after a specified term. Typically, the trust has made periodic annual payments to another non-charitable beneficiary, such as the donor or another family member.

Q 7:179   What is a CRAT?

A CRAT, or charitable remainder annuity trust, is a type of charitable remainder trust that provides a fixed dollar annual payment to the charity.

Q 7:180   What is a CRUT?

A CRUT, or charitable remainder unitrust, is a type of charitable remainder trust that provides a variable payment to the charity based on the value of the trust as determined annually. If the trust fund has depreciated, then the actual payout amount is reduced. Conversely, if the funds have appreciated in value, then the actual payout amount for that year is increased.

Q 7:181 What are the advantages of implementing a charitable remainder trust?

The donor receives a current income tax deduction based on the amount of money initially transferred into the trust. The life interest (*i.e.*, the periodic annual payments that can be made back to the donor) is valued to the taxpayer and the remainder interest is valued to the charity. The present value of the remainder interest is deductible to the taxpayer for federal income tax purposes.

Q 7:182 In what type of scenario would an individual use a charitable remainder trust?

Charitable remainder trusts provide a tax-favored means of sheltering highly appreciated property prior to its sale. In a charitable remainder trust the money flows into the trust when the property is sold. In a typical scenario, individuals have highly appreciated stock or land first put into a trust. When they later sell the property, any of the capital gains are deferred until the money is withdrawn from the trust.

Q 7:183 How is money flowing out of a charitable remainder trust taxable to a living donor recipient?

In order to conceptualize the tax implications on trust withdrawals it is helpful to think in terms of a bucket analogy. In the charitable remainder trust, there are basically four buckets of money, and one bucket of money must be exhausted before money is taken from the next.

- **In the first bucket is any ordinary income.** For example, a property is sold, generating $1 million in capital gains, and then reinvested at 5 percent, generating $50,000 in interest income. When a distribution is made, that $50,000 is the first $50,000 in taxable earnings to be drawn out of the trust.
- **In the second bucket are capital gains.** For example, with $1 million in a stock position in which a shareholder paid $1 for the stock itself, the additional $1 million or so that the stock is worth is subject to capital gains. These amounts are the second sums to carry out in terms of carrying out the tax attributes to the donor who is receiving the distribution from the trust every year.
- **In the third bucket is tax freeze.** The taxpayer would segregate the funds in a tax freeze because there potentially will be alternative minimum tax implications.
- **In the fourth bucket is the tax-free return of corpus principal.**

Q 7:184　What is a charitable lead trust?

A charitable lead trust is a type of charitable split interest trust in which the charity receives only the periodic annual payments from the trust. After the specified period of time has elapsed, then the remainder interest of the trust is transferred to the noncharitable beneficiary.

Q 7:185　In what type of scenario would an individual use a charitable lead trust?

Charitable lead trusts are normally set up post-mortem. A charitable lead trust created while the donor is still alive is considered a grantor trust. It produces income that goes directly to the charity. Generally most individuals do not wish to pay income tax based on the distributions.

Generation Skipping

Q 7:186　What is a generation skipping trust?

A generation skipping trust, more commonly referred to as a generation skipping transfer, is a transfer of property from an individual's estate to the estate of a beneficiary who is at least two or more generations removed from the transferor. For example, a grandparent sets up a trust naming a grandchild, grandniece, or great-grandnephew as the beneficiary. The generation skipping transfer technique was originally implemented as a technique to avoid federal gift and estate taxes by keeping property out of the taxable estates of the second generation. The trust allowed the beneficiaries to make use of the inherited property while enjoying protection from creditors, divorce courts, and bankruptcy.

Q 7:187　When would a generation skipping trust be used?

Generation skipping trusts are used when one or more of the following conditions are present:

- When the client wishes to make a gift directly to the grandchildren, instead of gifting or entrusting the property to the parents.
- When the client's children already have substantial estates of their own and wish to avoid an increase to the size of their taxable estates.
- When the client's children are no longer living and the client is interested in passing property down to a subsequent generation.
- When the client is interested in insulating the property transfer from potential loss in divorce or bankruptcy proceedings.

Q 7:188　Are taxes applicable to property transferred in a generation skipping trust?

Yes. In particular the GSTT (generation skipping transfer tax) was specifically created to obtain at least one transfer tax per generation. The GSTT applies only if the transfer avoids estate and gift tax on the "skipped genera-tion." Following the Tax Reform Act of 1986, the IRS imposes a flat tax rate of 55 percent on all taxable transfers. For 2005, the amount is capped at the maximum estate tax rate of 47 percent. In addition to the GSTT, estate or gift tax may also be applicable on the transfers. Consequently, the transfer could conceivably generate enough taxes to completely negate the value of the trans-fer or even create a situation where money is owed in taxes beyond the value of the gift.

Q 7:189   May generation skipping transfers be exempted from GST?

Yes, the GST exemption, which is indexed annually for inflation, is $2,000,000 for 2006.

Q 7:190   What are the three types of transfers that may be taxable for GST?

The following three types of transfers may be taxable for GST:

2. **Direct skips.** These are also known as outright gifts.
3. **Taxable distributions.** These are typically distributions from a trust to a skipped person.
4. **Taxable terminations.** This occurs when a trust terminates and pays out its remainder to a skipped person.

Q 7:191   What is a skipped person?

A skipped person in the family context is an individual who is one generation below the transferor. Transfers that occur from an individual in one generation to an individual more than one generation below (*i.e.*, a grandchild) are subject to GST.

Q 7:192   What is the predeceased parent exception for GST?

If the parent is not alive at the time of the transfer to the grandchild, for example, no GST is due on the transfer. However, the IRS must determine when the transfer occurred. If the money was transferred into the trust when the parent was still alive, GST still applies to any amounts paid out of the trust to the grandchild.

Q 7:193   What is the GST requirement in nonfamily situations?

A transfer to an individual who is more than 37½ years younger than the transferor is deemed to be a generation skipping transfer subject to GST. Note that there is no generation skipping transfer in a marital context (*i.e.*, between an older transferor and a much younger spouse).

Q 7:194 Is there any point in planning for an excess of the GST transfer amount?

Absolutely not. It is possible that among the estate tax, the gift tax, and the GST, the individual may effectively lose the entire value of a transfer to payment of taxes. Remember that the GST applies in addition to any estate tax and the gift tax amounts already applied.

Q 7:195 What is the EGTRRA and how does it affect GST and estate tax exemptions?

The EGTRRA, or Economic Growth and Tax Relief Reconciliation Act of 2001, repeals both the generation skipping transfer tax and the estate tax for one year in 2010. Following 2010, the GSTT exemption and the unified credit both return to their original 2001 levels of $1 million for each.

Q 7:196 What is the ETIP?

The ETIP or estate tax inclusion period is a period of disqualification during which time a transferor may not allocate any GST exemption. This period of time is equivalent to the amount of time that the underlying transfer would be recapturable in the transferor's estate for federal estate tax purposes.

Q 7:197 What are some examples of the ETIP exclusion?Example 1: If the insured transfers an existing life insurance policy, the exclusion period is three years subsequent to the date of the transfer.

Example 2: If the transferor puts a vacation home in a QPRT for a term of ten years following the transfer, the grantor may not allocate his or her GST exemption until the end of the trust term. Stated simply, if the grantor dies at some point within the term of the trust, the home is includable in the grantor's estate. Hence in this example the 10-year term is considered the "inclusion period." (*See* Q 7:167–169.)

Dynasty Trusts

Q 7:198 What is a dynasty trust?

A dynasty trust is a generation skipping trust designed to exist for the maximum period permitted by applicable state law (the rule against perpetuities). (*See* Q 7:201.) The intent of the trust is to pay a life income to each succeeding generation of the family while retaining the corpus in the trust so that the corpus of the trust will pass estate tax-free to subsequent generations.

Q 7:199   What drafting provisions should be included in a dynasty trust?

When drafting a dynasty trust, the following provisions should be included:

1. **A merger clause.** A merger clause allows different portions of the trust to be merged together.
2. **A dissolution clause.** A dissolution clause allows the trustee to split portions of the trust.

This clause permits a trustee to split the trust into disparate portions and recombine the portions at a later time. This can be useful given that a certain branch of a family may vehemently disagree over how a trust is being managed and may want to pursue a different means of holding funds. Rather than force these beneficiaries into the fold, the trustee may split this group off from the other beneficiaries. At a later date, this dissident group could rejoin the trust, provided the trustee consents. Given the undoubted changes that will occur in the future, this type of provision is absolutely essential to the effective administration of a dynasty trust.

Rule Against Perpetuities

Q 7:200   What is the rule against perpetuities?

The rule against perpetuities (RAP) states that an interest must vest in the hands of the ultimate transferee within an applicable period of time or the interest will fail, thereby vesting immediately. The purpose behind this rule was to prevent decedents from "ruling beyond the grave."

Q 7:201   What is the common law rule against perpetuities?

The common law rule against perpetuities states that an interest will fail unless it vests within a "life in being" plus 21 years. Lives in being include persons alive at the time the interest was created, which includes children in gestation. Unborn children count for the purposes of this rule.

Q 7:202   Does the common law rule against perpetuities apply in all states?

No. A state may repeal the common law rule against perpetuities by statute, which, for example, Alaska has done. Thus, a trust created in that state may exist indefinitely.

Chapter 8

Characteristics of Retirement Plans

For many clients, one of the most important questions is "Will I be able to retire in comfort?" This chapter discusses the various types of retirement and pension plans, plus IRAs and annuities, all to help the financial planner choose the right course for the client.

Q 8:1   What is a retirement plan?

A retirement plan is any plan or program maintained by an employer and/or an employee organization that provides retirement income to employees or results in the deferral of income by employees for periods extending to the end of employment or beyond, regardless of how plan contributions or benefits are calculated or how benefits are distributed.

Retirement planning can offer a variety of benefits to both employers and employees. As one of the most sought after employee benefits following health insurance, retirement plans serve as a powerful incentive to employers to attract and retain a superior quality workforce. Retirement plans also offer attractive tax-deferral opportunities for both owners and highly compensated employees. Profit-based and stock purchase retirement plans provide an added incentive to employers by encouraging direct employee productivity through plan participation.

Retirement plans in general fall into two basic categories: qualified and nonqualified. Beyond these two classifications, we will also discuss a third category that includes personal or individual retirement plans, commonly referred to as IRAs.

Characteristics of Qualified Plans

Q 8:2   What is a qualified retirement plan?

A qualified plan is a retirement plan that is afforded special tax treatment for meeting more stringent Internal Revenue Code requirements. With its goal of serving as a savings tool for retirement, a qualified plan allows the employer to deduct annual plan contributions and employees are able to defer the income until receiving the distributions.

The government loses a great deal of money annually in lost tax revenues as a result of the available tax benefits in qualified retirement plans. Stringent federal regulatory and statutory requirements were established in an attempt to ensure that plan benefits go where they are needed most. Regulation is primarily aimed at discouraging plans that discriminate in favor of highly

Retirement Planning Flow Chart

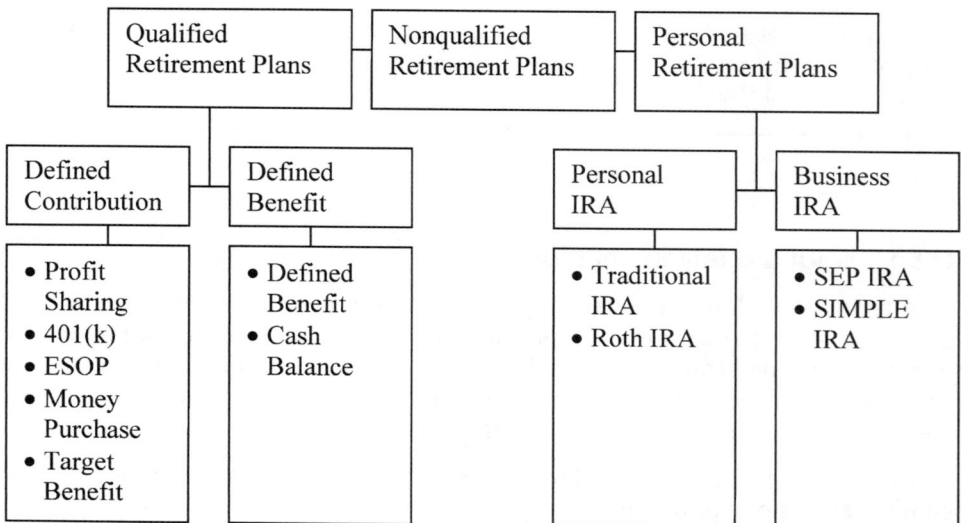

Qualified Retirement Plans	Nonqualified Retirement Plans	Personal Retirement Plans

Defined Contribution	Defined Benefit	Personal IRA	Business IRA
• Profit Sharing • 401(k) • ESOP • Money Purchase • Target Benefit	• Defined Benefit • Cash Balance	• Traditional IRA • Roth IRA	• SEP IRA • SIMPLE IRA

compensated or executive employees who have other sources of retirement income. In addition, as retirement plans typically receive a large amount of funding, federal regulation ensures that the funds set aside for plan benefits are managed in the exclusive interest of plan participants and beneficiaries. The administration of qualified retirement plans is governed concurrently by both federal tax law and federal ERISA law.

Q 8:3   What are the advantages of a qualified retirement plan?

- The employer is allowed an immediate tax deduction for amounts contributed to the plan for a particular year.
- The employee plan participant pays no current income tax on the amounts contributed by the employer on the employee's behalf.
- Earnings are tax-exempt. This allows for tax-free accumulation of income and gains on investments, which can significantly increase the effective investment return on plan assets.
- Reduced income tax may apply to lump-sum distributions to certain participants.
- Income taxes on certain types of distributions may be deferred by rolling over the distribution to an individual retirement account (IRA) or other qualified or nonqualified retirement plan.
- Income taxes on certain types of distributions to a deceased participant's spouse may be deferred by rollover distributions to an IRA.
- Installment or annuity payments are taxed only when they are received.

Q 8:4   What is ERISA?

ERISA is an acronym that stands for Employee Retirement Income Security Act of 1974. Congress intended ERISA to be the sole source of law regulating employee benefit plans to establish national uniformity in plan administration. This measure was an attempt to simplify plan administration. By enacting federal legislation, plan administrators would no longer need to focus on the complexities involved in complying with the laws of each individual state.

ERISA was enacted shortly after the bankruptcy of automobile manufacturer Studebaker. The bankruptcy of this company left many long-term employees without any pension benefits. Congress realized that legislation was needed to ensure that pension plans contained more than unfunded promises to pay plan benefits.

Many commentators have argued that the primary (and original) purpose of ERISA was to create a minimum funding standard for pension plans. Creation of such a standard forced employers to put money away each and every year, thus ensuring that a company that fell upon hard times would have funded its retirement plan every year except the last year of the company's pension liability.

Financial planners should expect ERISA to grow in its importance to the financial services industry. Just as the statute has expanded to encompass fiduciary investment selection and more, planners should expect a commensurate expansion in the knowledge required to coexist professionally within this complex area of the law.

Q 8:5   How does ERISA apply?

ERISA is a federal statute. Its application depends on whether the issue relates to a welfare benefit plan or a qualified retirement plan. With respect to a qualified retirement plan, Congress has effectively preempted state regulation in this area. ERISA is said to "occupy the field" with respect to qualified plan regulation. Consequently, no state may pass a law that would survive constitutional challenge if the statute attempted to regulate qualified retirement plans.

Interestingly, Congress permits concurrent jurisdiction with respect to welfare benefit plans. Therefore, a participant in a group health plan may sue his HMO doctor in either federal or state court.(There is a strong likelihood that the matter will be decided in federal court for reasons beyond the scope of this book.)

Q 8:6   To what types of plans does ERISA apply?

ERISA applies to the administration of both welfare benefit plans (*e.g.*, group health, disability, and life insurance plans) and qualified retirement plans (*e.g.*, 401k, profit plans, and defined benefit plans). In order for an arrangement to be subject to ERISA, it must be shown that there is a plan, fund, or program that is established or maintained by an employer or employee organization.

Q 8:7   What ERISA requirements must be met for qualified plans?

1. **The agreement must be in writing.** Generally, the courts will not enforce amendments that are adopted in a manner that is inconsistent with a plan's amendment provisions or amendments that are oral and informal.

2. **Benefits must be definitely determinable.** Either the benefits going into the plan (*i.e.*, defined contribution) are determinable or the benefits coming out of the plan are determinable. For example, even if no contribution is made to a plan during the year, as long as a formula exists (*e.g.*, based on salary) to allocate any subsequent contributions, the plan remains tax-qualified.

3. **The plan must be communicated to employees.** This communication can be in the form of a summary plan description (SPD).Plan documents are quite voluminous and difficult for nonlawyers to understand.

Therefore, often an employer will issue an SPD to employees to communicate the terms of the plan. However, if the SPD and the plan document are in conflict as to funding, the employees always get the more generous of the two amounts.

4. **Discrimination is prohibited.** In particular, Code Section 401(a)(4) provides that benefits may not discriminate in favor of highly compensated employees. However, this statement should not be taken too literally. One should think in terms of maximum allowable discrimination, not an absolute prohibition on discrimination.

5. **The plan must be for the exclusive benefit of employees and their beneficiaries.** This is ERISA's anti-alienation provision, which prevents creditors (but not the IRS) from seizing assets in an ERISA plan.

6. **Funding must be made on a regular annual basis under all circumstances.** Maintaining the minimum funding standard is arguably the primary purpose of ERISA. The bankruptcy of automobile manufacturer Studebaker left many long-time employees without pension benefits because the employer failed to put money aside to fund its pension responsibilities. Fearing similar situations in the future, Congress passed ERISA to force employers to fund their pension liabilities on an annual basis based on the present value of a company's projected future costs.

7. **Vesting must meet or exceed federal tax requirements.** Under current tax law, employees must be vested in employer contributions under either a three-year cliff or a two-to-six-year graded vesting schedule.

Q 8:8   What if an SPD and a master plan document are in conflict?

In any case where an SPD and a master plan document are in conflict with one another, the more favorable of the two documents will govern. For example, if an SPD promises $3,000 in plan benefits while the master plan document promises $2,500, then the plan participant is entitled to $3,000 in plan benefits. The reason for this rule is simple when one realizes that most plan participants never receive the master plan document or have an opportunity to read it. Instead, plan participants often rely exclusively on the SPD. If employers were allowed to inaccurately communicate the benefits actually offered, the results could be disastrous. Under this rule the employer now has every incentive to draft the communications to plan participants clearly and accurately.

Q 8:9   Who may participate in a qualified plan?

Participants in a qualified plan are all of a company's employees unless otherwise excluded. Qualified plans may have almost any kind of initial eligibility provision except for specific restrictions based on age or service in the company. The minimum age must be 21 or under, and the minimum time must be one year of service or less. Some examples of valid exclusions include employees working less than 1,000 hours a year or for employees under age 21.

Plans may not be used exclusively to shelter income of highly compensated employees for income tax purposes. Required coverage tests ensure that average, nonmanagement employees are sufficiently included in the plan for the plan to retain its qualified tax status. In general, the plan must cover at least 70 percent of all nonhighly compensated employees.

Q 8:10 What constitutes a highly compensated employee?

"Highly compensated employee" (HCE) is defined as one who meets at least one of the following criteria:

- Individuals who are 5 percent owners of the company during the current or previous year;
- Individuals earning income at a level of at least $100,000 in 2006; or
- Individuals in the top 20 percent of all employees (those who can make a tax election on an annual basis).

Note that in an organization that has a large group of employees who earn more than $100,000 per year, the employer may elect to limit the group to only those individuals whose earnings put them in the top 20 percent of all employees.

Q 8:11 Why would an employer choose not to make the top 20 percent of employees election?

The reason for an employer to make this tax election is to pass discrimination testing.

Example: At a top Wall Street law firm, even the first-year associates make in excess of $100,000, while the paralegals and legal secretaries make less than $100,000 annually. As the saying goes, a good secretary is hard to find, but hiring and firing of associates creates a revolving door through the firm's professional ranks.

An employer may choose to treat all its employees making $100,000 or more as HCEs. The employer would be able to create two job categories of HCEs, partners and nonpartners. The paralegals and legal secretaries would each be in another category of non-HCEs. The company would pay the maximum amount to the partner HCEs while making no contributions at all to the nonpartner HCEs. The paralegals and legal secretaries would receive a contribution sufficient to pass discrimination testing. For example, assuming there are 100 HCE partners and 400 HCE nonpartners. If the partners receive 10 percent each, the average for all HCEs is only 2.5 percent, given that all 400 HCE nonpartners receive no contribution. Simply contribute 2.5 percent to the accounts of the paralegals and legal secretaries and the company has fulfilled its responsibility.

This election is used quite frequently to disenfranchise non-owner HCEs who receive high salaries. By including these non-owner HCEs in the HCE group, the owner HCEs will receive a much larger qualified plan contribution while still minimizing contributions to the non-HCEs.Of course, competitiveness in the job marketplace may limit or eliminate entirely an employer's ability to apply this technique.

Q 8:12   What are the exceptions to the nondiscrimination requirement?

Valid exceptions to discrimination in favor of HCEs include contribution variables based on employee compensation or length of service. These variables may indirectly result in more favorable benefits to HCEs.

Q 8:13   What is Social Security integration?

Qualified plans may also be integrated with Social Security so that a greater contribution or benefit is available to employees whose compensation is greater than the current Social Security taxable wage base levels. This results in employers being able to limit or eliminate entirely contributions to employees whose taxable wages are at or below the Social Security wage base in a given year.

Q 8:14   How does Social Security integration work in a defined contribution plan?

For example, under a defined contribution plan, employee Adams makes $220,000 in compensation. If the annual wage base for Social Security taxation is $94,200 (for 2006), then the $125,800 in compensation in excess of the wage base may receive up to an additional 5.7 percent more annual employer contribution to the plan.

Q 8:15   What are the funding requirements in a qualified retirement plan?

Qualified plans are generally funded by employer contributions to an irrevocable trust fund for the employees' benefit under an insurance contract. The employer is specifically limited in exercising control over the fund. Control of the fund is maintained by the fiduciary of the trust and must be managed solely for the benefit of plan participants and beneficiaries.

Q 8:16   What is a vesting schedule?

A vesting schedule is a timetable for when an employee acquires ownership (*i.e.*, vests) in the employer's contribution to the employee's account.

Q 8:17   What are the vesting requirements of a qualified plan?

Under the vesting rules, an employee must be given a nonforfeitable or vested benefit at the normal retirement date specified in the plan or after a specified number of years of service. Vesting applies only to employer contributions. An employee is always 100 percent immediately vested in his or her own contributions.

Q 8:18   What are the two types of vesting schedules?

"Cliff" and "graded" vesting are both permitted methods. However, an employer's plan must pass either one or the other method in each and every plan year or the plan will be disqualified. For example, assume a plan whose vesting schedule passes cliff vesting in years 1 and 2 and fails cliff vesting in years 3, 4, 5, and 6. The same plan passes graded vesting in years 1 and 2, then passes graded vesting in years 3, 4, 5, and 6. This plan would be nonqualified even though it passes one of the required vesting schedules in each year.

Q 8:19   Why do employers want to use vesting schedules?

Employers are concerned that employees will take the money and run after the employer puts the contribution into the plan. A vesting schedule allows employers to reward those employees for staying with the company while penalizing those employees who terminate employment too soon.

Q 8:20   What is a "cliff" vesting schedule?

A cliff vesting schedule vests the employee fully in his or her qualified plan account by the end of five years. Stated differently, five years = 100 percent vesting. Prior to that time, the employee could have zero percent vesting. This is an all or nothing approach to vesting that is intended to reward employees for longevity.

Q 8:21   What is a "graded" vesting schedule?

Graded vesting occurs according to the following schedule:

Year	Vesting Percentage
3	20%
4	40%
5	60%
6	80%
7	100%

Q 8:22   May an employer alter the timetables in either vesting schedule?

Yes. An employer can be more generous than the statutory vesting schedules but may not be less generous or the plan will be disqualified.

Q 8:23   What are the two types of qualified retirement plans?

Qualified retirement plans are classified as either defined contribution plans or defined benefit plans. Basically, the classification is dependent on whether the plan specifies an employer contribution rate or guarantees a specified benefit level.

Q 8:24   What is a defined contribution plan?

Defined contribution plans provide benefits based on the amounts contributed to an employee's individual account. In a defined contribution plan, the employer contributes a fixed amount to each employee account. Thus, the employee bears all the investment risks of the market. This concept can be compared to opening up a savings account at a bank where the investor makes regular contributions and the account grows based on the rate of investment return.

In a defined contribution plan the retirement benefit to an employee is uncertain. The retirement benefit is dependent on both the length of service with the employer (and thus the number of regular payments made to a particular individual's plan) and the investment earnings on the money contained in the plan. Using this type of formula, defined contribution plans favor younger employees, who have a longer period of time to accumulate funds for retirement. Older employees are disadvantaged due to the reduced number of years in which to accumulate funds.

Q 8:25   What are the types of defined contribution plans?

Examples of defined contribution plans include:

- Profit-sharing plan
- 401(k)
- ESOP—employee stock ownership plan
- LESOP—leveraged employee stock ownership plan
- Money-purchase pension plan
- Target benefit pension plan

Q 8:26   How much money may the employer contribute in a defined contribution plan?

Employers are eligible to contribute 100 percent of the employee's compensation up to a maximum of $44,000.

Q 8:27   What is a defined benefit plan?

Defined benefit plans provide a set level of benefits regardless of employer contributions and investment experience. In a defined benefit plan the employer specifies the benefits that each employee receives at retirement. In most plans the benefit is based on a percentage of the employee's salary. This type of plan functions in a manner similar to an insurance policy for the employee. The risk being insured is the loss of income due to the employee's inability to continue working. The additional risk of the employee running out of money during retirement is also addressed: the benefit is payable for the retired employee's entire life.

The amount of funding is determined each year by the plan's actuary and may vary depending on economic factors and market fluctuations. Therefore, if a defined benefit plan experiences significant investment losses, the employer must make additional tax-deductible contributions to the plan to provide the predetermined benefit amount.

Defined benefit plans are advantageous to older employees who continue their employment through retirement, as the benefit is dependent on both length of service and final income prior to retirement. In a defined benefit plan the burden of providing an adequate retirement income is placed entirely on the employer.

Q 8:28   What is the maximum benefit an employee may accrue under a defined benefit plan?

The maximum benefit an employee may accrue is $175,000 per year based on a normal retirement age of 65. If an employee retires after age 65, the benefit may be greater.

Characteristics of Personal Retirement Plans

Q 8:29   What are personal retirement plans?

Individual retirement accounts or annuities, more commonly known as IRAs, are personal retirement plans that are available for an individual to contribute pre-tax and defer earnings until retirement, in a manner similar to qualified plans. A personal retirement plan can be a useful supplement or alternative to a qualified plan adopted by an employer.

These nonqualified but tax-favored savings plans are intended for middle class individuals to encourage the personal accumulation of savings for retirement. These plans are also for those individuals who are not active participants in another pension program or are below a certain income level.

Q 8:30   What if an individual is already participating in a qualified retirement plan offered by an employer?

Employee participants in a qualified plan may be limited or excluded from receiving a tax deduction when they contribute to an IRA. In addition, if spouses file a joint return, one spouse may be limited by the other spouse's participation in a qualified plan.

Q 8:31   What are the contribution limits for IRA funding?

The annual IRA deduction limit for an individual is the lesser of $4,000 or earned income. If a joint return is filed with a spouse, this amount increases to $8,000 annually.

Q 8:32   What are the different types of retirement plans available for individual funding?

IRAs can be further subdivided into two distinct categories: business and personal. Among the personal IRAs are traditional and Roth IRAs. Business IRAs include SEP and SIMPLE IRAs. While each functions as a personal retirement vehicle, not all IRAs are created equal. Each of the individual types of IRAs is subject to different contribution and taxation rules and regulations. Often, contributions to a business IRA may limit contributions to a personal traditional IRA.

Characteristics of Nonqualified Plans

Q 8:33   What is a nonqualified plan?

A nonqualified plan is one that fails any one or several of the ERISA requirements of a qualified plan. Common examples of nonqualified plans include rabbi trusts or secular trusts. In a nonqualified plan the employer is not allowed to deduct the contributions made to the plan until the benefits are received by the employees. The employee is allowed to defer income taxes until the receipt of the benefit.

In addition, employers are able to discriminate in nonqualified plans. In a nonqualified plan participation may be limited to executives or the senior management team. ERISA refers to this type of arrangement as a "Top Hat" plan, which is not permitted for qualified plan eligibility.

Nonqualified plans are designed for key employees to provide customized retirement or savings benefits beyond the limits allowed in qualified plans. As a result, the employer may find a reduction in the costs associated in providing a qualified plan, which must be designed to cover a broader range of employees.

Q 8:34   What are the advantages of a nonqualified plan?

Advantages of nonqualified plans include:

- **Discrimination is allowed.** This lack of restriction would allow the plan to be made available to a small number of employees or even limited to a single employee.

- **The benefit is unlimited.** Nonqualified plans may provide unlimited benefit to any one employee, subject to the reasonable compensation requirement for deductibility.
- **There is customization and versatility.** The employer may provide different benefit amounts for different employees based on different terms and conditions.
- **There are minimal regulatory requirements.**
- **Payment of taxes by employees is deferred.** The employer's deduction is also deferred.

Q 8:35   What are the disadvantages of a nonqualified plan?

Disadvantages of a nonqualified plan include:

- **The employer's tax deduction may not be taken for the year in which compensation is earned.** The deduction is deferred until income is taxable to the employee.
- **Funding is limited to the employer's unsecured promise to pay.** Most of the protections of the federal tax and labor law, including ERISA requirements, are not applicable to enforce compliance in nonqualified plans. The reason for this is that members of the "Top Hat" group are deemed sufficiently sophisticated to protect themselves and therefore require minimal interference with ERISA. *Caveat emptor*—clients should be cautioned that many executives have been very disappointed with their results under these plans and often find themselves without legal recourse pursuant to the terms of the plan.
- **Not all employers are eligible.** Some examples of potentially ineligible employers may include S corporations and partnerships that use a pass-through tax structures, many closely held or family businesses that may not last long enough to make promised payments, and tax-exempt or government organizations.

Profit-Sharing, Stock Bonus Plans, ESOPs

Q 8:36   What is a profit-sharing plan?

A profit-sharing plan is a qualified, defined contribution plan that allows an employer to contribute to the plan under either a discretionary or formula provision.

Q 8:37   Is a profit required in order to fund a profit-sharing plan?

No. A business may contribute to a profit-sharing plan even during periods in which the business experiences a loss for tax purposes.

Q 8:38   Where did the profit-sharing plan get its name?

Businesses traditionally seek out tax deductions when taxable profits are high and tend to make higher contributions to a profit-sharing plan, thus sharing the profits; hence the name.

Q 8:39   How does a profit-sharing plan differ from other types of qualified plans?

Profit-sharing plans are often designed to function more in the context of a tax shelter for business earnings than as an employee retirement plan. Profit-sharing plans are generally not structured to provide a pension benefit at retirement but rather to offer employee participation in company profits. Funding of the plan may vary greatly from year to year.

Q 8:40   What are the two types of funding methods for a profit-sharing plan?

Profit-sharing plans may be funded according to either a discretionary or a formula provision.

Q 8:41   What is a discretionary provision?

Under a discretionary provision, the employer may determine each year the amount to be contributed to the plan. Any amount up to the maximum deductible limit (the lesser of 100 percent of compensation or $2,000) may be contributed by the employer, even if the business does not make any profit that year. While the amounts of the contribution may vary, including omitting a contribution for a given tax year, tax law requires evidence of recurring and substantial contributions to the plan or the IRS will terminate it.

Q 8:42   What is a formula provision?

Under a formula provision, the employer must contribute a specified percentage or amount to the plan whenever certain conditions occur. For example, there may be a company formula that provides 5 percent of business profits in excess of $100,000. The employer has the authority to specify any appropriate formula for funding; however, once a formula is adopted, the employer is legally obligated to contribute the amounts as outlined in the formula.

Q 8:43   When would a profit-sharing plan be used?

Some of the leading indicators for implementing a profit-sharing plan include:

- When company profits tend to vary widely from year to year (*e.g.*, in a cyclical business).

- When the employer would like to supplement an existing defined benefit plan to provide a more balanced employee retirement plan.
- When the employer wants to implement a qualified plan that includes an employee incentive to participate in the increase in company profits.
- When the employee group is relatively young, with the ability to accumulate several years of contributions, and is willing to accept a certain degree of investment risk on their individual accounts.

Q 8:44   What are the tax implications of a profit-sharing plan?

By meeting the tax law qualification requirements, the employer is able to take advantage of tax-favored benefits, including being able to deduct employer contributions to the plan when made. In addition, contributions and subsequent earnings are not taxable to the employee until distributed.

Q 8:45   Is a profit-sharing plan subject to ERISA?

Yes, a profit-sharing plan is subject to ERISA.

Q 8:46   Are there any tax incentives for establishing a new plan?

Certain employers may also be eligible to obtain a business tax credit of up to $500 for qualified start-up costs in implementing a new profit-sharing plan.

Q 8:47   What is an age-weighted profit sharing plan?

An age-weighted profit-sharing plan is one where contributions are allocated in favor of older employees. This is a popular plan among business owners because they tend to be the oldest participants in the plan.

Q 8:48   What are the tax implications of an age-weighted profit-sharing plan?

Applying age-weighting to a plan is a type of plan that permits age discrimination, which enables the plan to obtain the advantageous tax treatment of a full qualified plan under current federal tax laws. Effectively, the older owner and employees may receive a full tax deduction for their plan contributions despite the plan discriminating in their favor.

Q 8:49   How does an age-weighted profit-sharing plan benefit older employees?

Using an age-weighted profit-sharing plan, an older employee may receive an increased contribution amount. Older employees receive a higher percentage contribution relative to younger employees for a given level of compensation. This allows older employees to accumulate a greater amount of money to apply to retirement in a shorter period of time.

Q 8:50   What is a stock bonus plan?

A stock bonus plan is a qualified employer plan that functions in a manner similar to the profit-sharing plan with the exception that employer contributions are invested in company stock. Employer contributions can be in the form of direct shares of stock or cash that will be used by the plan to buy the stock. Like profit-sharing plans, stock bonus plan contributions by the employer may also be discretionary and need not be made every year. Similarly, contributions are also typically based on company profits and may also be allocated by a formula provision.

Q 8:51   What is the advantage of adopting a stock bonus plan?

The employer is able to use its own stock to fund the plan. This minimizes the amount of cash flow required to fund the plan contributions, given that an employer could simply issue more stock to fund the plan.

Q 8:52   What is the disadvantage of adopting a stock bonus plan?

From the employer's perspective, the potential disadvantage of adopting a stock bonus plan is the dilution of the shareholder's equity, given that the employees will own more and more stock each year. Employees have their own agenda relative to the interests of nonemployee shareholders. From the employee's perspective, the disadvantage of a stock bonus plan is that all of an employee's eggs are in one proverbial basket—all retirement assets are concentrated with the employer. Especially when the employer's stock is doing well, employees may be lulled into a false sense of security, not perceiving the actual risk of their situations. A financial planning should keep in mind how many dotcom millionaires are now unemployed and their companies are bankrupt.

Q 8:53   Does the employer have any liability for buying only employer stock?

No. Under a stock bonus plan, the employer is legally permitted to purchase only employer securities and is therefore absolved of fiduciary liability. The policy reason for this is that otherwise the employer would offer no retirement plan at all.

Q 8:54   What is an ESOP?

An ESOP (employee stock ownership plan) is a type of stock bonus plan that an employer may use to leverage against to borrow money from a bank or financial institution to purchase employer securities, which are in turn allocated to the accounts of employees. The securities are placed into an ESOP trust account. The trustee may then use the employer's stock as collateral to place a loan in order to buy a block of stock. In this type of loan transaction the future employer contributions may be used to pay off the outstanding loan balance used to purchase the employer securities.

Q 8:55   How does an ESOP loan work?

Step 1: The trustee of the company ESOP borrows money from a lending institution. The loan is guaranteed by the employer, using the purchased stock as collateral.

Step 2: The trustee then uses the proceeds of the loan to purchase company stock from the employer or from the principal shareholders of the company. The collateralized stock is placed in a suspense account.

Step 3: The employer makes annual tax-deductible contributions to the ESOP, enabling the trustee to pay off the loan. As the loan is paid off, the stock is released from the suspense account.

By borrowing against the ESOP the employer receives the loan proceeds up front and is able to repay the loan with tax-deductible money. When an ESOP is used for this purpose it is also known as a leveraged ESOP (LESOP).

Q 8:56   When would an employer use a stock bonus plan?

Some of the leading indicators for implementing a stock bonus plan include:

- When the company is interested in providing a means for employees to acquire company stock at low cost to the employer for a tax advantage.
- When the company wants to broaden its ownership. The argument is that employees who own company stock will start to think more like shareholders and less like employees.
- When the employer is interested in enhanced cash flow. Using a stock bonus plan or ESOP, the employer is effectively making a cashless contribution to the retirement plan if the employer issues more stock.
- When the company's shareholders would benefit from the additional market created for company stock. This increased market generates capital for the corporation and can be used to finance a company's growth. Existing employees are the best buyers of a small company's stock because they have the greatest appreciation for the current value and future potential of the business.
- When the company is a corporation. Partnerships are ineligible. S corporations are permitted to establish a stock bonus plan or ESOP, but a Subchapter S corporation loses its eligibility to be taxed as a Subchapter

S corporation when the corporation exceeds 75 shareholders, including the employees in the ESOP.

Q 8:57   When would an employer use an ESOP?

Some of the leading indicators for implementing an ESOP stock bonus plan include all of advantages of a stock bonus plan, with the additional consideration of allowing the employer to borrow money from a lender in order to provide contributions.

Q 8:58   What are the tax implications of a stock bonus plan or an ESOP?

Dividends on shares purchased in a stock bonus plan can be reinvested to increase the employee's total number of shares in the account or they can be paid directly to the employees in cash. The employer receives a tax deduction for cash dividends, which is a quite compelling motivation because the dividends are typically nondeductible (*i.e.*, they are an after-tax payment) to the corporation. If the employee takes the dividend in cash, then these amounts are currently taxable to the employee. The employee also enjoys a tax deferral on employer contributions to an ESOP or stock option plan, as with any qualified plan.

Q 8:59   Are there any tax advantages on distribution of employer securities from the ESOP?

The employee is able to defer tax on the unrealized appreciation of stock received in a lump-sum distribution.

Example: In year 1, an ESOP buys stock for $1,000 and allocates it to employee Smith's account. By year 25, employee Smith is ready to retire and the stock purchased in year 1 is now worth $6,000. If Smith elects a lumpsum distribution from his plan, he only pays tax on the "cost basis" of $1,000. The $5,000 on unrealized appreciation of the stock (capital gain) is not taxable until Smith sells the stock. If Smith holds the stock for an additional year after distribution, he would have to pay long-term capital gain on the appreciation in the employer securities.

Q 8:60   Are there any advantages to a shareholder who sells his or her shares to an ESOP?

Shareholders also receive favorable tax treatment from a sale of stock to an ESOP. If the shareholder purchases a portfolio of common stock (not mutual funds) with the proceeds, the shareholders recognize no gain on the sale of the securities to the ESOP. Of course, the shareholder will recognize gain or loss of the subsequent sale of securities in the replacement portfolio. To qualify for this special treatment, the shareholder must also comply with numerous regulatory requirements.

Q 8:61   What are the tax implications of an ESOP loan?

A C corporation may deduct dividends paid on stock with an ESOP loan, if the corporation meets one of the following conditions.

Dividends must be:

1. Paid in cash to plan participants or beneficiaries as elected, or
2. Paid to the plan and distributed within 90 days to plan participants and beneficiaries as elected, or
3. Used to make payments on certain loans incurred to acquire company stock.

Q 8:62   What are the disadvantages of stock bonus plans or ESOPs?

One of the primary disadvantages of stock bonus plans or ESOPs is the employee's inherent market risk due to lack of diversity. If the company's stock falls drastically in value, the availability of adequate retirement funds is severely reduced, and perhaps even eliminated.

Q 8:63   What statutory protections exist to protect long-term employees who participate in an ESOP?

To avoid the potential disaster concerning the lack of diversification, federal regulation requires that participants who are aged 55 and over and who have completed at least ten years of participation in the ESOP may elect to diversify funds by moving up to 50 percent of the account balance into other investments.

A disadvantage to an employer is that if the stock is not readily tradable on an established market, the employer is required to offer an option to repurchase the stock. This feature is known as a "put" option. This put option can create potential administrative and cash flow problems for the employer.

Q 8:64   What actions may an employer take to minimize the risk of put options in the employer's securities being exercised?

Employers often implement the ESOP with the expectation that the company will be part of an initial public offering within the next ten years. That way, by the time any employees are eligible to exercise a put option, there will be an established market for the employer's securities.

401(k) Plans

Q 8:65   What is a 401(k) plan?

A Section 401(k) plan, also known as a cash or deferred arrangement (CODA) plan, is a qualified profit-sharing or stock bonus plan that contains a salary deferral feature. Participants in a 401(k) plan have the ability to defer taxation on a portion of their salaries by electing to contribute money into the plan rather than receiving that portion as taxable compensation. Contributions to the plan are tax-deferred until distribution.

Q 8:66   What is the distinguishing feature of a 401(k) plan?

A 401(k) plan uses employee contributions. All other types of qualified plans use employer contributions exclusively.

Q 8:67   Why is it called a 401(k) plan?

The 401(k) plan gets its name from Section 401(k) of the Internal Revenue Code of 1986 as amended. Interestingly, Congress may not have conceived of the 401(k) plans in their present form. The financial planner may attribute the current explosion in 401(k) plans to a crafty planner who saw the potential in this single Code section.

Q 8:68   How do 401(k) plans operate in conjunction with profit-sharing plans?

Note that a 401(k) plan is not a stand-alone plan. It must be combined with a qualified profit-sharing plan, although often the employer will not contribute to the profit-sharing plan. Stated differently, all 401(k) plans are profit-sharing plans while not all profit-sharing plans have a 401(k) feature.

Q 8:69   Is employer matching mandatory in a 401(k) plan?

No, but most employers do offer some form of matching for competitive reasons or to encourage employee participation. The primary reason for the matching is to stimulate employee participation in the plan by offering an instant return on the investment. By encouraging employee participation, an employer will have a simpler way of passing discrimination testing.

Q 8:70   When would an employer implement a 401(k) plan?

Some of the leading indicators for implementing a 401(k) plan include:

- When the employer is interested in supplementing an existing defined benefit or other qualified retirement plan to provide an additional employee savings vehicle.

- When the employer is interested in providing a qualified retirement plan for employees but cannot afford a significant investment beyond plan installation and administration costs. While employers may make contributions to a traditional 401(k) plan, the plan may be funded almost entirely from employee salary deferrals. In this way, employees can take matters into their own hands and save for retirement despite the inability or unwillingness of the employer to make plan contributions for the benefit of the employee.

- When the employee group is relatively young, has the ability to accumulate several years of contributions, and is willing to accept a certain degree of investment risk on their accounts.

- When the employee group is interested in a certain degree of choice in the amounts that they wish to tax-defer for retirement savings.

- When the organization is private taxpayer or is tax-exempt. Government employers are not eligible for 401(k) plans. However, certain tax-exempt organizations such as a not-for-profit hospital are eligible to offer 401(k) plans to their employees as a substitute for 403(b) files. (*See* Q 8:205.)

Q 8:71   What are the tax advantages of a 401(k) plan?

Participants in a 401(k) plan enjoy abundant tax savings. The doctrine of constructive receipt typically requires an employee who has the choice of cash or deferral to pay tax on the full amount of cash even if the employee elects the deferral. A 401(k) plan allows an employee to have his or her cake and eat it too, given that so long as the employee makes a deferral election in advance of the period in which the compensation is earned, the employee will reduce his or her federal taxable wages by the full amount of the deferral.

Example: Jim knows that he needs to save more toward retirement. Jim makes $75,000 annually and is in a 30 percent marginal federal tax bracket. Jim can save $12,000 for retirement annually and reduce his federal taxable wages to $63,000, which will save Jim an additional $3,600 when he files his taxes. In addition, the money in the plan can accrue tax-deferred interest until retirement so Jim will not be taxed on the earnings until the money is withdrawn.

Q 8:72   How are 401(k) deferrals taxed?

Although uncommon, a 401(k) plan may also include employee after-tax contributions in addition to pre-tax salary deferrals. Withdrawals of after-tax contributions are not subject to the same withdrawal restrictions of pre-tax contributions. Employees may elect to defer up to $15,000 annually, plus any permitted catch-up contributions. These amounts are considered deferred for federal income tax purposes, but are taxable for Social Security and Medicare tax purposes.

Employer contributions are not subject to FICA (Social Security and Medicare) taxation.

Q 8:73   What is the maximum amount that an employee can elect to defer into a 401(k) plan?

For 2006, an employee is permitted to defer $15,000 into a 401(k) plan. If the employee is 50 years old or older, the employee may defer an additional $5,000, for a total deferral of $20,000.

Q 8:74   May an individual make an early withdrawal on a 401(k)?

Yes, but only for a documented financial hardship. Otherwise, no withdrawal is permitted. (Note that a loan is not a withdrawal for purposes of the tax law but that a loan is not required to be offered by an employer.)

If the participant withdraws funds prior to age 59½, Code Section 72(t) applies. The participant pays a 10 percent excise tax on the early withdrawal in addition to regular federal income tax liability. Permissible early withdrawal conditions include death, disability, retirement, termination, and hardship. A hardship withdrawal is intended for immediate and heavy financial need purposes only. The withdrawal must be deemed as necessary to satisfy the hardship requirement, and the participant must show that he or she has no other reasonable alternatives available.

Q 8:75   What are other permissible exceptions to the Section 72(t) 10 percent excise tax on early withdrawal?

Other permissible exceptions for early withdrawal include:

- Medical expenses for the participant, a spouse, or a dependent.
- Education expenses, including tuition, fees, room, and board for the next 12 months of post-secondary education.
- Purchase of a principal residence, not including mortgage payments.
- To prevent eviction from a principal residence or mortgage foreclosure.

Q 8:76   What types of nondiscrimination testing is a 401(k) plan subject to?

Traditional 401(k) plans are subject to two nondiscrimination tests, actual deferral percentage (ADP) tests, or actual contribution percentage (ACP) tests. In a nutshell, the testing is performed in order to ensure that highly compensated employees may not contribute a significantly larger amount of money than nonhighly compensated employees actually contribute.

While employers are able to discriminate in favor of highly compensated employees to a slight degree, if the percentage is found to be too much at variance, the plan is considered discriminatory, and excess contributions must be returned to the highly compensated employees or recharacterized as after-tax contributions. ADP and ACP testing forces an employer to design the 401(k) plan in a way to attract participation by lower-paid employees by making the amount that higher-paid employees can tax-shelter conditional on the amount that lower-paid employees actually tax-shelter.

Q 8:77　What is a safe harbor 401(k) plan?

In a safe harbor 401(k) plan the employer matches 100 percent of the first 3 percent, and 50 percent of the 4 to 5 percent on the employee elective deferral percentage amounts. The advantage of the safe harbor 401(k) plan is that it is not required to conduct ADP or ACP testing. Generally, these types of plans are considered so advantageous to employees that they are deemed to satisfy the testing requirements for fairness.

Alternatively, the employer may provide a flat 3 percent to each employee's account. The problem with this election is that now the employer has increased administrative costs of tracking more accounts. Also, many employees will terminate employment and have small amounts to roll over to another plan. Last, the employer is allocating contributions to employees who may not value the contribution, given that the employee chose not to participate on an election basis.

Q 8:78　What happens when an employee terminates employment with a 401(k) plan?

An employee may leave his or her money on deposit in the plan if the employee's account balance exceeds $5,000. If the employee's balance is less than $5,000, then the employee must roll over his or her account, or the employer has the option to distribute the moneys in the plan to the employee in a taxable transaction where the employee pays federal income tax and potentially a 10 percent excise tax under Code Section 72(t) for premature distributions (*e.g.*, because the employee is under age 59½).

Q 8:79　How are 401(k) funds invested?

Although fund investment options are limited by the 401(k) plan, employees are almost always able to select their investment selections. However, under Section 404(c) of ERISA, the employer has a duty to educate the employee so that the employee is reasonably able to direct the investment of the employee's funds in the plan. An employer could also choose to direct employee investment accounts, but the employer would be assuming fiduciary liability for the investment selections, which, understandably, most employers do not wish to voluntarily undertake.

Q 8:80　What types of investments should be offered under ERISA to 401(k) participants?

When drafted in 1974, ERISA required that at least three options be provided to plan participants. These options were cash, bonds, and stock. Although

ERISA has never been formally amended, the Department of Labor has released guidance not as to how many options are sufficient, but rather that three options are too few.

Money Purchase Pension Plans

Q 8:81   What is a money purchase pension plan?

A money purchase plan is a type of defined contribution qualified plan whereby employees making the same amount of money receive the same amount of employer contribution to the plan. The employer makes annual contributions to each employee's individual account in the plan based on a nondiscriminatory contribution formula. This formula is typically a fixed percentage of each employee's annual compensation up to a maximum of 100 percent, based on $220,000 of salary.

> **Example:** The formula for XYZ plan is 10 percent of an employee's salary. Employee Smith, with an annual salary of $50,000, receives $5,000 in employer contributions to her account. Employee Jones, with an annual salary of $40,000, receives $4,000 in employer contributions to his account. Contributions are made regardless of the employees' age or length of service.

Q 8:82   What is the distinguishing feature of a money purchase pension plan?

Unlike a traditional defined benefit plan where the employer retains both the risk of investment loss and the investment direction, a money purchase plan typically allows an employee to select a more aggressive asset allocation. However, because a money purchase pension plan is a defined contribution plan, any investment loss is borne by the employee absent a showing of liability on the part of the employer.

Q 8:83   What is the effect of a money purchase plan on older employees?

Money purchase pension plans are not overly friendly to older employees compared to other forms of qualified plans. All employees regardless of age receive the same contribution for the same level of compensation. If the employer wants to attract a younger workforce, adoption of a money purchase pension plan is a legal way to accomplish this goal.

Q 8:84   What is the maximum employer contribution to a money purchase pension plan?

The maximum percentage of compensation that an employer may contribute is 25 percent.

Q 8:85 What is the maximum salary level that may be used to fund a money purchase pension plan?

For 2006, the maximum salary level that can be considered is $220,000. The financial planner should keep in mind that the overall funding limit of 100 percent and $44,000 still applies. Therefore, even if an employee makes $220,000 in a plan to which the employer makes a 25 percent contribution, the employee receives only $44,000 in contributions. A planning consideration for the employer may be to reduce the company contribution down to 20 percent so that the $220,000 employee receives the maximum $44,000 contribution while reducing contributions to other employees in the plan.

Q 8:86 May an employer change its percentage of contribution?

Yes, but any change requires IRS approval and involves the payment of an application fee. Generally, requests to decrease the funding percentage may be denied on the first request, whereas requests to increase the funding level are generally approved.

Q 8:87 What effect has the current tax law had on money purchase pension plans?

As a pension plan, all contributions are mandatory each and every year, contrasted with profit-sharing plans whereby an employer may vary the level of plan contribution each year. The change in tax law permitting profit-sharing plans to have a maximum 100 percent of payroll contribution level (up from 15 percent under prior tax law) may likely signal the end for the money purchase pension plan.

Q 8:88 How did the money purchase pension plan get its name?

Money purchase pension plans are so termed by their design. Money in the account is used to purchase annuities for retirement, hence the money to purchase a (traditional) pension plan.

Q 8:89 When would an employer or employee want a money purchase pension plan?

Some of the leading indicators for implementing a money purchase pension plan include:

- When the employer is interested in simplicity. The money purchase pension plan is one of the simplest qualified plans to design, administer, and explain to employees.
- When the employer is interested in predictable costs. With its fixed-rate formula based on a percentage of employee annual compensation, contribution amounts are relatively easy to predict.

- When the employee group is relatively young, has the ability to accumulate several years of contributions, and is willing to accept a certain degree of investment risk on their individual accounts.
- When participants are seeking a certain degree of retirement income security. Accounts are not guaranteed, but annual employer contributions are required. The employee does assume the investment risks of the plan's earning performance.

Q 8:90　What are the tax implications of a money purchase pension plan?

An employer enjoys an immediate tax benefit on contributions to a money purchase pension plan. Contributions to the plan are deductible when made. In addition, certain employers are eligible to receive a business tax of up to $500 for qualified start-up costs on implementing a new plan.

Employees are able to defer taxes on plan contributions until funds are distributed at retirement.

As a qualified plan, money purchase pension plans are subject to both ERISA requirements and IRS regulation. Code Section 412 requires minimum annual contributions to the plan, subject to an employer penalty if minimum contribution levels are not met. These minimums are typically calculated by the plan's established contribution formula.

Q 8:91　Can the employee make withdrawals from the plan while employed by the employer?

No, employees are restricted from making "in-service" withdrawals, with certain hardship exceptions.

Q 8:92　What is the amount of employee benefit at retirement?

The amount of benefit at retirement in a money purchase pension plan is equal to the employee's account balance at the retirement date, or the valuation date near retirement. Although each employee has an administratively separate account, account funds of all employees are commingled for investment purposes and may increase or decrease in accordance with the investment performance of the fund as a whole. Therefore, the employee is unable to make an exact prediction of benefit amounts available at retirement.

Q 8:93　Are older employees disadvantaged in a money purchase pension plan?

Yes. The nature of the fixed-formula approach to employer contributions makes it impossible for the plan to provide enhanced benefit to older employees. The plan cannot provide for past service. Employees who begin the plan at younger ages receive the best benefit because they have a longer period of time in which to accumulate contributions and compound investment earnings.

Target Benefit Plans

Q 8:94   What is a target benefit plan?

A target benefit plan is a type of qualified defined contribution plan that functions in a manner similar to a defined benefit plan. In a target benefit plan, the employer chooses a target level of employee retirement benefit and funds the plan accordingly each year to achieve that target objective.

At the start of the plan, the employer uses an actuarial calculation of the amount that would be required to fully fund this benefit at the participant's anticipated retirement date. Using these data, the employer makes an appropriate level annual contribution each year to fund the individual's account.

The way this plan differs from a traditional defined benefit plan is that the employer is not required to make any adjustments in the contribution amount to guarantee the target amount if actual investment return varies from the original assumptions. Therefore, the actual benefit amount is not as predictable as a defined benefit plan.

Q 8:95   What is the distinguishing feature of a target benefit plan?

A target benefit plan functions like a defined benefit plan where the contributions are age-weighted but the employee bears the risk of investment loss. Older employees get larger contributions for a given level of compensation. These contributions are put into individual accounts where either the employer or the employee directs the investment of the account.

Q 8:96   Where does a target benefit plan get its name?

The intent of this plan is that the employer makes sufficient contributions to an employee's account so that for a given investment return assumption, the employee would be able to enjoy the "targeted" benefit. For example, if an employer wanted all employees to receive 25 percent of their final pay in retirement income, an employer would fund the plan so that at a 6 percent rate of return, the employee would achieve his or her target.

Q 8:97   Does a target benefit plan favor older employees?

Yes. All else being equal, an older employee receives a greater contribution to the plan than a younger employee at the same compensation level because the older employee has less time to earn investment return on the money in order to achieve the desired target benefit.

Q 8:98   Are there any aspects of a target benefit plan that do not favor older employees?

Yes. Because a target benefit plan is a defined contribution plan, the risk of investment loss is borne by the employee. Consequently, an older employee must bear the risk if the plan investments perform poorly in the capital markets and consequently there are not sufficient plan assets available to the employee to achieve the targeted plan benefit.

Q 8:99   How does investment performance affect the plan?

Remember that a target benefit plan is a defined contribution plan. Therefore, all investment risk of loss is borne by the employee. The funding of the target benefit plan is generally equivalent to a balanced investment fund. If an employee takes greater investment risk and makes a return in excess of the underlying plan assumption, the employee would enjoy a benefit greater than that which the employer originally targeted in the plan.

Q 8:100   Who directs plan investments?

Typically, an employer allows an employee to direct contributions to a target benefit plan. However, some employers choose to direct the investments for the employees, perceiving that employees do not have the requisite level of knowledge to adopt an appropriate asset allocation and ride out fluctuations and volatility in the capital markets.

Q 8:101   When is a target benefit plan used?

Some of the leading indicators for implementing a target benefit plan include:

- When the employer is interested in providing a defined contribution plan that would not disadvantage older employees who have relatively few years of plan participation available prior to retirement.
- When the employer is interested in a comparable, and less costly, alternative to a defined benefit plan without the assuming all of the risks associated with market variance. In a target benefit plan, as with all defined contribution plans, the employee assumes the investment risk of the plan.
- When the employer needs to receive the largest amount of available tax deduction on plan contributions and is financially able to fund large contribution amounts for employees nearing retirement age.

Q 8:102   What drives an employer to adopt a target benefit plan?

Generally, an employer who would like to adopt a defined benefit plan but simply cannot afford to pay for investment losses in that type of plan will adopt a target benefit plan. Financial planners should keep in mind that shareholders want to make or lose money in the widget business and do not want to lose millions of dollars in the employee retirement plan.

Q 8:103   What are the tax implications of a target benefit plan?

Target benefit plans allow employers to deduct greater amounts in annual contributions than other qualified plans, as the annual additions limit does not apply. These contributions to the plan are deductible when made.

The employer may deduct up to the full amount available under Code Section 415 limits. This plan remains qualified for tax purposes even though older employees receive substantially greater benefit. In addition, certain employers are eligible to receive a business tax deduction of up to $500 for qualified start-up costs on implementing a new plan. Employees may defer taxes on plan contributions until funds are distributed at retirement.

As a qualified plan, a money purchase pension plan is subject to both ERISA requirements and IRS regulation. Code Section 412 requires minimum annual contributions to the plan, subject to an employer penalty if minimum contribution levels are not met. These minimums are typically satisfied if the employer contributes to each participant's account the percentage of compensation required by the plan.

Q 8:104   Are older employees advantaged over younger employees in a target benefit plan?

Yes. A target benefit plan may use an age-weighted factor in calculating its employer contributions to achieve the desired target benefit for an older employee's retirement. Older employees are favored in target benefit plans because they can accrue as great a sum over a reduced number of years compared to younger employees, whose benefit is spread out over a larger time span, thereby reducing the annual contribution amount.

Example: Under a target benefit plan employee Clark and employee Brown each make the same salary working at the same position, with the same years of service at the company. Employee Clark, aged 50, receives twice as much annual contribution in his plan as Brown, aged 25, who will have more years under which to allocate the same benefit amount. This concept can be a difficult one for younger employees to accept.

Q 8:105   What is the maximum annual contribution that an employee may receive in a target benefit plan?

The maximum annual deductible contribution is the lesser of 100 percent of the employee's salary or $44,000.

Q 8:106   Is a target benefit plan an ERISA plan?

Yes, target benefit plans are covered by ERISA.

Defined Benefit Pension Plan

Q 8:107   What is a defined benefit pension plan?

A defined benefit pension plan is a qualified defined benefit pension plan that specifies the amount of benefit promised to the employee at retirement. As with any other defined benefit plan, the employer assumes the risk of providing the anticipated benefit amount to the employee at retirement.

A defined benefit pension plan functions in a manner similar to the target benefit plan, with the exception that the funds are guaranteed by the employer. In both pension plans, the amount of employer annual contribution is determined by an actuary to meet the specified benefit goal. Annual employer contribution is required in each; however, if the amount of money in the fund fluctuates due to market depreciation or some other occurrence, the employer is required to make adjustments to the amount of annual contribution to make up for the deficit.

In addition, unlike a defined contribution plan in which an employer makes contributions to individual participant accounts, defined benefit plans do not have individual participant accounts. In a defined benefit pension plan, each participant has a percentage claim on the overall fund. These fund amounts are typically distributed in the form of a lifetime annuity for the participant at retirement.

Q 8:108   When would an employer or businessperson use a defined benefit pension plan?

Some of the leading indicators for implementing a defined benefit plan include:

- When the employer is interested in, and capable of, guaranteeing a specific benefit amount to employees at retirement.
- When the business owner is an older participant who needs to defer a large amount of taxable income. Defined benefit pension plans provide the maximum tax shelter potential available under any qualified plan.
- When the employer is interested in providing an attractive retirement benefit for highly compensated or older participants, regardless of length of service.

Q 8:109   What are the tax implications of a defined benefit pension plan?

Like target benefit plans, defined benefit pension plans allow employers to deduct greater amounts in annual contributions than other qualified plans, as the annual additions limit does not apply. These contributions to the plan are deductible when made. The employer may deduct up to the full amount available under Section 415 limits. This plan remains qualified for tax purposes even though older employees receive substantially greater benefit. Additionally, certain employers are eligible to receive a business tax deduction of up to $500 for qualified start-up costs on implementing a new plan, and employees may defer taxes on plan contributions until funds are distributed at retirement.

As a qualified plan, a defined benefit pension plan is subject to both ERISA requirements and IRS regulation. Code Section 412 requires minimum annual contributions to the plan, subject to an employer penalty if minimum contribution levels are not met. These employer contributions may fluctuate in order to guarantee the specified employee benefit at retirement.

In addition to the standard qualified plan requirements, defined benefit plans are subject to mandatory insurance coverage by the government-sponsored Pension Benefit Guaranty Corporation (PBGC).

Q 8:110   What is the maximum benefit under a defined benefit pension plan?

An employee retiring at age 65 would be entitled to receive a benefit of no more than $175,000 annually.

Q 8:111   What if an employee delays retirement?

Pursuant to the Age Discrimination in Employment Act (ADEA), an employer cannot force an employee to retire. Consequently, the employee would be entitled to receive a benefit that would be actuarially increased in excess of the $175,000.

Q 8:112   What is the maximum deductible contribution to a defined benefit pension plan?

It depends on a number of factors, including investment return and employee turnover, payroll, ages, etc. It is not uncommon for a defined benefit pension plan deductible contribution to be many times that of a defined contribution plan funding limit. The enhanced deductibility of the plan contribution often leads cash-rich employers to adopt this type of plan.

Q 8:113   What if an employer never had a defined benefit plan in the past?

If an employer never had a defined benefit plan before, he or she could adopt a defined benefit plan and fund a tax-deductible supplemental liability for past service. This allows the business owner to make deductible contributions to the plan to cover prior years even though no retirement plan was then in place.

Q 8:114   What is the risk to a supplemental liability?

Generally, the IRS only permits in practice for employers to pay in a supplemental liability to a plan over five years. Technically, the statute permits up to

30 years to pay in the supplemental liability for prior service. If an employer misses any of the payments, the plan is terminated and ceases to be qualified. Consequently, the employer should be very careful before undertaking a supplemental liability.

Q 8:115 What is the Section 412(i) variation to a defined benefit pension plan?

Under Section 412(i) of the Internal Revenue Code, a defined benefit plan could be solely funded using whole life insurance and fixed annuities. Because the rate of return is lower in these products, the amount of the employer contribution is increased substantially. This is a great advantage to an employer who has the cash to fund the tax-deductible contributions.

Q 8:116 What is the exit strategy for a 412(i) plan?

Generally, the 412(i) plan is adopted by a business owner who desperately needs to fund retirement after years of neglect. The business is doing fantastically well, and cash flow is not an issue. The employer may also incur a supplemental liability. The owner may fund the plan for five years, then terminate the plan and retire. The owner often takes a rollover of the large plan account balance to a personal IRA where he or she invests in a more aggressive asset allocation. The IRS is likely to challenge plan terminations made before the five-year mark as a sham transaction.

Q 8:117 How does an employer calculate employee benefit in a defined benefit pension plan?

A formula is typically used to calculate the benefit amount that the employer will provide to the employee on retirement. As a general rule, this benefit typically amounts to 40 to 60 percent of the employee's final average salary. The formula is based on a percentage of earnings over time or based on years of service. Two formulas used for this purpose are the unit-benefit formula and the fixed-benefit formula.

Q 8:118 How does a unit-benefit calculation work?

Of the two types, the unit-benefit formula is the more commonly implemented. The unit-benefit formula bases the benefit amount on a percentage of the employee's earnings per year.

Example: Company *A* implements a defined benefit plan whereby each plan participant receives a monthly pension beginning at the standard retirement date. This benefit is paid in the form of a life annuity that is equal to 2 percent of the final average monthly salary multiplied by the years of service, not to exceed 25 years. As a participant in this plan, employee Michaels is able to calculate his benefit after 20 years of service and at an average $5,000 per month compensation at retirement using the following calculation:

$$2\% \times \$5,000 \times 20 = \$2,000 \text{ per month}$$

The unit-benefit calculation rewards experienced employees and highly compensated owners and executives.

Q 8:119   How does a fixed benefit calculation work?

In a fixed benefit formula, the benefit can be calculated using a flat percentage of amount. This can be either a flat percentage of earnings (*e.g.*, 40 percent of final average monthly salary) or a flat amount per year of service (*e.g.*, a monthly benefit of $12 for every year worked). In the percentage-ofearnings method, employees are not rewarded for length of service; in the flatservice method, benefit could be disproportionate to previous employment earning levels.

Q 8:120   Why should a financial planner read a client's summary plan description for a defined benefit plan?

Often, plans pay the benefit based on the five highest years' pay or the last five years' pay. If the financial planner's client was downsized in a merger and elected a demotion instead of severance, it is possible that the client would actually receive substantially less retirement plan benefits by continuing to work for an employer after a demotion in light of a merger. Please note that employers may change their formula in the plan from time to time, albeit subject to substantial anti-cutback statutes in the tax law. Bottom line—the financial planner should read the plan documents carefully.

Q 8:121   May a defined benefit plan permit early retirement under the plan?

Yes, the plan may have an early retirement program that allows employees to retire with fully accrued benefits prior to normal retirement age. However, the plan must have sufficient assets to ensure that the payment of benefits to early retirees will not jeopardize the financial security of remaining plan participants.

Q 8:122   May a defined benefit plan permit loans?

Surprisingly, the answer is yes. However, since an actuarial computation is required, the reality is that no plan permits loans because offering this option is cost-prohibitive.

Q 8:123   May an employee take a lump-sum distribution from a defined benefit plan?

Only if the employer permits this type of distribution.

Q 8:124   Why would an employer prohibit a lump-sum distribution?

An employer may prohibit a lump-sum distribution if:

- The employer perceives that an employee is unsophisticated and would lose the lump-sum assets quickly if self-directed. (Interestingly, the IRS has ruled that an employer may allow salaried employees to take lumpsum distributions while hourly employees are prohibited from taking lump sums from the plan.)
- The employer believes that if the he or she retains the assets in the plan that the employer will be able to achieve an investment rate of return in excess of that required to fund plan benefits, thus lowering the employer's required plan contributions. (If the investment returns alone pay all plan benefits, the employer may never need to make plan contributions.)

Q 8:125   Are defined benefit plans covered by ERISA?

Yes, defined benefit plans are ERISA plans.

Q 8:126   What is the argument against using defined benefit plans?

According to most economic theorists, a business exists to make a profit. Generally, if the business makes widgets, then the shareholders either want to make or lose money in the widget business. The shareholders expect the management of the widget company to minimize any risks that could make the enterprise unprofitable provided that the widget market is good.

Defined benefit plans shift the risk of investment loss squarely onto the employer. Consequently, an employer could be liable for massive investment losses should there be a severe and extended market downturn, as has occurred in recent history. While paternalism toward one's employees is perhaps an admirable goal, will a business that has higher widget costs (as a result of making additional cash payments to the pension plan to make up for investment losses for which the employer is liable under ERISA) be able to compete in the marketplace? Probably not.

In a twist of recent legislative fate, a defined benefit plan that is terminated results in the surplus funding reverting to the plan, not to the employer. A 50 percent excise tax applies to all amounts that revert to the employer (in addition to ordinary federal income tax, usually at a 35 percent rate).This congressional modification has brought an abrupt halt to the merger frenzy that involved terminating overfunded defined benefit plans to pay down the debt in the leveraged buyout debt load.

Cash Balance Pension Plan

Q 8:127   What is a cash balance pension plan?

A cash balance pension plan is a qualified pension plan in the defined benefit category that provides a specified employee benefit, which is funded by annual employer contributions to hypothetical individual employee accounts. The accounts themselves are fictitious. The actual employer contributions are commingled in a large trust account with money allocated at a specified rate to individual employee accounts by means of an accounting entry. Investment returns on contributions are also hypothetical and are based on a fixed rate specified in the plan or on a floating rate based on an external index.

A cash balance pension plan is a "smoke and mirrors" type of defined benefit plan that is designed to look and function like an employee-defined contribution plan. Unlike the traditional defined benefit plan, participants in a cash balance pension plan receive an annual statement that shows their specific account balances. Individual account statements provide the "look and feel" of defined contribution plans, such as a 401(k), but in a cash balance pension plan the individual participant does not actually own the plan outright; the individual merely holds an ownership interest in a commingled hold.

What this means is that while the participant is guaranteed a specific rate of return from the plan, allocations and investments are controlled solely by the employer. While this plan insulates the employee from market risk, it also prevents the employee from profiting in a favorable market.

Q 8:128   What is the distinguishing feature of a cash balance pension plan?

As a defined benefit plan, the risk of investment loss is borne by the employer. Consequently, the plan has a stated crediting rate on all plan investments that is wholly independent of actual investment returns. However, all employees receive the same contribution regardless of age for a given level of compensation.

Q 8:129   Where does a cash balance pension plan get its name?

The name comes from the fact that each employee gets an annual statement showing a cash balance that is a benefit accrued for that individual employee's benefit.

Q 8:130   Why is the "cash balance" so important?

The problem with a traditional defined benefit plan is that employees have no concept and consequently no appreciation of the value of their benefits under a defined benefit pension plan. An employee sees the contribution to and the growth on a cash balance plan on an annual basis. Consequently, employers are able to make employees perceive exactly how much money is going toward the employee's retirement plan account. Nothing is worse from an employer's perspective than spending millions of dollars on employee benefits programs that employees perceive as being of little value, which has been the problem with the traditional defined benefit pension plan.

Q 8:131   May an employee withdraw his or her "cash" balance?

No, an employee may not withdraw the account balance unless the employer gives the employee a lump-sum distribution option. Technically, this makes the annual statement detailing the cash balance a bit of "smoke and mirrors" deception, given that this balance is merely an interest in a commingled trust fund for the plan.

Q 8:132   How does a cash balance pension plan favor older employees?

The cash balance as a defined benefit plan shifts the risk of investment loss to the employer. This is advantageous to older employees, who may not have the investment time horizon to ride out volatility in the capital markets.

Q 8:133   Are there any aspects of a cash balance pension plan that do not favor older employees?

Yes, older employees receive the same plan contribution that younger employees receive for a given level of compensation.

Q 8:134   How does investment performance affect the plan?

As a defined benefit plan, all investment risk or loss is borne by the employer. The plan sets a crediting rate on all plan assets, which is the investment return on plan assets for the year.

Q 8:135   When is a cash balance pension plan used?

Some of the leading indicators for implementing a cash balance plan include:

- When the employer is a mid-size or larger corporation who is interested in a less costly alternative to a traditional defined benefit plan.
- When the employer is interested in providing a defined benefit plan that is simpler to explain to its employees. In a cash balance pension plan employees receive an annual statement showing their allocated account balance.
- When the employee group is relatively young, with the ability to accumulate several years of contributions and prefer a guaranteed rate of return on their accounts.

Q 8:136 What are the tax implications of a cash balance pension plan?

In a cash balance pension plan, the employer makes annual contributions and interest credits to the fund. The employer has a certain degree of flexibility in the amount and frequency of the required contribution. These contributions to the plan are deductible when made. Specifically, in a cash balance pension plan the employer is allowed to specify the crediting rate of the fund (*e.g.*, a hypothetical annual earnings rate of 2 percent).

The employer may deduct up to the full amount available under Code Section 415 limits. This plan remains qualified for tax purposes even though older employees receive substantially greater benefit. In addition, certain employers are eligible to receive a business tax of up to $500 for qualified startup costs on implementing a new plan. Employees are allowed to defer taxes on plan contributions until funds are distributed at retirement.

A cash balance pension plan, as a qualified plan, is subject to both ERISA requirements and IRS regulation. Code Section 412 requires minimum annual contributions to the plan subject to an employer penalty if the minimum contribution level is not met. These employer contributions may fluctuate in order to guarantee the specified employee benefit at retirement.

In addition to the standard qualified plan requirements, cash balance pension plans are subject to mandatory insurance coverage by the government-sponsored PBGC.

Q 8:137 How does a cash balance pension plan compare to a traditional defined benefit pension plan?

A cash balance pension plan is a fairly recent addition to retirement planning options. First introduced in 1984, this plan has quickly gained in popularity as a more cost-effective alternative to traditional defined benefit pension plans. The modern trend in large organizations has been to convert a traditional defined benefit pension plan to a cash balance pension plan in an effort to provide a defined benefit plan option that is easier for employees to understand and appreciate. Unlike a traditional defined benefit pension plan, employees are able to see at a glance their annual accumulated earnings and "cash balances" of the plan at the end of a particular year, similar to a savings account.

The cash balance pension plan's simulated individual account allocation gives the appearance of segregated individual accounts as seen in a defined contribution plan. Depending on what the plan document specifies, the employee may even be able to receive a plan payout on termination of employment, prior to retirement. In this way, the employee feels a sense of ownership not easily found in having a traditional benefit pension plan, which accumulates its balance in the background, where amounts are not seen or given final calculation until retirement.

Older employees fair more favorably in a traditional defined benefit pension plan than in a cash balance pension plan. With their flat contributions and earnings credits, cash balance benefit plans favor employees who have a greater period of time in which to accumulate earnings.

Q 8:138   Is a cash balance pension plan covered by ERISA?

Yes, a cash balance pension plans is covered by ERISA.

Q 8:139   How does a cash balance pension plan compare to a defined contribution plan?

While a cash balance pension plan appears to be more like a defined contribution plan than a defined benefit plan, the cash balance pension plan does have some inherent differences. Besides the more obvious comparisons of the risk of the employee benefit assumed by the employer (in a defined benefit plan) versus the employee (in a defined contribution plan), an easily overlooked strength of a cash balance pension plan over defined contribution plans is that the cash balance pension plan can provide credits for past service. A cash balance pension plan offers greater rewards and incentives to longer tenured employees.

While both types of plans benefit younger employees, who have more time in which to accumulate several years of contributions, the levels of market risk and investor control differ widely. In defined contribution plans employees assume all the risk of the market and as a result also enjoy all of the benefits of a long-term stock portfolio investment, which over time generally provides for a greater level of average return than the guaranteed fixed rates found in cash balance pension plans.

The reduced risk of defined benefit plans does not mean an entire lack of risk, as the PBGC-required guarantee for all defined benefit plans does not guarantee all benefits to an employee. In a worst-case scenario, the benefit could be lost entirely if the company folds at a time when the plan has insufficient assets. Also, unlike the "cash and carry" nature of defined contribution plan accounts, cash balance pension plans benefits are also within reach of the employer's creditors.

Q 8:140   Why have cash balance plans been replacing defined benefit plans in corporate America?

There are likely two reasons for this transition. First, cash balance plans are still defined benefit plans, which cause the employer to bear the risk of investment loss. Consequently, the employer invests the funds under a defined benefit arrangement. For a paternalistic employer who traditionally has operated the business under a model where employees have usually worked all their lives, it may be difficult, if not impossible, to abandon the corporate culture where the employer not only used the qualified retirement plan to recruit, reward, and retain, but also used the plan to successfully retire the employee.

The second reason for transitioning over to the cash balance plan from a defined benefit plan is consistent with the desire of U.S. business to remain competitive. If two employees performed the identical job with an identical level of skill and identical pay, should not the two employees receive identical pension plan contributions? Under the new cash balance plan design, the two employees would receive the same plan contribution. However, under the old defined benefit design, the older employee would always receive a greater (often substantially greater) monetary contribution to the pension plan. At issue is the concept of equal pay for equal work. The cash balance pension plan does a superior job of achieving this result for an employer.

Traditional IRAs

Q 8:141 What is a traditional IRA?

Unlike the qualified retirement plans discussed in our previous chapters, IRAs are not technically categorized as qualified plans; they are examples of personal retirement plans that enjoy some of the same tax deferral advantages of qualified plans.

A traditional IRA, which stands for either individual retirement "account" or individual retirement "annuity," is a type of personal retirement savings plan that allows an individual to contribute pre-tax (if the taxpayer is eligible) and defers earnings until retirement in a manner similar to qualified plans. An IRA may be used as a supplement or an alternative to an employer-sponsored qualified retirement plan.

Although the funds are taxed on distribution, this ability to deduct contributions reduces the amount of an individual's taxable income. Combined with the ability to defer taxation on earnings, IRAs function like an interest-free loan from the government. IRAs have thus been called Congress's greatest gift to working Americans. This "gift" from Congress should be carefully examined to ensure appropriate compliance with federal eligibility, contribution and deduction limits, and distribution rules. Generally, these rules were intended by the federal government to foster retirement savings for the middle classes or below or those who are not considered active participants in another pension program.

Q 8:142 What are the advantages of an IRA?

The general advantages of funding an IRA are:

- Eligible individuals may deduct their annual contributions to a traditional IRA up to the maximum amount ($4,000), or up to the maximum annual contribution amount for a spouse ($8,000 joint contribution) if a traditional spousal IRA is available. If the individual is age 50 or older, an additional $1,000 may be contributed.

- Investment incomes earned on the assets held in traditional IRAs are not taxed until distributed as ordinary income from the account. This can be an advantage to individuals whose current compensation places them in a higher tax bracket than they are likely to be in during retirement years. Deferrals may also be made on investment income such as interest, dividends, rents, or capital gains.

- IRA funding allows individuals an alternative or supplemental retirement savings vehicle to qualified plans. For example, highly compensated employees who have not yet reached their annual contribution maximum with their employer's qualified retirement plan are allowed to contribute additional eligible funding to an IRA for maximum tax deferral.

- Individuals are free to make their own selections on the specific investments used to fund an IRA. The only types of investments that are not eligible for IRA funding are life insurance and collectibles. This ability to exercise individual control over the plan is an advantage to the more limited qualified plan options.

Q 8:143   What are the disadvantages of an IRA?

The general disadvantages to funding an IRA are:

- Compliance with stringent annual contribution limits. If the individual or spouse is an active participant in a tax-favored employer retirement plan, the IRA deduction may be unavailable.

- Premature (prior to age 59½) withdrawals to traditional IRAs are subject to a 10 percent penalty, except under limited cases of specified hardship conditions. These early withdrawal penalties may cancel out the benefit of the tax deduction and negate the advantages of tax deferral.

Q 8:144   Who is eligible to fund an IRA?

Any person under age 70½ who receives compensation, in the form of either salary or self-employment earned income, may make a contribution to an IRA. Depending on several factors, including the individual's adjusted gross income and individual or spousal participation into an employer's retirement plan, the contribution may or may not be deductible, but in all instances interest earnings will be tax-deferred. A financial planner should keep in mind that a taxpayer must have earned income equal to or greater than the IRA funding amount. For example, if a taxpayer has only $250 in earned income in one year, then the he or she may contribute only $250 to an IRA even if the he or she has another $1 million in dividend income.

Q 8:145   Are annual contributions required?

No, annual contributions to an IRA are not required and in any year in which contributions are not made, the taxpayer is not eligible to carry an allowance forward to the following year. For example, if the taxpayer is eligible to fund an IRA for $4,000 in one year and no contribution is made, the taxpayer is not allowed to contribute an additional $4,000 to the following year's contribution. Catch-ups are not permitted from year to year.

Q 8:146   Are minimum distributions required at age 70½ in a traditional IRA?

Yes, distributions from a traditional IRA must begin by April 1 of the year following the year in which the participant reaches age 70½. These minimum distributions must be amounts calculated to exhaust the account over the participant's life expectancy. For joint accounts, the joint life expectancy of the participant and the beneficiary is calculated. Life expectancy may be recalculated once per year.

Q 8:147   What if minimum distributions are not made?

Excess accumulations are subject to a nondeductible excise tax equal to 50 percent of the difference between what was paid out (if any distributions were made) and what should have been paid out.

Q 8:148   May distributions on a traditional IRA be made prior to age 59½ without penalty?

Generally, no. Early withdrawals (those that occur prior to age 59½) are subject to the 10 percent tax penalty, with a few valid exceptions. The following events are considered exceptions to the early withdrawal penalty:

- The participant's death or disability;
- Medical care;
- Health insurance premiums for unemployed individuals;
- Post-secondary education expenses for the individual, spouse, child, or grandchild;
- Acquisition costs associated with purchase of a first home, up to a $10,000 lifetime maximum; and
- Substantially equal periodic payments.

Q 8:149   What is a transfer IRA?

A transfer IRA is a vehicle whereby moneys are typically transferred from a qualified plan (*e.g.*, 401(k) plan) into an IRA. Of course, an employee could transfer funds from one 401(k) to his employer's new 401(k) plan. However, given that investment options in the 401(k) are limited, often an employee will roll his or her funds over into an IRA where there are more investment choices.

Q 8:150   Are there any disadvantages to an IRA transfer from a qualified plan?

This is a question that depends on state law. Some states protect IRAs from creditors in bankruptcy while other states do not. The financial planner should be knowledgeable about the rule of law for the jurisdiction where the IRA contributions are funded. Of course, there is no guarantee that a law suit may arise in Florida even if a client is a Florida resident. Consequently, rolling moneys over to an IRA may be a risky proposition from the standpoint of liability and asset protection.

Q 8:151   Are IRAs covered by ERISA?

No.

Q 8:152   What if an individual makes a cash withdrawal from an IRA?

Here is an interesting twist in the law. An individual may actually withdraw cash from an IRA for a 60-day window one time during any calendar year. Provided that the funds are redeposited in the IRA prior to the expiration of the 60 days, there is no taxable distribution. Of course, if someone takes advantage of this option twice during one calendar year, the second withdrawal will be taxable.

Q 8:153   What is a commingled IRA?

This is an IRA that has traditional IRA contributions as well as qualified money contributions. Under the old law, any nonqualified money was ineligible to be rolled back into a qualified plan. This was important because creditors generally often reach IRAs but are barred from attaching qualified plan assets under ERISA's anti-alienation provisions.

Q 8:154   Who is eligible to deduct a traditional IRA contribution for federal income tax purposes?

For single taxpayers not covered by a pension plan: Regardless of the taxpayer's AGI, the taxpayer may deduct the full amount of the his or her IRA contribution.

For married taxpayers where one spouse is covered by a pension plan: If one spouse is covered by a pension plan while the other spouse is not, the noncovered spouse may deduct only his or her IRA contribution if the AGI on the joint return is less than $150,000. No deduction is available when AGI exceeds $160,000 and is phased out pro rata between $150,000 and $160,000.

For single taxpayers covered by a pension plan *or* for married taxpayers where both spouses are covered by a pension plan: Single taxpayers whose AGI is less than $50,000 are eligible to deduct their traditional IRA contribution for federal income tax purposes. Married taxpayers who file a joint income tax return are eligible to deduct their traditional IRA contributions for federal income tax purposes if their AGI is less than $75,000. Both single and married taxpayers phase out their eligibility to deduct their contributions over the succeeding $10,000. Therefore, at $60,000 and over for single taxpayers and at $85,000 and over for married taxpayers, the ability to deduct the contribution to the IRA is lost.

Q 8:155　Why would a taxpayer fund a nondeductible IRA?

Assuming a taxpayer is ineligible to fund a Roth IRA, he or she may still want to fund a traditional IRA even if the contribution is not deductible for federal income tax purposes on the basis of asset protection. State laws generally shelter IRAs over nonqualified annuities in bankruptcy proceedings.

Q 8:156　What is an advantage of a nonqualified annuity over an IRA?

There are two primary advantages of a nonqualified annuity over a traditional IRA. First, the annuity has an unlimited contribution level regardless of earned income, unlike a traditional IRA, which is limited to $4,000 per year provided the taxpayer has at least that amount in earned income. Second, a nonqualified annuity has no required minimum distribution (RMD), unlike an IRA, which requires taxable withdrawals beginning at age 70½.

Q 8:157　When is the deadline for making a contribution?

The deadline for making a contribution is April 15 of the next year for a contribution for the previous tax year. For example, a taxpayer would need to fund an IRA by April 15, 2008 for the 2007 tax year.

Roth IRAs

Q 8:158　What is a Roth IRA?

Like a traditional IRA, a Roth IRA is a type of IRA within the personal retirement planning category. A Roth IRA is a specialized form of IRA that is not eligible for a tax deduction on contributions, unlike its traditional IRA cousin. However, distributions in a Roth IRA are tax-free within certain limits. This method of retirement savings allows an investor's taxed distributions to accumulate earnings that are not taxable when withdrawn. In a Roth IRA, the annual IRA contribution limits and early withdrawal penalties are the same as a traditional IRA.

Q 8:159　What are the differences between Roth IRAs and traditional IRAs?

The main differences between Roth IRAs and traditional IRAs are:

- **Traditional IRAs are tax-deferred.** Contributions to a traditional IRA are not taxed until distribution, allowing the investor to defer taxes on compensation until retirement, when his or her annual income level may be lower and thus taxed at a reduced rate. Roth IRAs function in a reverse manner: contributions are taxed immediately but distributions are not taxed. This method may be preferred for younger or nonhighly compensated participants who anticipate higher income levels at retirement and wish to put off deferrals until they are needed most.

- **Roth contribution eligibility is not restricted by active participation in an employer-sponsored retirement plan.** Traditional IRAs have restrictions on eligibility if a husband or wife is an active participate in an employer-sponsored retirement plan.

- **Contributions may be made after age 70½ in a Roth IRA.** Investors in a traditional IRA may not make contributions after age 70½.

- **No minimum distribution requirements at age 70½.** Unlike a traditional IRA, which requires minimum distributions starting at age 70½, owners of Roth IRAs may accumulate contributions until death.

Q 8:160　When may withdrawals be made in a Roth IRA without penalty?

In order for a withdrawal to be tax-free, one of the following conditions must exist:

1. The holder of the Roth IRA must be at least age 59½;
2. The withdrawal must take place after a five-year period beginning with the first year of taxable contribution; or
3. In the event of a hardship condition, such as death, disability, or for firsttime home buying.

Premature withdrawals in excess of contributions are fully taxable and may be subject to a 10 percent early withdrawal penalty.

Q 8:161　Who is eligible to contribute to a Roth IRA?

Single taxpayers whose adjusted gross income is less than $95,000 and married taxpayers who file a joint income tax return whose AGI is less than $150,000 may contribute to a Roth IRA.

Q 8:162　At what level of income is a taxpayer prohibited from contributing to a Roth IRA?

Single taxpayers reduce their allowable Roth IRA contributions pro rata between $95,000 and $110,000. Married taxpayers who file a joint income tax return reduce their allowable Roth IRA contributions pro rata between $150,000 and $160,000. For example, a single taxpayer having an AGI of $100,000 would be allowed to contribute a maximum of $1,333 to a Roth IRA for that tax year. The calculation would be $5,000 (over the $95,000 limit)/$15,000 phaseout corridor that results in one-third of the $4,000 maximum contribution being eliminated for the tax year.

Q 8:163   May a taxpayer convert funds from a traditional IRA to a Roth IRA?

A taxpayer may convert moneys from a traditional IRA to a Roth IRA provided the taxpayer's AGI is less than $100,000 in the year of conversion. The AGI is exclusive of the amount of the conversion to the Roth IRA. For example, if a single taxpayer makes only $80,000 in AGI for a given year, that individual could convert any amount (*e.g.*, $1 million) from a traditional IRA to a Roth IRA.

Q 8:164   What criteria should be used in deciding whether to convert moneys from a traditional IRA to a Roth IRA?

A financial planner would need to model various scenarios for a client to determine under what sets of assumptions a conversion from a traditional to a Roth IRA would be advisable. As an overbroad general rule, in order to make the conversion profitable, the client needs to convert at a lower tax bracket than the tax bracket at which the client takes the withdrawals from the Roth IRA. The problem with this type of analysis is that the planner must make many assumptions regarding future tax policy, which is best predicted using a crystal ball.

Q 8:165   Are minimum distributions required at age 70½ in a Roth IRA?

No. This is a major advantage of a Roth IRA compared to a traditional IRA.

Q 8:166   What happens at the death of the IRA owner?

The beneficiary may make withdrawals of the Roth IRA moneys income taxfree over the child beneficiary's life expectancy. This tax advantage is why Roth IRAs are often used as an estate planning tool to leave an inheritance to the decedent's wealthiest children so that the beneficiary is able to enjoy a lifetime of tax-free income.

Q 8:167   Can Congress change the laws regarding the Roth IRA taxation?

Yes, the only prohibition against ex post facto laws in the U.S. Constitution is regarding criminal laws. Consequently, just like with the Social Security laws,

Congress could change the tax laws regarding how or how much of a Roth IRA distributions is taxable. It is prudent for planners to advise clients regarding this potential for tax treatment on Roth IRAs.

Q 8:168   Are Roth IRAs covered by ERISA?

No.

Q 8:169   May a taxpayer deduct contributions to a Roth IRA for federal income tax purposes?

No. Because the income is tax-free, the contribution is never deductible.

Q 8:170   When is the deadline for making a contribution?

The deadline for making a contribution is April 15 of the next year for a contribution for the previous tax year. For example, a taxpayer would need to fund a Roth IRA by April 15, 2008, for the 2007 tax year.

SEP IRAs

Q 8:171   What is a SEP IRA?

A SEP, or simplified employee pension, IRA is a type of business IRA within the personal retirement planning category. SEP IRAs were designed for use by employers and self-employed individuals who are interested in adopting a retirement plan with features similar to a qualified retirement plan, but wish to simplify the administrative requirements of a qualified plan. The documentation, reporting, and disclosure requirements are easier to administer than a qualified plan, making SEPs attractive to smaller businesses or to the self-employed.

SEPs are a type of employer-sponsored retirement plan in which the employer contributions are made directly into each participant's IRA. Each participant has a separate IRA established in the plan. The participant's benefit may then be easily established as the balance of his or her own individual IRA account. SEPs specify that a participant is fully vested as soon as contributions are made but loans on the account balances are not allowed.

Q 8:172   What are the differences between SEP IRAs and traditional IRAs?

The main differences between SEP IRAs and traditional IRAs are:

- **Annual deduction limit for a SEP IRA is higher.** The limit on deductions for a SEP is higher than the traditional IRA $4,000 limit. A SEP limit for deductible contributions for each employee is the lesser of $44,000 or 25 percent of employee compensation.

- **Minimum participation is required and discrimination is not permitted.** In some ways, participation mandates are more stringent than even those of qualified plans. Generally, SEPs must cover all employees who are at least 21 years of age and who have worked for the employer for three out of five years. The years are not defined by a 1,000-hour work definition, but rather by calendar years of service.

- **Employer contributions can be made for employees over age 70½ in an SEP.** Investors in a traditional IRA are unable to make contributions after age 70½.

Q 8:173 What are the differences between SEP IRAs and qualified plans?

The main differences between SEP IRAs and traditional IRAs are:

- **SEPs are subject to Code Section 408(k) rules.** Qualified plans are controlled by a different Code section, Section 401(a). Section 408(k) provides some additional requirements that are unique to SEPs.

- **Coverage requirements are different for part-time employees.** SEPs require the inclusion of all part-time employees making over $500 who have three or more years of service. As a result, SEPs may be more attractive to employers with a larger number of part-time employees who are short-term.

- **Contributions are discretionary.** Unlike qualified plans, SEPs do not require the employer to make annual contributions, and there are no minimum contribution requirements. The primary requirement of the contribution formula that the employer establishes is to avoid discrimination in favor of highly compensated employees.

- **Participants may make in-service withdrawals.** Unlike qualified plans, which typically do not permit in-service withdrawals, SEPs are required to allow participants the option of making withdrawals at any time. Early withdrawals and large distributions are still subject to penalties, just like a qualified plan. Distributions are treated as ordinary income and are taxed in the same way as traditional IRAs are. To avoid a tax penalty, distributions can be rolled over into another IRA.

- **Vesting is immediate on contribution.** All contributions to a SEP must be immediately vested to the employee. However, employers may exclude employees from plan participation. who have fewer than three calendar years of employment.

- **Contribution allocations do not favor older, highly compensated employees.** Unlike certain qualified plans, SEPs may not take into consideration age-weighting or years of service. SEPs must receive allocations as a level percentage of compensation (*e.g.*, 5 percent of compensation).

Q 8:174 What is a SARSEP?

A SARSEP is a type of SEP plan in which the employee may make pre-tax contributions to the plan in a manner similar to a 401(k). Its stringent requirements, however, make it unduly burdensome to small businesses. Under the Small Business Job Protection Act of 1996, the SARSEP was replaced by the SIMPLE plan, which is detailed below. All currently existing SARSEP plans must have been established prior to 1996. Existing SARSEP plans may be retained or converted into a SIMPLE.

Q 8:175   What is the deductibility advantage of a SEP IRA?

Unlike a traditional IRA, which must be funded by April 15, or a qualified plan, which must be funded by year end for a cash basis taxpayer to realize a federal income tax deduction, a SEP IRA needs to be funded prior to the due date of the return plus extensions, if any. For example, a sole proprietor could fund a SEP IRA on or before the automatic four-month extension to August 15. This can be quite useful for a taxpayer who needs additional time to raise the cash to fund the contribution.

SIMPLE IRAs

Q 8:176   What is a SIMPLE IRA?

A SIMPLE, or savings incentive match plan for employees of small employers, IRA is a type of business IRA within the personal retirement planning category. SIMPLE IRAs replaced the more complicated SARSEPs in 1997. Like the old SARSEPs, SIMPLEs allow eligible employees to make their own pre-tax contributions to the plan.

Another departure from the old SARSEP plans is that SIMPLEs do not require discrimination testing to ensure that highly compensated employees are not unduly favored. As a result of this favorable treatment, the SIMPLE does require that the employer make mandatory contributions to the plan, subject to strict funding requirements. Also like SEPs, SIMPLEs specify that a participant is fully vested as soon as contributions are made, but loans on the account balances are not allowed.

Q 8:177   What are the employer contribution requirements in a SIMPLE?

The employer is required to make annual contributions to the plan using one of the following two options:

1. Dollar-for-dollar matching contribution of up to 3 percent of the employee's compensation; or

2. A nonelective contribution of 2 percent compensation for all eligible employees earning at least $5,000.

If the employer chooses the matching option, the employer is able to elect a lower contribution of no less than 1 percent of compensation for no more than two out of five years. The employer must also notify participants of the lower contribution within a reasonable period of time before the 60-day election period before January 1.

Q 8:178   What are the employee contribution rules?

Employees who earned at least $5,000 in any of the two previous years and are reasonably expected to earn $5,000 in the current year are eligible to contribute up to $10,000 annually to a SIMPLE, plus any catch-up amounts for participants who have reached the age of 50 during the plan year.

Q 8:179   May participants over age 70½ make contributions to a SIMPLE?

No, a participant is unable to make a contribution to his or her own IRA account after reaching age 70½. However, the employer may make contributions, including matching contributions and salary reductions, for employees over age 70½.

Q 8:180   May SIMPLE IRAs be combined with another employersponsored retirement plan?

Employers are prohibited from adopting a SIMPLE if any one of the following retirement plans is also maintained:

1. Qualified plans
2. SEPs
3. 403(a) annuity
4. 403(b) tax-sheltered annuity
5. Government plans other than a Section 457 plan

Q 8:181   Why would a small employer choose a SIMPLE over a 401(k)?

Because 401(k) plans are full-fledged qualified plans, there is a substantial amount of administration in a 401(k) plan. A SIMPLE by comparison is quite simple to maintain and administer. A 401(k) plan could cost $1,000+ annually for a small employer to administer, whereas the SIMPLE IRA is typically provided free of charge save for the employer enrolling eligible employees.

Nonqualified Plans

Q 8:182   What is a nonqualified plan?

A nonqualified plan is one that fails any one of several of the ERISA requirements of a qualified plan. Common examples of nonqualified plans include rabbi trusts or secular trusts. In a nonqualified plan the employer is not allowed to deduct the contributions made to the plan until the benefits are received by the employees. The employee is allowed to defer income taxes until the receipt of the benefit.

In addition, employers are able to discriminate in nonqualified plans. In a nonqualified plan participation may be limited to executives or the senior management team. ERISA refers to this type of arrangement as a "Top Hat" plan, which is not permitted for qualified plan eligibility.

Nonqualified plans may be designed for key employees to provide customized retirement or savings benefits beyond the limits allowed in qualified plans. As a result, the employer may find a reduction in the costs associated in providing a qualified plan, which must be designed to cover a broader range of employees.

Q 8:183   What are the advantages of a nonqualified plan?

Advantages of nonqualified plans in a nutshell include:

- **Discrimination is allowed.** This lack of restriction would allow the plan to be made available to a small number of employees or even limited to just a single employee.
- **There are unlimited benefits.** Nonqualified plans may provide unlimited benefits to any one employee, subject to the reasonable compensation requirement for deductibility.
- **There are customization and versatility.** The employer may provide different benefit amounts for different employees, based on different terms and conditions.
- **There are minimal regulatory requirements.**
- **Taxes may be deferred by employees.** The employer's deduction is also deferred.

Q 8:184   What are the disadvantages of a nonqualified plan?

Disadvantages of a nonqualified plan include:

- **Employer's tax deduction cannot be taken for the year in which compensation is earned.** The deduction is deferred until income is taxable to the employee.
- **Funding is limited to the employer's unsecured promise to pay.** Most of the protections of the federal tax and labor law, including ERISA requirements, are not applicable to enforce compliance in nonqualified plans.
- **Not all employers are eligible.** Some examples of potentially ineligible employers may include S corporations and partnerships that use a pass-through tax structure, many closely held or family businesses that may not last long enough to make promised payments, and tax-exempt or government organizations.

Q 8:185   How are most nonqualified plans designed?

The two most common nonqualified plan designs include the salary continuation formula and the salary reduction formula.

Q 8:186   What is the salary continuation formula?

The salary continuation formula is designed to function in a manner similar to a defined benefit in a qualified plan. In both plans, a specified benefit amount is provided to a plan participant. However, unlike in qualified plans, in a nonqualified salary continuation plan, the formula used to calculate the retirement benefit is not subject to the same types of restrictions or limitations on its benefit amounts.

Salary continuation plans may be offered as a supplement to employee participation in other qualified plan offerings, like a 401(k) or profit-sharing plan, without affecting the employee's participation amounts in the other qualified plans. Unlike qualified plans, salary continuation plans may be limited to only a select group of highly qualified employees. The prevalent use of these plans for retirement perks for executives have caused them to be referred to as SERPs, or supplemental executive retirement plans.

Q 8:187   What is the salary reduction formula?

The salary reduction formula, on the other hand, functions in a manner more similar to a defined contribution in a qualified plan. In both plans the employee may make annual elective salary deferrals to the plan. Unlike the salary continuation plan, which requires no reduction in employee salary amounts, the salary reduction formula requires that the employee forgo a certain percentage of annual compensation that he or she would otherwise have received from the employer.

The salary reduction formula's categorization as a nonqualified plan further distinguishes it from the more highly regulated requirements of defined contribution plans. The participation restrictions and individual account management of its qualified plan counterpart are not applicable in the nonqualified plan.

Q 8:188   What is a funded plan?

In a funded plan, money or property (such as a designated piece of land) is set aside typically in a trust account to insulate the plan funds from the employer's creditors. Generally, funded plans have unfavorable tax consequences.

Q 8:189   What is an unfunded plan?

In an unfunded plan, there is no specific account set aside to fund the benefits payable to the plan participants. This is not to say that the employer will not make investments to cover this plan liability. However, because the employer's investments are not specifically set aside for the purpose of plan funding, the assets remain subject to the claims of the employer's general creditors. Consequently, the unfunded plans receive a more favorable tax treatment than unfunded plans.

Q 8:190   What is a rabbi trust?

A rabbi trust is a type of unfunded nonqualified plan that is subject to the claims of the employer's general creditors. However, in a rabbi trust, unlike a traditional unfunded plan, the employer is barred from accessing participant funds. In this way, the participant in a rabbi trust receives more protection from the potentially unscrupulous actions of an employer. The employer likewise is not tempted by the easy access and availability of employee retirement plan funds.

Q 8:191   What is a secular trust?

A secular trust is a type of funded trust where specific funds are set aside for the employee. These funds are insulated from the claims of the employer's general creditors. However, all assets placed in the trust are taxable to the employee. Secular trusts are generally used as a conversion vehicle for rabbi trusts in instances where the employee participant may have concerns about the employer's ability to avoid creditor claims and prefers a greater level of asset security.

Q 8:192   What is the risk to an employee of participating in a plan of nonqualified deferred compensation?

There are two primary risks to an employee of participating in a nonqualified plan. The first and greatest risk is that in order to avoid income taxation, the plan assets must remain a general asset of the employer and consequently may be forfeited to general creditors of the corporation. General creditors include judicial lien creditors. So if, for example, a restaurant owner employer serves a particularly hot cup of coffee, a $100 million judgment could lead to complete forfeiture of the client's retirement assets contained in the nonqualified plan.

The second source of risk revolves around the contractual provisions contained in the nonqualified plan. If the vesting schedule requires ten years of service to vest in the plan, then nine years eleven months and eleven days is insufficient to acquire an interest in the plan assets. Courts are highly reluctant to protect top executives in these plans; they instead usually hold that the employee should have negotiated more favorable terms. A financial planner can be invaluable under these circumstances to determine if, for example, waiting ten years to acquire a $1 million benefit is better than waiting five years to acquire a $500,000 benefit. As the saying goes, a bird in the hand is worth two in the bush, and ten years is a long, long time to wait with everything to lose.

Qualified Plan Annuities, Distributions, and Loans

Q 8:193　Do qualified pension plans provide survivorship benefits for a surviving spouse?

Yes, all qualified pension plans must provide survivorship benefits to a surviving spouse if the deceased was a vested participant in the plan. These benefits are typically paid in the form of an annuity to the spouse on the death of the participant. The following two types of annuity options are provided in a qualified pension plan: the qualified pre-retirement survivor annuity and the qualified joint and survivor annuity.

In each type, the participant may elect to receive an alternative form of survivorship benefit, including a nonspousal benefit election. However, in order to implement an alternative benefit election (1) the spouse must waive his or her rights in writing; (2) the waiver must be notarized or witnessed by a plan representative; (3) the right to make such an alternative election must be communicated to all vested plan participants; and (4) the participant has the ability to change the election during a specified period (*i.e.*, for joint and survivor, a 90-day election period, and for pre-retirement survivor any time after the participant reaches age 35).

Q 8:194　What is a joint and survivor annuity?

A joint and survivor annuity is an automatic death benefit payable to the surviving spouse in the event that the participant dies following retirement. The amount payable in the annuity must be greater than or equal to 50 percent and less than 100 percent of the annuity payable during the joint lives of the participant and the spouse. This annuity is payable to the spouse even on remarriage.

Q 8:195　What is a pre-retirement survivor annuity?

A pre-retirement survivor annuity is an automatic death benefit payable to the surviving spouse of a vested plan participant who dies prior to retirement. In a defined benefit plan, the amount payable to the spouse is equal to the amount that would have been paid under a joint and survivor annuity if the participant (1) retired on the day before his or her death or (2) separated from service on the date of death and survived to the plan's earliest retirement age, then retired with an immediate joint and survivor annuity.

In a defined contribution plan, the annuity is for the life of the surviving spouse at an amount that is the actuarial equivalent of at least 50 percent of the participant's vested account balance as of the date of death.

Q 8:196　What is unusual about annuity options in qualified plans?

ERISA anti-alienation generally prevents any restriction on the use of a plan participant. Yet Congress has decided that in the interest of public policy, spouses should receive the right to a survivorship benefit under their spouses' qualified plans.

Q 8:197   May qualified plan participants elect a lump-sum distribution?

Yes, the participant may elect a lump-sum distribution from a qualified plan at retirement; however, depending on the specific plan, these distributions may be subject to mandatory tax withholding at 20 percent. Additionally, lump sums may not be tax-advantageous to the participant who may be in a relatively high tax bracket.

Lump-sum distributions may be subject to early withdrawal penalty.

Q 8:198   When is a participant eligible to elect ten-year averaging on capital gain for lump-sum distributions?

A participant is eligible to elect ten-year averaging on capital gain only if he or she was born prior to January 1, 1936.

Q 8:199   May qualified plan participants take out a loan against plan funds?

Yes, plan participants are eligible to borrow from plans that specifically permit such loans. In particular, loan options are most commonly found in defined contribution plans but are not permitted from SEPs and traditional IRAs. With the 10 percent penalty on early withdrawals, participants may wish to consider taking out a plan loan rather than withdrawing funds prior to retirement. Loans must meet the following regulatory requirements to avoid penalties:

1. Equal availability to all plan participants.
2. No unequal preference given to highly compensated employees.
3. Adherence to the specific plan provisions.
4. Reasonable rate of interest provided.
5. Adequate security of the loan.

Q 8:200   What types of plans may offer plan loans?

All types of qualified plans may offer plan loans. Certain other types of plans, such as SEP IRAs and SIMPLE IRAs, do not permit plan loans. Defined benefit pension plans generally do not permit plan loans due to the cost of accurately calculating the participant's account balance.

Q 8:201   Are qualified plans required to offer plan loans?

No, offering plan loans is entirely elective on the part of the plan sponsor/ employer.

Q 8:202   What amounts are available to be borrowed under a qualified plan loan?

At a minimum, plan participants may borrow 100 percent of the vested account balance up to $10,000. At a maximum, plan participants may borrow up to 50 percent of the account balance up to $50,000.

Q 8:203   May owners borrow money from their qualified plans?

Yes, borrowing money from an owner's qualified plan is no longer considered a prohibited transaction.

Q 8:204   May a qualified plan benefit be assigned as part of a domestic relations dispute?

Yes. While generally retirement plans are immune from creditors, the exception to the rule occurs in domestic relations disputes. Qualified plan benefits may be assigned under qualified domestic relations order (QDROs) as defined in Code Section 414(p). A QDRO is a decree, order, or property settlement under state law relating to child support, alimony, or marital property rights that assigns part or all of the participant's plan benefits to a spouse, former spouse, child, or other dependent of the participant.

Q 8:205   How does a QDRO work?

Earlier we discussed how ERISA preempts state regulation as it applies to qualified retirement plans. However, Congress permits a state divorce (*i.e.*, family) court to determine eligibility for qualified retirement plan assets. This is one of very few exceptions to exclusive federal control of ERISA assets.

In this case, a final order of a state court is controlling on who receives the benefits under a retirement plan. The nonparticipant spouse must deliver to the plan administrator the QDRO issued by the court that entitles the nonparticipant spouse to plan benefits. However, a word of caution applies to planners. First, planners should not get creative with the drafting of a QDRO. QDROs have been held to be ineffective for making small changes in the statutory language. Second, without a QDRO in place, all distributions made from the plan, including those to a nonparticipant spouse, will be taxable to the participant spouse under the assignment of income doctrine.

Other Types of Plans

Q 8:206   Why were Keogh plans so popular in the past?

In the past, professionals were not allowed to incorporate their practices under state law. However, only corporations were allowed to adopt qualified plans. Keogh plans allowed unincorporated business owners to deduct contributions to (Keogh) plans. Now that professionals are free to incorporate, Keogh plans are largely obsolete.

Q 8:207   What are 403(b) plans?

403(b) plans are offered by § 501(c)(3) organizations (*i.e.*, charities) and schools ranging from the local elementary school to colleges and universities.

Q 8:208   Why are 403(b) plans often called tax-sheltered annuities?

Tax deferred annuities are the only approved funding vehicles (save for a special exception for mutual funds under Code Section 403(b)(7)).

Q 8:209   Are 403(b) plans subject to nondiscrimination testing?

No. This is a significant advantage of 403(b) plans over 401(k) plans.

Q 8:210   What are the contribution limits of a 403(b) plan?

The contribution limits are the same as in a 401(k) plan: $15,000 per year plus a catch-up contribution of $5,000 for participants age 50 or older in 2006.

Q 8:211   What is a 457 plan?

A 457 plan offers deferred compensation to employees of municipalities.

Q 8:212   What is the contribution limit of a 457 plan?

A participant may contribute up to $15,000 to a 457 plan in 2006.

Q 8:213   What is the purpose of Code Section 457?

The congressional intent behind Code Section 457 is to limit the amount of money employees of local governments may defer into a tax-deferred compensation arrangement. For example, when an employee in a taxable entity places money into a nonqualified deferred compensation arrangement, the employer pays tax on the amount of money deferred given that the deferral is not deductible to the employer. Tax-exempt employers would not owe any tax on the employee deferral. Without Code Section 457, there would be no incentive for tax-exempt employers to limit employee deferrals, and thus valuable tax revenue would be lost by the federal government.

Bibliography

Beam, B.T., Bickelhaupt, D.L. & Crowe, R.M. (2000). *Fundamentals of Insurance for Financial Planning*. Bryn Mawr, Pennsylvania: The American College.

Bernstein, P.W., Editor. (2002). *The Ernst & Young Tax Guide 2002*. Ernst & Young LLP and Peter W. Bernstein Corporation.

Bost, J.B. (2001). *Estate Planning and Taxation* (2001–2002 Ed.). Dubuque, Iowa: Kendall/Hunt Publishing Company.

Brazelton, J.K. & Campbell, A.D. (2000) *Tax Strategies for the Self-Employed*. Chicago, Illinois: CCH Incorporated.

Buffett, M. & Clark, D. (2001). *The Buffettology Workbook*. New York, N.Y.: Simon & Schuster.

CCH (2001). *CCH Financial and Estate Planning Guide* (13th Ed.). Chicago, Illinois: CCH Incorporated.

CCH (2002). *CCH Guide to Tax Planning for Individuals and Small Businesses* (2nd Ed.). Chicago, Illinois: CCH Incorporated.

CCH (2002). *CCH Tax Planning Strategies* (2002–2003 Ed.). Chicago, Illinois: CCH Incorporated.

College of Financial Planning (2002). *Retirement Planning and Employee Benefits*. Denver, Colorado: College of Financial Planning.

Cordell, D.M. (1999). *Fundamentals of Financial Planning* (4th Ed.). Bryn Mawr, Pennsylvania: The American College.

DeFusco, R.A., McLeavey, D.W., Pinto, J.E. & Runkle, D.E. (2001). *Quantitative Methods for Investment Analysis*. Baltimore, MD: United Book Press, Inc.

Evensky, H.R. (1997). *Wealth Management: The Financial Advisor's Guide to Investing and Managing Client Assets*. Chicago, IL: Times Mirror Higher Education Group, Inc.

Fabozzi, F.J. & Fabozzi, T.D. (Eds.). (1995). *The Handbook of Fixed Income Securities* (4th Ed.). Chicago, IL: Irwin Professional Publishing, Inc.

Fowler, L., Mears, W.H. & Rattiner, J.R. (1994). *Evaluating Life Insurance Decisions*. New York, N.Y.: Harcourt Brace & Company.

Gear Up, Inc. (2002). *1040 Individual Income Tax* (2002). Portland, Oregon: Gear Up, Inc.

Graber, R.S. & Woerheide, W.J. (2002). *Fundamentals of Investments for Financial Planning* (2d Ed.). Bryn Mawr, Pennsylvania: The American College.

Graves, E.E. (1994). *McGill's Life Insurance.* Bryn Mawr, Pennsylvania: The American College.

Groopelli, A.A. & Nikbakht, E. (2000). *Finance* (4th Ed.) Haugppauge, N.Y.: Barron's Educational Series, Inc.

Hearth, D. & Zaima, J.K. (2001). *Contemporary Investments: Security and Portfolio Analysis* (3rd Ed.). Fort Worth, Texas: Harcourt, Inc.

Hoyle, B.J. (2001). *Wiley CPA Examination Review Fast Track Study Guide* (2nd Ed). New York, N.Y.: John Wiley & Sons, Inc.

Ivers, J.F. III, (2002). *Fundamentals of Income Taxation* (3rd Ed.). Bryn Mawr, Pennsylvania: The American College.

Jones, C.P. (2000). *Investments: Analysis and Management* (7th Ed.). New York, N.Y.: John Wiley & Sons, Inc.

Jones, M.J. (2002). *The Pension Answer Book* (Special Supplement—Final Regulations Governing Minimum Required Distributions). New York, N.Y.: Aspen Publishers.

Jones, S.M. (2002). *Principles of Taxation for Business and Investment Planning* (2002 Ed.). New York, N.Y.: McGraw Hill Irwin.

Keir, J.C. (1999). *CFP^{TM} Certification Examination Review Volume1; Revised June 2002.* Middletown, Ohio: Keir Educational Resources.

Keir, J.C. (1999). *CFP^{TM} Certification Examination Review Volume21; Revised June 2002.* Middletown, Ohio: Keir Educational Resources.

Krass, S.J. (2002). *The Pension Answer Book* (2002 Ed.). New York, N.Y.: Aspen Publishers.

Kurlowicz, T., Ivers, J.F. & McFadden, J.J. (2002). *Planning for Business Owners and Professionals* (8th Ed.). Bryn Mawr, Pennsylvania: The American College.

Leimberg, S.R. & Doyle Jr., R.J. (1999) *The Tools & Techniques of Life Insurance Planning* (2nd Ed.). Cincinnati, Ohio: The National Underwriter Company.

Leimberg, S.R., Kasner, J.A., Kandell, S.N., Miller, R.G., Rosenbloom, M.S., Levy, H.L. & Polacek, T.C. (2001). *The Tools & Techniques of Estate Planning* (12th Ed.). Cincinnati, Ohio: The National Underwriter Company.

Leimberg, S.R. & McFadden, J.J. (2001). *The Tools & Techniques of Employee Benefit and Retirement Planning* (7th Ed.). Cincinnati, Ohio: The National Underwriter Company.

Leimberg, S.R., Riggin, D.J., Howard, A.J., Kallman, J.W. & Schmidt, D.L. (2002). *The Tools & Techniques of Risk Management & Insurance.* Cincinnati, Ohio: The National Underwriter Company.

Leimberg, S.R., Satinsky, M.J., LeClair, R.T. & Doyle, R.J. (2002). *The Tools & Techniques of Financial Planning* (6th Ed.). Cincinnati, Ohio: The National Underwriter Company.

Lesser, G.S. & Diehl, S.D. & Kolojeski, G. (2000). *Roth IRA Answer Book* (2nd Ed.). New York, N.Y.: Aspen Publishers.

Lesser, G.S. Starr, L.C. (1998). *Life Insurance Answer Book.* New York, N.Y.: Aspen Publishers.

Littell, D.A. & Tacchino, K.B. (2001). *Planning for Retirement Needs* (5th Ed.). Bryn Mawr, Pennsylvania: The American College.

Lockwood, S.G., Levy, D.R. & Fleisher, M. (2002). *Individual Retirement Account Answer Book* (8th Ed.). New York, N.Y.: Aspen Publishers.

Martin, A.R. (2001). *Limited Liability Company & Partnership Answer Book* (2nd Ed.). New York, N.Y.: Aspen Publishers.

Mayo, H.B. (2002). *Investments: An Introduction* (6th Ed.). Mason, Ohio: South-Western College Publishing.

Mercer. (2002). *2003 Guide to Social Security and Medicare* (31st Ed.). Louisville, Kentucky: Mercer Human Resource Consulting, Inc.

Mitchell, W.D. (2001). *Estate and Retirement Planning Answer Book* (3rd Ed.). New York, N.Y.: Aspen Publishers.

Mittra, Sid (2002). *Practicing Financial Planning for Professionals* (7th Ed.). Rochester Hills, Michigan: RH Publishing.

Rattiner, J.H. (2005). *Getting Started As A Financial Planner* (2nd Ed.). Princeton, NJ: Bloomberg Press.

Reilly, F.K. & Brown, K.C. (2000). *Investment Analysis and Portfolio Management* (6th Ed.). Orlando, FL: The Dryden Press.

Reilly, F.K. & Norton, E.A. (1999). *Investments* (5th Ed.). New York, N.Y.: Harcourt, Inc.

RIA. (2001). *RIA Federal Tax Handbook* (2002 Ed.). New York, N.Y.: Research Institute of America.

Ross, S.A., Westerfield, R.W. & Jordan, B.D. (1995). *Fundamentals of Corporate Finance.* Chicago, IL: Irwin Professional Publishing, Inc.

TMI Tax Services. (2005). *Form 1040 Quickfinder—2005 Tax Year* (2006 Ed.). Minnetonka, MN: TMI Tax Services, Inc.

The National Underwriter Company. (2006). *Social Security Manual* (2006). Cincinnati, Ohio: The National Underwriter Company.

The Options Institute. (1990). *Options: Essential Concepts and Trading Strategies*. Burr Ridge, IL: Irwin Professional Publishing, Inc.

Schweser Study Program. (2002). *Asset Valuation: Market, Equity, Debt, Derivatives & Alternative*.

Shilling, D. (2001). *Financial Planning for The Older Client* (5th Ed.). Cincinnati, Ohio: The National Underwriter Company.

Soule, C.E. (2002). *Disability Income Insurance: The Unique Risk* (5th Ed.). Bryn Mawr, Pennsylvania: The American College.

Vaughan, E.J. & Vaughan, T. (2003). *Fundamentals of Risk and Insurance* (9th Ed.). New York, N.Y.: John Wiley & Sons, Inc.

Wiley & Sons, Inc. (2005). *J.K. Lasser's Your Income Tax 2006*. New York, N.Y.: John Wiley & Sons, Inc.

Index

A

A. M. Best Company, 3:10

ABA (American Bar Association), 7:21

Accelerated sinking fund provision, 5:19

Accidental death benefit, life insurance, 3:66

Accountants during tax time, 6:105, 6:106

Accrual bond, 5:2

Accrued interest, 5:58, 5:61

Accumulated earnings credit, 2:3

Accumulated earnings tax, 2:23

Accumulation phase of life cycle, 1:22

Achievement awards, 6:65

Activity ratios
defined, 4:79
inventory turnover ratio, 4:81
receivables turnover, 4:80

Actual return on investments, 1:24, 1:26

ADEA (Age Discrimination in Employment Act), 8:111

Adhesion, 3:32

Adoption expense tax credit, 6:4, 6:63

ADRs (American depository receipts), 4:10

Age Discrimination in Employment Act (ADEA), 8:111

Age-weighted profit-sharing plan, 8:47, 8:48, 8:49

Alaskan trusts, 7:131

Aleatory, 3:33

Alimony, 6:13, 6:14

Alternative minimum tax (AMT), 2:8

Alternative valuation date for estate taxes, 7:134, 7:135

American Bar Association (ABA), 7:21

American depository receipts (ADRs), 4:10

Amortizing securities, 5:13

AMT (alternative minimum tax), 2:8

Annual renewable term insurance, 3:39

Annuity
annuity due, 1:29
charitable remainder annuity trust, 7:179
future value, 1:29
joint and survivor, 8:194
nonqualified annuity vs. IRA, 8:156
ordinary, 1:29
pre-retirement survivor, 8:195
present value, 1:29
private annuity, 2:55, 7:98–7:99
property transfer to charity in exchange, 2:15
qualified joint and survivor annuity, 2:60
qualified pension plan, 8:196
qualified preretirement survivor annuity, 2:60
taxation of payments, 6:47
tax-sheltered, 8:208
time value of money, 1:29

Any occupation, defined, 3:120

Approximate duration, 5:67

Arithmetic average, 4:14

Asset management
closed-end investment company, 4:41, 4:42

Preliminary meeting, 1:10

Prepayment provision, 5:18, 5:26

Pre-retirement survivor annuity, 8:195

Present interest gifts, 2:58

Present value
  annuity, 1:29
  of a fixed sum, 1:27
  irregular cash flows, 1:32
  net present value calculation, 1:30

Price-to-book value of common stock, 4:34

Price-to-cash flow ratio of common stock, 4:36

Price-to-sales ratio of common stock, 4:35

Price-weighted series, 4:11

Primary market, 5:44

Primary security market, 4:1

Primogeniture, 7:34

Private annuity, 2:55, 7:98–7:99

Private charity income tax deduction limits, 2:8, 2:11

Probate
  advantages of use, 7:16
  alternatives, 7:15
  ancillary, 7:14
  generally, 7:12
  process, 7:13

Process of financial planning. *See* Financial planning process

Profit-sharing plan
  age-weighted, 8:47, 8:48, 8:49
  background of name, 8:38
  discretionary provision, 8:41
  ERISA regulations, 8:45
  formula provision, 8:42
  funding, 8:37, 8:40–8:42
  generally, 8:36, 8:39
  tax implications, 8:44, 8:46, 8:48
  used with 401(k) plans, 8:68
  uses for, 8:43

Property
  common law, 7:33
  community. *See* Community property
  cost basis, 6:87
  domicile, 7:39
  equitable ownership, 7:37
  estate, 7:24
  estate for a term of years, 7:35
  fee simple or fee simple absolute, 7:27, 7:32
  four unities of joint tenancy, 7:28

  individual ownership, 7:27
  joint tenancy, 7:28, 7:138
  legal ownership, 7:37
  life estate, 7:32, 7:34
  personal. *See* Personal property
  quasi-community property, 6:20
  real estate. *See* Real estate
  remainder interest, 7:36
  residency, 7:39
  settlement tax issues in divorce situations, 6:9
  situs, 7:38
  sole ownership, 7:31
  tenancy by the entirety, 7:30, 7:31
  tenants in common, 7:29
  transfer to charity in exchange for annuity, 2:15
  trustee's duty to make property productive, 7:124
  Uniform Marital Property Act, 6:20
  valuation, 7:139–7:142

Protective call, 5:88

Protective puts, 5:83

PRT (personal residence trust), 2:54

PS-58 costs, 3:95

Public charity income tax deduction limits, 2:11

Purchasing power risk, 5:30

Put provision
  at-the-money, 5:74
  covered put selling, 5:87
  defined, 5:20, 5:71, 5:83
  in-the-money, 5:74, 5:83
  out-of-the-money, 5:74, 5:83
  price, 5:76
  protective puts, 5:83
  put-call parity, 5:81
  put-call ratio, 4:37
  risks, 5:52
  writing naked puts, 5:85
  yield to put, 5:66

Q

QDRO (qualified domestic relations order), 6:18, 8:204, 8:205

QJSA (qualified joint and survivor annuity), 2:60

QPRT (qualified personal residence trust), 2:54, 7:167–7:169

QPSA (qualified preretirement survivor annuity), 2:60

R

U